THE SECRETS
OF FACILITATION

THE SECRETS OF FACILITATION

The SMART Guide to Getting Results with Groups

Michael Wilkinson

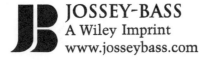

JOSSEY-BASS
A Wiley Imprint
www.josseybass.com

Cover design: John Miller
Cover art: Shutterstock (RF)

Published by Jossey-Bass
A Wiley Imprint
989 Market Street, San Francisco, CA 94103-1741—www.josseybass.com

Jossey-Bass books and products are available through most bookstores. To contact Jossey-Bass directly call
our Customer Care Department within the U.S. at 800-956-7739, outside the U.S. at 317-572-3986, or fax
317-572-4002.

Wiley also publishes its books in a variety of electronic formats and by print-on-demand. Not all content
that is available in standard print versions of this book may appear or be packaged in all book formats. If
you have purchased a version of this book that did not include media that is referenced by or accompanies
a standard print version, you may request this media by visiting http://booksupport.wiley.com. For more
information about Wiley products, visit us www.wiley.com.

Library of Congress Cataloging-in-Publication Data

Wilkinson, Michael.

 The secrets of facilitation : the SMART guide to getting results with groups / by Michael Wilkinson.— New
and Revised.

      pages cm. —(The Jossey-Bass Business & Management Series)

 Includes bibliographical references and index.

 ISBN 978-1-118-20613-3 (pbk); ISBN 978-1-118-22857-9 (ebk); ISBN 978-1-118-23330-6 (ebk);
ISBN 978-1-118-26573-4 (ebk)

 1. Group facilitation—Handbooks, manuals, etc. 2. Business meetings—Handbooks, manuals, etc. I. Title.

 HM751.W55 212

 658.4'56—dc23

                                                                                    2012020198

Printed in the United States of America
SECOND EDITION   V10016845_010920

THE JOSSEY-BASS Business & Management Series

To Mom, who taught me, and Pop, who inspired me

CONTENTS

INTRODUCTION TO THE SECOND EDITION

It has been eight years since the publication of the first edition of *The Secrets of Facilitation*. As the world around us has changed, so has the world of facilitation. This edition reflects some of these changes.

From many who read *The Secrets of Facilitation* I have heard comments about how the book has provided real foundation techniques for how to guide a team through a facilitated process. People frequently said they liked the numerous case studies and how the sample dialogues put them right into the room. I have been especially pleased with the numerous emails from people telling us how they have put the Secrets to use. We have also heard from many who have attended The Effective Facilitator, the training course that teaches the principles and techniques found in *The Secrets*. At the end of this Introduction to the Second Edition, I have included two of these letters.

Along with the positive feedback on *The Secrets,* we also have heard that more and more people are finding themselves facilitating "virtual meetings" where most of the people are not in the room. We also heard of extreme cases where the only one not in the room was the facilitator. People said they wanted more tips on how to facilitate large groups, more information about making meetings more productive, and greater guidance on preventing dysfunctional behavior.

Information from various surveys and research studies supports these needs.

- As an example, a landmark study on meetings by MCI (*Meetings in America: A Study of Trends, Costs and Attitudes Toward Business Travel and Teleconferencing, and Their Impact on Productivity,* 1998) revealed that busy professionals attend more than sixty meetings a month. Yet nearly all surveyed admitted to some sort of dysfunction during meetings: 91 percent admitted to daydreaming, over 70 percent said they have brought other work to meetings, and 39 percent said they have dozed off during meetings.

- In a study by Carlson Wagonlit Travel's Travel Management Institute (*Meetings and Events: Where Savings Meet Success*, 2010), over 80 percent indicated that the number of virtual meetings is growing in their organizations.
- In my article "The Case for Masterful Meetings" (2006), I have documented that with a team of twenty people who spend an average of thirteen hours a week in meetings, just a 15 percent increase in the productivity of meetings is equivalent to adding another person to the team.

What's New in the Second Edition?

A lot! *The Secrets of Facilitation—New and Revised* responds to the aforementioned needs and more. I have kept the features people have said they liked, and in this edition you will also find

- Four new chapters, covering
  - Virtual meetings
  - Facilitating large groups and conferences
  - Facilitating cross-cultural groups
  - Building an in-house network of facilitators
- Ten engagement strategies that we teach to advanced facilitators:
  - Brief encounters
  - Dump and clump
  - Elevator speech
  - Forced analogy
  - Future letter
  - Last person standing
  - More of / Less of
  - Start / Stop / Continue
  - Talking stick
  - The whip
- Ten new secrets covering the following topics:
  - Defining the session product: the 3 Hs
  - Managing a sponsor's presence
  - Exciting people in the opening
  - Gaining consensus on wording
  - Preparing for a virtual meeting
  - Facilitating large groups

- Facilitating conferences
- Managing time with speakers
- Facilitating cross-cultural groups
- Establishing an internal facilitator cadre
- Fifteen additional case studies, including
  - The facilitator's role in civic leadership groups
  - The starting question to engage the VP's number two
  - Preparing for vision councils
  - The power of the pen, ELMO, and parking boards
  - The low-key facilitator
  - The virtual strategy monitoring session
  - Facilitating a conference on spirituality
  - Facilitating the strategic plan for a Caribbean government
  - The pull strategy at Hydro One
  - The facilitator development program at Saudi Aramco
- Expanded information on handling dysfunctions, including how to prevent the dysfunction, what to do in the moment when you are facing the dysfunction, and what to do after the moment
- An expanded list of dysfunctions, which adds the following five:
  - Cell phone junkie
  - Topic jumper
  - Interrupter
  - Low-energy group
  - Time-pressured group
- New material on numerous topics, including
  - Applying the Secrets to running a simple meeting
  - Applying the Secrets to the first meeting of a task force
  - Should the sponsor be in the room?
  - When should you arrive for a meeting?
  - How to get executives to turn their power over to you
  - How facilitators abuse the pen
  - The informed majority decision-making process
  - Energy and authenticity
  - Crossing the River: my favorite team building activity
  - Defining what can be communicated following the session
  - A tool for improving your cross-cultural awareness by identifying your cultural biases
  - Interrupting the effects of institutional power through facilitation
  - Facilitator neutrality: fact or fiction?
  - Facilitator certification

- A new feature answering the question, "Why do this?" to highlight why a particular approach or strategy is so critically important
- Recommended exercises at the end of each chapter to suggest ways to practice one or more key concepts covered in the chapter

In summary, you will find in this second edition a wealth of new information, along with the foundational structure that made the first edition such a big success. I am excited about this new edition and what it has to offer. Our company's tagline is "Sharing the Power of Facilitation with the World." We fundamentally believe that facilitation is a powerful tool for helping people reach better decisions, often faster, with much higher levels of buy-in and commitment.

- Better decisions . . . because a diversity of views were openly shared and considered
- Often faster . . . because the processes used promote productive and efficient communication
- Much higher levels of buy-in and commitment . . . because those impacted by the decisions were involved in creating them

My hope is that this second edition will both empower you and inspire you to "share the power" with the groups you serve.

Michael Wilkinson

Managing Director, Leadership Strategies

Sharing the Power of Facilitation with the World™

CASE STUDY: The Secrets in Action—How Two Practitioners Have Put the Secrets to Work

Andy Weavill is a freelance management and training consultant based in the United Kingdom.

The Secrets of Facilitation delivered success for me at a recent series of conferences. I had been engaged on a project with a large public sector organization going through a tremendous period of change. They had commissioned me to put together a series of three large group conferences (260 people, 200, and 150) to engage their people in discussion about the changes, to share information and celebrate past successes.

My primary role on the day was to open the conference and engage delegates in thinking about the future and formulating questions and observations to put to various speakers throughout the day. Thereafter my role was to facilitate the question-and-answer sessions and generally keep the conference moving along. Getting the opening right was crucial to the success of the day.

The first two conferences were deemed to be successful, but I knew that although the level of participation was reasonable, it could be better, with more questions and more people asking them from the floor. Also I felt, due to the uncertainties of change, I hadn't managed to create the rapport and warmth in the room I would have liked. By the end of the day it was still a little frosty!

Prior to the third conference, I had ordered and received *The Secrets of Facilitation.* The book arrived on the Monday, two days before the last conference. I read it Monday evening and Tuesday in readiness for the third conference on Wednesday. My motivation: Were there any secrets I could apply to improve my opening pitch, generate more involvement, and more questions? By Tuesday afternoon I had read the book, and my attention was focused on Chapters Two and Four, The Secrets to Questioning and The Secrets to Starting, and to some extent on Chapter Three, The Secrets to Preparing. I also had in mind secret 19 (using PeDeQs for my direction giving) and secret 30 (the secret to Q&A sessions). Late Tuesday afternoon, I rewrote and replanned my opening to better focus it around the IEEI outline and set up the participation for Q&A by following the steps outlined in secret 30.

I applied the Secrets on Wednesday morning at the third conference and noted the reactions. The opening flowed better, and a greater level of rapport was achieved. The opening also established greater involvement and participation in the pre-questioning process and sequence. During the Q&A, more questions were asked than at the other two conferences—and these kept coming throughout the day. The PeDeQs sequence for giving directions also improved understanding and execution of activities throughout the day.

I might be biased, but at the end of the day I felt the mood of delegates was not as frosty as it was at the other two conferences, and subsequent analysis of conference evaluations showed that, in comparison to the other two conferences, we had improved on *all* our ratings. The client also thought that this had been the best of the three conferences. Of course, I could put this improvement down to familiarity with the conference process (it was the third one, after all)—but I don't think so. I had made sufficient changes (based on my reading of *The Secrets of Facilitation*) to the way I facilitated the third conference to know that these changes—some process, some change in words and/or emphasis—had made the difference.

As I sit here and reflect on all three conferences, I would also like to make the point that had we really followed the five Ps of preparation with the client, putting together the conference agenda would have been easier; and if we had focused on probable issues to a greater extent than we did, I am convinced our conference process would also have been different.

So overall, I have had a great learning opportunity and experience helped in no small measure by *The Secrets of Facilitation*—the book really does deliver!

Jason Kean is a project coordinator with one of the largest used car Web sites in the United States, with more than two million used vehicles listed for sale by private owners, dealers, and manufacturers. Jason attended The Effective Facilitator, the training course that covers the content in The Secrets of Facilitation.

Let me start by telling you how much I truly appreciated The Effective Facilitator class. I have used the principles I learned during this course in all aspects of life, both personally and professionally. The only instance in my life that has remained unaltered by the class is my relationship with my dog (she just doesn't get it!).

Having facilitated several meetings with executives and coworkers, I now run more effective idea meetings and accomplish specific objectives. I've learned it's highly effective when the goal is clearly stated and used to keep the group focused.

In addition, I ask direct questions and am getting better responses. I've also found I'm better able to read audience "nonverbal cues" and now have a toolbox full of strategies I can use to engage audience participation in conversations. This makes for highly effective meetings and works great on Sunday mornings when I'm teaching high school kids who are still waking up!

Not only do I feel a personal change as a result of the course, but others have seen a change in me as well. My boss has noticed a difference in the way I conduct sessions. My meetings are more successful because I know how to address and resolve conflicts immediately, I can identify distracting behaviors and redirect them before they are out of control, and I know my process cold so I can take a tangent, come back to my original point, and end my meetings on time, every time.

When not leading meetings, I find I'm a better listener and more active participant because I now recognize what it takes to turn a "good" meeting into a "great" meeting. It's awesome that my company understands the value of offering this kind of training to our staff. It is knowledge I can use in every aspect of my life.

INTRODUCTION: A POWERFUL SECRET

Professional facilitators know a *powerful secret*.

What makes it a secret? Certainly not the number of people who know it. In fact, there are probably many who would say they are aware of the secret. Yet very few truly understand how to use it. Therein lies the secret.

What makes it powerful? If "power" is somewhat synonymous with "getting results," then this secret is extremely powerful. The secret can increase your ability to achieve results simply because it is linked to effectiveness and human motivation.

CASE STUDY: Learning the Powerful Secret

I began understanding the secret during my career with the management consulting division of what was then one of the Big 8 accounting and consulting firms. In the eight years I spent in that consulting practice, we had a standard way of addressing a client's problem. We might be called in to review a particular department or activity. We would arrive with our army of bright people, interview those who we believed were the key stakeholders, develop a set of recommendations based on our interviews and experience, and create what might be called the "100 percent solution." We would go away and come back a year later, and, if we were lucky, perhaps 15 percent of our recommendations would be implemented.

In my final years with that organization, the practice in which I worked began taking a different, more facilitative approach. We would come in with a smaller group of consultants and work shoulder to shoulder with client personnel. Together we would convene group interviews (facilitated sessions), which typically included eight to twenty people. In the facilitated sessions, the participants—not the consultants—would create the recommendations. In most cases, they would come up with what we might consider only the 60 or 70 percent solution.

So we would float ideas based on our experience. Some they would accept; others they would reject as "not beneficial" or "not implementable" in their environment. When all was done, they might have created what we would consider the 85 percent solution. Yet when we came back a year later, amazingly 80 to 90 percent of the solution would be implemented!

Why wasn't more of the 100 percent solution implemented? Why did the 85 percent solution gained through facilitation achieve far greater success? Therein lies the secret and the power behind it.

Secret #1	**The Fundamental Secret of Facilitation** You can achieve more effective results when solutions are created, understood, and accepted by the people impacted.

Prior to my grasping the secret, facilitating groups was about 10 percent of what I did on a day-to-day basis. Once I understood the power and effectiveness achieved through facilitation, I wanted to spend my time focused on this skill. In 1992, I left that consulting organization and founded Leadership Strategies— The Facilitation Company. An example from the work of Leadership Strategies may make the power of the secret even more apparent.

Case Study: The Sanitation Workers

After reading the independent recommendations of an outside consulting firm (which didn't use facilitation), the mayor of a major metropolitan city issued a directive indicating that the Sanitation Bureau would move from three-person to two-person garbage pickup crews. Yet the director of the Sanitation Bureau believed strongly that the implementation of two-person crews would fail without the support and involvement of the workers. Therefore, the director called us in to help facilitate the development of a plan for implementing the directive.

We recommended that the employees at each of the bureau's three operating facilities elect four representatives to serve on the planning team. The director appointed several other team members, including one person each from the finance office, the human resources office, and the union. In total, there were fifteen members on the team.

We facilitated the team through a series of eight half-day meetings using a project planning process to help focus on purpose, key outcomes, critical success factors, approach, scheduling, and budgeting, among other topics. Although many of the team members had limited education, they understood sanitation issues and quickly were able to grasp the process as a vehicle for working through problems and alternatives.

As the team's facilitators, we often used questioning techniques to challenge what appeared to be recommendations that might undermine the goals of the team. Some challenges led to refinement of recommendations; other challenges proved irrelevant; and still others, though perhaps beneficial, the team consciously chose to ignore. In the end, the team created a comprehensive plan whose benefits were clearly delineated. They were very proud of their work.

The team members (not the facilitators) presented their plan to the mayor and his cabinet. We coached the team on presentation skills, group question-and-answer techniques, and other methods to help ensure effectiveness. One member of the team bought a suit specifically for this meeting with the mayor. At the end of the presentation, the chief operating officer for the city announced that it was the best presentation, set of recommendations, and justification he had ever received from an employee work team. The recommendations, almost in their entirety, were implemented.

Consider the sanitation workers and their state of mind after investing their hearts and souls in creating their solution. They had two major concerns the night before the presentation. Of course, there was the internal fear of presenting so poorly that they would fall flat on their faces—an emotion well known to most of us. But outside of that fear, *their greatest concern was that the mayor would not accept their recommendations!* Yet it was the mayor's idea in the first place to go to two-person crews. By putting the workers in charge of developing the plan for implementation, the director of sanitation had made it *their* plan: they owned it, and they were ready to sell it to the mayor and to their coworkers.

In contrast, before the Big 8 firm implemented facilitation techniques, the consultants created the solution. It was, in essence, the *consultants'* solution. The employees felt little ownership. When the workers created it, it was *their* solution. Admittedly, the workers agreed to only the 85 percent solution. But which results would you rather have? Very little of 100 percent or nearly all of 85 percent?

In his book *Transforming the Mature Information Technology Organization,* Dr. Robert Zawacki from the University of Colorado put the secret this way:

$$ED = RD \times CD$$

That is, an **E**ffective **D**ecision equals the **R**ight **D**ecision *multiplied by* the level of **C**ommitment to the **D**ecision. The multiplication sign in Dr. Zawacki's formula means that even the best decision can be rendered completely ineffective if commitment to the decision is lacking. A group of consultants might have created the 100 percent solution for the Sanitation Bureau, but if the workers did not buy in to the solution, the effectiveness of the solution would have been near zero.

Learning to Apply the Fundamental Secret

Of course, the secret is not complicated. Remember, however, that although many know the secret, few truly understand how to apply it and how to unleash the power that is available when you get people together to develop solutions that will work for them. For example, few understand

- How to get people excited about participating in a solution process
- How to keep people focused and engaged
- How to ask questions that challenge without alienating
- How to guide a team without overpowering it
- How to address disagreements and build consensus
- How to deal with people who drop out, dominate, or demonstrate other dysfunctional behaviors that can be disruptive
- How to ensure that you gain commitment to action

These are foundational facilitation skills that help groups achieve amazing results. In early 1993, we at Leadership Strategies set out to find a facilitation training course that taught these skills. We found many courses that focused on facilitating higher-level processes, such as strategic planning and requirements analysis. We also found courses that provided instruction in building-block methods and processes, such as quality tools and problem-solving techniques. For the most part, they were terrific courses. Yet generally they did not thoroughly address the foundational skills that made great facilitators superb at their trade. Some courses covered concepts related to group dynamics. But often these courses explained the result that was desired (for example, helping the group move to consensus) without providing details on how to create the result. The foundational skills seemed to be missing, as shown in Figure I.1.

We believed that facilitation was an art but that there was a science to the art. We believed that at the foundation of facilitation there had to be a methodology that facilitators use, even if they were unaware of it. We were intent on discovering the methodology and developing training materials to support it.

To learn what we needed, we interviewed veteran facilitators who were considered among the best in their areas of expertise. We asked them four specific questions:

FIGURE I.1 THE FOCUS OF MOST FACILITATION COURSES.

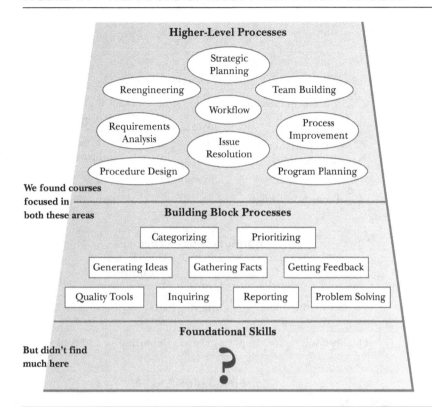

Our Questions to Veteran Facilitators

- When you are facilitating and things are going well, what are you doing? What are the techniques and processes you use to get the group involved, interacting, and achieving results?

- If you were going to send those who worked with you to a facilitation class, what are the key topics and techniques you would want them to learn?

- What are some of the classic mistakes you have seen facilitators make? During those times when you were in the back of the room and someone else was facilitating, what were the things that the facilitator did or didn't do that made you uncomfortable, irritated you, or made you want to jump up and run the session yourself?

- Although you are considered a very good facilitator, surely there are areas in which you would like to be better skilled. What are the situations for which you need better techniques? Consider sessions you facilitated where something didn't go as well as you would have liked. What are those areas for which additional tools would make you an even better facilitator?

FIGURE I.2 FOUNDATIONAL SKILL AREAS.

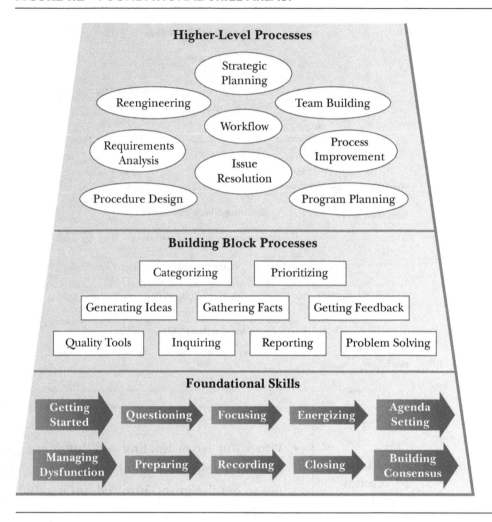

From the information gained in these interviews, we identified what we believe are the foundational skill areas for facilitators, as shown in Figure I.2.

The Principles of SMART Facilitation

We were very excited to uncover these foundational skill areas. From this base, we formulated a structured facilitation methodology that we call SMART Facilitation: **S**tructured **M**eeting **a**nd **R**elating **T**echniques. SMART Facilitation is based on eleven principles that provide SMART facilitators with a clear vision of facilitation excellence. Supporting the principles are specific strategies and techniques that demonstrate how SMART facilitators execute the principles in practice. Together, the principles and techniques constitute a comprehensive methodology for SMART Facilitation that can be used to produce consistent, repeatable results. Figure I.3 shows the overall structure of SMART Facilitation.

FIGURE I.3 THE PRINCIPLES OF SMART FACILITATION.

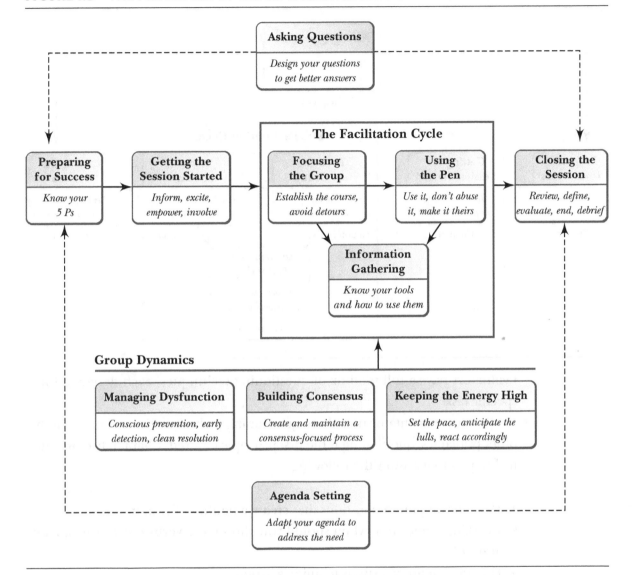

Because this diagram has many components, I am going to break it down into the primary parts. Following Chapter One, which covers the role of the facilitator, each of the next eleven chapters of this book focuses on one of the principles. Chapters Two through Eight cover the principles that serve as the basic flow for a typical facilitated session, as shown in Figure I.4. Let's preview the chapters and the insights found in each.

Chapter Two: The Secrets to Questioning

Design Your Questions to Get Better Answers

SMART facilitators know that the most important facilitation tool is questioning. Rather than using only open- and closed-ended questioning techniques, SMART

FIGURE I.4 THE FLOW OF A FACILITATED SESSION.

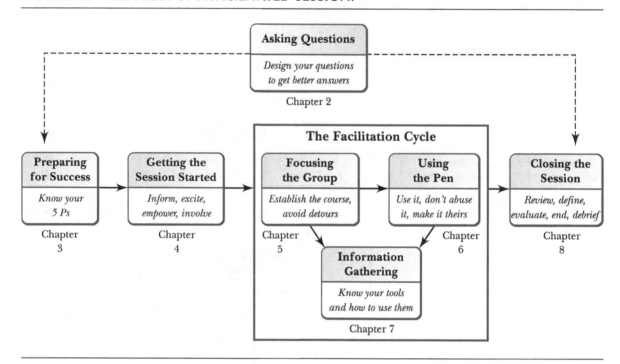

facilitators have a full toolbox of questioning techniques, each designed for a specific task.

Because a facilitator uses these questioning techniques in executing all the other principles, questioning is the first principle covered. Chapter Two provides techniques that answer the following:

- How do you phrase questions that create a bonfire of responses?
- In asking a question, when should you choose the verbs *could, should, must,* and *will?*
- How do you use questions to guide a group?
- How do you react to responses without overpowering the group?
- How do you float an idea without unduly influencing the group?
- How do you use questioning techniques when you are not facilitating?

Chapter Three: The Secrets to Preparing

Know Your 5 Ps

SMART facilitators know that preparation is critical for success. They know the questions to ask to fully understand the need that will be addressed in the session, and they know the steps to take to fully prepare to meet the need. They make sure they understand the 5 Ps of preparation: purpose, product, participants, probable issues, and process. Chapter Three answers these questions:

- What are the most important steps in planning for a facilitated session?
- What are the key questions that you need to have answered?
- With whom should you speak to get prepared?
- What do you ask participants about the session?
- How do you know if you are well prepared?

Chapter Four: The Secrets to Starting

Inform, Excite, Empower, Involve

SMART facilitators know that the opening of any facilitated session is critical. During this time, you set the stage for everything that follows. Start well, and the group is ready to work with you to achieve the desired outcome. Start poorly, and you are fighting an uphill battle. Questions answered include the following:

- What are the four most important things to do in the opening?
- How do you get the participants excited about participating?
- How do you get buy-in to the agenda?
- What is the purpose of ground rules?
- What parking boards should you use?
- How do you get the session started on time?
- What is the appropriate order of the steps in the opening?

Chapter Five: The Secrets to Focusing

Establish the Course, Avoid Detours

Chapters Five, Six, and Seven make up what I call the Facilitation Cycle. After getting the session started (as discussed in Chapter Four), you are now ready to begin the first agenda item. You first focus the group (Chapter Five), use the power of the pen (Chapter Six), and perform information gathering (Chapter Seven). When you are done with the first agenda item, you return to focusing the group and go through the cycle for the second agenda item, and so on, until you have covered all the agenda items.

Chapter Five contains the Secrets to Focusing, including the answers to these questions:

- What should you do at the beginning of every agenda item to get the group focused?
- When significant time has passed since the last session, how do you restart and get the group focused?
- How do you avoid asking your first question and getting complete silence?

- How do you give directions that are accurate, clear, and concise?
- What techniques are there for keeping a group on track?
- How do you effectively use breakout groups?
- How do you keep groups focused during report-back sessions following breakout groups?

Chapter Six: The Secrets to Recording

The Power of the Pen—Use It, Don't Abuse It, Make It Theirs

Most facilitators aren't aware that they can propel a group to the brink of dysfunction simply by abusing the pen. Often facilitators unintentionally devalue a participant's comments either by failing to record a remark with which they disagree or by waiting until the remark is validated by other people. Other times, they reword the participant's comment, then record the reworded version (tacitly implying that the original words were not good enough!). In time, group members can lose complete ownership over the recorded comments simply because the comments aren't theirs, but rather the facilitator's. In Chapter Six, you will learn the answers to the following:

- What is the most important information to document from a facilitated session?
- How do you avoid abusing the power of the pen?
- How do you manage the recording process while still facilitating the group?
- What do you do when a participant gives you a long monologue?
- How do you prevent lulls while you are writing?
- How do you effectively use a scribe during the session?
- What is an appropriate format for the documentation?
- What are the seven deadly sins of facilitation?

Chapter Seven: The Secrets to Information Gathering

Know Your Tools and How to Use Them

Facilitators must have a wealth of information gathering and processing tools at their disposal in order to address a variety of needs. Some tools are for gathering facts, others for generating ideas, and still others for categorizing, prioritizing, reporting, and evaluating. This chapter covers the following questions:

- What are the major information gathering and processing functions?
- How do you maximize question-and-answer (Q&A) sessions to ensure that the most important questions get asked?

- What is the most important thing to do in a brainstorming session?
- What are the three critical activities in prioritizing?
- How do you ensure quality feedback during a report-back process?
- How do you perform an evaluation of the session without allowing the comments of one or two people to bias the feedback?

Chapter Eight: The Secrets to Closing

Review, Define, Evaluate, End, Debrief

Often meetings end without a clear understanding of what was accomplished or what will happen going forward. SMART facilitators know that in closing a session, it is important that everyone is clear on what was done, the benefits of what was done, the actions that must occur once the meeting is over, and the method for ensuring that the actions have been accomplished. In Chapter Eight, you will find answers to these questions:

- What are the most important activities to do before closing a session?
- What do you do with the participants' personal objectives identified at the beginning of the session?
- How do you ensure buy-in and commitment to the decisions made in the meeting?
- What do you do with the items remaining on the Issues list?
- What are guidelines for assigning responsibility for the Actions list?
- What feedback is needed from the team and the sponsor of the meeting?
- What do you do if it looks as though you are going to exceed the scheduled ending time?

Chapter Nine: The Secrets to Managing Dysfunction

Conscious Prevention, Early Detection, Clean Resolution

Whereas Chapters Two through Eight lay out the flow for a facilitated meeting, Chapters Nine through Eleven focus on group dynamics. A facilitator skilled in the techniques covered in Chapters Two through Eight will understand the mechanics of facilitation. The group dynamics information in Chapters Nine through Eleven provides the tools for managing group behavior, as shown in Figure I.5.

FIGURE I.5   THE PRINCIPLES OF SMART FACILITATION BY CHAPTER.

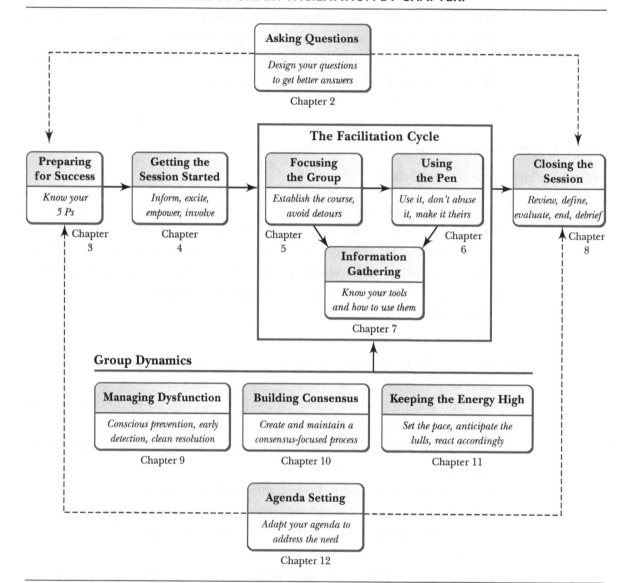

How do you deal with someone who is constantly saying, "No, that won't work. We've tried it before, and it won't work. It's a bad idea. It's not practical. It's not realistic. It just won't work"? What about the people who want to dominate the discussion? Or—just the opposite—the people who sit there and say nothing, until they go out the door and then tell everyone how much a waste of time the meeting was?

Many facilitators fear dysfunctional behavior and seek a wealth of techniques to address dysfunction should it occur. SMART facilitators, however, know that the key to dysfunction is to address it *before* it occurs (conscious prevention), detect it early if it does happen (early detection), and cleanly resolve it so that it goes away for good (clean resolution). By the end of this chapter, you will be able to answer the following:

- What is dysfunctional behavior?
- How do you identify potential dysfunction during the preparation stage?
- What are strategies you can take prior to the session to prevent dysfunctional behavior from occurring?
- How do you detect dysfunction early?
- What are the needs and typical dysfunctions of the different communication styles?
- How do you address some of the more common dysfunction types, such as the dropout, the naysayer, the whisperer, and the verbal attacker?
- What do you do when something unexpected happens in a session, such as an emotional outburst?
- How should you respond when one or more participants indicate that you have made a mistake or suggest a change to the process that you don't want to make?

Chapter Ten: The Secrets to Consensus Building

Create and Maintain a Consensus-Focused Process

SMART facilitators know both the good news and the bad news about consensus building. The good news: people disagree for only three reasons. The bad news: if you use an inappropriate consensus building strategy, you are likely to fail. Level 3 disagreements can't be solved with a level 1 technique, and level 1 disagreements can't be solved with a level 2 technique. SMART facilitators know the three reasons people disagree, and they have consensus building tools for addressing each one. Questions covered in Chapter Ten include the following:

- What is the definition of consensus?
- Why might full consensus not be the recommended goal of a group?
- What are the three reasons people disagree?
- How do you address a disagreement in which the argument appears to be irrational?
- How do you slow down a conversation to ensure that everyone is getting the facts?
- How do you resolve a disagreement that is based on different values or experiences?

Chapter Eleven: The Secrets to Energy

Set the Pace, Anticipate the Lulls, React Accordingly

Whether you are leading a single two-hour meeting or a series of half-day meetings, a degree of energy is essential to keeping the group interested and engaged. In Chapter Eleven, you will learn the answers to the following questions:

- What is the impact of energy on the session topic, the session participants, and the participants' view of the facilitator?
- How do you start a session with energy?
- What are the lullaby times during the day, and what should you do about them?
- How do you maintain energy throughout a session?
- When are team building activities appropriate? How do you use them well?

Chapter Twelve: The Secrets to Agenda Setting

Adapt Your Agenda to Address the Need

The last of the core principles ends at the beginning, with methods for constructing agendas using the techniques covered in the other chapters. Chapter Twelve answers the following questions:

- What is a standard agenda, and why do you need it?
- How do you customize a standard agenda to meet a specific need?
- How do you create an agenda from scratch?
- How do you ensure that you know your process cold?
- How does an agenda differ from a detailed facilitation guide?
- What should be included in a facilitation guide?
- How do you estimate time?

Whereas Chapters Two through Twelve lay the foundation for the eleven principles, the remaining chapters focus on specific topics and specific areas for applying the Secrets.

Chapter Thirteen: The Secrets to Facilitating Virtual Meetings

Keep Everyone Focused and Engaged

Virtual meetings have become a reality of today's business world; people attend meetings from anywhere in the world by telephone, smartphone, videoconference, or Internet. Although these technologies can reduce the cost of meetings, they also present significant challenges to the facilitator in keeping people focused and productive. In Chapter Thirteen, you will find answers to the following questions:

- How do you help people who are not in the room "see" what is going on?
- What are common technologies available to support virtual meetings?
- How do you keep people fully engaged and participating in virtual meetings?
- What special ground rules can be used to help with virtual meetings?

- How do you apply the various Secrets of Facilitation in the virtual setting?
- How do you facilitate a virtual meeting when you are the only person *not* in the room?
- How do you address anonymity in a virtual meeting?

Chapter Fourteen: The Secrets to Facilitating Large Groups and Conferences

Use the Power of Process to Guide and Engage

Many of the same techniques that you would use with a group of sixteen or fewer are also applicable when facilitating one hundred or more as part of a large group or conference. However, how you apply the techniques will vary depending on the size of the group, the session purpose, whether you have cofacilitators, and so on. This chapter describes best practices for maximizing engagement with large groups and conferences while maintaining control. Chapter Fourteen answers the following questions:

- What are the key strategies for facilitating large groups?
- How is planning the facilitation for a large group different from planning for a smaller group?
- When is it best to have professional facilitators, rather than volunteers, lead the breakout groups?
- How do you prepare the breakout group leaders?
- What are best practices for facilitating conferences?
- How do you maintain high levels of participant engagement when you have speakers and no control over how engaging they are?
- How do you manage time during the conference, given that many speakers run over their allotted time?

Chapter Fifteen: The Secrets to Facilitating Cross-Cultural Groups

Recognize Your Own Biases to Better Adapt to the Culture of Others

How do you facilitate groups from a culture different from your own? In Chapter Fifteen, I team with three other veteran facilitators to provide approaches for understanding your own cultural biases and for applying the Secrets appropriately to adjust for cultural differences between you and the group you are facilitating. This chapter also includes a powerful section on interrupting the effects of institutional power through facilitation, and answers the following questions:

- What is meant by cross-cultural competency?
- How does a national culture differ from an organizational culture or a team culture?

- How do generational cultures impact facilitation?
- How do you recognize your own cultural biases?
- What are major dimensions that define different cultures?
- How do you adapt the Secrets to the culture you are facilitating?
- How do you facilitate groups whose culture encourages participants to defer to their leaders?
- What is the dominance effect, and how does it play out in the groups you facilitate?

Chapter Sixteen: The Secrets to Building an Internal Facilitator Capability

Build the Case, Raise Awareness

Many large companies determined several years ago that having an internal consulting group that helps various areas of the organization could significantly raise overall performance; similarly, an increasing number of organizations are establishing an internal cadre of facilitators who are available to design and facilitate important meetings. This chapter answers key questions concerning how to get an internal group started:

- What is an internal facilitator capability, and how might it work?
- What are the benefits to an organization of having a facilitator cadre?
- How do you get a facilitator cadre started?
- How many facilitators might you need? How do you recruit them and build their skills?
- Who manages the cadre? How are the facilitators assigned to engagements?
- How do internal customers learn about the cadre? What do they "pay" for the service?
- What pitfalls must you avoid?

Chapter Seventeen: Special Topics

In the final chapter, I discuss applying the Secrets to special situations, such as running a simple meeting, working with a small group, and acting as a consultant or subject matter expert. The chapter answers the following key questions:

- How do you apply the Secrets to running a simple meeting?
- How do you apply the Secrets as a meeting participant?
- How do you apply the Secrets to very small groups?
- How do you apply the Secrets as a consultant or subject matter expert?
- How do you become a certified facilitator?
- Facilitator neutrality: fact or fiction?

More Ways to Apply the Secrets

Since first releasing our facilitator training course, The Effective Facilitator, two decades ago, we have trained more than fifteen thousand facilitators, managers, analysts, and consultants around the world in applying the power of facilitation to work with teams and task forces. We knew that this course would be a big help to this audience, especially in aiding them in facilitating meetings. However, what we didn't expect was how enthusiastic participants were about applying the skills to other areas inside and outside the business world.

- In one of the early classes, a consulting manager from IBM suggested that these techniques could be extremely effective for their sales force. She felt that if her sales representatives used a more facilitative approach with their clients, they could avoid common problems, such as misunderstood needs, unrealistic expectations, and resistance from the client's staff.
- A chapter of the American Society for Training and Development thought that the techniques were ideal for trainers and presenters and asked that we present a special workshop for beginning trainers on how to use facilitation techniques in the classroom. Since that time, we have been asked to present similar techniques in-house to nationwide training organizations.
- During classes, managers frequently asked questions about how to address the various personalities and dysfunctions they face in the workplace.
- A participant from a software firm confided that after just the first day of the three-day class, she began using the techniques to relate better with her husband. She was very pleased with the difference in his response to her.

The more that class participants shared about ways to apply the techniques, the more we were convinced that people in general—not just facilitators, managers, analysts, and consultants—could benefit from understanding how to use the power of facilitation in their interactions. By publishing *The Secrets of Facilitation,* I hope to make these concepts and techniques accessible to a much wider audience.

What This Book Will Do for You

Facilitation works. You *will* achieve more effective results when solutions are created, understood, and accepted by the people impacted. You *will* be more successful, have more effective group interactions, and gain better results. This book shows you how.

The Secrets of Facilitation delivers the concepts and strategies you need in order to make facilitation work more effectively for you. What does the book give you?

- *A comprehensive methodology—the principles.* Until now, there has not been a book written specifically to show the professional facilitator and the layperson alike a comprehensive methodology for facilitating any situation. Whether you lead a cross-functional work team or head up a committee for your church or PTA, *The Secrets of Facilitation* gives you a step-by-step approach to group facilitation. You can be confident that you know what to do and how to do it.
- *Detailed techniques—the Secrets.* This book details the seventy concepts and techniques that I have termed "the Secrets." Each secret represents a tool or technique that you can use to achieve amazing results with teams, groups, and individuals. Collectively, the Secrets comprise a set of best practices that you can begin using tomorrow in one-on-one interactions, short meetings, full-day retreats, and multisession task forces.
- *Underlying insights—group dynamics.* The book is chock-full of key insights—such as the three reasons people disagree, the causes of dysfunction, and the ways to ask a question to enable participants to visualize answers—that go beyond merely explaining what to do. These insights give you the underlying understanding that enables you to create your own techniques to address various problems and issues that can occur in a facilitated session.
- *Real-world learning—case studies and sample dialogues.* The numerous case studies and sample dialogues will put you in the room witnessing the facilitator in action. You will learn what the facilitator did, why the facilitator did it, and how the group responded. You will also read about mistakes facilitators made and the ramifications of those mistakes.
- *Immediate usability—application tips and checklists.* There are numerous applications of the Secrets, and each chapter describes sample situations for applying them in business and everyday life. The application tips, coupled with the checklists that end each chapter and the sample meeting agendas in Chapter Twelve, will help get you thinking about ways to apply the information in your professional and personal life.

In short, this book delivers the Secrets that SMART facilitators use for consistently achieving amazing results through groups.

Where to Start

Chapter One defines facilitation and the role of a facilitator. Following that overview, the book takes you through each of the principles. Each chapter covers methods used by SMART facilitators, those facilitators who know the Structured Meeting and Relating Techniques.

Starting with Chapter Two and going through Chapter Sixteen, the chapters are generally organized in a similar way.

- The chapter-opening page includes a list of questions answered in the pages that follow.
- Most chapters begin with an example from a facilitated session that illustrates the power of the Secrets found in the chapter.
- Multiple facilitation Secrets are highlighted in each chapter.
- Each chapter ends with a checklist for using the Secrets found in the chapter along with an exercise for practicing your skills.

The final chapter, Special Topics, discusses how you can apply the Secrets in several special situations.

To make the most of this book, consider the following suggestions:

- Start by reading Chapter One, What Is the Role of a Facilitator? It will give you an overview of facilitation and a framework for understanding how facilitators operate.
- If you work with groups frequently but are new to facilitation, consider reading the book chapter by chapter. Although each chapter is somewhat discrete, the facilitation methodology builds on itself. Therefore, I make frequent references to techniques presented in earlier chapters.
- If you are a veteran facilitator, you may want to read the questions at the beginning of each chapter and scan the chapter for the Secrets contained in each. (They are set off visually from the regular text.) If you can answer the questions and are fully familiar with the Secrets and how to apply them, move on to the next chapter. When you find particular Secrets intriguing, I would encourage you to go back to the case study at the beginning of the chapter to get an immediate flavor for the Secrets in the chapter and then read forward from there to understand how SMART facilitators apply the techniques.

My greatest desire for *The Secrets of Facilitation* is that it will inspire you to use the Secrets as we do: to achieve amazing results through groups.

CHAPTER ONE

WHAT IS THE ROLE OF A FACILITATOR?

Questions Answered in This Chapter

What is the definition of a facilitated session?

Why must the participants "create, understand, and accept" the results?

What is the role of a facilitator?

What are the attitudes that make up the "soul" of a facilitator?

When is facilitation not appropriate?

What's next for the field of facilitation?

CASE STUDY: The Facilitator's Role in Civic Leadership Groups

In major cities throughout the United States, there are civic organizations, such as Leadership Atlanta and Leadership New York, that specialize in bringing together business, religious, community, and government leaders once a month in small groups to discuss key issues facing the urban area. These civic leadership organizations are designed to break down barriers and create networks across racial, socioeconomic, and business sector lines. Participants are part of a small group for a year and then become graduates and are able to assist with incoming classes.

The small groups are typically facilitated by a local volunteer who is a program graduate. The volunteers often differ widely in their level of prior facilitation experience. We were called in by one civic leadership organization to assist by providing facilitation training for the group facilitators.

Through our review of feedback we received from the first group we trained following their eight months of facilitation, we realized that there was a wide variance in the role each facilitator played.

- In some cases, the facilitator simply played the role of a *meeting adviser.* In this role, the facilitator did not lead the meeting planning or execution, but instead primarily sat on the sidelines and stepped in only when asked or when a situation occurred that the participants could not handle themselves.
- In other cases, the facilitator played the role of a *meeting manager.* In this role, the facilitator set the agenda, established ground rules, and initiated the discussion, but stepped in only when needed.
- A third role we saw was that of *meeting leader.* In this role, the facilitator set the agenda, established ground rules, and initiated the discussion just as the meeting manager did. In addition, however, the meeting leader was active in getting participants excited about participating. The facilitator described the purpose of the session in terms that gave the participants a much bigger picture of the importance of each session in the overall "Leadership" experience. In addition, the facilitator challenged the participants when the discussion appeared to remain at a conceptual level instead of delving into personal application, and the facilitator was very active in ensuring that all participants engaged in the discussion.
- Finally, we saw the role of the *participating leader.* In this role, the facilitator started out much like a meeting leader, by setting the agenda, establishing the ground rules, and initiating the discussion. But the facilitator also actively engaged as a participant in the discussion, frequently offering his own views, giving his opinions on topics, and expressing disagreement with various comments.

We believed that it was important for the organization to determine the role they wanted facilitators to play, so as to increase the level of consistency in the experience each small group received. On the basis of the feedback from the participants, the organization concluded the following:

- The participating leader was not an appropriate role because it tended to disempower the group and negatively impact the experience of the participants.
- It was best for facilitators to start as meeting leaders to help the group engage and to establish a high level of energy and interaction.
- Over time, facilitators were expected to move into the meeting manager and meeting adviser roles as participants took more control of the process and meeting execution.

What is the appropriate role of the facilitator? Is it meeting adviser, meeting manager, meeting leader, or participating leader? Let's start with some foundation information first, then we'll revisit this question when I cover the responsibilities of a facilitator.

SAMPLE SCENARIOS: Group Solutions Needed

What would you do if you were faced with one of these situations?

Human Resources Organization—Hiring Process

The vice president of human resources is fed up with all the complaints she has been receiving about problems with the hiring process. Some departments complain that it takes too long to get people hired. Other departments are concerned that their people don't have enough involvement in the screening process. Still others believe we are hiring people who lack some of the basic business skills needed for success. The vice president has appointed you to lead a twelve-person, cross-functional task force to research the problem and recommend a revised hiring process, including an implementation plan and timeline.

Food Processing Plant—Quality Plan

The general manager of your plant announces, "We have been asked by our largest customer [a fast-food chain] to develop and implement a plan for ensuring that our beef patties, buns, and sauces will be able to keep up with the customer's rising quality standards. If our plan is unacceptable to them, or if our people fail to implement the plan successfully, we stand to lose over 50 percent of our business. I know this won't be a small task, but I want you to make it your number-one priority. Just let me know what you need, and who you need, to get it done."

Transportation Company—Systems Project

You are leading a systems development project for your transportation company. The consulting firm developing the computer programs estimated that the system would cost $10 million and require three years to implement. Two-and-a-half years and $12 million later, the consulting firm is estimating that another $10 million and two years will be needed to complete the job. In two days, the chief information officer wants a recommendation to take to the company's executive committee. You and your eight-person management team need to decide whether the company should continue to invest in the project, salvage what it can from what is currently finished, or cancel the project completely.

Managers in both the private and public sectors are frequently faced with handling situations such as these. Yet they are often ill-equipped to plan, execute, and follow through on these efforts. Many don't know the steps to take or the pitfalls to avoid. For example, if you were faced with one of these situations, how would you answer the following questions?

- What overall approach should you take to address the issue; specifically, what should the group do first, second, third, and so on? Is a "strategic planning" approach beneficial? Or perhaps an "issue resolution" or "process improvement" approach would be better?

- Who are the right people to participate in the decision making?
- When the participants meet, how do you get them interacting and working together right from the beginning?
- What do you do to prevent one person from dominating the discussion, or to keep people from dropping out, or even to prevent two people's disagreement from derailing the entire meeting?
- How do you ensure that the group stays focused and on task? What do you do when people attempt to focus on side issues or "hidden agendas"?
- How do you keep the energy high throughout the session?
- What techniques do you use to encourage participants to reach consensus on a final solution?
- How do you ensure at the end of the effort that everyone is clear about what was done, the resulting benefit, and the next steps to be taken?

When Is Facilitation Appropriate?

Although the three scenarios described earlier are not identical, they have several key elements in common.

- *An important issue has been detected.* There is an issue that needs to be addressed: an inefficient process, a client seeking assurances of continued quality, a project that has exceeded its budget.
- *The solution to the issue is not readily apparent.* If the solution were obvious, more than likely it would have been implemented already. To develop a solution will require a deeper understanding and analysis of the situation with input from a number of people.
- *Buy-in is needed for the solution to be successful.* The solution will require acceptance—and often a change in behavior—by a number of people. Without acceptance, even the best solution will fail.
  - If the revisions to the hiring process are unacceptable to the hiring departments or personnel, the hiring process will continue to be ineffective.
  - If the general manager allows the quality director to develop the quality plan without the involvement of key people on the plant floor, the chances of successful implementation are significantly decreased.
  - The decision on whether to continue or cancel the systems development project must take into account all relevant information from all sides of the issue. If critical information is withheld, or if key parties are left out of the decision-making process, the decision may lack foundation and support.

I believe that situations with these characteristics cry out for a facilitated solution arrived at through one or more facilitated sessions. I have found that facilitation techniques are appropriate in any situation in which understanding and buy-in are needed from a group to achieve success.

The Secret of When to Use Facilitation

If more than a few people are involved, and understanding and buy-in are needed, so is facilitation.

Definition: What Is a Facilitated Session?

Although you hear "facilitation" used to define many activities, for the purposes of this book I define the term *facilitated session* in the following way:

> **A facilitated session is a highly structured meeting in which the meeting leader (the facilitator) guides the participants through a series of predefined steps to arrive at a result that is created, understood, and accepted by all participants.**

Let's look at some of the key aspects of this definition.

- Every facilitated session has a specific purpose or *result* to be achieved. For example, the purpose of a particular facilitated meeting might be to create a strategic plan for the organization, to improve the efficiency of a specific process, or to define a solution to a difficult problem.
- To create the result, the participants flow through a series of *predefined steps*. In the case of creating a strategic plan, for example, the facilitated session might include the following steps:
  - Situation assessment: Where are we now?
  - Visioning and goal setting: Where do we want to be?
  - Strategy development: How do we get there?
  - Action planning: How do we monitor our progress?
- The role of facilitators is to *guide* participants through the steps. Facilitators don't dictate the solution. Instead, they use their understanding of the process steps and of group dynamics to help the group achieve the desired results, given the specific needs and characteristics of the participants. If the group is successful, the final results will have been *created, understood, and accepted by all participants.*

Why Do This? | **Why must the participants "create, understand, and accept" the result?**

Recall from the Introduction that an effective decision equals the right decision multiplied by the level of commitment to the decision. Moving from three-person to two-person garbage crews may have been the right decision, but without commitment from the sanitation workers, its effectiveness would have been severely hampered. Likewise, even if you as the leader of a task force know the right solution, the effectiveness of the solution can be nullified if the other task force members are not committed to the solution. How do you build that commitment? That's what facilitation is all about.

What Are the Responsibilities of a Facilitator?

In the case study that opened this chapter, I indicated four distinct definitions of the role of a facilitator.

Different Definitions of the Role of a Facilitator

- **Meeting adviser.** The facilitator helps the leader plan the meeting; however, during the session, the facilitator primarily sits on the sidelines, stepping in only when asked or if a situation occurs that the participants cannot handle themselves.
- **Meeting manager.** The facilitator sets the agenda, establishes ground rules, initiates the discussion, and allows the session to flow, stepping in only when needed.
- **Meeting leader.** The facilitator sets the agenda, establishes ground rules, and initiates the discussion just as the meeting manager does. In addition, the facilitator provides a vision for why the session is important, gets participants excited about participating, keeps the discussion focused, asks challenging questions when appropriate, and ensures that all participants have an opportunity to engage in the discussion.
- **Participating facilitator.** The facilitator starts out much like a meeting leader, setting the agenda, establishing ground rules, and initiating the discussion. But the facilitator also actively engages as a participant in the discussion, frequently offering his or her own views, giving opinions on topics, and expressing disagreement with various comments.

Although the tools and techniques in this book will help you in any four of the roles, this book assumes that you will be playing the role of meeting leader as I've described it here.

As the facilitator, you are active in both planning and executing the session. In this role you are both exciting people and challenging people. Under this definition of a facilitator as meeting leader, you have several responsibilities, as delineated in Table 1.1.

After having fulfilled so many responsibilities, is there any wonder why facilitators are typically exhausted after a facilitated session?

TABLE 1.1 THE RESPONSIBILITIES OF A FACILITATOR.

Motivator	From the rousing opening statement to the closing words of cheer, you must ignite a fire within the group, establish momentum, and keep the pace.
Guide	You must know the steps of the process the group will execute from beginning to end. You must carefully guide the participants through each of the steps.
Questioner	You must listen carefully to the discussion and be able to quickly analyze and compare comments and to formulate questions that help manage the group discussion and challenge the group when appropriate.
Bridge builder	You must create and maintain a safe and open environment for sharing ideas. Where other people see differences, you must find and use similarities to establish a foundation for building bridges to consensus.
Clairvoyant	Throughout the session, you must watch carefully for signs of potential strain, weariness, aggravation, and disempowerment—and respond in advance to avoid dysfunctional behavior.
Peacemaker	Although it is almost always better to avoid a direct confrontation between participants, should such an event occur, you must quickly step in, reestablish order, and direct the group toward a constructive resolution.
Taskmaster	You are ultimately responsible for keeping the session on track; this entails tactfully cutting short irrelevant discussions, preventing detours, and maintaining a consistent level of detail throughout the session.
Praiser	At every opportunity, you should praise participants for the effort they put forth, the progress they make, and the results they achieve. Praise well, praise often, praise specifically.

The Soul of a Facilitator

To perform these roles requires considerable skill and expertise in the numerous techniques you will find in this book. SMART facilitators know, however, that knowledge and experience in using techniques are not enough. SMART facilitators also bring a caring persona to their work that I like to call the "soul" of a facilitator. What are the characteristics of this soul?

- *Facilitators care about people.* They value people, their views, and their input. They want each person to walk away from a facilitated event feeling welcome, heard, and understood. They model positive affirmation and demonstrate their caring through their words and actions.
- *Facilitators want to help.* The word *facilitator* comes from the Latin word *facil,* which means "to make easy." Facilitators get great pleasure from being of assistance. They genuinely enjoy using their expertise to help others succeed.
- *Facilitators put their egos aside.* Facilitators recognize that they are servants of the group. They understand that their presence is secondary, that their personal views are inconsequential, and that their value is defined by their ability to help the group achieve the group's objectives, not the facilitator's. They don't get upset with a participant's difficult behaviors. They don't take concerns personally. They are willing to play as little or as great a role as necessary to help the group be successful.

The Secrets of Facilitation will provide you with numerous tools and techniques for executing successful facilitated sessions. These same methods, however, can be used for group manipulation and selfish pursuits if not coupled with the characteristics that make up the soul of a facilitator. Facilitators don't "facipulate"; that is, they don't use their facilitation skills to attempt to manipulate the group to accept a predefined outcome.

When facilitating a group, try asking yourself this question: "Am I trying to achieve my own outcomes, or am I seeking an outcome that will maximize the group's buy-in and success?" The essential difference between a manipulator and a facilitator is in the intention of the soul.

When Is Facilitation Not Appropriate?

Recall the definition of a facilitated session: a highly structured meeting in which the meeting leader (the facilitator) guides the participants through a series of predefined steps to arrive at a result that is *created, understood,* and *accepted* by all participants. Given this definition, you can see there are several instances when a facilitated session is not appropriate:

- When there is nothing to "create"
  Example: A decision has already been made by the manager to move in a certain direction. In this case, *a facilitated session on what direction to choose would be a waste of time and would border on facipulation.* In fact, the participants could perceive such a session as deceptive and misleading, as the decision has already been "created." However, a facilitated session on how to implement the decision might be appropriate.

- When a situation or the related information is too complex or too confidential for the group to "understand"
Example: An organization is developing a computer system to track a customer order from the time that a telephone operator takes the order over the phone through the time that the order is delivered to the customer's home. Through facilitated group sessions, the team identifies the tasks the system needs to do and perhaps the general designs for the screens and reports. However, because of the complexity and wealth of information involved, the design analysts work individually to define the details that will support the screen and report layouts. The analysts then hold facilitated meetings to review the design with the other members of the team.

- When the participants don't have a reason for, or are not open to, "accepting" a common solution
Example: A relatively random group of people attending a conference are discussing which sessions each will attend. The "result" of the discussion is that each person "creates" a list of sessions to attend, and each person has an "understanding" of what sessions others will attend. Yet there is *no need for any one person to "accept" the selections of the others.* A facilitated session, per se, is not appropriate. In contrast, a facilitated session would be appropriate if, for example, the group members were all part of the same department, and the desire was for the department to walk away with at least one person experiencing each of the conference sessions deemed most important. In this case, a facilitated session would be helpful in defining the important sessions and selecting the most appropriate person to attend each.

- When time does not permit a facilitated approach
Example: A project team has been working on developing recommendations to improve the hiring process. The chief HR officer from a different Fortune 500 company, who happens to be in town for the day, offers to meet with the team leader and available team members to describe her organization's hiring process. Although all other decisions have been made as a team, *time does not permit a team gathering to decide whether the meeting is desired.* The team leader accepts the invitation, notifies all members of the meeting, and requests all team members who can attend to do so. Of course, decisions on how to use the information gained will still be made through facilitation.

Warning: Keep in mind that facilitation builds buy-in and that for some situations—though time critical—buy-in is so essential that you can't afford *not* to use facilitation.

TABLE 1.2   A CHECKLIST: WHEN TO USE FACILITATION.

Has the decision already been made?	Yes →	Don't use facilitation
	No →	Use facilitation
Is the issue important enough to justify the time and expense of a facilitative approach?	Yes →	Use facilitation
	No →	Don't use facilitation
Will the development of a solution require a deeper understanding and analysis of the situation with input from a number of people?	Yes →	Use facilitation
	No →	Don't use facilitation
Will the solution likely require buy-in or a change in behavior by a number of people?	Yes →	Use facilitation
	No →	Don't use facilitation
Are the likely participants open to, or do they have a reason for, accepting a common solution?	Yes →	Use facilitation
	No →	Don't use facilitation
Is the situation or the related information not too complex or too confidential for a group to address?	Yes →	Use facilitation
	No →	Don't use facilitation

When facilitation is not used appropriately, the result can be frustrating and quite ineffective. When used appropriately, however, facilitation can yield better results with greater buy-in and stronger commitment to action. Table 1.2 summarizes when facilitation is and is not appropriate.

The first question trumps all others. If the decision has already been made, then holding a facilitated session to come up with a decision is not appropriate. If, however, the answer to the first question is no, ideally you would use facilitation in situations for which the responses to all the other questions are yes.

What if the responses to one or two of the other questions are no? This means that the conditions are not optimal for facilitation. You might choose not to use facilitation, or you may be able to change the focus or the conditions so that the use of facilitation is more appropriate.

Facilitation: Where Is the Industry Today?

Facilitation has come a long way since the founding of the International Association of Facilitators more than fifteen years ago.

- People around the world are using facilitation and group facilitators in a wide array of applications, including strategic planning, total quality management, issue resolution, performance improvement, lean processing, system design, communication engagement, visioning, partnering, requirements analysis, focus groups, and town hall meetings, just to name a few.

- By the start of 2012, there were nearly five hundred Certified Professional Facilitators representing forty-six countries around the globe.
- A master-level certification has been established by the International Institute for Facilitation, and by 2012, there were eighteen who had achieved the Certified Master Facilitator designation.
- The term "certified facilitator" has begun showing up in requests for proposals and government solicitations. The Canadian government essentially requires contract facilitators to hold a facilitation certification to provide government services.
- Each year, international conferences are held regionally around the globe to bring facilitators and nonfacilitators together to network and build their skills.
- Organizations have begun establishing internal facilitation cadres—people who can be called on to facilitate important meetings in areas outside their own. Although in some cases members of the cadre serve as full-time facilitators, in many cases they are full-time members of a department but have a percentage of their time designated to facilitating in other areas for the good of the organization. These organizations recognize the benefit of having an internal function that brings unbiased facilitation expertise to benefit others.
- An entire subindustry has grown up around facilitation. Today you can hire a facilitator to run a meeting, receive face-to-face training in facilitation skills, attend a webinar on facilitation, receive coaching in facilitation, do online facilitation training, take an online self-assessment of your facilitation skills, become a certified facilitator, purchase tools and templates for facilitation, buy facilitation software and apps, get assistance preparing to become certified, license materials so that you can train others to facilitate, and so on.

What's Next for Facilitation?

I asked fifteen leaders in the facilitation industry to provide their input on what the next decade might look like for facilitation.[1] Several key themes emerged.

- **Facilitation as a skill rather than a role.** For the most part, facilitation today is seen as a role played by people with considerable expertise in process design and managing group dynamics. In the future, I expect that facilitation will be seen as a skill, much like leadership, that is cultivated in people playing various roles in all types of organizations. Wouldn't you want your children taught by a teacher who used facilitation skills? Wouldn't you want the managers in your company to use facilitation when supervising their people? Wouldn't it be great if politicians understood the value of empowering people and each other with unbiased information that promoted informed choice? (Okay, maybe I'm really dreaming on this last one.) The point is that leaders in the facilitation industry see facilitation as moving toward being a skill that many share rather than a role for a select few.

- **Expanded awareness of facilitation and its value.** To expand facilitation into much more of a skill than a role, the industry must learn to focus on proving value and return on investment and expanding the number of people who are aware of what facilitation is. Even today, when I say I run the largest meeting facilitation company in the United States, I get blank stares. Many think that this means we are a facilities management company that manages the buildings, factories, and other facilities of different businesses. Then, if I explain that when executives go on those two-day retreats, we are the ones up front taking the executives through strategic planning or issue resolution, they then think we are the ones arranging the room and keeping the water pitchers filled. But when they finally get that we design the process, ask the questions, and manage the group dynamics, I often hear, "So you're the ones that get them to hold hands, do group hugs, and sing 'Kumbaya.'" Today, few know what facilitation is, and even fewer understand its value. Over the next decade, I expect the industry to change this. Already there is a groundswell of support for a noncompetitive awards program that highlights organizations that use facilitation to produce amazing results. I expect that eventually there will be research papers published that show the positive impact that facilitated solutions bring when compared to solutions arrived at without facilitation.

- **Areas of focus.** Leaders in the industry believe that over the next decade, facilitation will be used in additional areas not common to facilitation today, including
  - Addressing ethical issues and other differences in order to move away from the "either-or" thinking that currently polarizes many communities and our political process
  - Building resilience against economic turmoil
  - Facilitating sessions in the highest level of government, including sessions for the United Nations, G7, and cabinet-level decision making

- **Virtuality.** Over time, a much larger percentage of group sessions will be held virtually. I would not be surprised if by the end of the decade, the number of virtual facilitated sessions exceeds the number of face-to-face ones. This means that facilitators will need to be skilled in the technologies and strategies for making virtual sessions effective, productive, and engaging. (Chapter Thirteen provides insights on facilitating virtual meetings.)

- **Youth.** The first generation of certified facilitators is aging, and in the next twenty years, the majority of this group is unlikely to be active in the profession. Over this next decade, there will need to be a conscious effort to bring more youth into the facilitation industry. Facilitation skills will need to be embedded in colleges, universities, business schools, and other areas of academia to raise awareness and attract younger professionals.

I invite you to join with me and others to help make the next decade one in which the awareness, application, and impact of facilitation soars.

Applying the Secrets to Gain Buy-In to a Strategic Plan

How do the Secrets apply to strategic planning? Suppose you were the CEO of an organization of 250 people. You and your twelve-member senior team want to develop a strategic plan. The plan will establish a vision with three-year, measurable targets; first-year milestones; specific strategies; and activity timelines.

- You have read the Introduction and Chapter One of this book and recognize the benefits of gaining the buy-in of those who will be impacted by the plan.
- You have concluded that all 250 people in your organization will be impacted by the strategic plan.
- You are convinced that the organization can implement the plan more effectively if the people impacted by the plan "create, understand, and accept" it.
- You are also convinced that it would not be productive to have 250 people at a strategic planning retreat with you and the other executives. They don't *understand* all the issues, they may be concerned about only their areas of focus (*acceptance*), and it would just take too long for the entire group to *create* it.

The Fundamental Secret of Facilitation still applies: you can achieve *more effective results* when solutions are created, understood, and accepted by the people impacted. You just apply the secret differently to match the situation.

They Understand It

Hold a briefing for the employees on the strategic planning process. Ensure that they are briefed on the steps in the process and their role. Provide all employees with summarized information about the current state of the organization and future opportunities, challenges, and threats.

They Create It

At the briefing, ask the employees (in groups, for the sake of anonymity) to build lists of what they see as the primary issues the organization needs to address in the strategic plan. Gather additional information by giving every employee the opportunity to respond to a detailed written survey to make specific suggestions and recommendations. Consider using employee focus groups to follow up on specific areas requiring additional insight. Supply the planning team members with the survey results, issues, and recommendations provided by the employees.

They Accept It

Once the planning team has drafted the plan, hold a second session with employees to walk through the proposed plan. Bring back the list of issues the employees identified. Ask them (in teams) to identify where in the plan the issues are addressed. In instances where an issue is not addressed, ask the employees to determine if the issue is a priority (compared to the other priority strategies). If the issue is deemed a priority, ask a group of employees to take on developing a specific set of recommendations, including expected costs and justification, for consideration by the senior team. Finally, ask employees to identify the strategies for which they would be willing to join with others to work on developing detailed action plans.

Facilitator's Checklist for Understanding Facilitation and the Roles of a Facilitator

☐ A facilitated session is a highly structured meeting in which the meeting leader (the facilitator) guides the participants through a series of predefined steps to arrive at a result that is created, understood, and accepted by all participants.

☐ The roles of the facilitator include that of motivator, guide, questioner, bridge builder, clairvoyant, peacemaker, taskmaster, and praiser.

☐ Facilitators bring a caring persona to their work: they care about people, they want to help, and they put their egos aside.

☐ Facilitation techniques are appropriate in any situation in which understanding and buy-in are needed from a group.

☐ Facilitation is not appropriate when one or more of the following conditions exist:

- There is nothing to create; the decision has already been made.

- The situation or the related information is too complex or too confidential for the group.

- The participants are not vested in accepting a solution.
- Time does not permit a facilitated approach.

Exercise Your Skills

If you will be making a decision, developing a plan, or implementing a program, project, strategy, or initiative, ask yourself the questions in Table 1.2 to determine if facilitation is appropriate. If it is, what steps can you take to ensure that those impacted "create, understand, and accept" what is done? For ideas, review the section on applying the Secrets to gain buy-in to a strategic plan in this chapter and the two case studies in the Introduction.

Note

1. The fifteen leaders with whom I consulted are as follows:
    Gary Austin, past chair, International Association of Facilitators
    Ingrid Bens, author, *Facilitate with Ease*
    Gil Brensen Lazan, past president, Global Facilitators Serving Communities
    Eileen Dowse, chair, International Institute for Facilitation
    Cameron Fraser, past chair, International Association of Facilitators
    Martin Gilbraith, chair, International Association of Facilitators
    Dale Hunter, author, *The Art of Facilitation*
    Danuta McCall, partner, Facilitate.com
    Jo Nelson, past chair, International Association of Facilitators
    Gary Rush, past chair, International Association of Facilitators
    Sandy Schuman, editor, *The IAF Handbook of Group Facilitation*
    Roger Schwarz, author, *The Skilled Facilitator*
    Carol Sherrif, convention chair, International Association of Facilitators
    Dorothy Strachan, author, *Making Questions Work*
    Simon Wilson, membership chair, International Association of Facilitators

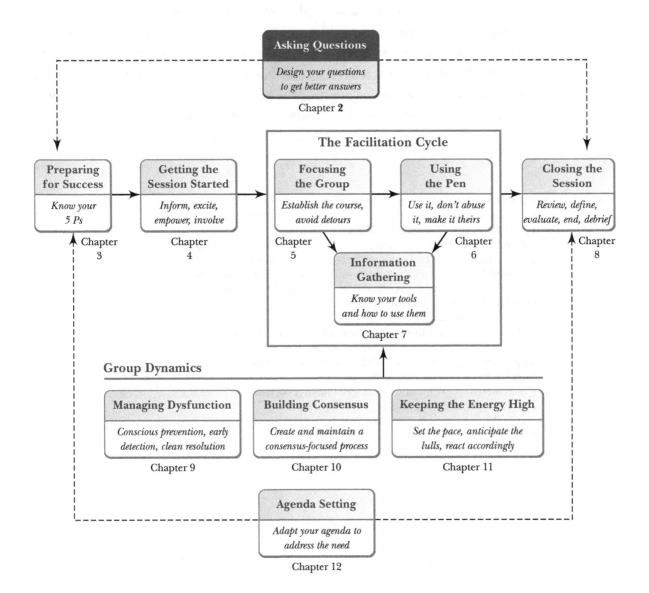

Asking Questions

Design your questions to get better answers

Chapter **2**

The Facilitation Cycle

Preparing for Success

Know your 5 Ps

Chapter 3

Getting the Session Started

Inform, excite, empower, involve

Chapter 4

Focusing the Group

Establish the course, avoid detours

Chapter 5

Using the Pen

Use it, don't abuse it, make it theirs

Chapter 6

Closing the Session

Review, define, evaluate, end, debrief

Chapter 8

Information Gathering

Know your tools and how to use them

Chapter 7

Group Dynamics

Managing Dysfunction

Conscious prevention, early detection, clean resolution

Chapter 9

Building Consensus

Create and maintain a consensus-focused process

Chapter 10

Keeping the Energy High

Set the pace, anticipate the lulls, react accordingly

Chapter 11

Agenda Setting

Adapt your agenda to address the need

Chapter 12

CHAPTER TWO

THE SECRETS TO QUESTIONING

Design Your Questions to Get Better Answers

Questions Answered in This Chapter

How do you phrase questions that create a bonfire of responses?

In asking a question, when should you choose the verbs *could, should, must,* and *will*?

How do you use questions to guide a group?

How do you react to responses without overpowering the group?

How do you float an idea without unduly influencing the group?

How do you use questioning techniques when you are not facilitating?

CASE STUDY: Starting Questions

During one of our early public training classes on facilitation, we learned what I believe is the single most important technique for facilitators to know. We call it the Secret of the Starting Question.

One of the case studies we used at that time involved facilitating a group of school schedulers through a process of identifying their requirements for a new school scheduling system. In one of the practice sessions, students facilitate groups of three through an exercise to create a list of inputs used in the scheduling process.

In this particular class, the first person who facilitated asked a question similar to the following:

"The first thing we want to talk about are inputs. What are the inputs to the scheduling process?"

After the person completed his practice session and received feedback, I moved on to the second practice team. The person facilitating in the second practice team was using the same case study, but she asked the question differently: "If you were about to develop the school schedule, what information would you need to have close by?"

The moment I heard this question, I interrupted the practice exercise and asked every team to listen to the two questions I had heard. I explained that I believed there was a powerful lesson here for us all if we could take a few minutes for examination. (Of course, I had no idea what the lesson was, so I was going to learn it with them.) The second question was clearly a much better question, and I asked their permission for us all to take the time to figure out why.

As a result of that discussion, we discovered an important skill that we teach to hundreds of people every year: the Secret of the Starting Question.

SMART facilitators demonstrate what appears to many as an innate ability to ask the right questions. They use questioning techniques when preparing, starting, focusing, gathering information, building consensus, and in every other stage of the SMART Facilitation methodology. Considering that facilitators ask questions throughout the facilitation process, let's begin with the first question, which I call the starting question.

The Starting Question

If I could teach every facilitator in the world just one tool or technique, it would be the Secret of the Starting Question. Why? Because if we ask better questions, we tend to get better answers, every time.

The *starting question* is what I call the question the facilitator asks to begin a discussion. Typically, you use a starting question at the beginning of every agenda item in a facilitated process. For example, for working with a team to create a plan to improve the hiring process, the facilitator might use the following agenda:

Agenda for Improving the Hiring Process	A. Getting started
	B. How does the process work today?
	C. What are the problems and root causes?
	D. What are potential improvements?
	E. How might we prioritize these improvements?
	F. How will the new process work?
	G. How will we implement this new process?
	H. Review and close

Agenda items B through G represent the core of the work for the facilitated session. For each of these agenda items, there is a time when the facilitator asks a question and expects the participants to begin responding. *The ability of the group to respond to a question is significantly affected by the quality of the question the facilitator asks.* The starting question is much like starting a fire. When facilitators use the wrong material to ask questions, they will get flickering flames that they have to blow on and feed continually just to keep the flames going. When facilitators use the right material, they quickly have a bonfire of responses, with people hardly able to wait to make their contributions.

What is the Secret of the Starting Question, and how do you get the bonfire of responses? Let's examine the two questions posed in the case study at the beginning of this chapter to understand the secret.

Question type A: "The first thing we want to talk about are inputs. What are the inputs to the scheduling process?"

Question type B: "If you were about to develop the school schedule, what information would you need to have close by?"

Why Is the Type B Question Better?

What is it about the second question that makes it better than the first? When we make this same inquiry of people we train in facilitation skills, these are some of the responses we get:

Why is the second question better?	• Uses their language ("school schedule," "information") • More personal; addresses them directly ("you") • Action oriented ("about to") • Open ended ("what information")

Although these are valid points, they don't quite focus directly on the Secret of the Starting Question. When we take the students through a quick exercise, they understand the secret in a way that helps them retain it. The facilitator asks the students to close their eyes and listen to the type A question. After stating the question, the facilitator asks them to open their eyes and to raise their hands if they saw something as the question was read. One or two typically say they saw a flowchart or diagram or something of that sort. Most indicate they saw nothing. In contrast, when the facilitator asks them to close their eyes a second time and listen to the type B question, there is a different result. Typically, two-thirds, if not more, see an image. The image described by most involves sitting at a desk with items they use for scheduling arranged on the desk. Herein lies the Secret of the Starting Question.

Secret #3

The Secret of the Starting Question
Great starting questions draw a vivid image of the answers.

Why is a vivid image key to the starting question? When you draw a vivid image, the participants can almost literally see the answers and can begin responding right away.

Type A Versus Type B Questions

Whereas a type B starting question draws a vivid image, a type A starting question simply asks what you as the facilitator want to know. If you want to know the inputs to the scheduling process, you ask, "What are the inputs to the scheduling process?" If you want to know the steps in the current hiring process, you ask, "What are the steps in the current hiring process?" Type A questions are easy for facilitators. They determine what they want to know and simply ask the question.

Unfortunately, after the facilitator asks a type A question, "What are the inputs to the scheduling process?" the participants have to put their hands to their heads and begin thinking of answers. What are they doing? They are probably trying to imagine themselves back at their school the last time they did scheduling. They are probably trying to draw the image that the facilitator did not draw for them! Unfortunately, this effort usually results in an awkward silence in the room for several moments—just at the time when the facilitator is looking for responses. In essence, because of the poor starting question, the facilitator has silenced the room! And this silence sometimes engenders a sense of unconscious disempowerment in the participants: "We should know the answer. What is wrong with us?" When we don't do our jobs as facilitators, the participants often look bad, not us. We made the mistake of asking a poor question, and they end up looking bad because they don't know the answer.

It is important to recognize that type A questions are the "default." If you do not think about your question in advance, more times than not you will ask a type A question. For example, suppose the agenda calls for the group to identify problems with the current hiring process. If you have not prepared an image-building type B question in advance, you will probably ask, "What are the problems you have encountered with the hiring process?"

How to Ask Type B Questions Every Time

How do you make sure that your starting questions are type B and not type A? The list that follows describes the steps for delivering great starting questions.

Delivering Great Starting Questions

Step 1	**Start with an image-building phrase.** Image-building phrases, such as "Think about . . . ," "Imagine . . . ," "If . . . ," and "Consider . . . ," put participants in the scenario and get them ready to see the answers.
Step 2	**Extend the image to their answers.** Provide two or more additional phrases or sentences that give the participants an image of their answers. Don't give the answers. Just set up an image that encourages the participants to clearly visualize their answers.
Step 3	**Ask the type A question.** Now that participants see the answers, ask the direct question that prompts them to respond with their answers.

The steps here describe how to deliver a great starting question. However, when you construct your starting question, you do step 3 first. To illustrate, let's say you are teaching a class on facilitation skills. At the beginning of the class, you want to know what people would like to learn from the class. Let's construct the type B question.

Constructing a Great Starting Question

- Start with step 3 by determining the type A question. In this example, because we want to know what people would like to learn from the class, the type A question would be "What would you like to learn from this class?" (Type A questions are easy, aren't they?)
- Next, let's go back to step 1 and create our image-building phrase. If you want people to visualize the things they want to learn in the class, what image could you use to help them visualize these answers? How about this: "Imagine facilitating your worst nightmare—a meeting that exposed all your facilitation weaknesses, all the things that you weren't good at."
- Next, you have to extend the image to their answers. To do this, use what I call the synonym trick. What are two or three synonym phrases for "things you would like to learn from this class"? How about these: things you know you want to be able to do better, skills that you could improve upon, techniques that would make you a better facilitator.
- Now you are ready to deliver your type B starting question:

    I want to get an idea of what you would like to get out of this class. Imagine facilitating a meeting that was your worst nightmare—a meeting that exposed all your facilitation weaknesses, all the things that you weren't good at. Think about the things you know you need to be able to do better, the skills that you would want to improve, or the techniques that would make you a better facilitator and prevent such a nightmare. What would you like to learn from this class?

There are several things to note from this example.

- Notice how the three parts of the starting question weave together.
- Note as well how in the example I telegraph my question to participants with my first sentence: "I want to get an idea of what you would like to get out of this class." *This gets the participants understanding where I am going with the question.*
- Finally, note that the hard part of the starting question is step 2, extending the image to the answers. This is the critical piece where you use two or three phrases that allow participants to visualize their answers before you ask the type A question at the end.

Why Do This?

Why use type B questions?

If you have ever asked a question to a group and gotten complete silence, you know how negatively it can impact a facilitated session. Perhaps you got silence because no one heard the question. But more than likely it was because you asked a type A instead of a type B question. And when the silence happens, it sucks the energy out of the room and typically makes the participants feel that they aren't too smart. I have even heard facilitators respond to silence by saying something like, "Come on, guys; you know the answer."

However, when you ask a type B question, participants can see their answers. As a result, the hands go up immediately because people can't wait to respond. With type B questions, you typically have many people ready to answer. I can honestly say that since learning about type B questions, I have never gotten silence when asking a starting question, except for when I forgot and asked a type A instead.

Common Mistakes with Type B Questions

There are common mistakes people make when they first begin formulating type B questions. Using the three parts to the starting question listed here as a reference, see if you can determine what is wrong with each of the questions that follow.

- Start with an image-building phrase.
- Extend the image to the answers.
- Ask your type A question.

What is wrong with each of these starting questions?

Question 1: I want to start by understanding what you would like to get out of this class. What are your objectives for the class?

Question 2: I want to start by understanding what you would like to get out of this class. Think about when you first saw the email about this class. What are your objectives for the class?

Question 3: I want to start by understanding what you would like to get out of this class. Think about when you first saw the email about this class. Think about the fonts that were used, how well the email was written, the tone of the email. What are your objectives for the class?

Question 4: I want to start by understanding what you would like to get out of this class. What are some of the things you would like to learn? What are the things that would make you a better facilitator? What would you find most helpful? What are your objectives for the class?

Each of the questions demonstrates one of the common mistakes people make when they first learn the Secret of the Starting Question.

Q1: Doesn't start with an image-building phrase; goes straight to a type A

Q2: Doesn't expand the image with two phrases

Q3: Gives a false image; the image and extension have nothing to do with the type A question

Q4: Asks more than one question; the only question should be type A; precede everything else with an image-building phrase (for example, "Think about," "Imagine," "Consider")

Sample Starting Questions

Let's run through a few examples of type A and type B questions based on the sample scenario of a session to improve the hiring process.

Type A: *How does the hiring process work today; what are the steps?*

Type B: Let's build a list of the steps in the current hiring process. Imagine for a second that one of your employees comes into your office, announces his resignation, and says he will stick around for up to thirty days until you get his replacement hired and trained. You know you have to get moving right away, so you begin listing the steps you have to go through to bring someone on board. You list all the actions you have to take, the things others have to do, and so on. Let's list some of these things; what are the steps you would have to take to get someone hired?

Type A: *What are the problems with the current process?*

Type B: Let's move now to the problems with the current hiring process. Think about the last time you had to hire someone. Consider the things that were real problems; the things that got you frustrated; the things that worked very poorly, took too long, or just seemed to be a waste of time. The things that made you say, "There's got to be a better way to do this!" What are some of those frustrating problems with the current hiring process?

Type A: *What are things we could do to improve the current process?*

Type B: We are ready to build a list of things to do to improve the hiring process. Look over the problems we need to fix. Consider things we could do to solve them. Think about things you have seen implemented in other places; consider how technology might be used to improve the hiring process or ways that we can better organize to get the work done. Let your mind see all the possibilities that we might consider . . . Let's list some of the ideas that could be put in place to improve our process. Who wants to start?

Throughout this book, you will see many examples of facilitator dialogue. You may want to take note of those cases that include additional examples of starting questions.

Avoiding "False Image" Starting Questions

Beware of the starting question that uses a false image, as indicated before. In our zest to create image questions, we may use an image-building phrase but make the mistake of failing to create an image that *leads the participants to visualize their answers.* We instead leave them visualizing something else, and participants therefore have to go silent in order to create their own image to find their answers. The following is an example of a starting question that creates a false image:

Type A: *What improvements should we make to the hiring process?*

Type B: *[false image]* Imagine that the president of your organization walks into your office, hands you a blank check, and says to you, "I want you to get whatever you need to create a world-class hiring process." What would you change about the current process?

This type B question draws a very vivid image. Unfortunately, the image (being handed a blank check by the president) does not help the participants visualize changes they would make to the hiring process. Instead, they are visualizing the president, the check, and the smile on their face as the president hands the check to them! Remember, the key to a great starting question is that you build an image that helps the participants visualize the answers to the question.

The Impact of Could, Should, Must, and Will

In several types of facilitated sessions, there are times when you take the group through a process of identifying possibilities. In strategic planning, for example, participants often identify possibilities when brainstorming strategies. In issue resolution, participants create possibilities when identifying alternatives. This same concept applies to our example of fixing the hiring process (process improvement) when participants identify potential improvements.

In the section "Sample Starting Questions," we looked at a type B question about identifying improvements in the hiring process. It ended with the instruction, "Let's list some of the ideas that *could* be put in place." How would the responses have been different if the facilitator had said one of the following?

"Let's list some of the ideas that *should* be put in place."

"Let's list some of the ideas that *must* be put in place."

"Let's list some of the ideas we *will* put in place."

Choosing the appropriate verb is essential for the facilitator to achieve the desired result.

Choosing the Question Verb

Could	"What could be done . . ." implies no limitations or restrictions. Use "could" to generate the maximum number of ideas.
Should	"What should be done . . ." implies a moral obligation for action, without implying responsibility for the action. Use "should" when the group is not yet committed to action.
Must	"What must be done . . ." implies that the group should identify only essential items. The number of items will likely be smaller, and a level of commitment is implied.
Will	"What will we do . . ." implies that we should include only actions we are willing to commit to doing. A smaller number of committed actions will likely result.

CASE STUDY: The Starting Question to Engage the VP's Number Two

Mike Dugas, an internal consultant for a digital technology industry giant in Portland, realized immediate success when he used a type B starting question with an executive.

I'd been working with the vice president on this organizational assessment project and had redesigned the project to fit his critiques of this assessment. We were piloting a new way to do the work, so in essence this was his baby. I was asked to present at the staff meeting where we would roll out the project, but it turned out that the vice president (who was the main champion of the organizational assessment) wasn't able to be at the meeting. This meant I would be presenting to the staff without him there to lend his support and backing for the project.

The vice president's number-two person would be present. Yet I had the impression this person wasn't entirely sold on moving forward with the project. This was significant because he had the clout to have a huge impact on how effective the assessment would be.

At the beginning of the meeting, I took the risk of having the staff decide whether to do the assessment, not do it, or postpone it, by using an engagement strategy with the VP's number two. I knew if his response was positive, we'd have a successful meeting. If it turned out his response was negative, I was prepared to recommend we table the assessment for a later date. I was willing to take a risk because even if things went awry, at least the underlying issue would be out in the open.

The meeting culture in our organization is one where you walk into a meeting and everyone has their laptops up and running. In some business arenas, this is considered rude, but in ours it is a very common practice. About ten minutes into the presentation, I used one of the techniques that I had just learned from a facilitation course. I wanted to be sure I was making it personal, so I paused and said to the group, "For the next five minutes I really need your attention because this is going to personally affect you and your credibility within your organization."

I then said to the number-two person, "Picture yourself in an elevator with an engineer who works for you. The engineer looks at you and says, 'Why are we wasting our time completing this assessment? We are already swamped working on several process qualifications, and now you're asking us to participate in this assessment. What gives?'"

I knew his response would set the tone for the rest of the presentation. He did surprise me with a very humorous wisecrack! It was extraordinary because I'd never seen him even crack a smile in a meeting before. He responded by insisting there was great value to the group in doing this assessment work and went on to explain in detail what their purpose for being there was. In essence, this exercise literally gave him the opportunity to deliver an "elevator speech" as to why we were having this meeting and how their participation would impact the organization. Once this key person was on board, the rest of the meeting went very smoothly. That was a personal breakthrough for me, having this individual respond like he did, because in any other meeting I've been in with him, he was consistently tough to convince. Using the WIIFM (What's In It For Me) model helped focus the group on the goal itself and highlighted the importance of their involvement with this project.

The Reacting Questions

The previous section discussed how to use starting questions to stimulate the group's responses. This section focuses on how facilitators react to what participants say. SMART facilitators use reacting questions to acknowledge, clarify, challenge, confirm, probe, and redirect.

Once you ask a starting question, participants typically begin responding. Some responses appear to be right in line with the discussion; other comments may seem to be unclear; still others may appear irrelevant to the discussion. You use reacting questions to help the group better process the comments participants have made.

To introduce the six types of reacting questions, let's compare how a nonfacilitator and a facilitator might respond to their perception of a situation or a participant's statement, as shown in Table 2.1.

Note that in each case, the nonfacilitator makes a statement, whereas the facilitator asks a question. By asking questions, the facilitator encourages

TABLE 2.1   FACILITATOR VERSUS NONFACILITATOR RESPONSE.

The Perception	Nonfacilitator Response	Facilitator Response	Question Type and Purpose
You don't think what was said is correct.	"I don't think that is correct."	*"Why is that important?"*	**Direct Probe** to challenge
You don't believe everyone understands what is said, but you think you do.	"Let me explain to everyone what he is saying . . ."	*"It sounds like what you are saying is . . . Is that right?"*	**Playback Question** to clarify what you believe you know
You don't understand what is said, and are not sure anyone else does.	"I don't understand your comment."	*"Is that important because . . . ?"*	**Indirect Probe** to provide a way for the participant to clarify
A potentially suitable solution has been overlooked.	"I think we should . . ."	*"Are there solutions in the area of . . . ?"*	**Leading Question** to seek other solutions
The point does not appear to be relevant to the current discussion.	"That point is irrelevant. Let's move on."	*"That's a good point. Can we put that on the Issues list so that we won't forget it, and then get back to . . . ?"*	**Redirection Question** to get the conversation back on track
The group has stalled.	"Let's move on to the next topic . . ."	*"We have covered (a), (b), (c) . . . What else might we do to improve the hiring process?"*	**Prompt Question** to help keep the group moving

Secret #4

The Secret to Guiding a Group

Guide the group's flow by asking, not telling.

Why Do This?

Why expand your toolbox of reacting questions?

Imagine being a carpenter with only one tool: when all you have is a hammer, every problem looks like a nail. Similarly, most of us have only one or two question types that we use most frequently. Before I learned this material, most of my reacting questions were direct probes ("Why is that important?" or "Tell me more about that") and prompts ("What else?"). This means that there may have been times when a redirection was more appropriate ("That's a good point; can we put it on the Issues list?") or when it would have been better to ask a leading question ("Are there solutions in the area of . . .") or a playback to move the group along ("It sounds like what you are saying is . . . Is that right?"). I was missing these opportunities to help the group simply because I had a limited toolbox.

participants to seek their own solutions—they create the solutions, they understand them, and they accept them.

The six reacting questions (direct, indirect, redirect, playback, lead, prompt) provide ways for facilitators to help keep the team focused and on track—all simply by asking questions. At the end of this chapter, I will suggest an exercise to help you consciously practice expanding your use of reacting questions.

Floating an Idea

For the sake of creating ownership and buy-in, it is almost always better for a group to come up with an idea rather than to have you feed it to them. That is why SMART facilitators use questioning techniques to challenge and probe. Sometimes, however, even the best questioning techniques fail to help the group "discover" a specific idea that the group appears to be overlooking. Recall that you should ask leading questions if you determine that a potentially suitable solution is being overlooked. Suppose, however, the leading questions don't work? Consider the sample dialogue here.

Sample Dialogue: The Leading Question That Leads Nowhere

The board of an association of women in accounting is reviewing information from its situation assessment and setting strategic priorities for the next three years.

Facilitator:	It sounds like we have concluded that one of the key needs members are looking to the organization to provide is a forum for the development of leadership skills to prepare them for becoming partners in their accounting organizations. Let's take a few minutes now to identify potential approaches we might consider for addressing this need. Imagine that we have become the top source for our members to develop leadership skills to enhance their careers in accounting. For this to happen, what's our role? What are we doing? How did we get there? Let's build a list of possible ways we could meet our members' desire for leadership skills. Who has one?
VP of Programs:	I suppose we could invest the time and energy in building a curriculum ourselves.
Facilitator:	That is one approach. Let's hear some others. What other alternatives are there? *[prompt question]*

The facilitator believes that the association could potentially partner with an organization specializing in leadership training to design a program specifically for women in accounting.

President-Elect:	If we are going to provide a leadership training program, we probably should make it accessible over the Web so that our members across the state can use it.
Facilitator:	That's a thought as well. Are there possible partnering opportunities with the training program? *[leading question]*
Treasurer:	We could probably save a lot of money by asking some of the larger accounting firms to provide the space for training classes.
Facilitator:	Are there other ways we could meet the need of our members for leadership training? *[prompt question]*
VP of Communications:	We could just maintain a list on our Web site of leadership training available.
Treasurer:	And we could probably charge the vendors for the listing!
Facilitator:	OK, we have several potential solutions listed here. Are there others, or are we ready to move on and discuss how we'll go about choosing one of these?
	The facilitator gives up!

SMART facilitators believe that they have a responsibility to be as helpful as they can be to their clients. This includes assisting the team if there are potential solutions that the team does not come to on its own. Yet facilitators must offer content suggestions in a way that is fair and unbiased. This leads us to our next secret.

The Secret to Influencing Idea Ownership

When you float an idea, ask participants to identify its benefits and how to record it.

The "floating an idea" technique is the seventh reacting question. Rather than allowing the idea to go unsaid, you have the option to float it to the group. To float an idea, you state the idea in a form of a question: "What about . . . ?" If the participants respond favorably, you ask the second part of the reacting question: "What do you see as the benefits?" If the participants see the benefits, ownership is locked down through the final question: "How do you want me to write it?" Following the sample dialogue, I will comment on whether floating an idea violates the common belief that facilitators should not involve themselves at all with content.

Sample Dialogue: Floating an Idea

This example picks up just before the previous dialogue left off. The board of an association of women in accounting is reviewing information from its situation assessment and setting strategic priorities for the next three years.

VP of Communications:	We could just maintain a list on our Web site of leadership training available.
Treasurer:	And we could probably charge the vendors for the listing!
Facilitator:	OK, we have several potential solutions listed here. If it is okay, I would like to take my facilitator hat off for a second. May I ? Let me ask, what about partnering with a firm that already offers leadership training and having senior accountants in the association coteach with their staff?
VP of Programs:	That's a great idea! I like it.
Facilitator:	What do you see as the benefits?
VP of Programs:	The base of the curriculum is already done. We will just tweak it by making sure all the examples and practice exercises apply to accounting.
President-Elect:	It is also a great way to get our senior members more engaged in the association. And it sets the foundation for implementing a mentoring program.
Treasurer:	On top of that, we can probably charge more if the training partner is a well-known firm!
Facilitator:	Those sound like great benefits. How do you want me to write the idea?

A note of caution: Many facilitators take great exception to floating an idea and even to asking leading questions. This very valid school of thought says that the role of the facilitator is to manage the process and that the content is the responsibility of the participants. Therefore, according to this view, any statement from the facilitator that influences the content is a confusion of the role. This school of thought also sets forth that facilitator involvement in the content can be an abuse of the power of the role: participants may tend to go along with the facilitator's views just because the facilitator is in a leadership role with the group.

I believe that these concerns are well founded; they should be carefully considered and, as appropriate, discussed in advance with the person responsible for the meeting or with the participants. In Chapter Seventeen, I address this topic of content neutrality more fully.

To avoid role confusion, consider three actions in particular.

- In advance of the facilitated session, ask the person responsible for the meeting if it is appropriate for you to float an idea if the group seems to be overlooking something. Explain the process of floating and how it is used.
- During the review of the ground rules, describe your role and explain that there may be times when you will float an idea for consideration, but only if you are aware of something that hasn't been said; explain what you will say and why.

- When you note that a potentially critical idea has not been mentioned that may be helpful to the group, first ask prompt questions, then leading questions, and only if neither of these approaches are fruitful, telegraph your attention ("I would like to float an idea here . . ."), then ask your floating question using all three parts.

My experience has been that when SMART facilitators ask leading questions and float ideas, participants appreciate the added input and react appropriately. At the same time, facilitators new to the skills and techniques of facilitation may do well to avoid these more advanced question types.

Applying the Questioning Techniques

You can apply the questioning techniques discussed in this chapter to a wide variety of situations. In this section, I have included two examples: drilling down in a disagreement and using the starting question when interviewing.

Using Questions to Drill Down to the Root of a Disagreement

When disagreements occur in a meeting, frequently the disagreement is due to a poor understanding of why each person supports his or her position.

Sample Dialogue: The Battle of "Yes It Will"–"No It Won't"

Optimist: I believe the best alternative to solving this problem is to pull a team of people together, let them develop a consensus solution, and present it to management for approval.

Naysayer: That's a bad idea.

Optimist: No it isn't. In my old company, we tried this same strategy on numerous issues with considerable success.

Naysayer: Nope. That stuff may work elsewhere, but not here. Not a chance.

Optimist: I don't understand why you're being so negative.

Naysayer: I'm not being negative. I'm just telling you like it is. And that idea of yours won't work.

When the naysayer blurts out, "That's a bad idea," it is natural for the optimist to feel he is being attacked. And when a person is under attack, the classic response is flight (concede the point) or fight (object). The optimist chooses to fight, and we have a battle on our hands. The optimist believes that his knockout punch is to explain the "considerable success" his approach had achieved elsewhere. Unfortunately, the naysayer easily deflects the knockout punch, and the battle rages on.

SMART facilitators know that most often neither flight nor fight is the appropriate response. When disagreements occur, often the appropriate response is to seek understanding by drilling down to the source of the disagreement. If someone believes that something is a "bad idea," the facilitator's goal is to ensure that the group has a chance to understand why. Let's try this discussion again.

Sample Dialogue: Drilling Down to Avoid the Battle

Optimist: I believe the best alternative to solving this problem is to pull a team of people together, let them develop a consensus solution, and present it to management for approval.

Naysayer: That's a bad idea.

Facilitator: You may very well be right. Help us understand: Why do you believe it's a bad idea? *[drill down]*

Naysayer: Two years ago we wasted six days in team meetings around improving the hiring process, and management didn't implement a thing.

Facilitator: What do you believe is the reason management didn't implement a thing? *[drill down]*

Naysayer: They said they didn't see the benefit.

Optimist: Well, it sounds like if we do this team approach, we will have to make sure that we get management's commitment up front to implement our recommendations if we can demonstrate adequate benefit.

Naysayer: I doubt if they will be willing to give that commitment. But if they do, I'm willing to call their bluff.

Using the Type B Question to Interview Candidates

The type B starting question is powerful because it helps participants see an image of their answers. The imaging technique can be quite effective when asking someone a difficult question. In the interviewing process, for example, candidates are often reluctant to be critical of themselves or give feedback about their weaknesses. Type B questions can be used to help alleviate this problem.

Sample Dialogue: The Interview

Interviewer: Jerry, think about the manager you have had who understood you the best. She knew your strengths, and she always wanted you to succeed. Imagine that I'm sitting across from her right now and asking her about your strengths, the things you do well. She would probably smile, wouldn't she, as she thought about your skills and the key things you bring to the table. What would she say are your key strengths?

Jerry:	She would probably say that I was . . .
Interviewer:	After she tells me all this, suppose I say to her, "You make this guy sound like he walks on water. Bring him down to earth a little bit. Surely there are one or two areas in which he could improve or things that he could do even better. So tell me this: What is it that if he were better at this or could do this better, would make Jerry even stronger than he already is?" What would this manager say?
Jerry:	She would probably say that she wished I could be . . .

In this example, putting the candidate in the mind-set of a former manager who liked him helped ease the discomfort of describing a weakness. The candidate has the opportunity to view himself from the perspective of someone else and uses the words of the other person to describe his areas for improvement.

A Final Note on Questioning

Considering all the various questioning techniques available, you can easily feel overwhelmed. Here are a few suggestions for applying this information.

- You may use a number of these techniques already, consciously or unconsciously. By giving names to the techniques and isolating where they are useful, I hope to enable you to apply the techniques more systematically when needed.
- For the question types with which you are less familiar, identify one or two that you want to begin using right away. Read through the sections on these question types once a week or so to keep the information fresh. In conversations, seek opportunities to employ the questioning techniques.
- If you are wondering which question types to start with first, consider the following:
  - Starting questions
  - Redirection questions
  - Drilling down
  - Floating an idea

Facilitator's Checklist for Questioning

- ☐ When asking a question for which you desire numerous responses, be sure it draws a vivid image in which the participants can see the answers.
  - Start with an image-building phrase (for example, "Think about . . .").
  - Extend the image so that the participants can see the answers.
  - Ask the direct question.

☐ Choose the appropriate verb for your question:

- Use *could* to create the maximum number of ideas.
- Use *should* to imply moral obligation without assigning responsibility.
- Use *must* to imply a level of commitment.
- Use *will* to lock in commitment.

☐ Guide the flow of the group by using reacting questions to acknowledge, clarify, challenge, confirm, probe, and redirect.

Reacting Questions

Ask a **direct probe** to challenge.	"Why is that important?"
Ask a **playback question** to clarify what you believe you know.	"It sounds like what you are saying is . . . Is that right?"
Ask an **indirect probe** to provide a way for the participant to clarify.	"Is that important because . . . ?"
Ask a **leading question** to seek other solutions.	"Are there solutions in the area of . . . ?"
Ask a **redirection question** to get the conversation back on track.	"That's a good point. Can we put that on the Issues list so that we won't forget it, and then get back to our question?"
Ask a **prompt question** to help keep the group moving.	"We have covered (a), (b), (c) . . . What else might we do to improve the hiring process?"

☐ Help a group gain ownership of an idea they did not create by floating the idea for their comments, asking them to describe the benefits of the idea, and then recording the idea in their words.

☐ When others are disagreeing, drill down to the source of the disagreement by asking "Why" questions.

Exercise Your Skills

Most of us, during a facilitated session, will naturally use the tools and techniques with which we are comfortable. Therefore it is important to build your comfort with new tools in advance of formally using them. In our classes, we have people use starting questions and reacting questions in six exercises during the class to increase their comfort in using these techniques.

Similarly, spend considerable time becoming familiar with reacting questions to improve your skills in guiding a group. Take a week to consciously use the questions in daily conversation to gain practice in probing, acknowledging, clarifying, and so on. You may be very surprised at how well these techniques can be used in everyday interactions: "Really, so why is that important? Is the reason you say that . . . ? It sounds like what you are saying is . . . Is that right? Are there solutions in the area of . . . ?" These examples can get you started—the exact wording isn't important.

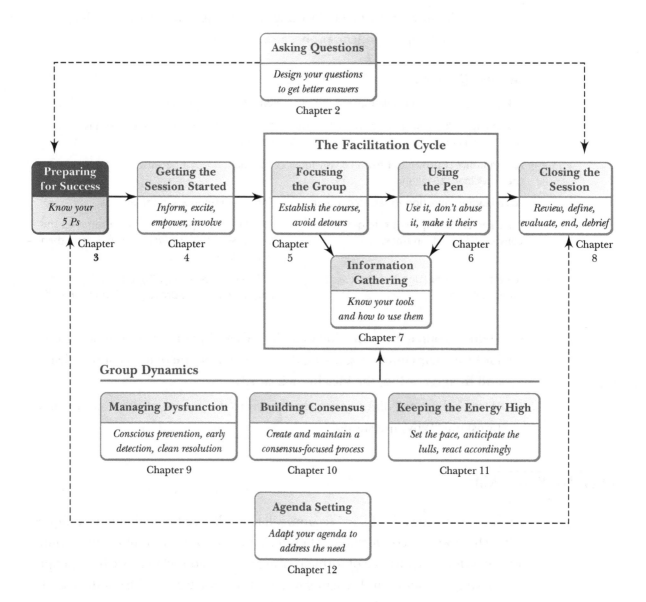

CHAPTER THREE

THE SECRETS TO PREPARING

Know Your 5 Ps

Questions Answered in This Chapter

What are the most important steps in planning for a facilitated session?

What are the key questions that you need to have answered?

With whom should you speak to get prepared?

What do you ask participants about the session?

How can you be sure that you are well prepared?

CASE STUDY: The Principals' Conference

We were working with a large urban public school system. The superintendent asked that we sit in on a meeting of a team that had been working for several weeks on the design of a principals' conference on academic standards. We were to review the conference agenda with the purpose of adding involvement segments to the program so as to keep people engaged and to maintain energy.

The committee had prepared a very detailed conference agenda and, using input from committee members in prior meetings, had identified speakers for each segment. Yet as I read over the agenda, I could not deduce the purpose of the conference. Nor could I determine the outcomes that were going to be accomplished. It was clear that the principals would be more informed about a number of topics as a result of the conference. It was not clear what they were expected to do with the information.

Twenty minutes into the meeting, I raised my hand, explained that I had several questions, and asked permission of the group to go through a fifteen-minute exercise that

I thought would lend additional focus to our efforts. We broke into three teams with a five-minute goal of creating a purpose statement for the conference. The statement was to answer, "Why are we holding the conference? What is the purpose to be achieved?" I was not surprised that the three teams created three very different purpose statements. Within ten minutes and after some debate, we had agreed on the overall purpose.

Next, I asked the entire group, "What do we want to have in our hands when we are done? What products, if any, should be created at this conference?" Although it took a little longer than expected, we were able to agree on the key deliverables: consensus on a general approach to standards, understanding of key strategies, and a high-level implementation timeline that included roles and responsibilities.

With this done, I suggested that we take another look at the agenda to ensure that every segment contributed directly to the purpose and deliverables for the conference. I could feel the excitement in the room rise. The committee members had discussed the conference for weeks without a clear guidepost to help them know if they were moving in the right direction. With the purpose and deliverables clear, the group could make decisions about what did and did not make sense. Nearly half the program was redesigned.

This story ends on a high note. One of the elected school board members unexpectedly attended the conference and remained for the duration. At the conference closing, she explained that when she had heard about the conference, she had been sure it was going to be a big waste of the school system's dollars. She went on to say, however, that she felt it was one of the most productive conferences she had attended in her twenty-plus years with the school system.

The 5 Ps of Preparation

What does it take to be prepared for a kickoff session, a task force meeting, a conference, or any other work session with a group of people?

Secret #6

The Secret to Preparation: The 5 Ps

During preparation, define your 5 Ps: purpose, product, participants, probable issues, and process.

SMART facilitators know that whether they are preparing for running a task force meeting, delivering a presentation, or meeting with a customer, the secret to preparation is the same: they must achieve a clear understanding of the 5 Ps.

The 5 Ps

- **Purpose.** Why are we holding this session? What are the key objectives?
- **Product.** What do we need to have when we are done? How will we know we have been successful?
- **Participants.** Who needs to be involved, and what are their perspectives?
- **Probable issues.** What are the concerns that will likely arise? What are the "gotchas" that could prevent us from creating the product and achieving the purpose?
- **Process.** What steps should we take during the meeting to achieve the purpose, given the product desired, the participants, and the probable issues we will face?

Of course, there are numerous logistics involved in preparing for a facilitated meeting, such as timing, location, and materials. It is nevertheless important to be aware of these five critical elements. SMART facilitators focus on them to gain a clear understanding of what is to be accomplished, why, by whom, and how.

It's All About Purpose

SMART facilitators know that clarity of purpose is essential for effectiveness. Whenever a group comes together, SMART facilitators are intentional about ensuring that they understand the purpose and that the purpose is communicated clearly to the participants.

Questions to
Identify the
Purpose

- Why are we having this session? What is the overall objective?
- What is telling you that this session is needed? What are the problems you are trying to solve?
- How do you know there is a problem? What are the symptoms?
- What are the implications of not solving this problem?

Purpose answers the questions, "Why are we doing this? What is our overall objective?" Whether you are designing a conference, giving a speech, or planning a vacation, it is important to have a clearly stated purpose that is shared by all involved. When the purpose is unclear or not shared, it is easy for an activity to go astray.

Secret #7

The Secret Power of Purpose
A clear purpose provides a solid basis for decision making.

Recall the principals' conference described earlier. The committee had created a full agenda before agreeing on the purpose of the conference. As a result, they had a conference agenda that was unfocused and potentially very ineffective. Once the committee defined purpose, they were able to ensure that all their activities focused on achieving their aims.

How important is purpose? Consider these examples:

- An organization is considering introducing a new product, and it is trying to decide whether to launch the product right away or delay the launch four months until the industry's annual convention. Which is the better strategy?
- A department head is considering giving the same annual compensation increase to each employee rather than varying the amounts. The department head believes that this will reduce the amount of "watercooler chatter" about raises. Is giving the same increase a good idea?
- A family is considering multiple options for vacation, including seven days on a beach, a tour of Italy, visiting Disney World, and hiking through the mountains together. Which should the family choose?

In all three cases, the answer lies in understanding the purpose of the activity.

- In the case of the product launch, the answer depends on the purpose of the launch. If the purpose of the launch is to gain exposure for the company as an industry leader, delaying until the convention may be appropriate. But if the purpose of the launch is to increase revenues to the company as quickly as possible, launching immediately may make more sense.
- For the department head considering giving the same annual compensation increase to each employee rather than varying the amounts, the question is, "What is the purpose of compensation increases?" If the purpose is to reward performance, a level increase for everyone might be appropriate only if everyone has performed at the same level. If instead the purpose is to promote teamwork and to reward people based on the performance of the company, a level increase may be appropriate.
- For the family deciding what to do for vacation, the answer also lies in the question of purpose. Is the purpose of vacations for this family to rest and relax, see sites the family hasn't seen before, make sure the kids enjoy

themselves, work through a challenging experience together, some combination of these, or something altogether different? Although members of the family may have different views of the purpose of vacation, once the family agrees on a shared purpose, the decision about where to go becomes much simpler.

SMART facilitators know that decisions great or small, professional or personal, should be made based on a clearly identified purpose. When groups focus on purpose, their decisions are likely to be more consistent, clear, and effective.

Defining the Product

SMART facilitators also understand the importance of a clearly defined product. Identifying the desired product allows you to transform what might be a highly nebulous purpose statement into a set of distinct deliverables that define achievement of the purpose.

Let's go back once more to the principals' conference case study. The basic purpose of the conference was to gain buy-in from the principals for implementing an approach to standards. Like most purpose statements, this one is a general statement of intent. By identifying the products that defined achievement of the purpose, the principals' conference became even more focused.

Desired Products for the Principals' Conference

- Consensus on a general approach to standards
- Key strategies
- High-level implementation timeline with roles and responsibilities

For most facilitated sessions, some products will be concrete deliverables, such as a report or an action plan. Other products may be intellectual or relational. Intellectual products might include knowledge of a topic or an understanding of a perspective. Samples of relational products include better interdepartmental communication or improved trust. When working with relational products, SMART facilitators attempt to identify the outward signs that can serve as evidence that the relational products have been achieved. For example, in the case of better communication within a department, evidence of improvement in this area might be such things as more frequent cross-collaborations and requests for participation early in the planning process.

Secret #8

The Secret to Defining the Session Product: The 3 Hs

To define the products desired from a facilitated meeting, ask the three H questions: What do you want people to have in their *hands* (deliverables), their *heads* (knowledge), and their *hearts* (beliefs) that they didn't have before the meeting started?

To better define the product you desire for a facilitated meeting, consider asking the following questions:

Questions to Identify the Product	• What is it that you are hoping to achieve from this session? • What specific tangible products or deliverables should people have in their hands when the session is over? • When the session is over, what do you want people to know that they may not have known before the session began? • When the session is over, what do you want people to believe that they may not have believed before the session began? • What other intangible products do you hope will be created? • Three months following the session, how will you know you have been successful?

Selecting Participants

There is a common saying in the facilitator world: "If you are not at the table, you could be on the menu!" The implication, of course, is that if you are not participating in the decision making, it is possible that decisions will be made that negatively affect you.

In helping an organization think through choosing the right people to have engaged in a group process, SMART facilitators ask three key questions:

Questions to Identify the Participants	• Who are the people who will be impacted by the decision? • What level of involvement should they have in the process? • Whose perspectives, involvement, and buy-in are so critical that they should be at the table or represented by someone who is?

The first question encourages you to consider all those affected by the decision. The second question helps you differentiate levels of involvement. For example, some people may need only to be informed of decisions after the fact. Others might provide input prior to the decision. Still others might be asked to participate in the decision making. The final question helps you consider preliminary criteria for selecting those to have at the table.

Team Size

The target size for a team is highly dependent on such factors as the amount of work to be accomplished, the nature of the work, the number of different departments or organizational units impacted by the work, and the sophistication and availability of personnel. Table 3.1 lists some suggested team sizes and general guidelines developed from my experience working with a variety of groups.

Desired Characteristics of Team Members

Who are the right people to have in a facilitated session? Once more, it depends on the meeting type. If the facilitated meeting is anything other

TABLE 3.1   SAMPLE TEAM SIZES.

Meeting Type	Target Size
Resolution Mode	**3–9**
You are attempting to resolve an issue by deciding between several specific alternatives for action.	Small enough to ensure that each individual is heard and that the perspectives can be discussed thoroughly to separate positions from underlying issues
Creation Mode	**7–16**
You are creating a solution or developing a new method (for example, process improvement).	Small enough to reach decisions on potential difficult issues, but large enough to have representation from all areas impacted
Direction Setting	**12–24**
You are establishing broad directions (for example, strategic planning).	Large enough to gain a diversity of ideas, yet not so large as to make discussions unmanageable
Review Mode	**2–100+**
You are reviewing and commenting on work previously performed (for example, a status meeting).	Because the session is primarily for review and comment (no resolution, creation, or direction setting) the size is limited only by logistical considerations (for example, size of room)

Sample Criteria
for Selecting
Participants

All participants should . . .

- Understand the issue under study
- Have a stake in the outcome
- Be empowered to make decisions or recommendations
- Be perceived as opinion leaders by peers
- Be open to solutions other than their own

As a group, depending on the session, the participants should . . .

- Represent diverse communication styles
- Be knowledgeable about all relevant activities under study
- Be cross-functional and representative of all groups with a major stake in the outcome
- Be drawn from various levels of the organizational structure (for example, managers, supervisors, and workers)

than a status meeting, I recommend that the participants have the following characteristics:

In selecting participants, other dimensions to consider are skills and authority. Consider asking, "Who has the knowledge, skills, or authority required to accomplish the objectives?" Skills may include technical skills related to the issue, or you may want participants with soft skills, such as "peacemakers" for volatile situations or "consensus builders" for difficult or complex issues.

Briefing the Participants

SMART facilitators prefer to hold a briefing with the participants prior to a facilitated meeting. Briefing the participants in advance has several advantages:

Advantages
of Briefing
Participants in
Advance

- You can identify, prior to the session, any issues participants have related to the facilitated session or the session topic. By knowing these issues in advance of the session, you can make adjustments to the process you will use to achieve the session's purpose.
- The participants can reach consensus on the agenda for the session and the key products they intend to create. By doing this prior to the session, participants have more ownership of the process.
- The participants can identify the steps to take and the information needed to better prepare for the session. This advantage is a necessity for some types of sessions,

such as strategic planning, for which a subteam will need to gather and disseminate a considerable amount of information prior to the session.

- All the points listed here have the additional benefit of increasing buy-in and commitment to participate in the session.

What should you do in a participant briefing? Consider covering the following points:

Questions to Ask and Points to Cover in the Participant Briefing

Describe: The session's purpose and product.

Ask: What are the issues you believe need to be addressed to achieve this purpose and product?

Describe: The proposed process.

Ask: Where in the process will the issues you identified be addressed?

Ask: Will this process achieve the purpose and product? or, What do you like about this process? What suggestions would you have to improve the process?

Ask: What are the potential problems that might surface that could hinder us from achieving our purpose and product?

Ask: How do we ensure that this session is not a waste of time?

Provide: A memo with logistical information (for example, date, time, location, suggested dress, items to bring to the session).

Request: Agreement from the participants to arrive at least ten minutes prior to the start time to allow for coffee and greetings before the on-time start.

Identifying the Probable Issues

Once you know the purpose, product, and participants, the next step is to identify the probable issues that are likely to have an impact on the success of the session. Probable issues tend to be of three different types.

Types of Probable Issues

- **Topics:** questions and other items that will need to be covered by the agenda in order to create the products and achieve the meeting purpose
- **Ditches:** difficult items that must be addressed, but that can derail the meeting if not handled well
- **Red herrings:** items that are not directly related to the topic and should not be addressed, but that may come up

You will likely discover probable issues during the sponsor interview and the participant briefing if you hold one. Consider asking questions similar to those covered during the participant briefing; in particular:

Questions to Identify Probable Issues	• What are the topics that must be discussed to achieve the meeting purpose and create the products? • What are the questions or concerns the participants will have about the purpose or products? • What are potential ditches or red herrings we will encounter in achieving the purpose and products?

Preparing the Process

The process, or agenda, that you will use in a facilitated interaction will depend on the other four Ps—the purpose, product, participants, and probable issues. The process will also employ many of the other secrets used in this book. Therefore, I will save the discussion of process until Chapter Twelve.

The Meeting Notice

The meeting notice defines the key information that participants need in order for them to arrive prepared for the meeting. If possible, distribute the meeting notice at least a week prior to the meeting. The meeting notice should contain several key items.

Contents of the Meeting Notice	• Meeting purpose, expected products, and proposed agenda • Location, gathering time, and start and end times • Invited attendees • Recommended items to bring

For recurring meetings, such as status meetings, the meeting notice may not be necessary if the same items are covered in every meeting. For other meetings, the meeting notice may be verbal (for example, a voicemail) or in writing.

To help the meeting start on time, make the first time on the agenda the gathering time, followed by the actual start time. In this way, participants will know that they are expected to arrive early so that the meeting can start on time.

If prior to the meeting there are items for participants to review or actions that need to be taken, distribute these in advance of the meeting as well.

Figure 3.1 is an example of a meeting notice.

FIGURE 3.1 SAMPLE MEETING NOTICE.

The Meetings Transformation Team
xx/xx/xx Gather 8:50 / End 11:30
1st Meeting—Conference Room A

Meeting Purpose
- To confirm the project objective and gain agreement on how we will go about accomplishing our work

Expected Products
- Work process, operating norms, meeting schedule

Proposed Agenda
8:50 Gather
9:00 Start
A. Welcome, purpose, and agenda.
B. Review the team's objective.
C. Identify critical lissues for accomplishing the team's objective.
D. Review the proposed work process (*The Master Plan*).
E. Define team norms and decision-making method.
F. Decide logistics for meetings.
G. Begin team work process (if time permits).
H. Define next steps.
11:30 End

Invited Attendees

- Cleve C.—Team Leader
- Bill G.—Documenter
- Katrina J.

- Ken M.
- Vanessa R.—Executive Sponsor
- Andrea T.

In Advance: Review the team charter sent to you last week. Identify any specific meeting issues you would like to see addressed.
Bring to the Meeting: The team charter and list of issues.

CASE STUDY: Preparing for Vision Councils

This case is from Deborah Crawford, an independent consultant and owner of Deborah A. Crawford Consulting in Columbus, Ohio. At the time of her facilitation training, she was the director of health at United Way of Central Ohio and expected to facilitate and plan for a "vision council," a group of area representatives and experts from various sectors of the community formed to have a positive impact.

The vision councils involved a lot of group decision making, problem solving, and priority setting. It's facilitation by design. I remember our course facilitator telling us that many facilitators don't understand that they may need to spend more time planning a session than actually conducting it. It's the first time it ever occurred to me that the time spent planning a meeting is just as vital as the actual meeting itself. I found it pays off enormously.

I spend a lot of time figuring out what the meeting sponsor wants. But it's not unusual for sponsors to be unclear regarding what key results they expect from the session. If the sponsor isn't clear, then there needs to be discussion around why the meeting is taking place, what we're going to have accomplished in the end, then arrive at consensus on what that is. I've learned if the sponsor and the facilitator aren't clear on what the meeting outcome is supposed to be, the meeting is kind of doomed, and as a facilitator you're dead in the water. So as the facilitator, it's up to me to hone down the process and meeting outcomes. I look at it as building blocks; if it's a multimeeting process, what do we have to get out of each meeting in order to achieve the end result for the process that is desired?

Since the training, it's easy to spot negative facilitation practices. The techniques don't only apply to extensive facilitation projects either; they can be utilized in simple meetings with great results. I have been told repeatedly that my meetings are very productive in comparison to many meetings that don't seem to be well thought out.

Special Topic: Managing a Sponsor

To whom do you address the 5 Ps? The *sponsor* of the meeting. The sponsor is typically the person who requests the meeting or the person with overall responsibility for ensuring that the purpose and product are achieved. Often, but not always, the sponsor is in the room when the meeting is held. If you are facilitating your own meeting, then you are the sponsor.

But if you are facilitating a meeting for someone else, it is important to have that sponsor answer the purpose, product, participant, and probable issues questions listed earlier in the chapter. Consider meeting with the sponsor in advance to cover key questions and other topics as well, including the role of the sponsor during the session. The overall goal of the sponsor meeting is for you to walk away with a clear picture of the sponsor's definition of success, suggestions for how to achieve success, the problems you are likely to encounter along the way, and any additional logistical information. During the meeting with the sponsor, consider asking the following additional questions:

Additional Questions About Participants

- Will the attendees know each other? Are introductions needed?
- Are there participants who are not in favor of holding the session or who stand to lose something if the session is successful?
- Are there attendees whose perspectives or ways of communication I should know about?
- Are there participants who are on unfavorable terms with one another?

Additional Questions About Probable Issues

- What are the potential problems or issues that may surface, and what challenges do you anticipate in addressing these issues?
- Are there specific topics you feel should not be discussed in the session?
- How should I go about becoming oriented on the session topics and the issues?

Questions About Process

- What types of facilitated activities has this group undertaken in the past? What were the results?
- What steps have you taken already to address the purpose and product?
- What are some of the steps that you feel we should consider taking during the session?

Questions About Logistics

- What is the time, date, and location of the session? Will the room be available for setup ahead of time?
- What is the dress code for the meeting?
- Will the materials needed to facilitate the session be made available (for example, flip charts, pens, pads, name tents)?
- What information should be distributed to the participants ahead of time? Who will distribute these items?
- Who will start the session?
- How will the results of the session be documented? Who is responsible for the documentation? How soon after the session will the information be needed?

Should the Sponsor Be in the Room?

What is the appropriate role of the sponsor during the session? Should the sponsor of the session be in the room while the team is meeting? For example, if you were leading the task force on the hiring process, should the vice president of human resources, the sponsor, be a part of the meeting?

The easy answer is, "It depends." But let's get to the more difficult answer by identifying the key factors on which the answer should be based, starting with the strengths and weaknesses of each alternative.

Strengths of Having the Sponsor in the Room

- The sponsor demonstrates support and commitment for the effort.
- The sponsor can provide history and rationale for decisions made in the past.
- The sponsor can prevent the task force from wasting time on potential recommendations that have obvious problems in terms of the "big picture" for the organization.
- At the completion of the session, the sponsor will understand, firsthand, the issues discussed by the task force and the reasons for its recommendations.

Weaknesses of Having the Sponsor in the Room

- The sponsor's presence may inhibit discussion and creativity. The participants may not feel free to make comments about the existing process and problems with it. They also may limit themselves to bringing up potential solutions that they feel would be acceptable to the sponsor.
- The sponsor may dominate the discussion and squelch ideas that she deems unacceptable.
- The sponsor's presence may hinder the task force from taking ownership of the work. Task force members may decide that their "work" is to make suggestions to the sponsor. It would be the sponsor's job then to decide which suggestions to undertake. Contrast this with when the task force takes ownership of the work and makes a series of specific recommendations, each backed up by supporting data, with documented benefits to be achieved. Typically, a task force that has taken ownership of the work has invested time, energy, and faith in its recommendations. Such a group usually wants answers if the recommendations are not implemented.

Let's sum up these pros and cons with the following guideline: When the sponsor must be a key implementer of the work done by the group or when the session is strategic in nature (for example, a strategic planning effort), have the sponsor in the room for most, if not all, of the discussion. When the sponsor is primarily an approver, limit the sponsor's involvement in the session.

Minimizing the Potential Negative Impact of a Sponsor's Presence

As noted in the previous section, for many meetings, it will be appropriate to have the meeting sponsor in the room during the meeting. How do you prevent the sponsor's presence from having a negative impact, such as inhibiting discussion or squelching creativity?

Secret #9

The Secret to Managing a Sponsor's Presence

Gain the sponsor's agreement not to be the first, second, or third person to speak on any issue.

To manage the sponsor's presence in the session, meet with the sponsor in advance to discuss the sponsor's role and the appropriate level of involvement. Describe the benefits of the sponsor's being in the room during the discussion and the potential negative impact as well. Ask the sponsor to agree to participate in a specific way, as described in the following sample dialogue.

Sample Dialogue: Sponsor's Role in the Session

Facilitator: The upcoming session can be an excellent opportunity for you to hear from your people. I'm a bit concerned that if you speak first on an issue, this may impact what others might say after you speak. So during the session, if you are okay with it, it might be very helpful if you would permit others to state their opinions first before you state your views. As an example, on any particular issue, please avoid being the first, second, or even the third person to speak. If you can add support to a position, feel free to state the support and indicate why. If you can add support to multiple positions, this is even better because it encourages the team members to look at all sides. But again, allow others to state their opinions before giving yours. If the group seems to be missing an idea, after several have spoken, please feel free to add your ideas. The key here is that we want the group to know that you are participating but not driving. Will this work for you?

Executive: It will indeed. I'm very interested in seeing who speaks up and what they have to say.

In most cases, I have found that these comments are well received and are enough to provide guidance to the sponsor. However, from time to time during a session, sponsors forget their role and begin dominating the discussion. In Chapter Nine, I address techniques for dealing with a dominant participant.

Beware of the Surrogate Sponsor

There have been occasions when the sponsor, who is the head of the organization, is too busy to meet with me, and a second in command asks me to facilitate a session. The second in command, or the "surrogate sponsor" as I call this role, usually does a tremendous job of explaining the sponsor's desired outcomes. Often the surrogate is even able to respond superbly to questions about the 5 Ps. I have learned, however, that my risk of failure increases significantly if I am unable to spend thirty minutes to an hour with the sponsor to discuss the session. What do you do in the abbreviated sponsor interview?

Abbreviated Sponsor Interview	<ul><li>During this time, confirm your understanding of what you have been told by the surrogate. If the surrogate and the sponsor have communicated badly and you haven't had this check-in time with the sponsor, you could end up having the session that the surrogate *thought* the sponsor wanted.</li><li>Ask the sponsor to respond to the process you have planned. Specifically ask what the sponsor likes about the planned process and what the sponsor's concerns are. The sponsor might be fully satisfied with the way the surrogate explained the process but not okay with the way you intend to execute it.</li><li>Be sure to ask how the sponsor will know that the session was a success and what the sponsor believes the early signs are likely to be if the session is failing.</li></ul>

If a sponsor is unavailable to meet in advance of the session, it may be wise to decline the facilitation due to the increased risk of failure.

Applying the 5 Ps

This chapter described the 5 Ps and their importance in effective preparation. But how do you go about defining these elements? Who is responsible for answering your questions about the 5 Ps? As you will see, these depend on the situation.

Applying the 5 Ps to a Task Force

If you have been asked to head a task force to address the hiring process or some other issue, the person who answers most of the 5 Ps will likely be the sponsor of the activity. This is typically the person who requests, initiates, or oversees the activity. The sponsor can typically provide answers regarding the purpose, product, participants, and probable issues. The process question (that is, How will we go about achieving the purpose and product?), however, is often answered by you and the members of the task force.

Applying the 5 Ps to a Customer Sales Call

How might one use the 5 Ps in a selling situation? Simply convert the questions:

- Why do I want to meet with this customer? (purpose)
- What specific outcomes do I want to occur as a result of the meeting? (product)
- Who will be in the meeting on the customer side, and who should be present from our organization? (participants)
- What are the key topics that the customer will want to hear covered? (probable issues)
- What are the steps I want to take in the meeting to ensure that this outcome is achieved? (process)

Perhaps the best salespeople think through these questions instinctively and know the answers intuitively. For the rest of us, however, it is important to focus on the questions explicitly to achieve more effective results!

Applying the 5 Ps to a Simple Meeting

If you are the meeting leader, then prior to the meeting you will need to identify the purpose of the meeting and the desired products. Understanding these two will help you determine the appropriate participants. To identify probable issues, you will want to consider the topic of the meeting, the participants, and the past history related to the topic. Once you have identified these other four Ps, you can then create the high-level process (an agenda) for the meeting. The agenda will need to achieve the purpose, create the product, and cover the issues you identified. As you will see in Chapter Four, it is important that you confirm the agenda with the meeting participants at the very beginning of the meeting.

Facilitator's Checklist for Preparing

- ☐ Interview the project sponsor to identify the session's purpose, the desired outcomes, the potential barriers, the session attendees, and any special personalities in the session.

- ☐ Develop and distribute a specific objective statement and an agenda.

- ☐ Prepare a sample deliverable to ensure that the participants can easily understand the target.

- ☐ Select and customize a process to use. Determine your starting questions, your examples, your recording method, and so on (see Chapter Twelve).

- ☐ Identify the people responsible for key roles (for example, the person responsible for meeting logistics, the person who will document the meeting).

- ☐ Educate the project team (if there is one) on the process and the role each individual will play.

- ☐ Interview the participants to build buy-in for the session and gain their perspectives on how to ensure that the session is successful.

- ☐ Receive an orientation on the business area in order to avoid wasting session time educating yourself.

- ☐ Assemble the materials you will need.

- ☐ Prepare the room and deal with other logistics.

- ☐ Prepare your opening words.

Exercise Your Skills

Chapter Seventeen contains a worksheet for planning and starting a meeting. The worksheet is also available at the Jossey-Bass *Secrets of Facilitation* Web page (www.josseybass.com/go/michaelwilkinson). To accustom yourself to using the 5 Ps, use the worksheet to plan your next three or four meetings.

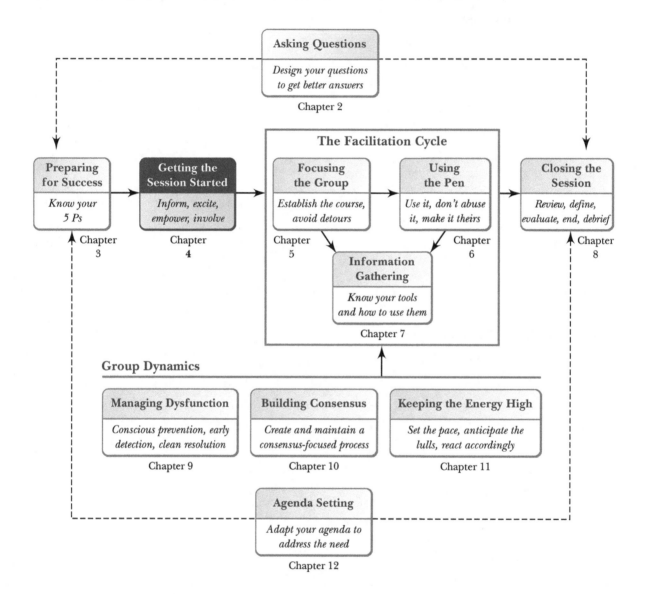

CHAPTER FOUR

THE SECRETS TO STARTING

Inform, Excite, Empower, Involve

Questions Answered in This Chapter

What are the four most important things to do in the opening?

How do you get the participants excited about participating?

How do you get buy-in to the agenda?

What is the purpose of ground rules?

What parking boards should you use?

How do you get the session started on time?

What is the appropriate order of the steps in the opening?

CASE STUDY: Kicking Off Vision 2020

I was working with the regional planning commission of a large metropolitan area on a project called Vision 2020. The goal of the project was to develop a strategic plan for where the community wanted to be by the year 2020. This ten-county metropolitan area had over three million citizens. The regional planning commission was intent on this being a community-based planning process and not the typical approach in which a few powerful people make the decisions. The commission wanted to give every citizen in the community an opportunity to contribute to the vision. They started by publishing surveys in each of the major newspapers in the area, including the major daily, the African American weekly journal, the Hispanic newspaper, and the various Asian newspapers.

To review the input and develop strategies to achieve the vision, the regional commission created ten groups they called collaboratives. Each collaborative was responsible for developing the strategic plan for a particular area of the vision, such as economic development, environment, housing, health, or transportation. The commission invited sixty to one hundred people to be a part of each one of the collaboratives. The collaboratives were to meet for three hours once a month for a twelve-month period to develop the strategic plan for that area.

As the head of the facilitation team leading the ten collaboratives, I recognized that the first meeting was vital. At this first meeting, we had to accomplish several tasks. Every member of the collaborative had to understand clearly the purpose of the collaborative and what was to be achieved, the role that collaboratives would play in the overall Vision 2020 process, and the process that would be used over the twelve months. We also recognized that, more important than anything else, we had to excite the participants about being involved in the process so that they would put the meetings on their calendars and make it a priority to return for all the meetings throughout the year.

As the team planned for the session, we wanted to be deliberate about what we would say and the environment we would create that would indeed get participants to return. Our opening words included, "Thank you all for choosing to be a part of this Vision 2020 collaborative. We have been tasked with an awesome responsibility. Over the next twelve months, we will be developing a plan for how to achieve our vision in this collaborative area. You were one of a hundred people out of the region of three million who have been asked to play a critical role in developing the strategic plan for this topic area. It is your ideas, your perspectives, and your creativity that will make a difference in this process. You have the opportunity to influence the direction that this city takes over the next twenty years. We ask that you fully commit to taking this responsibility seriously by being present at every session unless it's just not humanly possible."

Though not all collaboratives ended with a broad group still committed, most of them were able to maintain the interest and involvement of a sizeable core throughout the twelve-month process.

Opening the Session

As you will see, the order you use to open a facilitated session is critical. It is important that your opening addresses the most significant needs of the participants first. In my experience with literally hundreds of facilitated sessions, I have found the following order to be effective for most sessions. (The meaning of "inform, excite, empower, and involve" will be covered next.)

Recommended Order of the Opening for a Facilitated Session	1. Welcome 2. Session purpose and product (inform, excite, empower) 3. Participants' objectives (involve) 4. Agenda 5. Ground rules 6. Parking boards 7. Introductions 8. End of opening . . . on to the first major agenda item

Depending on the size of the group, the standard opening can be as short as twenty minutes and as long as ninety minutes. As you will see, SMART facilitators take the opening very seriously.

The Transfer of Power

When executives walk into a meeting that you are facilitating, they have the power. In your role as the facilitator, you typically have at most fifteen minutes to get them to voluntarily turn their power over to you. If this turnover of power doesn't happen, it can be a significant problem.

How Executives Respond When They Don't Give You Their Power	• The nice executives will simply ignore you. They will spend their time checking email on their cell phones, having side conversations with other executives, and engaging in other activities that result in their providing you with very little of their precious attention. • What will the not-so-nice executives do? They will fight you. They will challenge your process if they believe that it won't work for them. They will challenge the content if they believe that you are wasting time on irrelevant issues. And they will challenge you if they believe that you don't know what you are doing.

Achieving a Strong Opening

Conventional wisdom states that a good meeting should start with the agenda. The reason typically given is that the agenda answers the question, "What are we going to do?" SMART facilitators, however, know that participants in a facilitated session need answers to several questions *before* the agenda is discussed.

Questions Participants Want Answered	• Why are we having this session? • What do we need to have accomplished when we are done? • What is our role in the decision making? • Why should I invest the time?

SMART facilitators answer these questions, and more, in the first fifteen minutes of a facilitated session.

Secret #10

The Secret to a Strong Opening

Inform, excite, empower, and involve in the first fifteen minutes.

The opening sets the tone, pace, and expectation for the rest of the day. Your opening words should do four key things: inform, excite, empower, and involve (IEEI).

IEEI: The Four Parts of an Opening

- **Inform** the participants about the reason the session is being held by reviewing the **purpose** for the meeting and the **products** to be created.
- **Excite** them about the process by giving them a clear vision of the overall **result** to be achieved and the **benefits** to them.
- **Empower** them by discussing the important **role they play** in the process, the reason they were selected, or the authority that has been given to them.
- **Involve** them as early as possible by identifying their **personal objectives,** the issues that must be covered, the challenges that must be overcome, or some other topic that contributes to the overall goal of the session. Be sure to use a type B starting question.

You can consider using IEEI as an outline for your opening. For example, if you were facilitating a team to improve the hiring process, you might use IEEI in the following way.

Sample Dialogue: Using IEEI

Facilitator: I would like to thank you all for agreeing to be a part of this session. I would like to start by **informing** you about why we are here. As you all know, we've been having significant difficulty with our hiring process. We've had issues with the timeliness of the process as well as times when the wrong person was hired for a job, and we ended up with rapid turnover because it was a bad match. I'm sure there have been other problems as well. We have been called together to create a new process that will alleviate concerns like these. When we are done we will need to have the design of a new process and a plan for implementing it.

What is **exciting** about this? Today you may have people on your staff who don't have the skills or the attitude you need. As a result, you are having to work much harder to make up for what they aren't doing. This is your opportunity to put strategies in place to ensure that you hire the people you need to get the work done.

I want to make sure you know that you have been **empowered** to get this job done. Each of you was handpicked by the leadership team to be part of this process. They believe you have the knowledge as well as the vision needed to create a much better process. And they are looking forward to your recommendations.

Before we take a look at the planned agenda, I would like to get each of you **involved** by asking you to think about some of the things that you know we'll need to discuss during this process. Joe, why don't we start with you and go around the room. Think about the things in the hiring process you know need addressing, or solutions that you may have seen in other organizations, or topics you want to make sure we talk about. If we are going to improve the hiring process, what are some of the key things you want us to talk about? Joe, get me started . . .

Why Do This? | **Why should you start a session with IEEI?**

The IEEI opening is a powerful tool for making sure that your participants understand why they are there, what they are trying to achieve, and the benefits to them. IEEI lets participants know that they can turn their power over to you because what you are doing is important and takes into account the issues important to them.

Exciting the Participants

Although all four steps—inform, excite, empower, and involve—are important, I believe that the excite step is the most significant and also the area where facilitators tend to have the most difficulty. Therefore, let's delve a little deeper by examining two examples of excite.

Which of these two examples would you say would be better at exciting the participants?

Excite Example 1	Excite Example 2
Good morning, it's a pleasure to be here this morning. Our objective for the next two days is to walk away with a plan for improving the hiring process (inform).	Good morning, it's a pleasure to be here this morning. Our objective for the next two days is to walk away with a plan for improving the hiring process (inform).
What is exciting about this? If we are successful, we will walk away with a new hiring process that will help our organization get the right people hired and get them hired quickly.	What is exciting about this? Today you may have people on your staff who don't have the skills or the attitude you need. As a result, you are having to work much harder to make up for what they aren't doing. This is your opportunity to put strategies in place to ensure that you hire the people you need to get the work done.

Most people tell us that the second example is better. The reason they often cite is that the second one is more personal and better explains what the benefit is to the participants. And that is the key to excite—describing the participants' benefit. How does the second example do it? Very simply: Did you notice the number of times the words "you" and "your" appear in the second example?

What is exciting about this? Today **you** *may have people on* **your** *staff who don't have the skills or the attitude* **you** *need. As a result,* **you** *are having to work much harder to make up for what they aren't doing. This is* **your** *opportunity to put strategies in place to ensure that* **you** *hire the people* **you** *need to get the work done.*

The Secret to Exciting in the Opening

In the excite step of your opening, use the words "you" and "your" at least four times to ensure that you explain what is in it for the participants.

Involving the Participants

SMART facilitators engage participants in meaningful work right from the beginning. All too often, however, facilitators spend the critical beginning time on ground rules, introductions, and letting people know the location of the bathrooms. Of course, these are important, but these are not the vital things that engage participants and get them committed to achieving the purpose.

After informing, exciting, and empowering, get the participants involved right away in the work. Typically, for the involve step I ask the participants to indicate their objectives for the session or the most important topics they want to have discussed. Asking this type of involvement question at the beginning of the session serves several purposes:

Why Do This? | **Why ask the participants for their personal objectives?**

- Involves the participants immediately
- Lets participants know that their needs and desires are being considered
- Provides an opportunity to adjust the agenda if flexibility is possible

---

Quick Tip!

When it is time for participants to identify personal objectives at the beginning of the meeting, break the participants into teams of three to seven people each. Assign team leaders. Give the teams limited time (for example, two minutes) to identify the personal objectives, or issues, of the team. Have the team leader record each issue on a separate note sheet using a marker for easy visibility by all. Facilitate the entire group in categorizing the sheets into topic areas. Using teams has the additional benefit of increasing the energy in the room right from the very beginning. Identifying categories will be helpful later, as you will see, when the personal objectives are linked to the agenda.

Preparing Your Opening

Most facilitators know what to say once they have completed the opening and are flowing with the group interaction. Many of us, however, have a difficult time getting the session started. We tend to "hem and haw" a bit as we search for the right words to say to communicate our key points. And often we fail to make all the points that we intend to make. Although "making it up on the fly" in front of an audience may work 100 percent of the time for some, for the rest of us there's a better way.

For maximum impact, SMART facilitators memorize their opening statement so that they can focus on establishing maximum rapport with the group through eye contact, movement, gestures, and so on. It is not important that you actually say what you memorized; the point is that you know ahead of time exactly what you want to say so that you don't have to focus your attention on saying it.

Gaining Buy-In to the Agenda

After completing the opening statement and involving the participants in identifying their personal objectives, you should then review the agenda. Your agenda review should cover both the steps that the group will take and the deliverable or product that the group will create in each step. The review of the agenda should carefully lay out how each step contributes to the overall objective of the session.

The Secret to Gaining Agenda Buy-In

Gain buy-in to the agenda by having the participants link their personal objectives to the plan for the meeting.

How to Link
Personal
Objectives to
the Agenda

- After reviewing the agenda, review the participants' personal objectives, either by item or preferably by category if the grouping process described in the Quick Tip was done.
- Ask the participants to identify the agenda item that should cover each personal objective.
- Consider circling any personal objectives not covered by the proposed agenda.
- After reviewing all personal objectives, go back to the personal objectives that were not covered.
- Determine with the group whether these items will be saved for a later session or whether the agenda should be modified to ensure that these topics are discussed in the current session.

After reviewing the agenda and linking the participants' personal objectives to it, check in with the group for adoption of the agenda by saying such words as, "I would like to entertain a motion to adopt the agenda with the modifications made by the group. Is someone willing to make that motion? . . . Is there a second? . . . Any discussion? . . . All in favor of adopting the agenda with the modifications, please raise your hand. We have made our first decision of the day!"

Why Do This?

Why link the participants' personal objectives to the agenda?

Having the participants link their personal objectives to the agenda serves two powerful purposes: it helps ensure that they understand the agenda items and increases their buy-in to the agenda by showing them where their concerns will be covered.

At this point in the opening, we have informed participants about the purpose and product, excited them about what's in it for them, empowered them by explaining the role they play, and involved them by identifying their personal objectives and linking those objectives to the agenda. There are now three additional starting steps that you need to complete: establishing the ground rules, explaining the parking boards, and making introductions.

Using Ground Rules

Ground rules, or group norms, are used to set an agreed-on level of behavior that guides how the participants will interact with one another. Although some teams have worked together for some time and have established their own functional, unspoken ground rules, I have found that most groups benefit from a deliberate process of identifying in-bounds and out-of-bounds behavior. Over time, ground rules can help a group become self-correcting. Group members will begin correcting themselves on the basis of the norms that they have established and reinforced.

Sample Ground Rule List

1. Everyone speaks
2. One conversation
3. Take a stand!
4. Question first
5. ELMO
6. eManners
7. Recharge: _____
8. Your role / my role
9. Start and end on time
10. Use the parking boards
11.
12.

Secret #13

The Secret to Using Ground Rules

You start the list of ground rules; let them finish it.

SMART facilitators start by suggesting a set of ground rules, explaining each one carefully. They then ask the participants to use their knowledge of the group to suggest additional ground rules that will promote the group's success. Finally, they formally engage the group in a process to adopt the ground rules (as amended).

Why Do This?

Why have a starting list of ground rules and ask participants to add to it?

- Beginning with a starting point minimizes the time spent on developing the ground rules.
- Asking for additions "because they know each other better" empowers the group.
- Requesting adoption of the ground rules builds implicit consent to follow them.

Concisely explain the meaning of each ground rule and how to apply it. What follows is the explanation I give for each of the standard ground rules listed earlier.

Explaining the Ground Rules	
Everyone speaks	It is important that we hear from everyone during the session. The last thing we want to happen is for someone to be silent the entire day, until they walk out of the room and say, "Well, that was a waste of time." We want you to say that in the room. If we are wasting our time on an issue we don't need to discuss, please put up your hand; or if we are speeding through something that needs more time, please put up your hand. I'll check in with the group, and if the group wants to speed up or slow down, I'm fine with it. My only goal is that we maximize our time together to achieve the best outcome we can.
One conversation	We want everyone speaking, but not all at the same time! My momma told me that if someone is speaking, and I turn to my neighbor and start speaking, then I am saying that my words are more important than the other person's words. And my momma said that was rude and told me not to do it. So if you hear people speaking while someone else is speaking, just yell out, "Michael's momma's not happy!" So let's keep my momma happy today.
Take a stand!	To help move the conversation forward, it would be helpful if you would take a stand. As an example, if you were to say, "Well we could do X, or we could do Y, or we could do Z," I would respond, "Take a stand. Which do you think we should do? Let's focus on that one." Or if you say, "That won't work," you will hear me say, "Take a stand. What do you think will work?"
Question first	We want to always interact in a respectful way. Respect is like the oil that keeps ideas and communications flowing. When someone says something with which we disagree, instead of saying "That won't work," ask the question first: "Help me understand—how would that work? How would you address the issue of . . . ?"

Explaining the Ground Rules	
ELMO	We have limited time together, and we need to spend it focused on the most important topics. We don't want to major in the minors. If anyone believes we are spending too much time on a topic, you should yell, "ELMO!" ELMO means Enough, Let's Move On! However, just because one person yells ELMO, that doesn't end discussion. It does, however, call for an immediate group vote to end discussion, and we go with the majority of the group.
eManners	When we are in the room, we need everyone's full attention. So let's observe eManners. This means phones on vibrate, and work only on the session while we are in the session. No checking messages, no responding to emails. Will that work for everyone?
Recharge	I have to admit this is a little silly, but it works. A recharge is a quick activity intended to raise the energy in the room. Let me ask you: What is going to happen to the energy in this room at about 1:30 PM? . . . That's right, it will significantly drop off. But we want to keep everyone alert. So I would like for us to create a recharge activity, and anytime anyone senses that the energy in the room is dropping, that person can call for a recharge. The recharge activity can be anything we want. It just has to combine some body motion with something you say, and it can't last more than fifteen seconds. Let's take nominations for our recharge. [See Chapter Eleven for a fuller discussion of the recharge.]
Your role / my role	Your role during this session is to actively participate, share your ideas, and make sure that our time is being spent productively. My role is to provide clarity around purpose and deliverables, employ a process that helps us effectively achieve the purpose, and maintain an environment in which everyone has the opportunity to be heard.
Start and end on time	We want to start on time and end on time. We'll be breaking for ten minutes about every ninety minutes. When the time is up, I'll start back. If no one is here, I'll start back. I hope I won't be facilitating myself!
Use the parking boards	We have three parking boards for this meeting. If you have something to say that really should be discussed later or outside the room, let's go ahead and put it on the Issues list. Let's document all decisions we make on the Decisions list and all actions that will be taken on the Actions list. [The parking boards will be described in more detail later in this chapter.]
Additional ground rules	These are the ground rules I would suggest. You all know each other better than I do. Are there other ground rules you would recommend that would help our time together be effective and productive?
Adoption	I would like to entertain a motion to adopt the ground rules with the additions made by the group. Is someone willing to make that motion? . . . Is there a second? . . . Any discussion? . . . All in favor of adopting the ground rules with the additions, please raise your hand. We have made our second decision of the day.

CASE STUDY: Avoiding the Executive Feeding Frenzy

In the late 1980s and early 1990s, just about every major manufacturer of mainframe computers was facing the same critical problem: organizations weren't buying a lot of mainframes, but were instead investing in personal computers and servers. These manufacturers were structured and positioned to sell and deliver mainframes. (For example, they had worldwide sales forces and dedicated installation staffs.) Most large computer companies were not well positioned to succeed in the personal computer market.

We were called in by one of the major manufacturers to facilitate a one-day session that would include the CEO, his eight direct reports, and their thirty-one direct reports—the forty top executives in the organization. The purpose of the session was to develop a plan for addressing what had been identified as their three major barriers to growth. Three work teams had been commissioned in advance of the session to analyze the barriers and come up with specific recommendations that would be presented to the executive team.

The CEO had seen his leadership team be unsuccessful in group sessions before, especially when breakout groups were used and when there was not full agreement on the actions to be taken. Therefore, he established two "givens" in the design of the session: (1) the team of forty had to stay together the entire day, and (2) only those recommendations that had the consensus of all forty would be implemented.

These constraints were challenging enough by themselves: keeping the team together the whole day would make it harder to maintain the executives' attention, and avoiding going in-depth on subtopics for long periods of time in order to gain each person's consent would also be difficult. But during our preparation work, in which we interviewed a half-dozen of the executives, we discovered that there was a much bigger issue. We learned that members of the executive team had a tendency to tear apart recommendations brought before the group. They sometimes took pride in determining who could do the better job of finding holes in a presentation. Sometimes it would become an executive feeding frenzy, with one executive after another taking turns! One of the keys to the success of the meeting was to prevent this from happening.

Because of the information learned during preparation, we created a special ground rule for this meeting. Near the beginning of the session, I described the ground rule this way: "Today we will be hearing recommendations from three work teams. After the first work team, we *could* identify seven different reasons why the recommendation won't work. We then would go on to hear from the second work team, and we *could* spend a lot of time describing why their proposals were unacceptable as well. We *could* do likewise with the third team. Then we would be at the end of the day. And we would be no closer to a solution than we were when the day started, because we would have spent all our time discussing what would not work. In essence, discussing what won't work at this point is a waste of *our* time. So let's agree not to waste our time. We refer to talking about what doesn't work as 'looking down,' because it can keep us from looking up and moving forward. So we have created a ground rule called 'Always look up.' What this means is, any time a recommendation is made, we can say only two things: what we like about it and how to make it better. This way we are constantly improving solutions, and we avoid wasting time explaining why something won't work. Can we agree on this?" The executives accepted the ground rule.

At the end of the first presentation, we went around the room to talk about what we liked about it or how to make it better. We got to Darryl, who, I had learned, in the past had often served as the ringleader of the feeding frenzy. He started by saying, "Let me tell you why this won't work—" I interrupted and reminded him, "Darryl, remember our ground rule: always look up. Do you have a recommendation for improvement?" He responded, "Oh yes, sorry. Come back to me." After finishing around the room, I came back. "Darryl, any additional comments on this one?" He said, "No, my concerns were basically addressed." Perhaps someone else's suggested improvement had taken care of his concern. We went on to the next issue team. When we got to Darryl, he indicated what he liked about it. As I continued going around the room, Darryl raised his hand and asked, "When do I get to tell you what I don't like about it?" I could feel the tension in the room rising. My response was, "Now Darryl, that would be a waste of time, wouldn't it?" Darryl responded, "Yes, I guess that's right." He laughed, I laughed, the group laughed, and we moved on.

Of course, there were many issues with the recommendations, but the discussion focused on how to address them, not on why the solutions wouldn't work. A number of the recommendations changed considerably as a result of the discussion.

In total, the session was very productive. In fact, the CEO later said, it was their best executive session in many years.

As you can see from the case study, ground rules are a powerful tool for helping **take an issue off the table.** If from your preparation work you determine that the team may have difficulty with a particular issue, create ground rules that will help the group behave more functionally. There are three steps to using ground rules to take an issue off the table:

Using Ground Rules to Take an Issue off the Table	• State the issue up front. Don't wait for participants to say it or demonstrate the behavior. (In the "Feeding Frenzy" example, the facilitator stated the behavior: "We could identify all the reasons something doesn't work.") • Give the participants a reason to behave differently. ("This would be a waste of our time.") • Indicate the desired behavior. ("Always look up by telling us what you like about it or how to make it better.")

Quick Tip!

For sessions that run a day or longer, it's a good idea to review the ground rules at the halfway point (just after lunch or at the end of the first day) by asking the group to discuss how well they feel people are following the ground rules or whether there are adjustments needed to the ground rules or to our behaviors.

Using Parking Boards

In a facilitated session, there are a number of agenda items that must be covered sequentially. Most participants don't *think* sequentially, however. For example, if we were improving the hiring process, one of the early agenda items would be, "How does the hiring process work today?" During work on this agenda item, it is not unusual for participants to identify problems and potential solutions. Rather than tell a participant, "Hold that thought until we get to it later in the day," you can record the comment before bringing the group back to the current agenda item—but you need a place to record it. Facilitators typically call these places parking boards.

Secret #14

The Secret to Parking Boards

Have a place to park decisions, actions, and off-topic comments that come up prior to the time when you want to discuss them.

Why Do This?

Why use parking boards?

- Parking boards help the group avoid going off on tangents by providing a place to put topics that come up that are not the focus of the current discussion.
- Using parking boards helps participants become self-correcting by increasing their awareness of the types of comments not appropriate for the current discussion.
- Participants can easily review the parking boards to ensure that they have discussed topics previously brought up.
- By using the parking boards to record a comment, you convey to the participant that the input was valuable.

There are three standard parking boards that I include in most sessions.

The Standard Parking Boards

- The **Issues list** to post topics that need to be discussed later in the session or entirely outside the session.
- The **Decisions list** to post decisions made by the group that should be documented for future reference.
- The **Actions list** to post actions to be performed sometime after the completion of the session. The Actions list should be a three-column chart with the following headings: Action, Who, and When.

Although I recommend that you use the three standard parking boards for most sessions, you might also include additional parking boards depending on the nature of the session. For example, for issue resolution, you might have an additional parking board called Potential Alternatives or Additional Research Needs. For strategic planning, you might have a parking board called Potential Strategies.

Near the beginning of the session, and sometime after describing the agenda, you will want to identify the parking boards and explain how they are used. Before ending the session, you will need to review the content of each parking board. See Chapter Eight for more discussion of how the parking boards are used in the session closing.

Quick Tip!

I typically will have "Use the parking boards" as the last item on the ground rule list. This serves as a reminder to me to review the parking boards with the group at the beginning of the session.

Effective Introductions

As part of the session start, participants need to have a chance to become familiar with one another. This is especially important when a number of the participants don't know each other. For groups in which the members already know one another, it might suffice just to have a five- or ten-minute gathering period stated on the agenda prior to the official start of the session. For participants who don't know one another, a formal "get acquainted" process might be appropriate.

There are numerous techniques for increasing familiarity. The technique you use should be tied to the purpose of your session and the amount of time that can be allotted. For example, if the team will be working together for twelve months on an extensive project, consider taking a half day up front for initial team building. In contrast, for a team that will be working together for only a half-day session, ten or fifteen minutes may be all that can be afforded.

To increase familiarity, facilitators often engage participants in some type of detailed introduction that requires self-disclosure. Examples of this might include revealing something no one in the room knows about you, identifying your favorite movie, or sharing your most embarrassing moment. However, I recommend introductions in which participants are asked to provide information that will further the purpose of the session. For example, you might ask the participants to identify what they bring that will contribute to the success of the team.

Quick Tip!

One of my favorite introduction activities is *gifts and hooks* because the information gained from it can yield insight on team members while contributing to the success of the session. To use gifts and hooks, ask team members to identify three gifts they bring that can contribute to the success of the group, and one hook—the one thing that must occur in order to keep them engaged and coming back. (I first learned of gifts and hooks from Greg Brittingham when he was at the Center for Public Policy, Virginia Commonwealth University.)

Unfortunately, what often happens during introductions is that while a person is sharing his or her information, all the people who have yet to speak are preoccupied with figuring out what they will say. In addition, whereas the first person may take only twenty seconds, by the time you reach the last person, the time may have crept up to three or four minutes.

The Secret to Effective Introductions

Have participants write first; set an introduction time limit.

If you will be taking time for detailed introductions, consider the following steps.

Steps for Introductions	1. During your preparation stage, determine your purpose, the amount of time you have, and the process you will use for introductions.
	2. Record the questions on the flip chart to ensure that people understand what they are being asked to say.
	3. Give participants time (for example, one minute) to write down their thoughts in advance of your asking the first person to speak.
	4. Set a time limit for each introduction (for example, thirty seconds); consider using a clock with an alarm as a reminder of the time limit.

To introduce the time limit to the group, I try to be as respectful as possible to get the group to comply; for example, I say, "We have sixteen people in the room. If we all take three minutes to do introductions, it will require over forty-five minutes. Let's not do that. Can we agree to limit our introduction to thirty seconds? To help it along, I will use the timer. If you hear it beep, it means you have gone over your thirty seconds, so please go ahead and finish your sentence, but please avoid starting a new one . . . and I don't believe in semicolons!"

Opening Nonfacilitated Meetings

Recall that at the beginning of this chapter, I identified the following order for the opening of a facilitated session:

Recommended Order of the Opening for a Facilitated Session	1. Welcome 2. Session purpose and product (inform, excite, empower) 3. Participants' objectives (involve) 4. Agenda 5. Ground rules 6. Parking boards 7. Introductions 8. End of opening . . . on to the first major agenda item

How about for a meeting that doesn't have a facilitator? How should these meetings start? Nonfacilitated meetings should in essence start the same way, with purpose and product, but several steps are omitted after that, as follows.

Recommended Order of the Opening for a Nonfacilitated Session	1. The meeting leader gives the welcome and clearly states the meeting **purpose and product** at the beginning: "The purpose of this meeting is . . . When we are finished, we would like to walk away with . . . Are we agreed?" 2. The meeting leader then reviews and confirms the **agenda** and sets time limits: "The following agenda is proposed to achieve this purpose . . . Any recommended changes?" 3. End of opening . . . on to the first major agenda item

When Should You Arrive for the Meeting?

SMART facilitators recognize that they want to be completely set up and ready to start the session well before the first person arrives. If you are familiar with the room you are using, you may want to plan to be set up fifteen minutes prior to the start of the meeting. This way, as participants begin arriving ten minutes prior to the session start as you requested, you will be set up and ready.

However, if you are unfamiliar with the meeting room, you may want to plan to be set up thirty minutes prior to the start of the meeting just in case the room has to be rearranged or you have to track down flip charts, chairs, or other materials.

So when should you arrive? To calculate this number, first estimate the amount of time it will take you to set up, then add fifteen minutes if it is a familiar room or thirty minutes if an unfamiliar one, and finally subtract this sum from the start time.

| When Should You Arrive for the Meeting? | Familiar room = Session start time − Setup time − 15 minutes |
| | Unfamiliar room = Session start time − Setup time − 30 minutes |

For example, if the meeting starts at 9:00 and you estimate that it will take you ten minutes to set up and you are facilitating in a familiar room, you should plan to arrive at 8:35 (9:00 minus 10 minutes, minus 15 minutes). With this arrival time, you should be set up by 8:45 to be ready when the first participants arrive between 8:50 and 9:00. And if it takes you a little longer to set up than you had estimated, you still will be able to start on time.

Getting Started on Time

Getting the meeting started on time is a challenge for many facilitators. Consider the following three strategies for successfully meeting that challenge.

The Secret to Starting on Time

Make the first time listed on the agenda the gathering time; make sure the first speaker is ready; give a two-minute warning.

Schedule a Gathering Time

The first time that appears on the agenda that goes out to participants prior to the session should be the gathering time; the second time should be the start time. A separate gathering time has three advantages:

Advantages of Stating a Gathering Time on the Agenda	• Participants tend to focus on the first time listed and generally attempt to arrive at that time. • A separate gathering time acknowledges that you expect people to arrive early. • A separate gathering time communicates to those who tend to be prompt that the session will start on time.

Sample Agenda with Gathering Time

Session Purpose: To identify improvements to the hiring process

Agenda for Today: 7:50   Gather

8:00   Opening

How does the hiring process work today?

Problems and root causes

11:50   Review and close

Make Sure the First Speaker Is Ready

A second strategy for starting on time is to ensure that the person who will kick off the session is aware of this role in advance and that the two of you agree on the timing. During the gathering period, it is usually helpful to remind the person of this role and the agreed-on time.

Give the Two-Minute Warning

Just prior to the start time, give the two-minute warning. Encourage session attendees to take their seats by announcing, or asking the project sponsor to announce, that the session is about to begin. At the scheduled time, have the kickoff speaker begin the session.

Applying the Secrets to Starting

The Secrets to Starting apply to numerous areas professionally and personally. Consider the following examples.

Establishing Operating Principles

SMART facilitators use ground rules to help groups be self-correcting. Ground rules describe the behaviors that are expected and behaviors to be avoided.

Likewise, organizations can use ground rules, or operating principles, to communicate to everyone the behaviors that are expected and those to be avoided. If your people don't understand your operating principles, they are not likely to make the decisions or respond the way that you would want them to. Typically, when clear operating principles are absent, people base their responses on their own principles, which may or may not match yours!

Gaining Buy-In

The Fundamental Secret of Facilitation tells us that you can achieve more effective results when solutions are created, understood, and accepted by the people impacted. There may be times, however, when the solution has already been created and you are seeking buy-in. Is facilitation not appropriate then?

Let's take the example of an organization whose executive team has already created a draft strategic plan. At this point, the executive team desires to share the plans with middle managers to get their buy-in. Afterward, the middle managers will work within their departments and cross-functionally to develop the implementation action plans.

At the meeting with the middle managers, the executive team can use the Secret to Gaining Agenda Buy-In:

- They will first ask the middle managers to identify the most important issues they want to see addressed in the plan. These issues will be grouped into categories.
- After walking through the plan step-by-step, the executive team will ask the middle managers to match the issue categories to the parts of the plan where each is covered.
- In most cases when I have done this in the past, the draft plan covers all or nearly all the issues the managers identified. Those issues not covered are highlighted for consideration when the executive team reviews the draft.

Using this method for gaining buy-in allows the middle managers to see that the plan covers most of the areas that are important to them and that those areas not covered can be considered in a future draft.

Facilitator's Checklist for Getting the Session Started

☐ Arrive early enough to be completely set up fifteen to thirty minutes in advance of the session to allow for unexpected problems and to be available to greet participants.

☐ Set up the room: chairs and tables, charts, parking boards, markers, tape, name tents.

☐ Review the notes of your opening.

☐ Greet participants as they arrive.

☐ Meet with the sponsor briefly to review who will speak first and the planned start time.

☐ Give the two-minute warning to participants.

☐ Listen attentively to the sponsor's opening to be able to make reference back to the comments during your opening or later in the day.

☐ Give your opening: inform, excite, empower, involve.

- Review the session purpose and product.

- Excite the participants by explaining the benefits to them.

- Empower the participants by explaining the reason they were selected or the specific role they play.

- Ask the participants for their personal objectives or the key issues they want to see covered in the session.

☐ Complete the opening.

- Review the proposed agenda.

- Match the agenda to the participants' personal objectives; modify the agenda as needed; entertain a motion to accept the agenda.

- Review a preliminary set of ground rules; ask for additional ground rules to better help the group get its work done; entertain a motion to accept the agenda.

- Review the parking boards and their use.

- Ask for introductions.

☐ Start the next agenda item.

Exercise Your Skills

Chapter Seventeen contains a worksheet for planning and starting a meeting. The worksheet is also available at the Jossey-Bass *Secrets of Facilitation* Web page (www.josseybass.com/go/michaelwilkinson). To accustom yourself to the IEEI framework, use the worksheet to write out your opening for your next three or four meetings.

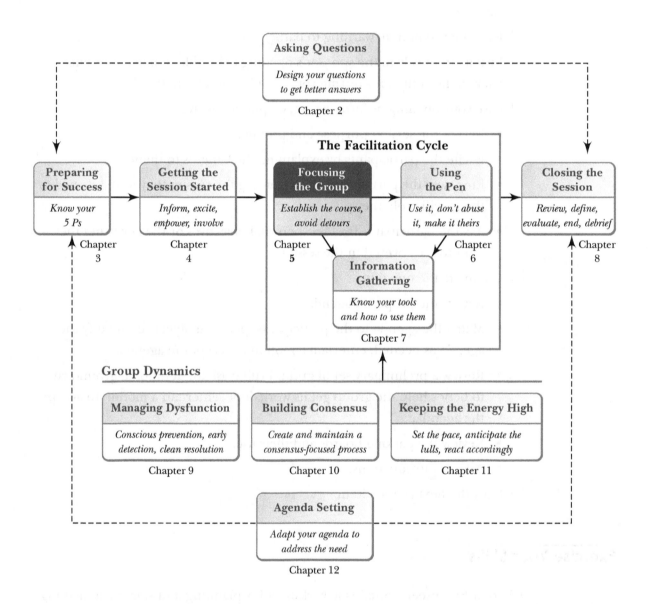

Asking Questions

Design your questions to get better answers

Chapter 2

The Facilitation Cycle

Preparing for Success

Know your 5 Ps

Chapter 3

Getting the Session Started

Inform, excite, empower, involve

Chapter 4

Focusing the Group

Establish the course, avoid detours

Chapter 5

Using the Pen

Use it, don't abuse it, make it theirs

Chapter 6

Information Gathering

Know your tools and how to use them

Chapter 7

Closing the Session

Review, define, evaluate, end, debrief

Chapter 8

Group Dynamics

Managing Dysfunction

Conscious prevention, early detection, clean resolution

Chapter 9

Building Consensus

Create and maintain a consensus-focused process

Chapter 10

Keeping the Energy High

Set the pace, anticipate the lulls, react accordingly

Chapter 11

Agenda Setting

Adapt your agenda to address the need

Chapter 12

CHAPTER FIVE

THE SECRETS TO FOCUSING

Establish the Course, Avoid Detours

Questions Answered in This Chapter

What should you do at the beginning of every agenda item to get the group focused?

When significant time has passed since the last session, how do you restart and get the group focused?

How do you avoid asking your first question and getting complete silence?

How do you give directions that are accurate, clear, and concise?

What techniques are there for keeping a group on track?

How do you effectively use breakout groups?

How do you keep groups focused during report-back sessions following breakout groups?

CASE STUDY: Facilitating the Senator and the Chief of Staff

A U.S. senator was considering implementing a series of business forums throughout his state to spur economic development. Although he had thoughts on how he might do it, he recognized that he needed some dedicated time to think through the idea and develop a plan for implementation. I was called in to facilitate him and his chief of staff through a three-hour session to outline the concept and build an implementation plan. I like to think of the session as "facilitation for two."

We were seated in a very small conference room. There was no space, no windows, and, worst of all, no flip chart! I did my IEEI (see Chapter Four), starting with informing them and getting agreement on the purpose and products to be created. I verbally reviewed the agenda because there was no place to write it down. As we started in on the first agenda item, I found

I was having a difficult time keeping the participants focused and on topic. Although there were just three of us seated around the conference table, the discussion would repeatedly flow into other topics. I remember thinking, "These are two really bright people. Why am I having so much trouble keeping them focused?"

It finally occurred to me that the lack of a flip chart was having a significant impact. The two participants couldn't see what I was recording; they couldn't see how their comments weren't staying on the topic. In complete exasperation, I took control of the meeting by holding my writing tablet on my shoulder, labeling the "chart," and recording their comments in a black marker on the pad.

This did the trick. After the first half hour of what felt like utter chaos, the rest of the meeting went very smoothly, as I was able to keep the senator and his aide focused on each agenda topic. What a difference a "flip chart" makes—whatever its shape or size!

In Chapter Four, I discussed how you would get the session started and the importance of informing, exciting, empowering, and involving in the first fifteen minutes. At this point in the session, you are ready to start the first agenda item. What do you do? How do you focus the group and keep them focused? How do you prevent the group from going off on long, unproductive detours? In this chapter, I identify strategies for focusing and for preventing detours. By the end of it, you will be equipped with tools for significantly increasing the productivity of groups and helping them achieve their desired ends.

This chapter includes four specific techniques for focusing a group and three techniques for avoiding detours. As you will soon see, I just used the preceding paragraph to demonstrate the most important of these techniques, the checkpoint.

The Secret to Using Checkpoints

Provide a review, preview, and big view at the beginning of each new agenda item or facilitated process.

Focusing the Group: Using Checkpoints

At the beginning of every agenda item or facilitated process, it is important to take a checkpoint by doing the following:

The Three
Parts of a
Checkpoint

- **Review.** Review quickly what has been done to date.
- **Preview.** Describe briefly what the group is about to do.
- **Big view.** Explain how the previewed agenda item fits into the overall objective of the session.

I will use the following agenda as an example to demonstrate the use of checkpoints.

Sample Agenda

Purpose: Define the changes necessary to increase the efficiency and effectiveness of the hiring process.

Agenda:
    A. Getting started

    B. How does the hiring process work today?

    C. What are the problems and root causes?

    D. What are the potential improvements?

    E. Prioritize the improvements

    F. Develop an implementation plan

    G. Review and close

Suppose you were about to start the second agenda item, "How does the hiring process work today?" Your checkpoint might sound like this:

Sample Checkpoint

Facilitator: We have just completed the getting started segment *[review]*. (*The facilitator puts a check mark next to this item on the agenda flip chart page.*)

Our next step is to identify how the hiring process works today *[preview]*. This is important, because if we can identify all the steps in the process, we can examine where in the process the problems are occurring and then identify ways to make it a much better process *[big view]*. The way we are going to do this is . . .

Why Do This? | **Why do a checkpoint?**

The checkpoint serves to ensure that all participants are aware that a transition is taking place. It also shows how vitally important the next step is by explaining how it relates to the overall purpose of the session.

Facilitators tend to be fairly good at the review and preview parts of a checkpoint. Unfortunately, they tend to leave out the key component, the big view. The big view explains why the step is important and why the participants should invest their time in the step. The big view should always tie back to the overall session objective by explaining how this step contributes to the purpose of the session. You might note that the big view is equivalent to the excite step in the IEEI technique for starting a session. In essence, with each agenda item, SMART facilitators re-excite people about the benefit of the session!

Quick Tip!

If a single agenda item has more than one facilitated process, you should use more than one checkpoint. For example, an agenda item such as "How does the hiring process work today?" could include three facilitated processes: a fact gathering process that identifies most of the steps, a categorization process to group the steps into major activities, and a review process to ensure that we have identified all the steps in each major activity. You should take a checkpoint when you transition from each of these facilitated processes as well as when you start the next agenda item.

What happens if you skip the big view? There could be repercussions. Let's go back to the hiring process example. Assume you were about to start the second agenda item, "How does the hiring process work today?" but all you gave were the review and preview and left out the big view.

Sample Dialogue: Dangers in Omitting the Big View

Facilitator: We have just completed the getting started segment. Our next step is to identify how the hiring process works today. The way we are going to do this is . . . *(At this point, your nightmare begins.)*

Participant: Excuse me, Ms. Facilitator. I agreed to be a part of this task force because the purpose is to come up with a *new* process. Let's be clear, we are not going to do the *old* process anymore. We are going to do the *new* process. So spending any time at all talking about how the *old* process works is a waste of our time, your time, and my time. Let's not waste time. If we are here to create a new process, let's get to it.

Facilitator: *(Rapid backpedaling ensues.)* I appreciate your concern about not wasting time. And if we don't need to talk about the current process, it will certainly save time to skip it. One reason perhaps to talk at least a little about the current process is that by identifying the current steps, it will make it easier for us to identify where the problems are. This typically helps us make sure that our new process fixes those problems. But maybe others agree that we don't need to talk about the current process. What do you think? And then let's check in with the rest of the group . . .

Participant: Let's not waste time checking in with the rest of the group. I understand now what you are trying to do. Let's just get to it.

In this sample, the facilitator didn't give the big view: she was about to start an agenda item without explaining why the agenda item was important. This participant happens to put a high value on time. The participant immediately objected to the idea of wasting time on an activity that wasn't contributing to the objective.

Notice what happened next: the facilitator acknowledged the recommendation and even gave a reason to do it (more on this in Chapter Eight), but she then gave the big view in an effort to resolve the situation! Once the facilitator gave the big view, the participant was basically satisfied. However, now there is a bit of tension in the air. Some of the other participants may perceive the vocal participant in a negative light. Yet he spoke up because the facilitator didn't give the big view. Note once more that when we don't do our job as the facilitator, the participants look bad. Had the facilitator given the big view in the beginning, this situation would probably have been avoided.

An additional benefit of the checkpoint is that it provides a smooth transition from item to item on the agenda. The big view is a key component for helping people understand how each part of the agenda fits into the overall session objective. Keep this in mind: if you find people asking you, "So why are we doing this?" it may mean you omitted the big view.

The Extended Checkpoint

Checkpoints are used to transition from one agenda item to the next. If, however, significant time has passed since you covered the last agenda item (for example, if you are restarting a session on a new day or after an extended break), use an extended checkpoint to get the participants "back in the room." There are four steps in an extended checkpoint.

The Four Steps in an Extended Checkpoint	1. **Remind** the participants of the overall session objective.
	2. **Review** all agenda items that have been completed to date; consider "walking the walls" by walking around the room and pointing to the flip chart pages or other output that has been posted on the walls.
	3. **Preview** all the agenda items remaining to be completed.
	4. If only a subset of the remaining items are to be done today, **explain** how the specific items to be completed in the current session relate to the overall session objective.

Warming Up a Group

I have talked about the checkpoint and the extended checkpoint. The third technique for focusing is warming up the group. It is typical for participants in a session to be initially reserved and very willing to allow others to speak first. As a result, it is not unusual for the first question you ask to be met with complete and utter silence! This can be demoralizing for you, especially when it occurs at the beginning of a session—that time when you are hoping for high energy and great interaction.

 **Secret #18**

The Secret to Warming Up a Group
Ask two questions that require a nonverbal response.

To avoid that resounding silence after you ask your first question, warm up the group by first asking at least two questions that require a nonverbal response. Plan these "pre-questions" carefully, as they should lead up to your primary question.

Sample Dialogue: Warming Up a Group

In this sample, the facilitator's primary question is, "What are the benefits of planning?" Note the questions the facilitator asks and the actions the facilitator takes before asking the primary question.

Facilitator: How many people here have been involved with a project that wasn't well planned from the beginning? *(Raises his hand.)*

It was somewhat difficult, wasn't it? *(Nods his head.)*

You may have had such problems as a lack of understanding of the purpose, people unclear about roles, lack of commitment to action, and so on. So there are some real benefits to planning, aren't there? *(Nods his head.)*

Let's name a few. What are the benefits of planning? Who can tell me one? *(Raises his hand. Calls on someone whose hand also goes up.)*

The warm-up technique is effective in getting people responding to you, first nonverbally, then verbally. By twice getting the participants to nod their heads or raise their hands, you have greatly increased the likelihood that when you ask that first question and raise your hand, one or more people will raise their hands to offer a response.

The timing of your gestures is important in the warm-up. You should raise your hand or nod your head *while* you are asking the question. This way, the participants will know what action you want them to take before you finish asking the question, and they can respond right away.

Delivering Accurate, Clear, and Concise Directions (PeDeQs)

After employing a checkpoint or an extended checkpoint, facilitators typically deliver instructions to the participants to begin the facilitated process. How well the facilitator delivers those instructions often affects how well the participants understand, execute, and enjoy the process. There is a science to giving directions so that you are accurate, clear, and concise. SMART facilitators use a standard process we call PeDeQs.

Secret #19

The Secret to Giving Clear Directions
When giving directions, use your PeDeQs.

When giving complex directions, always step through your PeDeQs:

PeDeQs—
Giving
Directions

1. State the overall **Purpose** of the activity.
2. When appropriate, use a simple **example,** outside the topic area, that helps participants understand how to complete the activity.
3. Give general **Directions** using verbal pictures and gestures.
4. Explain specific **exceptions** and special cases.
5. Ask for **Questions.**
6. Ask a **starting** question that gets participants visualizing the answers.

Suppose you want participants to identify the problems that occur in the organization's hiring process. You also want participants to identify the symptom and root causes for each of the problems. The table to be completed might have three columns, as follows.

Problem	Symptom	Root Cause

To give your PeDeQs, you might say the following:

Sample Dialogue: PeDeQs

Facilitator: We have just identified the steps in the hiring process. Our next step is to discuss the problems in the hiring process. This is important because it will help us understand what the problems are and the causes of those problems. This will lead us to strategies that will improve the hiring process. *[checkpoint]*

We will be using this table to help identify the problems, symptoms, and root causes. *[purpose]* For example, if we were cooking a turkey dinner, our problem might be "a burnt turkey." The symptom might be "turkey black." The root cause might be that we cooked it too long. What else might be a root cause? That's right, a root cause might be that the oven temperature was too high, the oven thermometer was broken, or a bad cook. *[example]*

Well, we're not cooking a turkey dinner. We are analyzing the problems with the hiring process. The way we're going to do this is, we will first list all the problems. Once we have all the problems listed, we will then identify the symptom and root cause for each. *[directions]*

Now, there are a couple of other things you need to know. While we are listing the problems, you may come up with a root cause. We will place it in the root cause column until we identify the associated problem. Likewise, after we list all the problems and are identifying symptoms and root causes, you may find an additional problem, and we will add it to the bottom. *[exceptions]*

Any questions? . . . *[questions]*

OK, let's think about the last time you hired someone. Consider the things you found frustrating, the things that upset you, the things that made you say, "We've got to fix this process." Let's build the list of the problems with the existing hiring process. Who will get me started? What problems are there with the hiring process? *[starting question]*

Why Do This?	**Why use PeDeQs when giving directions?**
	When you ask participants to do anything that is beyond the very simple, it is important that you empower them by giving them directions that are accurate, clear, and concise. By following PeDeQs, you can be sure that you have explained what you want them to do, why you want them to do it, and how to do it successfully. If you ever have your participants ask you, "Why are we doing this?" or "Could you explain that again?" more than likely, you haven't done your PeDeQs.

PeDeQs provide a systematic way to ensure that you give directions that are accurate, clear, and reasonably concise—every time. There are a few tips for giving PeDeQs.

Tips for Using PeDeQs

- Before the session, be sure to create a bulleted list that you will use to convey your directions to the group. Once you have developed your bulleted list, ask yourself, "Where might someone be confused?" Add verbal pictures, examples, or analogies to further facilitate understanding.
- After you state the purpose, use an example or analogy to help the participants better understand what is desired. In giving the example, you start it ("For example, if we were cooking a turkey dinner, our problem might be a burnt turkey"), but let them finish it ("What else might be a root cause?"). This helps them better understand the process and gain ownership of the activity. Avoid recording their responses to the example, however; recording typically takes more time than is warranted.
- Make sure the example you use is entirely unrelated to the session purpose or content. An example related to the topic can lead participants into debating the accuracy of answers to the example!
- After describing the example, give all the general directions first for how the facilitated process will work. To avoid confusion, leave out any exceptions or special cases until all of the general directions have been given.
- Your starting question is the question that will begin the process. Because this is the last thing you will say to the participants, it has the greatest effect on whether their subsequent responses will be on track. Plan the wording of this question carefully.

Note that for complex processes, you will likely use all parts of PeDeQs. For a simple listing or brainstorming exercise, however, you might just give the purpose and then jump straight to the starting question.

Keeping a Group on Track

Whereas the techniques in the previous section help get a group focused, the techniques I discuss here help the group stay focused and working productively. SMART facilitators have several simple techniques for keeping a group on track:

Strategies to
Keep a Group
on Track

- Label the charts.
- Ask extended prompt questions.
- Ask redirection questions.

The Secret to Keeping a Group on Track

Label, prompt, redirect.

Label the Charts

Before giving a checkpoint or delivering your PeDeQs, you should always label your flip charts or other recording media with the title of the agenda item, as shown in Figure 5.1. This simple technique helps remind the group of the topic being discussed. It also allows all participants to see when subjects are being discussed or information is being recorded that is not in line with this topic.

FIGURE 5.1   LABELING FLIP CHARTS.

Steps in the Hiring Process

Ask Extended Prompt Questions

In Chapter Two, I covered the technique of asking prompt questions, such as "What else?" The prompt question is sufficient for prompting a group that has stalled. To help ensure that the responses you receive are focused on the content, you should ask an extended prompt question.

Example of an Extend Prompt	If the group has been discussing the steps in the hiring process and the participants have stalled after giving several responses, instead of asking, "What else?" you would ask, "What other steps are there in the hiring process?"

The extended prompt better focuses a group by repeating the type A question.

Ask Redirection Questions

When the participants begin responding following a starting question, you should monitor the discussion carefully to ensure that all comments are related to the process under way. If the group begins to detour off on an unrelated discussion, you can bring the group back by asking a redirection question.

Sample Dialogue: Redirection Question

Facilitator: What other steps are there in the hiring process?

Carl: One of the things I think we really need to fix is the length of the process. It just takes too long to get people through the process from soup to nuts.

Facilitator: The length of the process certainly sounds like a problem we will want to address. Is it OK if we put it on the Issues list so we remember it when we talk about problems and then see if there are any other steps in the hiring process we still need to list?

Carl: Sure, go ahead. I just wanted to make sure we didn't miss this.

The traditional form of the redirection question is to affirm the value of the comment, ask permission to post it on the Issues list, and remind the group of the topic at hand: "That's a good point. Can we put that on the Issues list so we won't forget it and then get back to our question?"

When you use the redirection question, it is important to *ask for permission* to table the issue. By asking, you get the participant's buy-in. You may still get agreement if you *tell* the participant that you are going to table the issue, but if the person disagrees, you may be in for a power struggle.

What do you do if you ask for permission to table the issue and the participant disagrees? You put the question to the group, or to the meeting sponsor if more appropriate.

Sample Dialogue: Redirection Question—Denied!

Facilitator:	The length of the process certainly sounds like a problem we will want to address. Is it OK if we put it on the Issues list so we remember it when we talk about problems and then see if there are any other steps in the hiring process we still need to list?
Carl:	No, I think this is something we should discuss now.
Facilitator:	That would be a detour off our main course, but if the group is for it, we can do it. How much time do you think we'll need, Carl?
Carl:	Only about ten minutes.
Facilitator:	Let's check in. Group, the plan has been to talk about the hiring steps first and then the problems with the process. Carl would like to spend about ten minutes talking about the problem related to the length of the process and then we would get back to the discussion of the other steps. Carl, is that a clear description, or is there anything you would like to add?
Carl:	No, that's good.
Facilitator:	We typically go with a simple majority for these kinds of process decisions. Any other comments from anyone? . . . OK then, those in favor of taking ten minutes now to talk about the problem related to the length of the process, raise your hand . . . Those not in favor?

Managing Breakout Groups

So far, under the topic of the Secrets to Focusing, I have covered several techniques: checkpoints, extended checkpoints, PeDeQs, warm-ups, chart labeling, extended prompts, and redirection questions. Let's move now to the final technique for focusing: using breakout groups. As you will see, breakout groups can be a significant tool to enhance both engagement and productivity.

Breakout groups are especially appropriate when the agenda calls for a facilitated process to be performed several times (for example, when the group needs to come up with solutions to ten problems identified in the hiring process). In breakout sessions, the participants are divided into several teams, each of which has the responsibility to perform the facilitated process on one or more of the items.

Secret #21

The Secret to Effective Breakout Groups

Do, divide, direct: do one together; divide into teams; give final directions.

When used well, breakout groups can be quite effective. Consider the following steps:

Steps for Using Breakout Groups	1. Let the participants know that they are about to be broken out into groups.
	2. Complete the first element with the entire group.
	3. Divide into teams.
	4. Appoint team leaders, scribes, and reporters.
	5. Give final directions to the teams.
	6. Monitor the activity.
	7. Have each team report its results.

Let's take a look at each of the steps separately.

Step 1: Let the Participants Know That They Are About to Be Broken Out into Groups

Alert the participants that after completing the first element together as one group, they will be split into teams to complete the other elements. When you alert them ahead of time, the participants often pay a greater level of attention during the next step!

Step 2: Complete the First Element with the Entire Group

You should facilitate the entire group through the process of addressing the first element. For example, if each breakout team will be assigned the task of identifying potential solutions to one of the problems in the hiring process, you would lead the entire group in addressing one of the problems before breaking out. Doing this tends to increase the quality of each team's end result, because it gives the participants a chance to see the product to create and the process for creating the product.

Sometimes it is not helpful to do just the first item as a group because it does not give adequate guidance to the breakout teams. For example, in strategic planning, a common process is a SWOT analysis in which the group identifies the organization's strengths, weaknesses, opportunities, and threats. In theory, the entire group could focus on strengths and then each of three breakout teams could work on one of the remaining items: weaknesses, opportunities, and threats. The work on strengths as a group, however, would not guide the breakout teams in their work: knowing how to identify strengths does not guide the teams in identifying weaknesses, opportunities, and threats.

In cases like this one, in which each breakout team is working on a unique activity, consider a different approach. Instead of having the entire group work on one element, lead them in a minute or two of brainstorming answers to each breakout team's assignment. In this way the entire group will have given guidance and a starting point to each breakout team.

Step 3: Divide into Teams

Determine the number of teams to be used. Consider working with teams of three to seven members, though larger teams may be necessary. Typically, the smaller the team, the greater the level of individual responsibility and participation.

There are several methods for dividing into teams, depending on your purpose. Let's say that you have thirty people in the room, and there are five problems remaining in the hiring process after you have completed the first one as an entire group. Accordingly, you'll need five teams.

Methods for Dividing into Breakout Teams

- If your goal is to break into the teams as *quickly* as possible, you might designate teams based on where people are sitting.
- If your goal is to *mix* people who have been sitting together, you can have the group count off by fives (the number of teams you want) and have all the ones come together to tackle the first problem, all the twos come together to tackle the second problem, and so on.
- If your goal is to ensure *diversity* within each team, you might choose to assign the teams ahead of time and have the names available for viewing when it is time to break out into groups. Pre-assigning teams is often necessary when participants represent a wide range of levels within the same organization.
- If your goal is to have people address the problem to which they bring the most *expertise or passion,* you might have the participants choose the problem on which they wish to work. To avoid having only one or two people in a team, you might get agreement from the participants on a maximum and minimum number of team members.

In the strategy work that I do, I find that I use this last method most often. Let's say that I am working with an organization that has a twenty-person planning team with five goal areas: growth and profitability, customer service, brand awareness, products, and culture, and that we have completed the culture goal as an entire group. When we break out into subgroups, I would want the people with the strongest interest and expertise in marketing to work on the brand awareness goal, and those with the strongest interest and expertise in product development to work on the product goal. Yet at the same time, I would want a balance of people across all goal areas. The following sample dialogue describes what I might say to divide the group.

Sample Dialogue: Splitting into Teams

Facilitator: Now that we have gone through and defined objectives for the first goal area as a group, we are ready to divide into our breakout teams. This will allow a smaller group to give extended focus to each of these goals. We will be splitting into four teams to address the remaining four goals. In a minute, I am going to review the list of goals and ask you to indicate which goal you would like to address. But I would like for us to agree on something first. There are twenty people in the room. That means that each team will have an average of five people. Can we agree then that we don't want to have a team with fewer than three people or a team with more than seven? Also, can we agree that each person needs to be assigned to a team? OK, let's review each goal; put up your hand if you would like to be a part of that team.

Step 4: Appoint Team Leaders, Scribes, and Reporters

A lack of leadership can cause breakout teams to waste time; so can ambiguity around roles. When leadership is not clear, team members may have trouble getting the process started. Also, when team leadership is left to chance, the more dominant personalities are likely to take control, reducing the opportunities for shared ownership. When other roles are not defined from the very beginning, the reporter and scribe may not be told their responsibilities until late into the process.

As the facilitator, you can help the teams avoid these problems by defining for them a process for assigning roles. When I use multiple breakouts during a day, I ask for volunteers once the teams are divided and have the volunteers pick the first team leader. I then suggest that the scribe be the person to the right of the team leader and the reporter be the person to the left. I also encourage teams to adjust the process to meet their particular needs. In subsequent break-outs, I have the former team leaders name their successors.

Step 5: Give Final Directions to the Teams

When giving directions to the teams, make sure they know the following:

Items to Explain in the Final Directions	• What their deliverable is • How to judge the quality of the deliverable • What the process is for creating it • What the deadline is for completion

Consider setting an interim deadline (for example, "You should be record-ing your results on the flip chart by . . .") to help keep the teams on track.

Step 6: Monitor the Activity

As the breakout teams are working, you will want to move from team to team to monitor the activity. Specifically, you will want to ensure that each team is pro-gressing as expected, that the deliverables are reasonably close to what is desired, and that the team is working within the time frame.

Step 7: Have Each Team Report Its Results

Results from the breakout teams should be recorded in such a way that permits viewing by other teams. In some cases, you will use flip charts, other cases elec-tronic media or some other form.

Consider the following standard report-back process for reviewing the results following breakout groups.

The Standard Report-Back Process	• Each team is given a time limit (for example, three to five minutes) to report its results. The other teams listen without comment and give an ovation following the report. • The other teams comment on positive points first and then recommend additions or deletions. • Once all potential additions and deletions are identified, the entire group votes on each recommendation. For

each controversial recommendation, a suitable discussion period is permitted, with one or two persons speaking for and against the recommendation.

- Once all recommendations are decided, the next team follows in sequence.

Over the years, I have adopted an alternative process for report-back that I have found to be quite effective in achieving quality feedback on the work of breakout groups.

The Secret to Rotating Flip Charts

Have teams move from chart to chart to achieve a higher-quality review.

With the rotating flip charts process, each team has three to five minutes to review another team's work before moving on to the next team's charts, as described here:

Steps for Rotating Flip Charts

1. Assign team leaders and give a different colored pen and colored sticky notes to each team.
2. Have each team rotate clockwise to the next team's chart.
3. The teams review the other team's chart by placing a check mark on each item to indicate agreement.
4. If a team disagrees with an item, the team leader places an X next to the item and then records and posts a comment on a sticky note on how to improve the item. It is important that the focus of the note isn't to explain what is wrong with the item; the focus is on how to improve it.
5. The team can also add new items at the bottom of the other team's chart.
6. At the end of the allotted time, teams move to the next chart, performing the same review but also reviewing the comments of all past reviewers.

7. When the teams rotate back to their own flip chart, they will see multiple check marks in different colors to indicate those teams that agree with each item in their report. They will also see where disagreement resulted and the number of teams that concurred with that disagreement.

8. The teams then review all the disagreements (that is, the sticky notes) and indicate whether they agree (YES) or disagree (NO) with the written comment.

9. At this point, the entire group reviews all the NOs. The team writing the note explains why they did so, the team rejecting the note explains why they did so, and the entire group makes the final decision whether to accept or reject the written comment.

The rotating flip charts process allows each team to receive focused review from each of the other teams. This process also increases participation and the ownership of the entire work by all members. Surprisingly, it takes about the same amount of time as the standard report-back.

Why Do This?

Why use the rotating flip charts process?

One of the challenges with the standard report-back process is that people generally are not fully attentive to what other teams are saying. Some may be still preparing their own report-back. In other cases, with so many people involved, there may be little feeling of accountability on the part of any one person to give the other teams quality feedback. As a result, the standard report-back process typically yields very few comments and only from the more vocal participants. If you want quality feedback, I have found that the rotating flip charts process is far superior.

A Final Point About Breakout Sessions

Note that although breakout sessions are designed to increase participation and save time, they do not always save time. Because the group discusses and analyzes the results from each team, holding breakout sessions can take longer than remaining as one group! Often the key determinant of time saved is the quality of the results that come from the teams. If there are only a few strong sources of knowledge among the participants, it may be better *not* to use break-out sessions.

Applying the Secrets to Focusing

The Secrets to Focusing can be used quite readily in formal and informal settings. Consider the following examples.

Using Checkpoints in Speaking

Checkpoints are a fabulous tool to help groups understand where they are in an overall process. Facilitators use checkpoints at the beginning of each new agenda item to mark progress and to explain the importance of what's to come. In speaking situations, such as formal and informal presentations, use checkpoints liberally: give a quick review to tell your listener what you have covered already, give a quick preview to explain what's coming, and give the big view that explains why the next topic is important. Using this technique in speaking increases the ability of your listener to follow and value where you are going.

Redirecting a Conversation

In meetings, participants have a tendency to allow discussions to go off the main point. A facilitator uses the redirection question ("That's a good point; can we put it on the Issues list?") to prevent an unfocused comment from taking the group off on tangents. Just as facilitators use redirection questions, you can apply the same method to one-on-one conversations. When someone goes off topic in a conversation, you can wait for a pause or interrupt, and say, "Your point about . . . appears to be a good one; I don't want to lose it. But I was very excited when you were talking about . . . Can we get back to that?"

Facilitator's Checklist for Focusing a Group

☐ Use a checkpoint at the beginning of each new agenda item or facilitated process.

- Review. Review quickly what has been done to date.
- Preview. Describe briefly what the group is about to do.
- Big view. Explain how the previewed agenda item fits into the overall objective of the session.

☐ Use extended checkpoints when significant time has passed since the group worked on the last agenda item (for example, when you are restarting a session on a new day or after an extended break).

- Remind the participants of the overall session objective.

- Review all agenda items that have been completed to date; consider "walking the walls" by walking around the room and pointing to the flip chart pages or other output that has been posted on the walls.

- Preview all the agenda items remaining to be completed.

- If only a subset of the remaining items are to be done today, explain how the specific items to be completed in the current session relate to the overall session objective.

☐ To avoid getting silence in response to your first question, warm up the group by first asking at least two questions that require a nonverbal response.

☐ When giving complex directions, always step through your PeDeQs.

- Give the overall Purpose of the activity.

- When appropriate, use a simple example, outside the business area, that helps participants understand how to complete the activity.

- Give general Directions using verbal pictures and gestures.

- Explain specific exceptions and special cases.

- Ask for Questions.

- Ask a starting question that gets participants visualizing the answers.

☐ To help keep a group on track:

- Label the charts.

- Ask extended prompt questions.

- Ask redirection questions.

☐ Use breakout groups when the agenda calls for a facilitated process to be performed several times.

- Let the participants know that they are about to be broken out into groups.

- Complete the first element with the entire group.

- Divide into teams.

- Appoint team leaders, scribes, and reporters.

- Give final directions to the teams.

- Monitor the activity.

- Have each team report their results.

☐ Use the rotating flip charts process to achieve high-quality feedback on the work of breakout groups by having each breakout team study another team's chart, record detailed feedback on strengths and recommendations for improvement, and then move to the next team's chart.

Exercise Your Skills

Managing transitions and giving directions are two of the more important focusing skills. For the next three or four meetings you lead, write out the checkpoint you will use to transition between each agenda item. As well, for any activity that requires directions, write out your PeDeQs. The point of writing down these items is not so that you will read them but so that you will consciously train yourself to cover each of the elements.

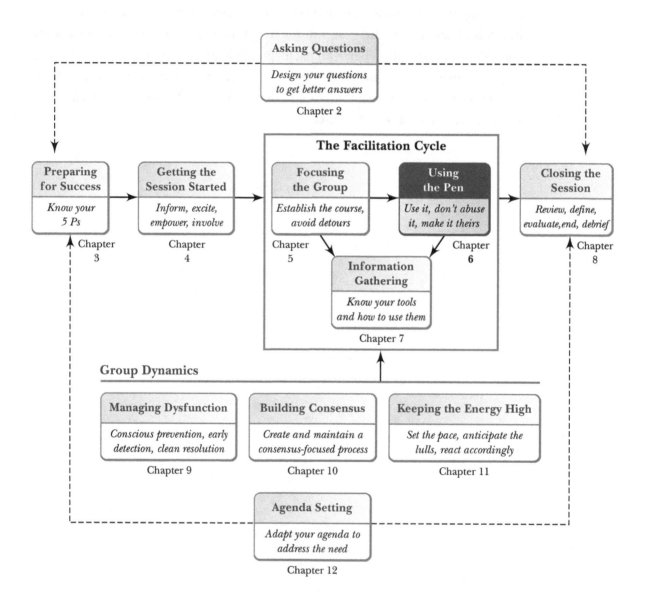

CHAPTER SIX

THE SECRETS TO RECORDING

The Power of the Pen—Use It, Don't Abuse It, Make It Theirs

Questions Answered in This Chapter

What is the most important information to document from a facilitated session?

How do you avoid abusing the power of the pen?

How do you manage the recording process while still facilitating the group?

What do you do when a participant gives you a long monologue?

How do you prevent lulls while you are writing?

How do you effectively use a scribe during the session?

What is an appropriate format for the documentation?

What are the seven deadly sins of facilitation?

CASE STUDY: Public Safety Collaborative

A member of our team was serving as coach and assistant to a facilitator from another organization. The lead facilitator was working with a group of forty people responsible for identifying methods to improve public safety in a large urban area. The task force included judges, police chiefs, sheriffs, district attorneys, juvenile court officers, and others who had an interest in public safety.

At this particular meeting, the lead facilitator got the session started and asked the participants to identify the key issues they wanted to see discussed during the collaborative process. One of the participants, a police chief, said, "We need to address the recidivism rate." The lead facilitator responded, "So, what you are saying is that the recidivism rate is too high."

The police chief, just a bit annoyed, responded, "No. What I said was that we need to address the recidivism rate."

Rather than write what the participant said, the facilitator once more responded, "OK, you're saying then that too many criminals have repeat crimes." "No," said the police chief, "that is *not* what I said. I said we need to address the recidivism rate!" The facilitator then turned to the other participants and asked, "What other concerns do we have about the recidivism rate?"

At this point, you could see the police chief become totally exasperated. He pulled back in his chair and didn't say a word for the rest of the session. The facilitator coach added later, "I could see the chief of police getting upset. All I could think was, 'Write it. Just write it. The man's got a gun. Write it!'"

How Facilitators Abuse the Pen

You may find the content in this chapter more challenging to your existing beliefs about facilitation than the content in any other chapter in this book. For I have found that often facilitators don't truly understand the power of the pen and how they frequently abuse it. As evidenced by the public safety case study that opened this chapter, a facilitator can cause participants to become dysfunctional simply by abusing the pen. Abuse of the pen can very easily lead to participants' dropping out, arguing with the facilitator, or not buying into the overall result.

There are several ways that facilitators commonly abuse the pen, often without knowing it. Let's take a look at each of these common abuses.

Common Ways That Facilitators Abuse the Pen	<ul><li>The facilitator chooses which comments merit recording on the flip charts.</li><li>The facilitator asks for the group's agreement before recording someone's words.</li><li>The facilitator interprets the words that are spoken and records the interpretation, instead of recording what is said.</li><li>The facilitator asks the person for permission to record the facilitator's words instead of the words the person spoke.</li><li>The facilitator waits until a comment is "perfect" before recording it.</li></ul>

The Facilitator Chooses Which Comments Merit Recording on the Flip Charts

Facilitators who don't understand the power of the pen frequently abuse it in this way. They will quickly record those comments with which they agree. When they hear comments with which they disagree, they will engage in a conversation with the participant to try to get the participant to change the comment or agree that it is not necessary to record. As you will see in this chapter, there are far more empowering techniques for addressing this situation.

The Facilitator Asks for the Group's Agreement Before Recording Someone's Words

As an example, I was in a practice session that someone else was facilitating. When Sally and Joe made comments, the facilitator immediately recorded them. However, when Pete made a comment with which the facilitator disagreed, instead of writing what Pete said, the facilitator turned to the group and asked, "What do you all think about what Pete just said?" I remember thinking, "What, is Pete the outcast or something? You wrote down everyone else's comments. Why does Pete's comment require the validation of the group?"

The Facilitator Interprets the Words That Are Spoken and Records the Interpretation, Instead of Recording What Is Said

Facilitators often are in the habit of listening to a participant's statement, then transforming what was said into words more "acceptable" to the facilitator. Why change the words? Some facilitators say that they change the words to summarize the idea. Others say they transform the words to promote clarity. Still others say they are just trying to shorten the comment to make it easier to write. As you will see in this chapter, changing participants' words disempowers them completely. It implies, "You all don't know how to speak. Let me speak for you." This can result in participants' losing ownership of both the session and the results, because the results represent your words, not theirs.

The Facilitator Asks the Person for Permission to Record the Facilitator's Words Instead of the Words the Person Spoke

A more subtle form of the prior abuse occurs when facilitators ask the person for permission to write their own words instead of the person's words. In essence, these facilitators are asking for permission to abuse their participants. Like the prior form of pen abuse, this one can lead to disempowerment and lack of ownership of the result.

The Facilitator Waits Until a Comment Is "Perfect" Before Recording It

In this form of pen abuse, the facilitator only records comments once the group has discussed and agreed to what will be done. I have found that this can lead to a failure to consider good ideas because they were never written down, and can also lead to considerable unfocused discussions because people aren't "seeing" where the discussion is going. Recording comments serves as a significant focusing tool to keep the conversation on track. When the focusing tool isn't there, people will often go off on side conversations.

Using, Not Abusing, the Pen

The best strategy I have found for preventing abuse of the pen is to get in the habit of *using*, not abusing, it.

The Secret to Using, Not Abusing, the Power of the Pen

Write first, discuss second; write what they said; write so they can read it; ask, don't tell.

There are four primary strategies that will build a strong foundation for preventing abuse of the pen.

Strategies for
Using the Pen

- Always write first, discuss second to ensure that you don't selectively record.
- Write what they said, not what you heard, to ensure that you use their words, not yours.
- Write so the group can read it, using large, legible writing.
- Ask, don't tell, so that you stay in your facilitator role.

Write First, Discuss Second

One of the ways a facilitator prevents abuse of the pen is to write first and discuss second. Here are some rules of thumb:

Rules of
Thumb for
Write First,
Discuss Second

- If what is said is incomplete, write it anyway.
- If what is said can be improved on, write it anyway.
- If what is said is not the answer you were looking for, write it anyway.
- If what is said is obviously wrong, write it anyway.

By recording what participants say, you as the facilitator are implicitly telling them, "Thank you for making a contribution." It is vital to positive group dynamics that you do this regardless of whether the contribution was good, bad, or indifferent. Each time you record a contribution, you are saying thank you. If you stop saying thank you, participants may very well stop contributing!

There are other benefits to writing first:

Other Benefits to Writing First	• Writing first prevents you from allowing your opinion of a comment to influence whether you record the comment. • Writing first prevents you from slowing down the activity because of your having to ask, "What did you say again?" • Writing first helps make sure you record their words and not yours. • Writing first helps you, the facilitator, stay on track. Should a long discussion ensue, you will always be able to refocus by looking at the last thing you wrote.

Write What They Said, Not What You Heard

Writing first and discussing second is important for empowering the participants. An equally important empowerment technique is to write what the participants said, not what you heard. Whatever the reason for changing a participant's words, the potential negative impact on empowerment may far outweigh the benefit.

Why Do This?	**Why write what they said instead of what you heard?** If you try to "clean up" the speaker's words by writing words he or she did not say, you as the facilitator are implicitly saying, "You don't know how to speak; let me speak for you." Over time, less assertive participants will tend to get lazy and look to you to "make all their words better"; more assertive participants will tend to compete with you to come up with suitable words for the other participants. Rewriting comments in your own words decreases the likelihood that participants will be able to understand what was meant after time has passed. This effect is typically a result of your using words and expressions in ways that are familiar to you but that might not be the way the participants express these same ideas. Writing your words can decrease the participants' sense of ownership of the result, because the words are yours, not theirs.

Write So the Group Can Read It

Clear documentation helps keep the group engaged and focused. And because it is your responsibility to ensure that participants agree with the documentation of the session before the session ends, it is important that participants be able to read what you write. Sometimes, however, even the best facilitators can't read their own writing. When recording on flip charts, consider the following to keep your charts legible:

Strategies for Keeping your Charts Legible	• Use large print; about ten lines should fill a page. • Write straight; use lined paper if necessary. • Leave plenty of space; allow for corrections between your lines. • Use dark pen colors for your primary writing (for example, black, dark blue, dark green); avoid using the lighter colors (orange, red, light green) for large blocks of text, as these colors are not as visible from a distance. • Consider alternating between two dark colors when a considerable amount of text is needed on a page. • Label or insert a header on *every* page for clarity and focus; draw a box or banner around the header to differentiate it from the rest of the text. • Edit and make additions using a lighter color pen to increase legibility.

Ask, Don't Tell

Recall that the Fundamental Secret of Facilitation is that the participants need to create, understand, and accept the solutions. To be effective in the facilitation role, you must strive to ask questions rather than to tell by making statements. Telling instead of asking has several potential pitfalls:

Pitfalls of Telling Versus Asking	• You may get verbal agreement on what you are saying, but the participants never own it. • You may not get agreement on what you are saying, and time is wasted while you try to convince one or more people that what you are saying is correct. • You may be perceived as taking a strong position and thus lose your credibility as an unbiased facilitator for the group.

Remember: if you say it, they can disagree with you. If they say it, it's theirs. Your job as a facilitator is to ensure that the conclusions reached are created, understood, and accepted by all participants. Even if you are both a facilitator and a participant, it is important to use questions to help the group achieve ownership. If you find yourself making statements instead of asking questions, you may have fallen out of the facilitator role into a participant role.

Refer to Chapter Two for examples of the differences between asking and telling using reacting questions.

CASE STUDY: The Power of the Pen, ELMO, and Parking Boards

Chad Klekar, with the global services organization of a major oil company, describes the difference he has found in using the "power of the pen" principles and other techniques.

One of my biggest personal learnings (I might even go as far as to call it a paradigm shift), is that I constantly wrote what I heard and not at all what was being said. Not only was I doing this, but I was making major changes in order to make comments and input align with what I personally wanted to present . . . all without realizing it. Since taking the facilitation course, I have completely broken this bad habit, and the results have been absolutely amazing. I receive ten times the amount of input from participants from what I used to, and I capture what the real issues are, versus what I "feel" they might be!

In addition, based on a story told about ELMO cards ("Enough, Let's Move On"), I decided to give them a try in a workshop that I facilitated with system users from all over the world. Some of them tended to be quite long-winded and would tell "war stories" nonstop. I was a bit reluctant to introduce the ELMO cards, because I didn't want to stifle participation if the cards were used incorrectly or too frequently. However, I took the risk, and it paid off.

I received a lot of compliments on how effective a tool it was and how it really helped to keep the group focused and on time. I had them laminated so that I can use them over and over. Depending on the size of the group, I usually say that we move an item to the Issues list if I see more than x number of ELMO cards being raised.

Another key tool is the use of the Issues list. Prior to the course, I used to have a "parking lot," but never took it to the level of categorizing each item as either an issue, an action, or a decision. Too often, parking lots were never really emptied or dealt with. Beginning each day by reviewing the Issues list and then categorizing every item has been a great help in ensuring that participants feel that their voices have been heard and are confident that their issues will be actively addressed.

Knowing What to Record

SMART facilitators know that it is the responsibility of the facilitator to ensure that participants agree with the documentation of the session *before the session ends*. SMART facilitators accomplish this by getting agreement from the participants that the information recorded by the facilitator during the session represents the official record of the session. In this way, the participants tend to pay closer attention to ensuring that all key information gets recorded during the session. After the session, the facilitator has the notes transcribed, edited, and distributed to all participants.

The Secret to Knowing What to Record

Record all decisions, actions, issues, and relevant analysis.

What should be documented in a session? SMART facilitators know that it is important to document four items in particular:

1. **Decisions** made during the session

   As described in Chapter Four, it is important to have a parking board for documenting decisions that are made during the session. Any time the group reaches a decision, you should note to the group that a decision has been made and record the decision on the Decisions list.

2. **Actions** assigned during the session

   Likewise, any time the group identifies an action that needs to be taken after the session, you should note to the group that an action has been identified, and record the action on the Actions list. As you will see in Chapter Eight, near the end of the session you will ask the group to identify the person who should be responsible for making sure each action occurs and the date by which the action is needed.

3. **Outstanding issues** as a result of the session

   You must also be alert to identify times when participants are discussing issues that are outside the scope of the meeting or the current discussion. Using the redirection technique discussed in Chapter Five, you should point out to the group that the issue is something that may be important to discuss but is off focus from the current topic. You should get agreement from the participant(s) to record the issue on the Issues list and then redirect the conversation back to the topic at hand. As you will see in Chapter Eight, when you review the Issues list at the end of the session, all issues will be either resolved or moved to the Actions list. Technically, therefore, there will be no outstanding issues to document in the session notes.

4. **Relevant analysis and comments** made during the session

   As the participants progress through the agenda, you will record comments that pertain to the topic under discussion. Note that with facilitated sessions, the goal is for *the group* to have ownership of the decisions, actions, issues, and analysis. Therefore, it is important *not* to identify in the documentation the individual who made a specific comment.

The final documentation will also include notes you have added to increase clarity or build context for the reader. Consider putting your added notes in italics to differentiate these notes from information provided by the participants. A sample of meeting documentation is presented as Figures 6.1, 6.2, and 6.3.

FIGURE 6.1   SAMPLE DOCUMENTATION, PART I.

The Hiring Process Improvement Team

Meeting xx/xx/xx

The Hiring Process Improvement Team held its first meeting on xx/xx/xx, from 9:00 AM to 11:30 AM. The session was held in Conference Room A. Attending the session were the following:

Anna H.	Karen L.
Jamie B.	Robert K.
Jeff C.	Sandra R.
Joe R.	Tony H.

Jeff C. served as the facilitator and documentor for the session. The following are the meeting notes from the session. *Items appearing in italics indicate information added by the facilitator for clarity or to provide context.*

Team Objective

The overall team objective is to improve our method for identifying, interviewing, and selecting candidates.

Team Agenda

A.   Getting Started—What are the most important topics to discuss?
B.   How does the hiring process work today?
C.   What are the problems with the current process?
D.   What are potential improvements?
E.   Prioritize the improvements
F.   Develop an implementation plan
G.   Review and close

During this meeting, the Process Improvement Team discussed agenda items A, B, and C.

FIGURE 6.2   SAMPLE DOCUMENTATION, PART II.

The Hiring Process Improvement Team xx/xx/xx

A.   What are the most important topics to discuss?
The participants were asked to identify the key items they wanted to ensure were discussed during the session. These items are listed below. Throughout the process, we will be coming back to this list to ensure that all topics are covered.

- The overall duration of the process
- The quality of the candidates hired
- The turnover rate
- Increasing the level of involvement from the hiring departments
- Saving money where possible
- Finding ways to access résumés of good candidates not hired in a prior search

B.   How does the hiring process work today?
After discussing the most important topics, the participants outlined the steps in the current hiring process.

1.   Department identifies need for personnel
2.   HR assists department in writing position description and requirements
3.   HR assists department in posting position and placing ad
4.   HR reviews résumés to select candidates to interview
5.   HR interviews candidates and selects finalists
6.   Department interviews finalists and selects person to hire
7.   HR prepares and sends offer letter
8.   Candidate negotiates/accepts offer letter and start date

FIGURE 6.3   SAMPLE DOCUMENTATION, PART III.

The Hiring Process Improvement Team xx/xx/xx

C.   What are the problems with the current process?
The participants reviewed each of the steps in the current hiring process and identified the problems that occur.

- Position descriptions take too long to write
- Department wants greater involvement in selecting finalists
- Money wasted placing ads for positions filled internally
- Don't save resumes of good people whom we previously interviewed
- Overall process takes too long

Next Steps
The team will meet again on yy/yy/yy from 9:00 AM to 11:30 AM to continue its work.

Decisions List
The following is an ongoing list of decisions made by the team, with the date that the decision was made.

1.   The hiring process begins when a hiring department identifies a need and ends when HR receives a signed acceptance letter from a candidate, pending acceptance by the sponsor. (xx/xx/xx)

Actions List
The following is an ongoing list of actions to be taken outside of the session, along with the date due and the person responsible. When an action is completed, it appears in the next meeting notes as "done" and is then removed from subsequent meeting notes.

1.   Get agreement from the sponsor for the start and end of the hiring process. (Robert K., yy/yy/yy)
2.   Document and distribute the session notes. (Jeff R., zz/zz/zz)

Managing the Recording Process

If during the session SMART facilitators are busy writing first and discussing second, and writing what was said, not what they heard, how do they manage the recording process? It seems as though a facilitator would be writing endlessly.

SMART facilitators have several techniques for making the recording process manageable. Take a look at the sample here and decide what you would record as the steps in the hiring process. Actual flip chart results are illustrated later in this chapter.

Sample Dialogue: Steps in the Hiring Process

Facilitator: Our next activity is to identify the steps in the hiring process. I would like to build a list of these steps. If you can, give me a "noun-verb-object" such as "Human resources does this; the department does that." Don't worry about the order; we'll order them later. So think about the last time you hired someone. Consider the things you had to do to get this person on board, all the steps you had to go through, the hurdles you had to jump over. Let's build a list. What were some of those steps?

Pat: Somewhere early in the process we in human resources place an ad in the paper.

Facilitator: OK, I got that. What other steps are there in the process?

Chris: Well, prior to placing the ad, the departments identify the need to hire someone. Then we get human resources to help us develop a job description and ad.

Facilitator: That sounds like two separate things. I got them both. Are there other steps in the process of hiring?

Sean: At the same time that we place the ad, the departments also post the position internally so that people on the inside have a chance to know about the position.

Pat: Do we actually do this at the same time, or do we post internally first?

Sean: I'm pretty sure we do it at the same time. But since most of our positions get filled internally, it's probably a waste of money to place an ad at the same time.

Facilitator: That's an excellent point, and sounds like something we want to talk about when we get to problems. Can we put that point on the Issues list so we don't forget it?

Pat: Sure, that's fine.

Facilitator: OK, are there other steps in the hiring process that we've left out?

Sean: Yes. Human resources receives the résumés, and boy do they get a lot of résumés. There was an opening last year where they received over five hundred, just for one position. And they had to go through them one by one. They had people from all over the world wanting that position. I even understand that there were some applicants from Russia and Kuala Lumpur. Human resources had to screen all those résumés to come up with a handful of finalists. What a tough job they had.

Facilitator: Sean, you said a lot there. Can you headline it for me? We are talking about steps in the hiring process. If what you said was an article in the newspaper, what would the headline be?

Sean: I guess it would be "Human resources screens résumés and selects finalists."

Facilitator: Thanks, Sean; I got that. Is that it, or are there other steps?

Chris: Once human resources selects the finalists, we in the departments interview the finalists, and human resources does reference checks. Based on this final round, the departments select the best candidate.

Facilitator: Is this where the process ends, or are there other steps?

Pat: Of course human resources writes an offer letter and coordinates the negotiation with the candidate. The process ends when the candidate sends us a signed acceptance letter.

This example demonstrates several of the Secrets to Keeping the Recording Concise. Let's take a look at each one in detail.

Secret #25

The Secret to Keeping the Recording Concise
Use templates, headlines, and abbreviations.

To keep the recording concise, use the following techniques:

Keeping the Recording Concise

- Offer participants a template for their responses.
- Record only as many words as necessary to ensure that the participant's comments are clear and concise and can stand alone.
- Use common abbreviations where appropriate.
- Use the headline technique to shorten long comments.

Offer Participants a Template for Their Responses

One technique for managing the recording process is to give the participants a format for their responses. In the example, the facilitator asked for "noun-verb-object." Chris and Pat had no problem with the template. Over time, Sean may catch on as well!

The template method helps participants understand the information you are requesting. It also helps you listen for the information you desire and helps you know what to document.

Record Only as Many Words as Necessary

As the facilitator, you need to ensure that your record of the participants' comments are words that *they* said, clear to the reader and concise. The words you record must also be able to stand alone without having to rely on preceding comments to make sense.

To achieve these goals, you do not need to record all of the speaker's words. In fact, given the way most of us speak, recording all the words might reduce clarity! So, for example, you might record only words one, three, four, seven, and twelve. The key is to be sure that whatever words you do write are indeed words the participants said.

In the example, Pat said, "Somewhere early in the process we in human resources place an ad in the paper." The facilitator might record, "HR places ad in paper." Whereas fifteen words were spoken, only five words were recorded, and each of these were words that Pat said.

Use Common Abbreviations Where Appropriate

Another technique for managing the recording process is to use abbreviations. When using abbreviations, be careful that the abbreviations are clearly understood by the participants and will still be understandable days later when the documentation is finalized. In the example, the facilitator could use abbreviations for departments (Depts) and human resources (HR).

Use the Headline Technique to Shorten Comments

Have you ever been faced with a participant who has given you a long, wordy comment? There you stand, pen in hand, with no idea what to write. Use the headline technique for these situations. You might say, "If the comment you just made were an article in the newspaper, what would the headline on the article be? Would you headline that comment for me?" In our example, the headline technique was quite effective in helping Sean take an eighty-six-word comment and reduce it to seven words.

The headline technique can serve as a fail-safe mechanism for facilitators. When all other techniques fail, you can use it to bail yourself out when you have little idea what to write. Keep in mind, however, that it should be a fail-safe technique, not one you use after every participant's comment. The other techniques described earlier should prevent you from having to use the headline technique very often.

Using the techniques described in this section, the facilitator in the "Steps in the Hiring Process" example would have created flip charts similar to those shown in Figure 6.4.

Using Strategies to Avoid Lulls While Writing

As mentioned earlier, using—not abusing—the pen requires that you write first, discuss second, and write what participants said, not what you heard. It might seem that following these strategies could result in extended quiet periods while you take the time to record comments. Yet you are also responsible for the pace of the session; therefore, avoiding long lull times while you write is essential for the sake of the session's pace.

FIGURE 6.4 **SAMPLE FLIP CHART RESULTS: STEPS IN THE HIRING PROCESS.**

> ### Steps in the Hiring Process
>
> HR places ad in paper
>
> Depts. identify need to hire
>
> HR develops job description and ad
>
> Depts. post position internally
>
> HR screens resumes and selects finalists
>
> Depts. interview the finalists
>
> HR does reference checks
>
> Depts. select best candidate
>
> HR writes offer letter
>
> Candidate sends signed acceptance

> ### Open Issues
>
> 1. Is it a waste of money to place ad at same time we post internally?

What typically happens when there are extended and repeated lull periods? Dysfunctional behavior!

What Happens During Lull Times?

- Patient participants are likely to wait for you to finish writing.
- Participants who aren't as patient (often the majority) may fill in the lull by giving you additional answers before you are ready. This results in your having to say, "Hold on. Let me finishing writing this last one."
- The more vocal participants will begin talking to one another, as you are preoccupied and they cannot talk to you.
- The more aggressive participants may get irritated by the low efficiency of the process and start exhibiting intermediate dysfunctions: sighs of displeasure, doing other work in the session, making negative comments about the pace. (More on these and other dysfunctions in Chapter Nine.)

Secret #26	**The Secret to Avoiding Lulls While Writing**
	Reduce the lull and get the participants to fill it.

How do you avoid the lull period while writing? Let's use the following dialogue to demonstrate the techniques you can use.

Sample Dialogue: Avoiding Lulls

Participant: What I think we should do is utilize online directories to increase the size of the applicant pool.

Facilitator: So, you said we should "Utilize online directories . . ." to do what then? *(still writing)*

Participant: To increase the size of the applicant pool.

Facilitator: OK . . . to increase the size of the applicant pool. Why is that important? *(still writing)*

Participant: Well, the bigger the pool, the better chances we have of finding a qualified candidate.

Facilitator: Got it. What other improvements might we consider?

Consider the following five techniques for reducing lulls and getting the participants to fill them:

How to Avoid Lulls While Writing

- *Stay close to the writing boards* when you are brainstorming or recording a list of information. This will put you in position to begin writing early.

- *Begin writing at the first "recordable" word.* It is important to begin writing as soon as possible to minimize the lull time. If you wait until a participant finishes a comment to start writing, you will automatically extend the lull. At the same time, however, participants often give a preamble phrase as a start to answering your question. Therefore, it is important to listen for the first "recordable" word. In the example, you want to know ways to improve the hiring process. Given the participant's first statement, you would begin writing as soon as you heard the word "utilize."

- *Repeat what the participant said as you write.* Once a participant has finished speaking, repeat the words as you write them. Your words will fill in the lull time and help retain the interest of the group.

- *Ask participants to repeat their words.* After repeating parts of what the participant has said, ask the participant to repeat the parts remaining for you to record while you continue to write. "So you said, 'Utilize online directories to . . .' do what then?" You may already know the rest of what was said, but by responding to your prompt, the participant fills in the lull time.

- *Ask a direct probe* if you still need additional time. A probe such as, "Why is that important?" allows you to finish writing while the participant responds to your question.

With practice, you will be able effortlessly to use these effective techniques for avoiding lulls while writing.

Additional Techniques for Recording

I have included additional techniques here that you may find helpful in recording information.

Practice When Using a Scribe

Some facilitators find it helpful to have someone else do the writing while they facilitate. Using a scribe reduces the load on the facilitator and has the added advantage of allowing the facilitator to maintain greater eye contact and greater physical proximity to the group.

If you will be using a scribe to record comments on flip charts during the session, it is vital that the scribe understand fully the concepts of using, not abusing, the pen. Consider holding a practice session with the scribe, using one or more of the samples found in this chapter, to ensure that the scribe fully understands the power of the pen.

Have a Wall Plan

Establish a wall plan illustrating how you will post charts. The wall plan lays out a consistent approach so that you will know where charts are posted as the session progresses. Your wall plan should indicate the following:

- The flip chart pages that need to be displayed at the front of the room (for example, ground rules, parking boards, session objective) for easy accessibility
- The starting point for the remaining flip charts (for example, the right side wall) and the direction for posting them (for example, clockwise)
- The charts to be posted under one another to conserve wall space

Manage Flip Chart Pages

Try to have enough flip chart easels to allow all the pages for an agenda item to be viewed at one time without posting or flipping the charts. By being able to see all the points related to a topic, the participants can easily make reference to points previously made and can avoid repeating comments.

For the typical facilitated session, three flip charts allow you enough space to adequately view all the points from the process. Two flip charts are often acceptable. In most cases, one flip chart is not enough.

If you prepare charts in advance, leave one or two blank pages in front so you won't uncover the chart contents until you are ready. You can mark where the correct page is with masking tape or a small bright Post-it note, or by making a small fold in a corner of the top blank sheets. Use light pencil to mark "memory-jogger notes" (those only you will be able to see) on the charts.

Edit by Adding

Corrections are a fact of life when documenting large amounts of text on a flip chart. Therefore, leave plenty of space between the lines. When a correction is needed, maintain legibility by using a different color marker. When editing, line through the words that are not needed and add words for clarity. If you need to add your own words, add them in parentheses to distinguish your words from those of the participants.

Spell-Check

Many facilitators find it difficult to spell correctly while using flip charts during a facilitated session. As someone noted, "When you are standing in front of a group with a marker, your IQ immediately drops about forty points." However, if you are continually butchering the spelling of words, your participants can become distracted. Consider taking the issue off the table by letting the participants know in advance that spelling doesn't count.

Quick Tip!

If you are concerned about your spelling on flip charts, here is a tip. Make a bright red square in the right corner of the first flip chart and explain to the group, "This is the spell-check button. I will hit it when the session is over, and all the misspellings will be automatically corrected. So there's no need to be concerned."

Make the Perfect Tear

To tear a flip chart page cleanly, press down on the top of the chart while you make a small tear (about one inch) on each side. Then, using both hands, grasp each side of the page and pull straight down.

The Seven Deadly Sins of Facilitation

I conclude this chapter with a review of what I call the seven deadly sins of facilitation. More times than not, the following sins committed by a facilitator will lead to some form of dysfunctional behavior by one or more members of the group. If the facilitator continues his or her behavior, full-scale revolt by the participants is quite possible. I have included these sins in this chapter because, as you will see, the first two have to do with abusing the pen.

The Seven
Deadly Sins
of Facilitation

1. The facilitator chooses which comments merit recording on the flip charts.
2. The facilitator interprets the words that are spoken and records the interpretation, instead of recording what is said.
3. The facilitator permits the group to wander away from the stated objective for extended periods of time.
4. The facilitator permits the ground rules to be broken without taking visible corrective action.
5. The facilitator is perceived as losing neutrality and favoring one position over another.
6. The facilitator speaks emotionally charged words to a session attendee or permits a session attendee to speak emotionally charged words to another, without taking visible corrective action.
7. The facilitator allows an atmosphere of distrust or disrespect to build between himself or herself and the session attendees.

Applying the Secrets to Recording

Along with using the Secrets to Recording in facilitated meetings, you can apply these same secrets in other areas as well.

Documenting the Session

SMART facilitators know that only four items need documenting following a facilitated session. Likewise, in nonfacilitated meetings that you lead, consider documenting only the following:

1. Decisions made
2. Actions to be taken
3. Open issues
4. Relevant analysis

Documenting Decisions

SMART facilitators know that using flip charts to document the discussion is a great strategy for focusing the group and ensuring that everyone understands what decisions the group has made. Therefore, whether you are in a formal or informal meeting, consider using whiteboards, flip charts, or even notebook pads to document decisions to ensure that all participants understand the decisions they have made. In addition, when a group gets stuck and has difficulty making a decision between alternatives, consider documenting information about each alternative so that everyone can see the information and readily focus on the critical differences.

Facilitator's Checklist for Recording

☐ In a facilitated session, it is important to document the following:
- Decisions made during the session.
- Actions assigned during the session.

- Outstanding issues as a result of the session.
- Relevant analysis and comments made during the session.

☐ To avoid abusing the power of the pen, you should

- Write first, discuss second.
- Write what participants said, not what you heard.
- Write so the group can read it.
- Ask, don't tell.

☐ To make the recording process manageable, you should

- Offer participants a template for their responses.
- Record only as many words as necessary to ensure that the participant's comments are clear and concise and can stand alone.
- Use common abbreviations where appropriate.
- Use the headline technique to shorten long comments.
- Use strategies for avoiding lulls while writing.

☐ To avoid lulls while writing, you should

- Stay close to the writing boards.
- Begin writing at the first "recordable" word.
- Repeat what the participant said as you write.
- Ask participants to repeat their words.
- Ask a direct probe.

☐ Other recording techniques include the following:

- Practice when using a scribe.
- Have a wall plan.
- Use enough flip charts to allow all the pages for an agenda item to be viewed at one time.
- Edit by adding.
- Make the perfect tear.

Exercise Your Skills

It requires practice to get in the habit of using the techniques for writing first, writing what they said, and avoiding lulls while writing. One recommendation I give to students in our classes is to practice the techniques while watching the evening news program. Consider trying it daily for a week. Have a pen and pad with you as a news segment starts. In advance, label your page, "Key Points of the Story." As the news person gives the story, list the key points using that person's words. You can even pretend to play back what he or she says: "It sounds like what you are saying is . . . Is that right?" and to ask the person to repeat.

The point of this exercise is to get in the habit of writing their words, not yours, and to begin using lull avoidance techniques. As you increase your comfort with using these techniques in a practice environment, they will become more natural when you're working with a group.

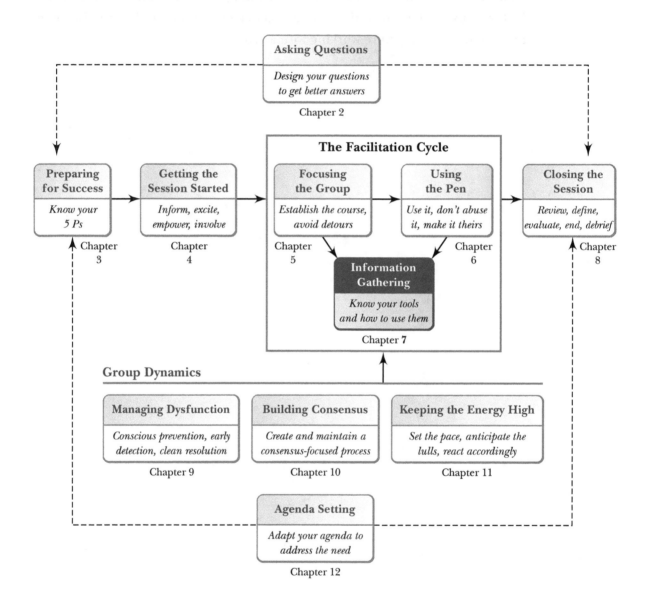

CHAPTER SEVEN

THE SECRETS TO INFORMATION GATHERING

Know Your Tools and How to Use Them

Questions Answered in This Chapter

What are the major information gathering and processing functions?

How do you maximize question-and-answer (Q&A) sessions to ensure that the most important questions get asked?

What is the most important thing to do in a brainstorming session?

What are the three critical activities in prioritizing?

How do you ensure quality feedback during a report-back process?

How do you perform an evaluation of the session without allowing the comments of one or two people to bias the feedback?

CASE STUDY: The Retailing Conference

A global developer of retail shopping malls requested our assistance in developing the program and facilitating their global internal conference, which they called "Retailing the Globe." The conference brought together 225 of their executives and managers for three days to discuss current and future strategies for developing malls around the world. In advance of the conference, we worked closely for two months with the program development team. The team used the overall conference objectives to identify high-quality speakers and program content; our role was to structure the session engagement strategies to ensure that the group produced a quality product. The pressure on us was high, for the board of directors of this global corporation was coming to town on the final day of the conference, and the participants would be giving the board members a presentation on the specific strategies and recommendations for board approval.

As you can imagine, the participants were highly intelligent and maintained high ownership and high engagement throughout the conference. Once the global strategies were identified, breakout teams worked well into the night on the final evening to estimate high-level numbers, develop scenarios, and prepare PowerPoint presentations. The recommendations were very well received by the board.

During the debrief with the project team, we learned a valuable lesson. At first we were surprised when participants indicated that the least beneficial activity was having each global region describe its accomplishments during the year. It was at these times, when members of the group were talking about themselves, that the rest of the group was least engaged. Upon reflection, we realized that the process was flawed. During that segment we had no engagement strategies, just pure presentation. In fact, the segment was information only. There was nothing that the participants were being asked to do with the information. This underscored for me the importance of ensuring that every process engages the participants in some type of meaningful activity. If a presentation is information only, it probably can instead be provided in written form.

SMART facilitators use numerous methods to engage participants in a facilitated session. In this chapter, I start with a *general* explanation of the various information gathering functions (such as gathering facts and generating ideas) and a description of different methods of processing (such as small group, round-robin). I then describe a variety of specific methods used in facilitated sessions. These methods will provide you with a full toolbox for constructing and executing a wide range of sessions.

Why Do This?	**Why use a variety of engagement strategies?**
	As the case study suggests, when there is no engagement, low value is often the result. Unfortunately, I have found that in most meetings, the only engagement method used is presentation followed by question and answer, over and over again. Is there any wonder why group sessions are often characterized by low energy and low engagement?

Quick Tip!

Please note that this chapter is one of the longest and includes seventeen methods for gathering and processing information, many of which you may already use. Although I have attempted to present the information in a way that is consumable, you may be overwhelmed by the number of tools presented. If you find yourself in this situation, I would recommend doing a quick read of the various tools so that you are familiar with the information and then adding one new tool a week or one new tool a month to your facilitation toolbox.

Understanding the Major Information Gathering and Processing Functions

A higher-level facilitated process, such as strategic planning or process improvement, uses a series of building-block processes to achieve its goals, as shown in Figure 7.1. In some cases, the participants provide information they already know. In other cases, they generate ideas. In still other cases, they categorize information or make decisions.

Although there are many types of information gathering and processing activities that serve as building blocks, for the purposes of this book I have broken them into seven major functions, as shown in Table 7.1.

FIGURE 7.1 HIGHER-LEVEL AND BUILDING-BLOCK PROCESSES.

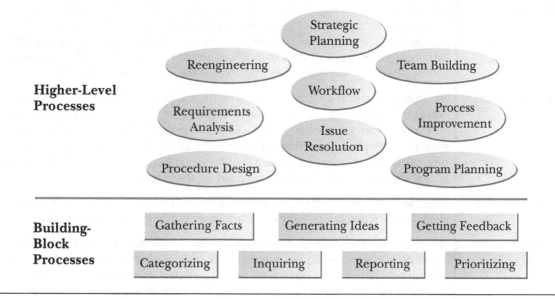

TABLE 7.1   MAJOR PROCESS FUNCTIONS.

Function	Sample Question	Purpose
Gathering facts	How does the process work today?	To gain greater detailed information; most appropriate when there are "right" answers
Categorizing	What are the key groupings represented by this information?	To group information into categories for further processing
Inquiring	What questions do we want to see answered?	To have participants create questions or ask questions of a speaker, a panel, or each other
Generating ideas	What are possible ways this problem could be solved?	To create possible solutions or approaches; most appropriate when there are multiple possibilities and creativity is desired
Prioritizing	Which of these solutions is best?	To rank, rate, or select
Reporting	What did your group come up with?	To inform about results of a breakout exercise or other activity
Getting feedback	What were the strengths and weaknesses of today's session?	To evaluate the session or other experience

Understanding Processing Groups

Along with choosing an appropriate information gathering and processing function, SMART facilitators choose the appropriate *processing group* to employ.

Full Group	With some processes and situations, it is more appropriate for the full group to process the information together. Full groups are typically used when it is important for all participants to hear the same information at the same time. It is also appropriate when each individual knows only parts of the topic, and all members are needed to provide the full picture (for example, when mapping the flow of a business process).
Breakout Groups	For other processes and situations, it may be more appropriate to process as breakout groups of three or more. As I described in Chapter Five, breakout groups are especially appropriate when the agenda calls for a facilitated process to be performed several times (for example, when seeking solutions to ten problems identified in the hiring process). Breakout groups can reduce the time required, increase the level of participation, and increase the feeling of responsibility for the outcome.
Pairs	Other times, the processing is best done in pairs. Pairs enable more intense one-on-one interaction and can be quite effective in team building and other activities.
Individual	Sometimes processing is best done by an individual. Individual processing allows time for introspection and reflection. Individual processing is often done prior to full-group or breakout-group processing to allow time for personal reflection before sharing information in the larger group (for example, when identifying critical issues to be discussed). Whereas extroverts tend to thrive in full-group processing, introverts often find it helpful to have individual processing before group discussions to give them time to gather their thoughts.

Understanding Processing Order

Once you have chosen the information processing function and the type of processing group, you choose the *processing order*.

Random Order	In many cases, people or teams are called on in random order or as they request to speak.
Round-Robin	In other cases, you might choose to use a round-robin technique to ensure that everyone has an opportunity to participate. To employ a round-robin, you start with one person and go around the room in sequential order. The round-robin technique is effective at preventing any one person from dominating the discussion and also encourages participation from reticent participants.
Assigned Order	You may choose to process in an assigned order. An assigned order is often used when breakout groups work on topics that have been previously ordered. The groups then report back in that assigned order.

Quick Tip!

When using a round-robin, make a point of calling the name of the person who will go first before you ask the question. This will help the person pay greater attention to the question and will give him or her time to prepare an answer.

Sample Dialogue: Alerting the Starter for a Round-Robin

Facilitator: I would like for us to go around the room starting with Sandra and ask each person to give me one step in the hiring process. So think about the last time you hired someone. Consider the things you had to do to get this person on board, all the steps you had to go through, the hurdles you had to jump over. Let's build a list. Sandra, get me started. What are some of the steps in the hiring process?

Gathering and Processing Information

SMART facilitators have a full toolbox of methods for addressing each of the information gathering and processing functions. They combine these tools with the most appropriate processing order and processing group to yield effective results, which brings us to the next secret.

Secret #27

The Secret to Gathering Information
Use the right tool in the most effective way to achieve your objective.

Although an exhaustive list of different information gathering and processing methods is beyond the scope of this book, in this chapter I provide a technique for each of the seven primary information gathering and processing functions, as shown in Table 7.2.

TABLE 7.2 SAMPLE PROCESSING METHODS.

Function	Sample Method	Purpose
Gathering facts	Listing	To gain greater detailed information; most appropriate when there are "right" answers
Categorizing	Grouping	To group information into categories for further processing
Inquiring	Pre-questioning	To have participants create questions or ask questions of a speaker, a panel, or each other
Generating ideas	Brainstorming	To create possible solutions or approaches; most appropriate when there are multiple possibilities and creativity is desired
Prioritizing	Dot voting	To rank, rate, or select
Reporting	Report-back	To inform about results of a breakout exercise or other activity
Getting feedback	Rated feedback	To evaluate the session or other experience

As a backdrop for this discussion, let's go back to the team that was looking to address the hiring process. Their agenda was as follows.

Sample Agenda

Purpose: Define the changes necessary to increase the efficiency and effectiveness of the hiring process.

Agenda:

A. Getting started

B. How does the hiring process work today?

C. What are the problems and root causes?

D. What are the potential improvements?

E. Prioritize the improvements

F. Develop an implementation plan

G. Review and close

I will use this agenda in examining methods for gathering and processing information. If when describing a method I refer to a technique described previously in the book, I will show that technique in **bold**.

Gathering Facts

Let's set the scene. You have completed agenda item A, "Getting started." You have just taken a **checkpoint** and indicated you are now ready to have the participants start agenda item B, "How does the hiring process work today?" To facilitate this activity, you need a technique for gathering facts. In this case, you choose to use the *listing* technique.

The Secret to Getting the Details
Ask, record, react.

Listing is the most common method used for gathering information from participants during a facilitated process. After **labeling** your charts, you take the participants through the steps described here:

Gathering Facts: Listing

1. Title your flip charts (or other recording device) ahead of time.

2. Describe the activity and purpose. (Note that you may have already done this through the **checkpoint**.)

    "Our next step is to identify the steps in the hiring process. This will get us all on the same page so that we will be able to identify where the problems are and how to address those problems."

3. Use **PeDeQs** to describe the general directions, with an example if necessary; offer a template response format if appropriate.

    "I would like for us to go around the room starting with Sandra and ask each person to give me one step in the hiring process. Don't worry about the order; we can order the steps later. If you can, give me a 'noun-verb-object' such as 'Human resources does this; the department does that.'"

4. Ask your **starting question** to help group members visualize their answers.

    "So think about the last time you hired someone. Consider the things you had to do to get this person on board, all the steps you had to go through, the hurdles you had to jump over. Let's build a list. Sandra, get me started. What are some of the steps in the hiring process?"

5. Record responses, being sure to **use, not abuse, the power of the pen** and to **manage the recording process**.

6. React appropriately using the **reacting questions** to acknowledge, clarify, challenge, confirm, probe, and redirect as needed.

    "Why is that important?"

    "It sounds like what you are saying is . . . Is that right?"

    "Are there steps related to . . . ?"

    "Is this related to that comment? Is it OK to combine them?"

7. Continue with **prompt questions** and **extended prompt questions** until no other information is offered.

"What else?"

"What other steps are there?"

Figure 7.2 shows a sample of the information that may have resulted from the listing activity.

FIGURE 7.2   STEPS IN THE HIRING PROCESS.

Steps in the Hiring Process

HR places ad in paper

Depts. identify need to hire

HR develops job description and ad

Depts. post position internally

HR screens résumés and selects finalists

Depts. interview the finalists

HR does reference checks

Depts. select best candidate

HR writes offer letter

Candidate sends signed acceptance

Candidate negotiates offer

Categorizing

Frequently, a process to gather facts will generate considerable information and often more than ten items or so. When this is the case, it is often helpful to consolidate the information into a smaller number of categories for further processing. There are a variety of methods for categorizing information. One such method is the nominal group technique, or *grouping*. The objective of grouping is to take a list of ten or more items and group them into like categories, usually no fewer than three and no more than eight.

Secret #29

The Secret to Categorizing

Ask, "Same or different?" one item at a time.

FIGURE 7.3   GROUPING STEPS IN THE HIRING PROCESS.

Group	Steps in the Hiring Process
A	1. HR places ad in paper
A	2. Depts. identify need to hire
A	3. HR develops job description and ad
A	4. Depts. post position internally
B	5. HR screens résumés and selects finalists
B	6. Depts. interview the finalists
B	7. HR does reference checks
B	8. Depts. select best candidate
C	9. HR writes offer letter
C	10. Candidate sends signed acceptance
C	11. Candidate negotiates offer

Steps in the Hiring Process

Group Categories

A. Announcement

B. Screening

C. Acceptance

During the grouping process, you must lead the participants through a process of discovery in which you and participants arrive at the "answer" at the same time. Because of this process of mutual discovery, many facilitators find grouping very difficult to master.

Let's go back to our example of the hiring process. We had used listing to identify the steps in the hiring process. We will now use grouping to categorize the steps. Figure 7.3 represents a sample of output from the grouping exercise described here.

Categorizing: Grouping

1. To prepare for grouping, arrange the information to be categorized near the front of the room, for easy viewing and marking.

2. Describe the activity and purpose. (Note that you may have already done this through the **checkpoint**.)

> *"Our next step is to take the items that we have created and group them into categories. We might end up with anywhere from three to eight categories. By doing this, we will be better able to identify the problems and develop solutions that will result in a much, much better hiring process."*

3. Use **PeDeQs** to give the general directions and specific exceptions.

> *"I will step through the items one by one and ask the group to name the category that the item should go in. If the category doesn't already exist, we'll create a new one. At the end we will review the categories to make sure we are all comfortable."*

4. Read the first item and ask the participants to define the category for it. You might suggest a category for the first item to get the participants started and check for agreement.

> *"The first item says, 'HR places ad in paper.' If I wanted to group other items in a category with this one, what would the category be called?"*

> *"It sounds like this first one has to do with the announcement; does that sound like a reasonable category?"*

5. Write the category name on a flip chart and label it *A*. Place an *A* next to the first item in the brainstorm list to indicate which group it was put in. Use a pen color different from the color used to create the original list so that the category label stands out.

6. Go to the next item on the original list. Ask the participants to determine whether it belongs in the existing group or whether a separate group is needed.

> *"Let's take a look at the next item, 'Departments identify need to hire.' Should this go into the 'Announcement' group, or is it different?"*

7. If the item belongs in the existing group, label the item with the category letter. If the item belongs in a new group, ask the participants for the name of the category, give the category a letter, and write the letter next to the item.

8. Repeat steps 6 and 7 until all items on the original list have been categorized.

Quick Tip!

It is easy for participants to become disengaged during the grouping process, especially when there are only two or three dominant personalities naming the categories or when only a few people can see the charts. One technique to help ensure full engagement is to divide the participants into teams where they are seated. Then, as you go through categorizing each item, rotate from team to team the responsibility of determining whether the item belongs to an existing category or should be assigned a new category.

9. Review the groups to determine if additional consolidation or category splitting is appropriate. In some cases, you will have a category that is very "crowded" compared to the other categories, and you may want to split it into two categories. In other cases, you may have a category that has very few items and can be combined with another category. Through the consolidation process, you might also become aware of additional items that may have been miscategorized.

> *"Let's review what we have. It looks like there are ten items in group A—Announcement, four in group B—Screening, but only two for group C—Acceptance. Should we consider consolidating group C, or should it really stand alone? OK, it sounds like we want to keep group C, and indeed we've added another item to it, 'Candidate negotiates offer.' OK, I've got that."*

10. As you become more comfortable with the grouping process, you may find it appropriate to prompt the participants to consider consolidating or splitting categories as you are grouping rather than waiting until the end.

Inquiring

Let's assume that you have gotten through the first three agenda items: A, "Getting started"; B, "How does the process work today?"; and C, "What are the problems and root causes?" Your next step is to focus on D, "What are the potential improvements?" Before you do this, however, the project sponsor has arranged for an outside recruiting specialist to present to the team about the latest techniques other organizations are using in their hiring processes.

Secret #30

The Secret to Q&A Sessions
Use teams to identify the questions in advance.

The objective of inquiring processes is for the participants to create questions or ask questions of a speaker, a panel, or each other. The *pre-questioning* process is an inquiring technique to prepare participants to listen. The technique also lets speakers know the most important points to stress in their presentation.

Inquiring: Pre-Questioning

1. Describe the activity and purpose. (Note that you may have already done this through the **checkpoint**.)

> *"Prior to hearing our expert on hiring processes, let's take a minute to identify the most important questions we want answered by this presentation. This will give us*

an opportunity to identify the most pressing issues and will let our speaker know what is most important to us."

2. Divide into teams and select a leader using in-place teams for **breakout**.

   "To do this, let's quickly divide into teams where we are seated. Anna, Jeff, and Tony, you will make up team one. Team two will include . . . Team three . . ."

   "We need team leaders. So I would like for the person from your team sitting closest to me right now to serve as the team leader. Team leaders, please grab the pad of sticky notes and marker that are at your table."

3. Use **PeDeQs** to give a two-minute time limit for the teams to write their most important questions on the sticky notes.

   "Team leaders, you will have two minutes in total to identify the most important questions that your team would like to see answered by this presentation. Please use the pen and marker and put only one question on each sticky note. When the two minutes are up, your pen should be capped and in the air. I will count down the time for you. Any questions?"

4. Ask your **starting question** to help the group members visualize their answers.

   "We are about to hear a presentation on the hiring processes used by other organizations. For this to be helpful to us, there are certain topics and issues that this presentation should cover. Think about the way our process works and the problems we are currently having. Since this specialist has experience with other hiring processes, there are probably some key insights you'd like to learn, some things you would like to hear about, some questions the specialist can answer for you about how other organizations address these problems. Take the time in your teams to write down those questions. Remember, one question per sticky note. What are the key questions you would like to see answered in this presentation? You have two minutes, starting now."

5. Use the **grouping** technique to create question categories by reviewing and grouping each sticky note.

   "It looks like we have six sticky notes from the first group. The first one says, 'Has any organization automated the résumé storage and retrieval process?' Let's create a category for this question, and let's give the category a name so that other questions similar to it will go in this same category. What would be an appropriate name for the first category? OK, so we have category A—Technology. What about the second question? It says, 'What is the average time from defining the need to having a person hired for the position?' Does this go with the technology category, or does it need a new category? OK, we have a new category, B—Timing. Let's go to the next question."

6. Do a **checkpoint** and turn it over to the speaker, alerting the speaker to the questions that have been asked. Be sure to set the expectation of the participants, and the speaker, that the presentation will not necessarily answer every question.

   "So, we have identified the key questions we want to hear answered. More than likely, only some of these will be answered by the presentation. After the presentation is over, we will go back over the questions to determine which additional ones can be answered and which have to be handled in a different way. Our speaker for today is . . ."

7. Following the presentation, divide the groups of questions among the in-place **breakout** teams. Have the teams assign a team leader. Give the teams three minutes to (a) review the questions, (b) identify those that have not been answered in the presentation, and (c) select up to three questions that they specifically want to direct to the speaker.

   "Now that we have heard the presentation, let's take a minute to review the questions and identify those that have not been answered. Current team leaders, please pass the marker on to another member of your team who will serve as the team leader for this exercise. New team leaders, you and your team will have three minutes to grab the sticky notes from the question category I will assign to you. Review each sticky note and decide whether the question has been answered. If it has, discard it. If it hasn't, decide whether you want to ask the question of the speaker. You will probably have enough time to focus on one to three questions. Team one, you are assigned the group of questions called . . . Come get it. Team two, you have . . . OK, you now have three minutes to identify the questions you want answered by the speaker. Team leaders, any questions? Let's go!"

8. Give each team up to four minutes for Q&A with the speaker.

   "OK, now that we have the questions, let's go around team by team. Each team will have a total of four minutes for Q&A with the speaker. Since you have only four minutes, I give you permission to be rude! Once you feel the question has been satisfactorily answered, feel free to interrupt the speaker and say, "I'm sorry to interrupt, but you've answered our question well, and I would like to ask one more question before our time is up." OK, let's start with team one. Team leader, ask your first question."

9. At the completion of the Q&A, have the teams take three more minutes to review their remaining questions and decide which, if any, still need to be addressed. Ask the teams to make notes on the sheets indicating how the question should be addressed (for example, discuss at team meeting, disregard for now). Collect these questions for documentation purposes.

"Now that we've gone through the Q&A, we should take a minute to review our remaining questions that haven't been answered. Team leaders, would you now review those questions with your teams and determine which, if any, still need to be addressed. Indicate on the sticky note the best method for addressing the question. For example, some questions are best handled in a team meeting, whereas other questions may need to be assigned to someone. And, of course, some questions will not be that important, and you may want to bypass them. It's your choice. You'll have three minutes to go back through the questions and note on them what should be done. We'll collect these and document them as part of the session notes. So we want you to identify any questions that still need to be addressed and then write on the sheet the best way to address it. Team leaders, any questions? OK, three minutes, let's go."

Generating Ideas

To help the hiring process improvement team address their fourth agenda item, D, "What are the potential improvements?" you will take them through a process for generating ideas.

Generating ideas and gathering facts are probably the most common functions performed by groups in facilitated sessions. In many sessions, generating ideas is crucial to arriving at creative solutions to the issue the team is tackling. I frequently use *brainstorming* as the technique for generating ideas.

Secret #31

The Secret to Generating Ideas
Ask, record, but don't react.

Brainstorming is an excellent vehicle for collecting a large number of ideas in a short period of time. In a brainstorming session, you state the objective, set a time limit, and use a flip chart or some other vehicle to record ideas that the session participants rapidly throw out. The sample flip charts shown in Figure 7.4 represent information that could have been generated as a result of the brainstorming session described here.

Generating Ideas: Brainstorming
1. Describe the activity and purpose. (Note that you may have already done this through the **checkpoint**.) Be sure to encourage creativity and out-of-the-ordinary ideas.

FIGURE 7.4   POTENTIAL IMPROVEMENTS TO THE HIRING PROCESS.

> ### Potential Improvements
>
> 1. If internal candidate identified in advance, allow for fast-track hiring process based on 14-day internal posting
>
> 2. Post all positions internally first; place external ads only if positions remain unfilled for 21 days
>
> 3. Scan résumés into computer to permit searching
>
> 4. Permit departments to be involved in screening process at their discretion
>
> 5. Publish interview schedules and allow department personnel to sign up
>
> 6. Track interviewers' comments and ratings
>
> 7. Provide interviewing training to all hiring managers and interviewers
>
> 8. Provide avenue for giving signing bonuses to attract top candidates

"Our next step is to brainstorm potential improvements to the hiring process. This is important because we don't want to be constrained by the way we do things now. Instead, we want to come up with creative solutions that can help us find and hire the best people available, quickly, effectively, and efficiently."

2. Set a time limit and use **PeDeQs** to describe the general directions, with an example if necessary; offer a response format if appropriate.

"We are going to take five minutes to do a round of intense brainstorming. I would like for us to go around the room starting with Joe and have each person give me one thing we could do that would move us toward our vision of a great hiring process. If you can, give me a 'verb-object' such as 'Implement this; develop that.'"

"We will probably go around four or more times, so if you can't think of anything the first time, just say 'pass.'"

3. Prohibit judgment of any type on an idea.

"Since we want to keep the creative juices flowing, it is important that during this phase we don't spend any time judging or analyzing the ideas. I will be writing as fast as I can, and we will be moving quickly from person to person. If you find yourself at any point thinking, 'That won't work,' ask yourself, 'What will work? How can I improve on it?' Some of the best ideas start out as impractical suggestions."

4. Ask your **starting question** to help group members visualize their answers.

    "Let's go back to our list of problems; they are the things we have to fix. Think about things you've seen other companies do, things that you have thought about us doing, things we could do to make our hiring process a much better process. Joe, get me started. Let's build a list of some of the things we could do to improve the hiring process. What are some of those things?"

5. Record responses being sure to **use, not abuse, the pen** and to **manage the recording process**. If an idea does not meet the objective, record it anyway. Remind the participants of the objective and keep moving.

Quick Tip!

During a brainstorming session, speed helps keep the energy going and the ideas flowing. Often, however, your ability to record creates a bottleneck. Consider soliciting responses while one or two other people record them on the flip charts.

---

6. Keep the pace moving. Go for quantity. The more ideas the better. Avoid silences by using a lot of fill-in words (such as "Give me more") if necessary, along with **prompt questions** and **extended prompt questions**.

    "Give me more. Who's next? More ideas, more ideas . . . What other ways could we improve the hiring process?"

7. End the brainstorming segment when the time limit is reached or when there is a round in which everyone passes. Ask for any last thoughts before closing.

    "We have reached our time limit. Any last-minute ideas to add?"

8. Always follow a brainstorming session with some type of **grouping** or prioritization activity (see the next section) to highlight the jewels.

Prioritizing

Facilitators often need participants to identify the most important items generated in a listing or brainstorming exercise. For example, prioritizing might indicate which items will be worked on further or the items to be processed first. If you are a veteran of strategic planning, you know that most planning efforts result in more strategies than you can possibly implement at once. Often teams end up with twenty-five to forty potential strategies, whereas most organizations would be fortunate to implement six to twelve strategic initiatives in a year. How do you go about deciding which strategies to undertake first? How do you determine your priorities? There are a number of approaches for prioritizing.

Some organizations use the dot method: each participant receives a small supply of sticky dots, the number of which is based on the number of strategies desired. The participants are told to place their dots on those that they believe should be started on first. The strategies with the most dots are given top priority.

Other organizations use a more elaborate, analytical approach, such as the weighted score method: the team scores each strategy against a predetermined list of criteria. The criteria are given weights, and the weighted score for a strategy is determined by multiplying the strategy's score for each criterion by the criterion's weight and then adding the results. Those strategies with the highest weighted scores are given top priority. I will talk more about the weighted score method in Chapter Ten.

Still other organizations take a hybrid approach. For example, they evaluate each strategy against a small number of criteria using a "high-medium-low" scale. They then use dots to determine the final selection.

Whatever approach you use for determining priorities, keep three basic principles in mind.

The Secret to Prioritizing

Secret #32

Define criteria; permit lobbying; check for consensus after scoring.

Define the Criteria to Use in Setting Priorities

When the group is setting priorities, even when using the dot method, have participants identify a common set of criteria. Consider using these three at a minimum:

Prioritization Criteria

- *Impact.* If the activity is successfully implemented, what will be the impact on achieving key objectives?
- *Probability of success.* What is the probability that the activity will be successfully implemented if we decide to undertake it?
- *Cost-effectiveness.* How do the tangible and intangible results expected from this activity compare to the costs and resources required to implement it?

Why Do This? | **Why have participants identify a common set of criteria?**

Without a set of common criteria, people will use what they believe is important. Unfortunately, in many cases a person's individual criteria may differ significantly from those of the organization. For example, one person's sole criterion for priority setting might be "support of my department." This person would give highest priority to those strategies that provide the greatest support to the department—a fairly myopic view.

Provide a Lobbying Period Prior to Voting or Dotting

Every participant should have an opportunity to explain why particular strategies should be given support. I call this lobbying. If strategies are scored against criteria, have lobbying occur after the scoring but before dotting or any other voting activity. I describe the lobbying process in this way:

We have just defined the criteria for prioritizing. Our next step is to vote. But before we vote, I would like to have a time of controlled lobbying. See, the last thing we want to have happen is for everyone to vote and then for Paul to say at the end, "You idiots! What is wrong with you all? Am I the only one with sense here? Clearly the most important item is . . . and I was the only one who voted for it. If we are going to have the slightest chance of achieving our objectives we are going to have to . . . and this strategy is the only one that addresses this. Why didn't you vote for it? What's wrong with you folks?" So we want to give Paul and everyone else an opportunity to express their support for an idea before the vote. So the way we are going to do this is, I will start with Jane, and each person will have sixty seconds to say to the entire group what that person believes are the most important strategies and why. The key is explaining the why. Of course if you don't want to lobby, just say "pass," and we will move on to the next person. Each time someone lobbies for an item, I'll place a small check mark on it, just so that everyone can see how many people lobbied for that item. After the lobbying, we will then vote. Any questions?

This controlled lobbying process gives each person the vehicle for influencing the opinions of others. The process also helps build consensus around particular solutions as participants repeatedly hear support for a small number of activities. One other significant benefit of lobbying: once the top priorities are identified and it comes time for people to sign up to implement them, those who lobbied for a particular item that "won" typically feel a sense of allegiance to volunteer to ensure that the item gets implemented! For these reasons, I nearly always use lobbying before any prioritization activity.

Check for Consensus After Scoring

Whether you are using the dot method, weighted scoring, or some hybrid method, the result is typically a score that indicates the level of support for a particular strategy. It is important to recognize that the score is not a decision. The score is just a result of the analysis that was done and should serve as input to the final decision. Once strategies are ranked by the scores received, it is still the job of the group to accept the scores as indicating the final priorities or to make adjustments as necessary.

For example, one organization, after prioritizing, realized that *none* of the internal activities (staff development, technology improvements, and so on) received high enough scores to be given priority. The team agreed, however, to place one of these strategies on the priority list because they believed it was essential to send the message to the staff that internal improvements were as important as external outcomes.

Let's take a look at the three principles in operation using the dot voting method as the team executes agenda item E, "Prioritize the improvements." Figure 7.5 represents information that could be generated as a result of the prioritization session described here.

FIGURE 7.5   PRIORITIZATION OF THE HIRING PROCESS IMPROVEMENTS.

	Priorities
3333331 (19)	1. If internal candidate identified in advance, allow for fast-track hiring process based on 14-day internal posting
1111 (4)	2. Post all positions internally first; place external ads only if positions remain unfilled for 21 days
3333311 (17)	3. Scan résumés into computer to permit searching
33331 (13)	4. Permit departments to be involved in screening process at their discretion
31 (4)	5. Publish interview schedules and allow department personnel to sign up
1 (1)	6. Track interviewers' comments and ratings
33111 (9)	7. Provide interviewing training to all hiring managers and interviewers
3331 (10)	8. Provide avenue for giving signing bonuses to attract top candidates

Note: 3s represent red dots, which count 3 points each;
1s represent blue dots, which count 1 point each.
The total score is shown as bold in parentheses

Prioritizing: Dot Voting

1. Describe the activity and purpose. (Note that you may have already done this through the **checkpoint**.)

   "Our next step is to prioritize these improvements in order to identify the ones that we should begin implementing first."

2. Use **PeDeQs** to describe the general directions.

   "We will start by identifying the most important criteria to use in our prioritization. I will then give each person a set of colored dots. Everyone will place their dots on those improvements that they feel will help improve the hiring process the most. The improvements with the most dots will be the ones that we will consider for initial implementation. Before we start voting, however, we will have a special lobbying period. See, if I were participating in the voting, I would want everyone to vote the way I would vote. I would hate it if we dotted, and the thing I believed was the most important received only my vote. The lobbying period is intended to address this. Before anyone votes, each of us will have one minute to share with the whole group what we believe are the most important items and why. After everyone who wants to has taken their sixty seconds in the sun, we will then vote. So to recap: first, we will talk about the criteria to use in selecting our priorities; second, we will have a lobbying period; and finally, we will vote and review the outcome. Any questions?"

3. Suggest criteria to the team and ask for others, before seeking acceptance.

   "There are three criteria that we typically like to keep in mind when prioritizing. The level of impact is perhaps most important: What will be the impact of this improvement on the overall hiring process? High, medium, or low? Probability of success is our second criterion. If we choose to implement this improvement, how likely is it that we will be successful, given the nature of the improvement, our skill sets, and other factors? Finally, we look at cost-effectiveness. How cost-effective is this improvement compared to others in terms of providing the largest bang for the buck? Are there other criteria that you suggest we keep in mind?"

4. Take a **checkpoint** and provide an opportunity for each person to lobby the group for support.

   "We have talked about the criteria. Now before we use our dots, we will all have the option of taking one minute to indicate which of those improvements we think should be given highest priority and to explain why. The 'why' is the most important part, because it will give each of us a better understanding of the value of the improvement. I would like to start with Tony and go around the room. Each person can 'pass or play.' Tony, what do you think? Would you like to pass or to lobby the group?"

5. After taking a **checkpoint**, distribute and explain the dots. Distribute a number of dots equal to 20 to 30 percent of the total number of items. To get a wider range of priority scores, consider using multicolored dots. I like making 50 to 60 percent of each person's dots one color (red) and the remaining dots another color (blue). The red dots count three points each; the blue dots count one point.

> *"Now that lobbying is complete, let's determine our priorities. This will tell us our focus for the next year. You have been given five dots. Three dots are red; the rest are blue. Place the red dots on the three improvements you believe are the most important. Place the blue dots on two other improvements that you would like to see happen as well. The red dots count three points each, while the blue dots each count one point."*

> *"You will have five minutes to place your dots on the ones that you feel are the best. You cannot place more than one dot on an item. As you are voting, keep in mind the criteria we have decided on. Any questions?"*

6. Review the results and ask for consensus to move forward with the voted priorities. If you do not have consensus, you will use consensus building strategies described later to resolve the issue.

> *"Of the fifteen improvements resulting from the brainstorming activity, it appears that only eight received any votes at all. Of the eight, the top five vote-getters are clearly the winners—improvements one, three, four, seven, and eight. Nine points was the lowest score among these five. From there, improvements two and five each received four points, which is a drop of over 50 percent."*

> *"Based on this, it appears that our priority improvements are the following . . . Let's go around the room and check for consensus. Give me a head nod if you're OK with these priorities."*

Reporting

Reporting processes are used to inform about results of a breakout or other activity. In Chapter Five, I talked about the **rotating flip charts** process as a method for reporting back. In this section, I will talk about a more standard report-back process.

At this point in your agenda, the hiring process improvement team has identified the top-priority improvements to implement and is in the middle of agenda item F, "Develop an implementation plan." Using breakout sessions, each of the five breakout teams has developed an implementation action plan for one of the five priority strategies. It is now time to report back.

As mentioned earlier, a challenge with report-back processes is that people generally are not as attentive to what other teams are saying. As well, with so many participants, there may be little feeling of accountability to give the other teams quality feedback. For these reasons, I prefer the rotating review process described in Chapter Five for breakout group reporting. However, if rotating flip charts is not an appropriate option, use the standard report-back process that follows.

The Secret to Reporting Back

Increase feedback quality by assigning teams to review report-back.

Reporting: Standard Report-Back

1. Describe the activity and purpose. (Note that you may have already done this through the **checkpoint**.)

   "Now that we have developed a starting point for the implementation plans in our breakout teams, it is time to hear from those teams. During the report-back, it will be important to take the starting points and improve on them the best we can."

2. Use **PeDeQs** to describe the general directions.

   "Teams will have four minutes each to give their report. You can use the time as you wish, but at a minimum we want to hear about the action steps, the responsibilities, and the timeline. As each team reports back, I am going to ask one of the other teams to serve as the primary commenters. This team's responsibility will be to give the first comments. They will say, first, what they like about the action plan and, second, how to make it better. Once the primary team has commented, all the other teams will have an opportunity to comment as well."

3. Before each team gives its report-back, let the members of the primary team know who they are. Ideally, the primary team in each case would be neither the team reporting next nor the team that reported previously. In this way, a team has an active role every other time or so.

   "Since the first team will be starting off, I am going to ask the third team to serve as the primary reviewer this time. Remember to listen for what you like and how to make it better."

4. After each team gives its report-back, prompt the primary team to identify strengths and ways to improve, and then open it up to the other teams.

   "Let's hear from the third team. What did you like about what you heard? Now describe any suggestions you have to make it better. Now let's open it up to the other teams to identify either things that you liked or ways to improve. Who would like to go first?"

5. After noting all suggestions to improve, go back and review each one and have the group decide whether to implement the suggestion.

> *"Now that we have all the suggestions, let's go back and review each one for agreement. The first suggestion is . . . Any additional comments? OK, since these are simply suggestions, are we comfortable with a simple majority as a way of making these decisions? OK, all those in favor of implementing the first suggestion, hands please? That suggestion was accepted. Let's move on to the next suggestion for improvement."*

Getting Feedback

In our agenda with the hiring process improvement team, you are on the last agenda item, "Review and close." You have reviewed the steps that occurred in the process as well as all decisions made, outstanding issues, and actions to be taken following the meeting. You are now ready for detailed feedback on the session itself.

Process feedback is an important part of ongoing learning, development, and application. People are often reluctant to give critical feedback, however. And sometimes, when feedback is given, it isn't clear whether the feedback is the view of one individual or the entire team. The *rated feedback* process is a vehicle to help ensure that you receive quality comments and that you can gauge the amount of support for those comments.

The Secret to Getting Quality Feedback

Ask for strengths, areas for improvement, and level of consensus.

The rated feedback process includes the following steps:

- *Ask the group to identify strengths first.* Having a discussion of strengths first makes it easier for participants who are reluctant to criticize to be more open to providing critical insights. When asking for strengths, use a **round-robin** or another technique to involve everyone.
- *Ask the group to identify ways to improve.* Note that you do not ask for weaknesses. Instead you ask for specific ways the session could have been improved. The "ways to improve" terminology serves to keep the discussion constructive, using the "Here is what I liked—here is how to make it better" format.
- *Test each improvement suggestion.* Once you have identified ways to improve, go back and ask for a show of hands of those who agree with each improvement suggestion.

Why Do This?

Why test each improvement suggestion?

When people make improvement suggestions, they are indicating how the session could have been better for them. And if you make each change recommended, you can be fairly certain that at least one person will enjoy the session more. But what about the rest of the people? By reading the requested change and asking people to raise their hand if they agree with it, you will know how strong the support is for each feedback suggestion and can respond accordingly. It may surprise you how often an improvement suggestion is supported by only one or two people.

Feedback: Rated Feedback

1. Describe the activity and purpose. (Note that you may have already done this through the **checkpoint**.)

   "We are nearing completion of the entire agenda. The last thing on our list is to evaluate the session so that we can identify what went well and what improvements can be made so that the organization can benefit from the process learning we have gained."

2. Use **PeDeQs** to describe the general directions.

   "The way I would like to do this is, we will first identify strengths—the things that we felt went well. We will then talk about ways that the session could have been improved. Finally, we will look back at those session improvement suggestions and identify the ones that have strong support for implementing."

3. Start with strengths. Ask a **starting question** and use a **round-robin** technique to include everyone. Checkmark similar comments.

   "Let's start with strengths. I would like to go around the room starting with Jamie. I would like each person to identify one thing they liked about the process and the way we worked. If someone has already said the thing you like, feel free to say "Ditto number one," and I'll put a check mark there to indicate that another person agreed with the comment. Jamie, get me started. Think about the entire process, starting on day one when we did gifts and hooks, and all the activities we did—documenting the current steps, talking about problems, potential solutions, priorities, and our implementation plan. Think about things you liked about the process, the way we worked, the results we achieved, and so on. Let's build the list. Jamie, get me started. What did you like? What went well?"

4. Move on to ways to improve. Instead of using a round-robin, have participants randomly indicate suggestions.

"We've talked about things we liked. Let's move on to ways to improve. I would like to open it up. We do not have to go in any order. During our time together, there were probably things about which you said, 'Well, I wish we had done that differently' or 'That certainly didn't go very well.' There may have been other improvement suggestions you thought about as well. If we had a chance to do this all over again, what would you do differently? What would you suggest to the team that we do differently that would have made the process even better? Who wants to go first?"

5. Go back and review each improvement suggestion and ask for a show of hands for the number of people who support each. If you are working with a small group, you might count the individual hands. With a larger group, it might be faster to estimate the percentage that agree.

   "Let's go back now over each improvement suggestion. I would like to get a rough indication of the level of support for each one. As I read each suggestion, please raise your hand if you agree with that suggestion. The first one says . . . How many people agree that this suggestion would have improved the session? That looks like about 80 percent. Let's move on to the next."

Additional Information Gathering and Processing Strategies

In the preceding sections, I have provided a separate method for each of the seven information gathering and processing functions. In this section, I briefly describe ten additional methods I have found helpful in our work. See the Resource Guide for where to go to develop your skills with these and other engagement strategies.

Brief Encounters	**Purpose** For participants to get feedback from others on their ideas **General Description** • The facilitator instructs the participants to develop a personal question (for example, "How do I give constructive feedback without sounding judgmental?"). • For ten minutes, the participants engage in as many one-on-one conversations as possible in which each asks and receives answers. Responding to the answers is specifically discouraged. **Benefits** • Gets participants up and moving • Allows participants to get considerable input into an idea • Gives participants an opportunity to hear about and make recommendations on the issues of others

Dump and Clump

Purpose
To gather and categorize information

General Description
- Participants work in teams to record (dump) on sticky notes their responses to a listing question (for example, "What are all of the steps in the hiring process?" "What are my objectives for this session?") or a brainstorming question (for example, "Where might we go for our company outing?").
- The facilitator collects the sticky notes and then uses a grouping activity to have the participants organize the items into categories using cells of a matrix drawn on flip charts (clumped).

Benefits
- Gets many people involved
- Organizes a large amount of input in a timely and efficient manner

Elevator Speech

Purpose
To summarize information or prepare a response to a question covered in a session

General Description
- Participants work individually or in teams to develop an elevator speech—a short statement presented in the time it takes an elevator to go from the first floor to the top floor of a building (about sixty seconds). The presentation should grab attention and say a lot in a few words.
- Topics for the elevator speech typically answer a question related to the work of the session (for example, "What's different about this strategic plan?" "What was most beneficial about the session?" "How did the team address the issue of . . . ?")
- Depending on the goal, participants can work as a full group to identify the key elements of the elevator speech before teams work separately to develop the speeches.

Benefits
- Takes very little time and gets all ideas or points of view on the table
- Keeps participants from sharing too much information or being repetitive

Forced Analogies

Purpose
To help teams come up with creative solutions

General Description
- After an initial round of brainstorming, choose an object that is completely unrelated to the activity at hand. For example, if the team is looking for ways to improve the hiring process, the facilitator might ask, "How is the hiring process like a cup of coffee?"
- The team then spends five to ten minutes responding to the question. A sample response might be, "You can spend a lot of money and not get what you want" or "What's right for one person might not be what's right for another; you have to understand what the buyer wants."
- After completing forced analogies, do a second round of brainstorming by asking, "Based on this exercise, what other solutions might we consider?"

Benefit
- Forces groups to think out of the box and consider possibilities that might not be readily apparent

Future Letter

Purpose
To help ensure follow-up action is taken

General Description
- When a session is complete and people have developed an action or commitment on how they will change their behavior, have the participants write a letter addressed to themselves that explains:
  - How they are feeling at the moment and why
  - The commitment that they have just made and why it is important to them and to their organization
  - Their recognition of the obstacles that they may face in fulfilling their commitment, and their determination to make it happen
  - Collect all of the self-addressed letters and tell everyone that you will mail them back three to four months after the session.

Benefit
- Despite the best of intentions, people often get buried with other priorities when they return to the workplace. Knowing that this letter will arrive is often a sufficient inspiration to keep their commitment alive and well. Receiving the letter will often rekindle any commitments that have deteriorated.

Last Person Standing

Purpose
To identify the unique information or ideas in a short and energy-filled period of time

General Description
- Participants work in teams to record on sticky notes their responses to a listing question (for example, "What are all of the steps in the hiring process?" "What are my objectives for this session?") or a brainstorming question (for example, "Where might we go for our company outing?").
- All team leaders are asked to come to the front of the room; team by team, the leaders post one of their answers to a flip chart. For example, team leader 1 posts one answer and moves to the back of the line, then team leader 2 posts one answer and moves to the back of the line, and so on.
- If a team leader gives a duplicate answer, the participants make a loud buzzer noise to indicate an error has been made.
- The first time a team leader gives a duplicate answer, the facilitator collects that sticky note, and the team leader goes to the back of the line. However, the second time the team leader gives a duplicate response, the team leader must sit down.
- The last team leader standing represents the winning team (that is, the team with the most unique answers).

Benefits
- Provides a competitive and energetic approach to identifying unique responses
- Is especially helpful during those lull times of the day

More of/ Less of

Purpose
To identify at a high level what is needed to bring about a vision or a change

General Description
- After completing a visioning or desired state activity, the participants identify what the organization must have more of and less of to achieve the desired state.
- Items identified might include activities, behaviors, attitudes, values, and so on.

Benefit
- Provides a way to identify high-level change before identifying specific actions to be taken

Start/Stop/ Continue	**Purpose**
	To identify at a lower level what must change in order to bring about a desired state

General Description
- After completing a visioning or desired state activity, or after a more of/less of activity, the participants compile a list of those activities they will start doing, those activities they will stop doing, and those activities they will continue doing to support the desired state.
- This activity can be done at whatever level is appropriate (for example, an individual, a team, a department, or an organization).

Benefit
- Provides a way for participants to think through their specific response to a change

Talking Stick	**Purpose**
	To promote discussion and listening

General Description
- The participants stand in a circle, with a stick in the middle of the circle.
- The facilitator asks a question. One person starts by walking into the circle, picking up the stick, and responding to the question. While the person is holding the stick, no one else can speak.
- Once the person finishes speaking, that person holds out the stick. When the next person steps into the circle to take the stick, the first person returns to the circle.

Benefit
- Encourages thoughtful consideration of ideas and a sense of community

The Whip	**Purpose**
	To allow all participants to quickly respond to a question

General Description
- The facilitator asks a question to the group that can be answered in one, two, or three words.
- After asking the question, the facilitator checks to ensure that all participants have determined their response.
- The facilitator then quickly rotates around the room having people give their responses.

Benefit
- Provides a quick way to take the temperature of the group or determine how a group feels about an idea or approach

Applying the Secrets to Information Gathering

This chapter includes numerous techniques for information gathering and processing. These same techniques are applicable across a wide range of activities. Let's take a look at four in particular, including a case study of how these techniques have been used in the classroom.

Pre-Questioning with Your Customer

SMART facilitators use the pre-questioning technique to ask participants, prior to a presentation, to identify the key questions that they want answered by the presentation. This technique prepares the participants to listen and also gives the presenter a preview of what the participants have on their minds.

You can use this same technique in a selling situation. Consider asking your customer one of the following questions. Be sure to convert the question to type B!

- What do you want to hear from us today?
- What questions do you want to see answered?
- What concerns do you have that, if they are addressed well in this presentation, would lead you to conclude that we are the organization with which you desire to partner?

Addressing Problems

When faced with a group whose job it is to solve a problem, SMART facilitators know to use a series of activities that first expand and then contract the possible actions. The participants move from "What can be done?" to "What will be done?"

Likewise, when working with a small team or one-on-one to address a problem, be sure to use processes, such as listing and brainstorming, that first expand the options. These kinds of activities allow participants to create a wide range of options and encourage them to seek creative solutions. After analyzing the options, use such processes as lobbying and prioritizing to contract the list down to the option or options the group will act on.

Getting Feedback

To receive quality feedback on a facilitated session, SMART facilitators don't ask for the strengths and weaknesses of the session; instead, they ask for the strengths and ways to improve. Doing so keeps the discussion positive and focused on improvement. You can use this same technique in any venue where a critique is helpful, whether reviewing a meal, a movie, a vacation, a meeting, or someone's management style.

CASE STUDY: Facilitation in the Classroom

I was going to be facilitating strategic planning for an affiliate of Project GRAD, an organization dedicated to improving public school education. With the financial support of the business community, the affiliate organization had implemented an entire approach for school reform based on having a dedicated focus on reading and mathematics, providing teacher training and support, establishing a classroom management methodology, providing a college scholarship incentive, and implementing an accountability process.

On this particular day, I was visiting an elementary school supported by Project GRAD to view the classroom management and reading techniques in action. As I walked through the school to the classroom, I noticed that posted outside the door of every classroom was a card labeled "Week 17, Day 4, Lesson XXX" along with a list of learning objectives for the particular lesson. It was clear that anyone visiting the class would know exactly what was being taught that Thursday.

When I walked into the classroom, the desks were grouped in teams of four to six young people. I noticed that each child was reading out of a booklet, and the teacher was standing in the front of the room with a manual and an open can of Popsicle sticks. I heard the teacher say, "Time for questions." She read the first question and then said "Pairs." The students immediately grabbed the hand of one of their neighbors. A buzz filled the air as each of these pairs began discussing answers. Quickly, pairs around the room began holding up their joined hands to indicate they had an answer. At this point, the teacher pulled a Popsicle stick from the can and read the name that was on the stick. That child stood up and gave the answer. The teacher said, "That's right. Let's give Tony a handclap cheer." All the children immediately, and in unison, began a syncopated clap that lasted five or six seconds. Tony was beaming. The teacher said, "Next question." After reading the question, the teacher said "Teams." Every member at each table joined hands and begun talking about the answer. Once more, joined hands began popping up around the classroom. The teacher pulled a stick and read the name. The student responded, and the teacher said, "That's correct. Let's tell Catherine, 'Way to go.'" All the students stood and gave each other high fives, saying, "Catherine, way to go!"

This activity continued for the full hour. I learned later that the young people had selected or made up their favorite cheers and that the Popsicle sticks were used to ensure that every student had the opportunity to speak. The teacher cleverly had a can within a can. The Popsicle sticks in the inside can had not been used. The Popsicle sticks in the outside can had been. That way she would always know which children had not been given a chance to respond.

I also learned that every day, for the same 60 minutes, in every class in this school, every teacher focused on reading based on a specific lesson for their reading level for that day. If the teacher didn't finish a lesson for the day, the teacher would still have to move to the next lesson to prevent the entire class from falling behind. I was also told that during that segment of the day, students moved into whichever class was appropriate for them. You could have a second-grade student in a fourth-grade teacher's class, and vice versa, depending on the child's reading level.

As a facilitator, I was very impressed to see sophisticated information gathering techniques and energizing strategies being used in the classroom by a truly facilitative teacher. That these same techniques were being used in every classroom in the school was inspiring. There was no question that students were engaged and that learning was indeed happening. Significant improvements in test scores over time reflected that the school was making great strides.

Facilitator's Checklist for Information Gathering

- ☐ To be effective, a facilitator must understand the different information gathering and processing functions and have a full toolbox of methods for addressing each one.

- ☐ Gathering Facts—Listing
  - In gathering detailed information through a listing exercise, use your reactive questioning techniques, rather than statements, to acknowledge, clarify, challenge, confirm, probe, and redirect as needed.

- ☐ Categorizing—Grouping
  - When categorizing comments, take the comments one at a time and ask, "Same or different? Does this one belong in one of the existing categories, or is a different category needed?" If it is different, create a new category and have the participants name it.

- ☐ Inquiring—Pre-Questioning

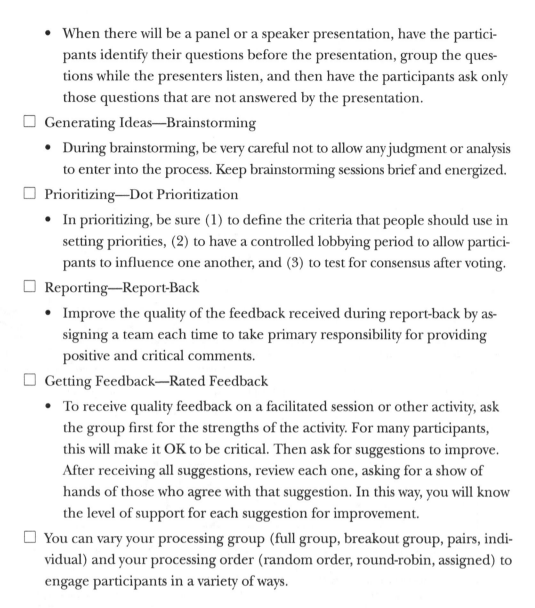

- • When there will be a panel or a speaker presentation, have the participants identify their questions before the presentation, group the questions while the presenters listen, and then have the participants ask only those questions that are not answered by the presentation.

☐ Generating Ideas—Brainstorming

- • During brainstorming, be very careful not to allow any judgment or analysis to enter into the process. Keep brainstorming sessions brief and energized.

☐ Prioritizing—Dot Prioritization

- • In prioritizing, be sure (1) to define the criteria that people should use in setting priorities, (2) to have a controlled lobbying period to allow participants to influence one another, and (3) to test for consensus after voting.

☐ Reporting—Report-Back

- • Improve the quality of the feedback received during report-back by assigning a team each time to take primary responsibility for providing positive and critical comments.

☐ Getting Feedback—Rated Feedback

- • To receive quality feedback on a facilitated session or other activity, ask the group first for the strengths of the activity. For many participants, this will make it OK to be critical. Then ask for suggestions to improve. After receiving all suggestions, review each one, asking for a show of hands of those who agree with that suggestion. In this way, you will know the level of support for each suggestion for improvement.

☐ You can vary your processing group (full group, breakout group, pairs, individual) and your processing order (random order, round-robin, assigned) to engage participants in a variety of ways.

Exercise Your Skills

As indicated at the beginning of this chapter, I have found that the only engagement method used in many meetings is presentation followed by question and answer, over and over again. This chapter has provided you a number of tools for achieving a variety of functions, from gathering facts to getting feedback.

To exercise your skills, think about a meeting you recently led or attended. Review each agenda item and identify the function the agenda item was serving and the method used. Then identify an alternative method that could have been used; choose from the seven methods described in detail or the additional ten methods summarized. If possible, use a different engagement method for each agenda item.

Do this same exercise for the next meeting you lead, and watch the difference in the level of engagement!

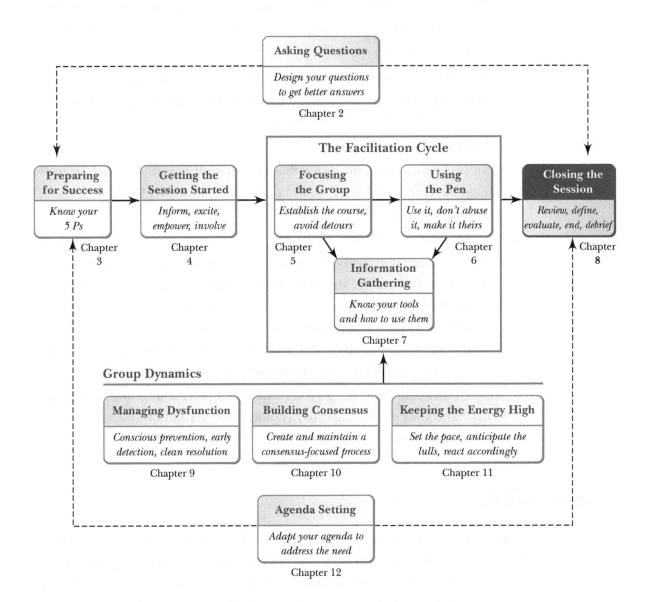

CHAPTER EIGHT

THE SECRETS TO CLOSING

Review, Define, Evaluate, End, Debrief

Questions Answered in This Chapter

What are the most important activities to do before closing a session?

What do you do with the participants' personal objectives identified at the beginning of the session?

How do you ensure buy-in and commitment to the decisions made in the meeting?

What do you do with the items remaining on the Issues list?

What are the guidelines for assigning responsibility for the Actions list?

What feedback is needed from the team and the sponsor of the meeting?

What do you do if it looks as though you are going to exceed the scheduled ending time?

CASE STUDY: Polling for Agreement at the Close

(*Note:* This is a continuation of the case study "Avoiding the Executive Feeding Frenzy" in Chapter Four.)

Recall that prior to the executive session on the three barriers to growth, the CEO of the mainframe manufacturing company had given us a ground rule that only those recommendations that had the consensus of all forty participants would be implemented. Throughout the session, we documented each of the decisions made as the executives discussed the issues and developed strategies. By the end of the day, there were a series of flip charts that documented the recommendations and the preliminary action plans.

To close the session, I used the "poll the jury" technique. I reminded the executives that we needed to confirm consensus on each element of the plan because we would move forward only on those elements that everyone in the room could live with and support. After reading the decisions and actions that were posted, I asked the first person in front of the group, "Can you live with these recommendations and support them through implementation?" The first person responded affirmatively. The positive responses continued around the room until we were about two-thirds completed. The next executive said, "Well, I pretty much can agree with it." I responded, "It sounds like you might have reservations about one or more aspects of the plan." The executive responded, "Well, it's not really a problem. I think I'm OK." I was concerned that we weren't hearing full commitment, so I probed again. "Let me ask you, is there something you could suggest that would make you feel more comfortable with the overall plan?" He explained that he did question whether a particular aspect of the plan was viable. He then recommended a change that he felt would increase the likelihood of success. I checked in with the group. "We just heard a suggestion of a change to one of the actions. Let's review it . . . Any questions or concerns about incorporating the change?" One person suggested a minor alteration to the change, with which the executive was very comfortable. When the entire group acknowledged acceptance of the change, I went back to the executive and asked, "Can you live with this and support it through implementation?" He responded, "Definitely."

All too often, meetings end with many dangling loose ends. As a result of the loose ends, within a day or two there can be differences of opinion as to what actually happened in the meeting. Sometimes the differences are so great that you are left wondering if everyone attended the same meeting!

When a meeting ends, participants should be able to answer the following:

- What did we accomplish?
- What decisions did we make?
- What can we tell others about the session?
- How will the session be documented?
- What's going to happen when we leave the room?
- Who is responsible for making it happen?
- How we will know that it has happened?
- When do we come back together?
- What will we do when we come back together?

SMART facilitators achieve these outcomes by using a five-step closing sequence:

The Closing Sequence	1. **Review** the activities performed, the participants' objectives, and the parking boards (issues, decisions, and actions).
	2. **Define** what can be communicated about the session.
	3. **Evaluate** the value of the session and the results achieved.

4. **End** by reminding of the next steps and formally ending the session.

5. **Debrief** with the meeting sponsor to identify strengths and areas for improvement.

The Secret to a Strong Close

Review what was done; define what can be communicated; evaluate the value; end with next steps; debrief with the sponsor.

Reviewing Activities Completed and Personal Objectives

Prior to ending the session, you start by reviewing the activities completed during the meeting. The review provides the team with a focused reminder of all that was covered in the session.

Two Ways to Review Activities Completed

- One way to review the activities completed is to step through the agenda, item by item.
- A different way, and the approach I recommend, is to "walk the walls." If you have posted the flip charts of information created during the session, you can review the work done by walking around the room, pointing out the results of each step in the process. This review typically takes two to three minutes and helps the participants have a sense of fulfillment as they see the output from the time spent.

After reviewing the activities completed, the next step is to review the participants' personal objectives documented early in the session.

Steps in Reviewing Personal Objectives

1. For each objective, ask the team, "Was this objective fulfilled?"
2. Encourage team members to be very boisterous in their response as a way to increase energy prior to ending the session. For example, ask them to give a rowdy cheer to indicate yes or a "gong" sound to indicate no.
3. Using a pen color that is different from the writing on the flip charts, check off each yes, circle each no.
4. Once you have reviewed all the objectives, go back to each circled one to discuss what, if anything, should be done as a follow-up action.
5. Be certain to place the follow-up action on the Actions list.

Confirming Commitment to Decisions Made

Recall that throughout the session, you used three parking boards to track important information.

The Parking
Boards

- The **Decisions list** identified decisions or recommendations made by the group during the session.
- The **Issues list** included topics that need to be discussed later in the session or entirely outside the session.
- The **Actions list** documented actions to be performed sometime after the completion of the session.

At the end of the meeting, review all three parking boards, starting with the Decisions list. The goal of the decision review is to remind the team of the decisions it has made. In addition, you can use this review to strengthen the commitment to action, identify potential issues, and develop strategies for overcoming those issues.

Secret #36

The Secret to Confirming Commitment to Decisions

Document the benefits, barriers, and success strategies for key decisions.

SMART facilitators have four steps for reviewing the Decisions list. *After completing the first step, you may choose to do one or more of the other steps,* depending on the amount of time you have available, the importance of the decisions, the need for commitment to action, and the level of resistance expected from others outside the meeting.

Steps in
Reviewing the
Decision List

1. Review the Decisions list.
2. Document the benefits of each decision.
3. Identify potential barriers to implementing the decisions and document success strategies.
4. Poll the jury.

Step 1: Simple Review of Decisions

The most straightforward method for reviewing decisions is simply to read through the list of items on the Decisions list and ask, "Does this list fairly portray the decisions we made in this meeting? Were there any other decisions that we made?" A sample Decisions list is presented in Figure 8.1.

FIGURE 8.1 DECISIONS LIST.

> ### Decisions
>
> If internal candidate identified in advance, allow for fast-track hiring process based on 14-day internal posting
>
> Provide interviewing training to all hiring managers and interviewers
>
> Scan résumés into computer to permit searching
>
> Permit departments to be involved in screening process at their discretion
>
> Provide avenue for giving signing bonuses to attract top candidates

Step 2: Documenting of Decisions and Benefits

After reviewing the Decisions list, you can document the benefits of each decision to help ensure that the team members understand the value to be gained. In some sessions, as part of the session design, you will have already documented benefits for each decision. If not, use the following steps:

1. Make sure the decisions on the list are numbered.

2. Create a two-column chart with the following headings: Decision and Benefit. The Decision column should be relatively small, about four inches.

3. Place a 1 in the first column and ask the participants to identify the benefits of the first decision, as shown in the sample dialogue that follows.

4. Continue until the team has documented the benefits of each of the decisions.

Sample Dialogue: Documenting Decisions and Benefits

Facilitator: Now that we have reviewed the decisions, let's take a minute to document the benefits of each of these decisions. This is important because, more than likely, one or more of us will be asked to explain why we made the decisions that we made. Documenting the benefits of each of our decisions will help ensure that each of us will be delivering the same message to everyone.

Let's take a look at this first decision. It says . . . Let's assume that this decision has been implemented. Think about the impact of this decision on the organization. Think about what we've gained by implementing this decision. Let's identify a couple of bullets. What are the benefits of implementing this decision?

Why Do This? | **Why document benefits to decisions?**

- By tracking and reviewing the decisions made, every person in the meeting will have a clear understanding of the results of the meeting.
- By also documenting the benefits, the participants will have a common vision of the value gained by the decisions. This common vision can be beneficial as participants communicate to others the reasons for the decisions.

Figure 8.2 is a sample flip chart page showing the results of documenting the benefits.

FIGURE 8.2   DECISIONS AND BENEFITS.

Decision	Benefit
1	Creates a fast-track process for internal candidates, while still making the position available to others in the organization
2	Increases likelihood of identifying stronger candidates and eliminating weaker candidates; reduces risk of legally inappropriate questions by interviewer during the interview process

Step 3: Barriers and Potential Strategies

After documenting decisions and their benefits, consider having the group identify potential barriers to implementing the decisions. Identifying barriers can be especially beneficial when implementing complex change or when a high degree of resistance is expected. Figure 8.3 shows a sample flip chart resulting from the discussion of potential barriers.

FIGURE 8.3   POTENTIAL BARRIERS.

Potential Barriers

1. Lack of management buy-in to the recommendations

2. Lack of participation in the interviewing training

3. Signing bonus budget wasted on people who are not top candidates

Sample Dialogue: Identifying Barriers

Facilitator: We have identified the benefits of each of our decisions. These are important benefits to achieve. At the same time, however, there may be barriers that are going to stand in the way of our implementing these decisions. These may be internal barriers, external barriers, or other things that get in the way of moving these decisions forward. Let's build a list of these. What are the barriers that might get in the way of implementing these decisions?

After you have recorded all the potential barriers, the next step is to define strategies for addressing the barriers.

Defining Potential Strategies	
	1. Create a four-column chart with the following headings: Barrier, Strategy, Who, and When. The Barrier column should be relatively small, about four inches.
	2. Place a 1 in the first column. Ask the participants to identify potential actions that can be taken to address the barrier.
	3. Document each success strategy identified by the group.
	4. Once you have documented all the success strategies, ask the group to decide who in the room should lead the implementation of each strategy. Have the leader of the strategy commit to a date by which the strategy will be completed.

Sample Dialogue: Potential Strategies

Facilitator: These barriers can certainly make it difficult to successfully implement the decisions we've made. It's important, therefore, that we take proactive steps to attempt to minimize the impact of these barriers. Let's walk through each one and determine what strategies we can take to address them.

Let's take a look at the first barrier. It says . . . Let's assume that we must prevent this barrier from negatively impacting the implementation of the decision. Think about the things we can do to prevent the negative impact. What actions can be taken? Let's build a list. What actions can we take to prevent this potential barrier from impacting the decision? . . .

Now that we have identified the strategies to overcome each barrier, let's go back and determine who the best person is to lead the strategy and by what date the strategy needs to be accomplished. Let's take a look at the first strategy. It says . . . Who is the best person to lead the strategy? . . . By what date will the strategy be completed?

It is important that the group first identifies the benefits of each of the decisions prior to documenting barriers and potential strategies. By documenting the benefits first, the team will be more likely to see the value of overcoming the barriers. If the participants identify barriers without documenting benefits, it is possible that they will get so discouraged by the barriers they have to overcome that they will begin second-guessing the value of the decisions. A sample flip chart resulting from the discussion of strategies to address barriers is shown in Figure 8.4.

FIGURE 8.4 SUCCESS STRATEGIES.

Barrier	Strategy	Who	When
1	Hold a management briefing on the recommendations and benefits to gain buy-in for implementation	Robert	Within 3 weeks
2	Hold briefing for supervisors to ask their help in defining what they would want to see in the interviewing training; have supervisors select three to serve as an advisory team for HR in developing the training	Sandra	Within 6 weeks

Step 4: Polling the Jury

In several types of facilitated sessions, it is essential to have a confirmation of agreement from all participants before beginning the implementation of solutions. Sessions related to strategic planning, process reengineering, and issue resolution (like the case study that opened this chapter) are three types in particular in which it can be helpful to ensure that you have the agreement of all involved. One method to ensure that you have full agreement is to poll the jury:

1. At the beginning of the session, define *consensus* as *"I can live with it, and I will support it."* (See Chapter Ten for a sample dialogue related to defining consensus.)

2. Also at the beginning, indicate that at the end of the session you will ask all participants if they can live with and support the solutions they create.

3. After reviewing the decisions made and, optionally, the benefits, potential barriers, and success strategies, go around the room asking each participant, *"Can you live with and support these decisions?"*

4. If anyone raises concerns, you might ask that participant the following: *"What is the minimum amount of change you would recommend to the group in order for this solution to be something you can live with and support?"*

5. Alternatively, if you believe the concerns to be less severe, you might first ask the following: *"Will these concerns prevent you from living with and supporting the solution?"*

6. If changes are recommended, suggest a time limit for discussing the recommendation and ask the participants if they are willing to enter into the discussion.

7. Once resolution is reached, ensure that you still have the consensus of the previously polled group members before continuing to poll the jury: *"We just heard a suggestion of a change to one of the decisions. Let's review it . . . Any questions or concerns about incorporating the change?"*

Clearing the Issues List

The Issues list was the place you parked topics that arose during the session that either needed to be covered at a later time or were completely irrelevant to the session. At the end of the session, it is important to clear all remaining items off the Issues list.

In some cases, the issue will have already been covered. In other cases, the team will conclude that the issue does not need to be covered at all. In still other cases, the issue will need to be covered, but in a later session. There may also be cases in which the issue needs to be covered before the meeting ends.

The Secret to Clearing the Issues List

Ask, "Have we covered it? Do we need to? Do we need to now?"

You can quickly and systematically process the Issues list by following the steps listed here. As you review each issue on the Issues list, ask these questions in the following order.

Clearing the Issues List

- "Have we covered it?" (If yes, move on to the next issue.)
- "Do we need to cover it?" (If no, move on to the next issue.)
- "Do we need to cover it now?"
  —Yes: set a time limit and facilitate the discussion.
  —No: move the issue to the Actions list.

By the end of this process, there will be no items remaining on the Issues list. Any items requiring additional action will have been moved to the Actions list.

Assigning Actions

The Actions list contains activities to be performed sometime after the completion of the session. As part of the closing process, the team should confirm that each action still needs to be done, assign a person to take responsibility for the action, and have that person establish a date by which he or she will make sure the action is accomplished.

 Secret #38

The Secret to Assigning Actions

Assign actions only to people who are present, with dates they have set themselves.

As described in Chapter Four, the Actions list should be a three-column chart with the following headings: Action, Who, and When. Consider the following steps in processing the Actions list:

Processing the Actions List

1. Review all actions to ensure that everyone is aware of all the actions on the list.
2. Prior to making assignments, remind the group of the following guidelines:
   - Accepting an assignment does not mean that you have to complete the assignment yourself; it means only that you are responsible for making sure that the action gets completed.
   - Assigning an action to someone not present in the room is not appropriate; that person may not feel committed to taking action or may not completely understand the action needed.
   - If the action is better performed by someone outside the room, assign the action to a person of authority in the room whose responsibility it is to delegate the action to the appropriate person and to follow up to ensure that it is accomplished.
3. Ask for volunteers for each action or have the team select a person.
4. Ask the person to establish a date by which the action should be completed. Having people assign their own dates helps build commitment to meeting the target.

Quick Tip!

When assigning actions, consider having participants sign their own name to the Actions list to reinforce the responsibility they are accepting. Any blanks that are left will then need to be filled by volunteers or the team.

Defining What Can Be Communicated About the Session

It is not unusual for the sponsor of a session to expect the entire results of the session to be openly shared with whoever finds the information of interest. It is also not unusual for the entire results of a session to be considered confidential and to be shared only with others who were in the room. More times than not, however, I have found that facilitated sessions contain a mixture of open and confidential information.

In these circumstances, difficulties may arise because the information that some participants view as open, others may view as confidential. Therefore, it can be important at the end of the session to identify what can be communicated to others about the session.

Depending on the nature of the session, I have used three different processes for developing what can be called "The Communication Plan."

Types of Communication Plans	• The simple list • The dual list • The communication plan matrix

The Simple List

With the simple list, the facilitator creates a one-column chart, "Items to Communicate," performs a checkpoint, and asks a type B question such as the following:

Facilitator: We have just completed a review of the parking boards; our next step is to talk about what we will communicate to others about this session. This is important because we need to be on the same page about what we will say about what we have done. So imagine that you walk out the door and one of your people asks, "So, what did you all do?" Think about the things you would want to say, the key points you would want to make, the thoughts you would want to leave with this person. What are some of those points?

You would then list on the flip chart the responses people give. It is not unusual for this list to include agenda items (what was done), decisions made, and next steps.

The Dual List

With the dual list, the facilitator creates a two-column chart, "Items to Communicate" and "Items NOT to Communicate Now." Use the dual list when you suspect that there is specific information that should not be communicated. You might use the following words to introduce the dual list.

Facilitator: We have just completed a review of the parking boards; our next step is to talk about what we will communicate to others about this session. This is important because we need to be on the same page about what we will say about what we have done. So imagine that you walk out the door and one of your people asks, "So, what did you all do?" Think about the things you would want to say, the key points you would want to make, the thoughts you would want to leave with this person. What are some of those points?

Now that you have identified some of the things you would say, let's identify anything that we know should not be shared with others at this point. Think about any topics that may be too sensitive or inappropriate for sharing at this point. Think about anything that was done or any decisions made that should be on this list. What might some of these be?

You would then list on the flip chart the responses people give. Note that there may be disagreement on whether an item should be on the left (to be communicated) or right (not to be communicated) column of the chart. You can use the informed majority process described in Chapter Ten to resolve these disagreements.

The Communication Plan Matrix

With the Communication Plan Matrix, the facilitator creates a five-column chart as shown here.

Audience	Information	Who	Vehicle	When

Communication Plan Matrix Definitions

- **Audience:** the various groups who need to have information about the session (for example, hiring managers, employees, candidates)
- **Information:** the specific information needed by that audience (for example, summary of the new process, detailed instructions)
- **Who:** the person responsible for ensuring that the communication is made to that audience

- **Vehicle:** the appropriate method for communicating the information (for example, email, hard copy report, presentation)
- **When:** the date by which the communication should occur

The Communication Plan Matrix is most appropriate when you have multiple audiences who should have significantly different information communicated to them about the session or who should be communicated with in significantly different ways.

Steps in Completing the Communication Plan Matrix	1. Identify each of the audiences who need to have information about the session.
	2. Starting with the first audience, identify the information needed and the most appropriate person to take responsibility for ensuring that the audience receives the information.
	3. The person responsible then defines the vehicle and the date by which the communication will happen.

Evaluating the Session

Feedback is a critical part of the continuous improvement cycle. Strive to gain documented feedback from every session you facilitate. Be sure to encourage specific comments, whether positive or negative, that tell you what you should continue to do and what you should consider changing.

If a written review is appropriate, Figure 8.5 provides a sample of a session evaluation form. If the group has demonstrated that anonymous communication is not necessary, consider taking a few minutes for a group review period at the end of the session. To execute the group review, consider the steps for getting quality feedback identified in Chapter Seven:

Steps in Evaluating the Session	1. Use a round-robin technique to have the group identify what they liked about the session. For many participants, this approach will make it easier for them to provide critical comments.
	2. Ask for suggestions to improve (random order).
	3. Review each suggestion and have the participants raise their hand to show support for it.

FIGURE 8.5   SAMPLE EVALUATION FORM.

Organization:	Date:
Facilitator:	Location:

SESSION	Excellent	Good	OK	Poor
1. Content of session (topics covered, depth, accuracy, etc.)				
2. Comprehensiveness of subjects covered				
3. Pace of session				
4. Allocation of time among subjects covered				
Overall Assessment of Session				

FACILITATOR	Excellent	Good	OK	Poor
1. Understanding of process (planning, analysis, etc.)				
2. Ability to facilitate group				
3. Ability to maintain appropriate pace				
4. Responsiveness to questions				
5. Sensitivity to needs of group				
Overall Assessment of Facilitator				

PERFORMANCE	Excellent	Good	OK	Poor
1. How well were the objectives of the session met?				
2. How likely is it that the session will lead to positive change?				
3. How beneficial was this session to you personally?				
Overall Assessment of Performance				

COMMENTS
1. What agenda topic was of most value to you?
2. What topic was of least value to you?
3. How could this session have been improved?
In one or two sentences, please comment on the overall session benefit (or lack thereof) and what caused the benefit (or lack thereof). Use the back of this form if you need additional space.

> ### *Quick Tip!*
> Consider using the group review technique described here to "take the temperature" of the group any time during a session, such as at the midway point or at the end of each day for multiday sessions.

Ending the Session

After all the open issues, decisions, and action items have been reviewed and the session has been evaluated, you are ready to formally end the session.

Steps in Ending the Session

1. Thank the participants for their involvement. Remind them of the part this meeting will play in achieving the overall objective.
2. Remind the team of the next steps, including the following:
   - Who will document the session
   - When and how the results will be distributed
   - The place, date, time, and purpose of the next session
3. Formally end the session.

Depending on the amount of work performed in the facilitated session, the review-evaluate-end portions of the closing process can require as little as ten minutes for a brief meeting and forty-five minutes, or even longer, for an all-day meeting. Be sure to plan adequate time for the closing.

Debriefing

As soon as possible after the session, meet with the sponsor to discuss the session process and the results. The debriefing session should answer the following questions:

Debrief Questions

- How well were the objectives of the session met?
- How well did the participants respond during the session?
- How sufficient are the deliverables from the session?
- What follow-up activities are needed?

What If the Session Is Running Behind?

Starting and ending a session on time are important ways to demonstrate respect for your participants. One of the responsibilities of the facilitator, described in Chapter One, is to serve as the taskmaster. The facilitator is ultimately responsible for keeping the session on track, making sure that the session accomplishes its objectives, and ending on time.

Yet some delays may be unavoidable. SMART facilitators use the following strategies to manage the session time:

Managing the Time in the Session	• Have a detailed agenda with start and stop times and the estimated duration for each process.
	• Track the start and end times of each process as the session progresses.
	• If the session begins to fall behind schedule, announce this to the participants. Solicit their assistance in keeping comments brief to help the session catch up with the schedule.
	• If the session continues to fall behind, set a specific time objective for each subsequent agenda item. Get agreement from the participants to stick to that objective. Remind participants periodically of the objective and the progress.
	• If the session continues to fall behind, meet with the sponsor at the next break to determine an alternate plan of action that can be proposed to the group.

Warning: avoid speeding up! Beginning facilitators may be tempted to speed up the facilitation in order to meet the time constraints. SMART facilitators know better. They understand that speeding up the facilitation has several potential negative results:

Negative Impact of Speeding Up	• For those participants who process at a slightly slower rate than others, your speeding up will leave them far behind. Their ability to create, understand, and accept the solution may be compromised.
	• Often when we as facilitators speed up, we cut out the engagement activities, eliminate feedback, and drop "nonessential" discussion. Unfortunately, even though eliminating these activities can save time, doing so also reduces participants' understanding and acceptance.
	• When we increase our pace, we can increase the level of stress in the room, causing others to become tense, short tempered, and less than cordial.

The overall impact of speeding up is to disempower one or more members of the group. Instead of speeding up, SMART facilitators reduce the scope. They get agreement from the group to reduce the amount of work that will be completed that day and look for alternative ways for the work to be done, without jeopardizing budget or time constraints, if possible.

What If the Session Is Going to Run Over?

If you determine that the ending time will slip, it is important to get permission from the participants *in advance* to continue past the agreed-on completion time.

Why Do This?	**Why ask for permission to run over?**
	• It shows respect for participants' time and avoids resentment about the time overrun.
	• Asking for permission maintains the integrity of the process by putting the decision about whether to extend the time in the hands of the participants.
	• It provides a forum for addressing the needs of anyone who must depart at the original time.
	• Asking allows an alternative action to be created and agreed on by the group if the session time is not extended.

Consider the following steps if the session is going to run over:

Actions to Take If the Session Is Running Over	
	1. Alert the participants.
	2. Conservatively estimate the additional time needed.
	3. Ask for alternatives.
	4. Assess the impact of continuing.
	5. Confirm the agreement.
	6. Hold firmly to the agreement.

If the decision is made not to extend the time, proceed with the appropriate closing activities. In cases where an additional session is going to be held, perform a partial close as described in the next section. If an additional session is not going to be held, execute all the closing activities, being sure to indicate how the outstanding activities will be completed.

Delivering a Partial Close

If a facilitated session spans multiple days or multiple meetings, as is often the case with process improvement and strategic planning activities, it may be appropriate to execute a partial close rather than a full close. In a partial close, you would typically not include a review of the participants' objectives, as the entire agenda has not been completed. You also might not formally evaluate the process, create a communication plan, or fully debrief the project team. Typically, you would perform the other closing steps, as follows:

Steps for a
Partial Close

1. Review the activities performed and the parking boards (issues, decisions, and actions).
2. Close by reminding participants of the next steps and formally ending the session.

Facilitator's Checklist for Closing

☐ Review the activities completed during the meeting by "walking the walls."

☐ Review the participants' personal objectives. For each objective, ask the team, "Was this objective fulfilled?"

☐ Review the Decisions list to remind participants of decisions made. (The second, third, and fourth steps listed here are optional.)

- Decisions list: review each decision made.

- Decisions and benefits: for each decision, ask, "If we implement this decision, what will the benefit be?"

- Potential barriers and success strategies: determine potential barriers to implementing the decisions and create success strategies that will overcome those barriers.

- Poll the jury: ask all participants if they will live with and support the decisions agreed on by the team.

☐ Clear any remaining items off the Issues list by asking the following:

- "Have we covered it?" (If yes, move on to the next issue.)

- "Do we need to cover it?" (If no, move on to the next issue.)

- "Do we need to cover it now?" (If yes, set a time limit and facilitate the discussion. If no, move the issue to the Actions list.)

☐ Make assignments to the Actions list.

- Make sure that each action on the list is assigned to an individual in the room and ask that person to establish a date by which the action should be completed.

- If the action is better performed by someone outside the room, assign the action to a person of authority in the room whose responsibility it is to delegate the action and to ensure that it is accomplished.

☐ Define what can be communicated about the session using one of the following methods:

- The simple list
- The dual list
- The communication plan matrix

☐ Have participants evaluate the session. Use an evaluation form or group feedback process:

- Ask the group first for what they liked about the session.
- Ask for suggestions to improve.
- Review each suggestion and have the participants raise their hand to show support for it.

☐ End the session.

- Thank the participants for their involvement.
- Remind the team of the next steps, including how documentation will be handled and the date, place, and time of the next session.
- Formally close the session.

☐ As soon as possible after the session, meet with the sponsor for a debrief to discuss the session process and the results.

☐ If you determine that the ending time will slip, it is important to get permission from the participants *in advance* to continue past the agreed-on completion time.

- Alert the participants.
- Conservatively estimate the additional time needed.
- Ask for alternatives.
- Assess the impact of continuing.
- Confirm the agreement.
- Hold firmly to the agreement.

Exercise Your Skills

As indicated earlier, it takes time to execute a formal closing process. For your next full-day or multiday facilitated session, consider reserving thirty minutes for the close. Create a flip chart page that you can use as the agenda for the close. Try to execute all the relevant closing components. Record the timing of each element so that you can better estimate your closing sequence in the future.

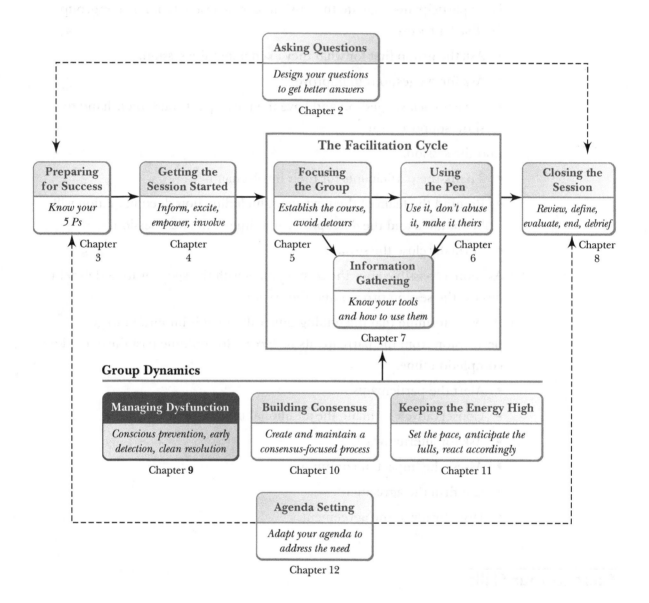

CHAPTER NINE

THE SECRETS TO MANAGING DYSFUNCTION

Conscious Prevention, Early Detection, Clean Resolution

Questions Answered in This Chapter

What is dysfunctional behavior?

How do you identify potential dysfunction during the preparation stage?

What are strategies you can take prior to the session to prevent dysfunctional behavior from occurring?

How do you detect dysfunction early?

What are the needs and typical dysfunctions of the different communication styles?

How do you address some of the more common dysfunction types, such as the dropout, the naysayer, the whisperer, and the verbal attacker?

What do you do when something unexpected happens in a session, such as an emotional outburst?

How should you respond when one or more participants indicate that you have made a mistake or suggest a change to the process that you don't want to make?

CASE STUDY: The Chairman and the COO

While a member of one of the national consulting firms (and before learning any of the material that makes up the Secrets of Facilitation), I was working with an oil and gas exploration company in the Southwest. We had been called in to guide an in-house team commissioned to implement an executive information system. The executive information system had been requested by the new CEO. The CEO had been appointed less than nine months before by the parent company. The prior CEO had been demoted and was serving as the chief operating officer (COO). The system would be used initially by the top executives: the CEO, the COO, and each of the eight executive vice presidents.

During the first phase of the project, we interviewed the executives individually to identify the type of information each desired in the new system. We aggregated the information from the various interviews and convened a facilitated review session with the executive team. The purpose of the session was to confirm that all key information needs had been identified and to determine which needs would be included in the first phase of the system. I served as the facilitator for the group review.

Early in the session, I noticed that each time the COO spoke, the CEO would shift in his seat, fold his arms, or exhibit other signs of uneasiness. As the session progressed, I noticed the CEO becoming increasingly irritated. Following a short break, the session continued. When the COO made his next comment, the CEO exploded, "That's the stupidest thing I ever heard. It's limited thinking like this that has caused us to be in the situation we're in now!" The room went silent. You could have heard a pin drop. Everyone looked at me, wondering what I was going to do. I had no idea what to do. I had not been trained in the Secrets of Facilitation. I asked, "Any other input?" The session was a disaster.

Facilitators often have high anxiety around encountering major dysfunctional behavior in a session, and for good reason. We typically are poorly prepared to handle dysfunctional situations. We typically are not trained and lack the tools and methods for addressing these difficult circumstances. And when we do encounter them, we often do as I did in the situation described in the case study; we employ the "ostrich technique" for problem resolution: stick our head in the sand and hope this situation goes away!

Unfortunately, as in the case study, dysfunctional behavior that is ignored usually doesn't go away. Sometimes it comes roaring back in a much worse form.

This chapter focuses on four topics:

1. Dysfunctional behavior: What is it?

2. Techniques for conscious prevention: How do you prevent dysfunction from entering the room?

3. Techniques for early detection: If dysfunction does begin to occur, how do you make sure you catch it early?

4. Techniques for clean resolution: Once you detect dysfunction, how do you address it effectively without alienating the individual or disempowering the group?

Dysfunctional Behavior: What Is It?

There are many different types of dysfunctional behavior. As Figure 9.1 indicates, dysfunctional behavior can range from dropping out and not participating to leaving the room in disgust and physically attacking someone.

Note, however, that *as the degree of the dysfunction increases, so does the severity of the disruption.* For example, you might not even recognize the mild forms of dysfunction, such as dropping out and doing other work during the session. The middle forms, such as negative physical reactions and audible sighs of displeasure, might be a bit irritating, but not completely disruptive. In the most extreme forms, however, such as verbal and physical attacks, the disruption is severe. And just as increases in the degree of dysfunction cause increases in the severity of the disruption, increases in the severity of the disruption cause increases in the level of intervention required by the facilitator.

The good news is that people don't walk into a room, sit down, and immediately start going at each other's throats. What usually happens is that there is an escalation period in which people get increasingly irritated, increasingly stressed, increasingly impatient, and more willing to allow their emotions to peak. Therefore, as facilitators we must understand the nature of dysfunctional behavior and have tools for preventing it, detecting it, and resolving it. Let's start by defining what dysfunctional behavior is and examining how it works.

FIGURE 9.1 DYSFUNCTIONAL BEHAVIOR.

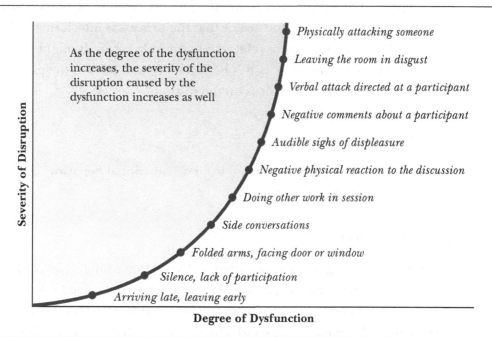

Our Definition

Dysfunctional behavior is any activity by a participant that is consciously or unconsciously a substitution for expressing displeasure with the session content or purpose, the facilitation process, or outside factors. Dysfunctional behavior is a symptom, not a root cause.

The Secret to Understanding Dysfunction

Dysfunction is a substitution and a symptom, not a root cause.

This definition has three important implications.

1. **Behavior, not the person, is dysfunctional.** In one meeting, a person may be actively and cooperatively participating, but in the next meeting, that same person's behavior may turn dysfunctional. In fact, the transition from functional to dysfunctional can occur in the same meeting, multiple times!

2. **Dysfunctional behavior may be conscious or unconscious.** Oftentimes, people exhibiting signs of dysfunction are not aware of the behavior. Other times, the behavior is intentional in an effort to bring about change, disruption, or some other action.

3. **Dysfunction is a substitution** for expressing displeasure related to the session content or process or to an outside factor. For example, the content issue might be that a comment was made with which the participant strongly disagrees. If the displeasure is with the process, it might be that the participant feels that the pace is too fast or that the process is interfering with the real work. If the displeasure relates to an outside factor, it might be that there is an issue in the participant's personal life that has left the participant distracted and unable to focus on the session.

Functional Versus Dysfunctional Behavior

How do you distinguish functional from dysfunctional behavior?

Take a look at this sample.

Sample Dialogue: Is This Dysfunction?

Carla: I am getting very irritated. This is beginning to look like another wasted meeting debating irrelevant issues. We need to stop what we're doing because we're way off base and focusing on the wrong stuff.

Facilitator: Help me understand. On what issues do you feel we should focus?

Carla: Look at your flip chart! All our potential solutions are just improvements to the current hiring process. We need to get way out of the box on this. We need to be discussing methods that will improve our

Facilitator: performance by a factor of ten or one hundred. Not just things that are going to give us a 5 percent savings or reduce our time by 8 percent.

Facilitator: You may very well be right that it is important for us to get out of the box and come up with solutions that can bring outstanding performance. We may or may not already be there. Let me check in with the group to see if there are others who share your concern. Carla seems to be saying . . .

SMART facilitators know that what Carla did was *functional* behavior. Carla was alerting the facilitator that she was not happy. No substitution was happening. She was giving the facilitator an opportunity to address the problem, and the facilitator responded by (1) asking a direct probe to clarify, (2) playing back what was heard, and (3) turning it over to the group for input and eventually a decision on how to respond to Carla's comment.

In contrast, dysfunctional behavior occurs when the displeasure is not expressed directly but instead comes out in a behavior that is not helpful to the overall goal of the session. For example, if instead of making a comment, Carla had pushed back from the table, folded her arms, and remained quiet for the rest of the day—that would be dysfunctional behavior. Or if Tom turns to Sheila and whispers, "This is a waste of time," or if Bob is busy answering emails on his smartphone and is not fully focused on the session, or if Kim stands up and leaves, slamming the door—these would all be considered dysfunctional behaviors.

Symptom Versus Root Cause

SMART facilitators treat dysfunctional behavior as a sign that the participant is asking for help. In essence, the participant is waving a red flag and saying, "I don't like what is going on, but I'm not ready to tell you yet." Of course, participants may not verbally tell you until their degree of dysfunction has gone through the roof! As you will see, it is very important for facilitators to recognize dysfunctional behavior and address it in its milder forms, before it does go through the roof.

A facilitator must also recognize that the dysfunctional behavior is a symptom that is masking the real issue (the root cause). As described earlier, the root cause is typically a problem with the information that is coming out of the session (content), the way the session is being run (process), or some outside factor that has nothing to do with the session.

Sample: Symptom or Root Cause?

The facilitator notices that Carla has pushed back from the table, folded her arms, and turned her body physically away from the group and toward the door. She appears to have lost interest in the session.

Facilitator: Carla, excuse me. It appears we may have lost you a bit. Would you mind unfolding your arms, leaning forward, and crossing your legs back toward the center of the group? Thank you.

Although the example is ludicrous, I believe it drives home the point. The facilitator has attempted to resolve the dysfunction by addressing the symptom (the behavior) while ignoring the root cause (possibly an issue with the session). When we address only symptoms and don't attempt to get at the root cause, we can be setting ourselves up for a much worse dysfunction later on. In essence, the facilitator is implicitly encouraging the participant to get worse! It is as if the facilitator were saying, "That dysfunctional behavior wasn't bad enough to get me to address the real issue. Give me another!" Sometimes the participant does just that.

Dysfunction Worsens over Time

If a dysfunctional behavior is not addressed, it tends to get worse over time. One reason is that participants' level of impatience increases with every additional minute that they feel you are wasting their time. Therefore, if you ignore dysfunctional behavior and hope it goes away, you are probably setting yourself up for a much larger problem later on. Fortunately, the earlier forms of dysfunction are much easier to address than the later forms.

Techniques for Conscious Prevention

Now that we understand what dysfunctional behavior is, let's move on to how to prevent dysfunction from occurring.

The Secret to Preventing Dysfunction

Secret #40

Identify potential dysfunction during preparation, then execute prevention strategies.

Identifying Potential Dysfunction

As indicated in Chapter Three, during the preparation stage you should talk with the meeting sponsor and, if possible, the session participants. In these interviews, you should inquire about issues and concerns that might cause problems during the session. Specifically, you are seeking to learn of the following:

- The concerns of any participant who is not in favor of holding the session
- Participants who perceive that they stand to lose something if the session or project achieves its objectives
- Participants who are not on favorable terms with one another
- Participants who tend to point out problems rather than create solutions

Executing Prevention Strategies

With the information you obtain from the preparation stage, you should develop and execute strategies for eliminating dysfunction before it can start. I frequently use the five prevention strategies that follow.

Assign Seats

In facilitated sessions, consider providing participants with name tents. The name tents I use are made with 8.5-by-11″ paper folded in half lengthwise, with the participant's first name in large, bold letters and his or her full name and affiliation in smaller print beneath the first name.

Before participants arrive for the session, place all the name tents on a single table and use colored dots or colored pens to mark each tent. The color indicates the team and table to which the person is assigned. When participants arrive, explain that you will be utilizing teams throughout the session and that people should sit in any seat that is free at the table with their color. (During setup, place colored tents at the center of each table to indicate the table color.)

This method of assigning seats has several advantages. For one thing, it gives participants some choice in selecting a seat. At the same time, you can carefully make team assignments to address potential dysfunction you identified during your preparation. For example, two people who aren't on favorable terms can be assigned to different teams. Likewise, highly vocal people can be spread out among the teams.

If necessary, you can assign specific seating by arranging the name tents in front of the seats. I have found, however, that arranging seating in this manner is less empowering to participants. Doing so can also cause distraction, as people ponder the rationale for the prearrangement. Some participants even switch the placement of their cards to a more preferred location!

Add Ground Rules

As described in Chapter Four, ground rules provide a self-correcting mechanism for keeping the participants functioning effectively. The case study "Avoiding the Executive Feeding Frenzy" described how adding the ground rule "Always look up" addressed the tendency of those executives to tear down rather than build up. Consider any potential issue identified during the preparation stage as a candidate for a ground rule. Some examples are shown in Table 9.1.

Interact with Particular People

If you know in advance that there are individuals who don't want to be present or who feel that they stand to lose something if the session is successful, you will

TABLE 9.1   ADDING GROUND RULES TO PREVENT DYSFUNCTION.

If the Potential Issue Is That . . .	. . . Consider Adding a Ground Rule
Participants like to discuss at a high level, but seldom get to the real issues.	Address root causes, not symptoms.
Arguments occur because people assume they understand when they don't.	Play back and confirm before stating a disagreement.
People stay silent rather than voice their disagreement.	Poll for consensus on all major decisions.
Participants tend to waste time tearing down alternatives rather than seeking solutions.	Comment only on strengths or make suggestions to improve.
Meetings end without a clear understanding of what was decided or what happens next.	Reserve fifteen minutes for review and action planning.

want to make a point of interacting with them prior to the session. As described in Chapter Three, key questions you will want to ask include the following:

- Why is the session being held? What is the real purpose?
- What are the key results that should be achieved?
- What are the potential problems or issues that may surface?
- How do we make sure the session is not a waste of time?

Your primary objective is to bring these participants' issues out into the open and get them involved with you in coming up with strategies to address those issues. This pre-session activity often helps the participants see that you are concerned about what is important to them and are open to working with them to address potential issues. The pre-session activity also can encourage them to interact in a functional way during the session.

Pay Close Attention to Particular Reactions

If you are aware that a particular person is not in favor of the session or that two people are not on favorable terms with one another, you will want to pay close attention to actions and reactions during the session. For example, if you notice that when a particular person speaks, two people pull back in their seats with expressions of disbelief or disdain, you will want to take action to turn this potentially dysfunctional situation into a functional one. I will cover the action to take later in this chapter.

Hold Informal Meetings During Breaks

Breaks are an excellent time to prevent dysfunction by privately discussing issues with people. For example, in the case of the participants who pulled back in their seats but did not choose to make a remark, you might engage them each in private conversation during the break: "How do you feel the session is going?" or, more directly: "I noticed your reaction to Randy's comment. Do you think that what he proposed is a realistic alternative? . . . Your point might be very valid. Would you mind bringing it up to the team so that we will get a number of different views?" The objective, once more, is to encourage functional instead of dysfunctional ways of addressing issues.

Techniques for Early Detection

I have talked about preventing dysfunction, especially steps you can take prior to the session. Now let's talk about detecting dysfunction once the session has started.

The Secret to Detecting Dysfunction
Take dysfunction checks at regular intervals.

Understand the Early Signs of Dysfunction

Facilitators must constantly be on the lookout for the early signs of dysfunction. What are the signs? Let's do some obvious comparisons by contrasting what people do when they are actively engaged in work they feel good about versus what they do when they are not engaged in work they feel good about, as shown in the following list:

When People Are Engaged	*When People Are Not Engaged*
Involvement in the discussion	Low involvement in the discussion
Words of encouragement	Complaints, objections
Laughs, smiles, head nods	Frowns, head shakes
Bodies leaning, and legs crossed, toward the center of the room	Bodies leaning, and legs crossed, away from the center of the room

As the list indicates, throughout the session you must look for

- Participants who are not speaking
- Participants who complain or object publicly to the group
- Participants who may be complaining or objecting privately to a neighbor through side conversations
- Participants whose outward expressions seem to indicate that they are not buying in
- Participants whose body language seems to indicate uneasiness with the session, such as folded arms, crossed legs, or bodies leaning away from the center of the room

Warning! Of course, just because people's arms are folded doesn't necessarily mean they are about to become dysfunctional. It could mean the temperature in the room is too cold for them. Likewise, just because people's legs are crossed away from the center of the room doesn't necessarily mean they are dissatisfied with the session. It could mean their legs are more comfortable in that position. Over the course of the session, however, you will be able to construct an idea of "baseline behaviors" for individuals. You will want to be on the lookout for changes. For example, you will want to notice when, after a comment, someone pulls back or shifts away from the room or when people who normally are smiling and nodding their heads change to frowning or inaction.

Routinely Take a Dysfunction Check

To help ensure that you detect these early signs of dysfunction, frequently and routinely execute a *dysfunction check* in which you actively look for signs of dysfunction. To aid you in remembering to do a dysfunction check, consider linking the dysfunction check with an agenda activity. For example, just before announcing each break, do a dysfunction check: look around the room specifically to observe any nonverbal cues that you may have previously missed.

Recognize the Communication Styles at Their Best and Worst

As a facilitator, you should have a model for recognizing different communication styles. People communicate differently and have different needs in a meeting. By having a mental model of the different communication styles, as well as an understanding of the needs and typical dysfunctions associated with those styles, you will be better able to prevent, detect, and resolve dysfunctional behavior.

There are a number of models for understanding behavioral and communication styles, including Meyers-Briggs Type Indicators, Hermann Brain Dominance Indicators, and DISC Communication Styles. In our organization, we use the DISC Communication Styles from TTI Performance Systems to focus on communication styles. We find that it is an insightful, yet simple, model that is easily understood, retained, and applied by casual users of the information.

In this model, there are four basic communication styles, referred to as Drive, Influence, Steadiness, and Compliance (DISC). Although all of us communicate using each of the four styles, we do so to varying degrees. And for most of us, we tend naturally to communicate in one of the four styles most of the time. Table 9.2 is a very abbreviated summary of each of the styles. The summary describes the styles at their best and worst in a facilitation session and lists additional strategies for preventing dysfunction that address the characteristics of each style.

TABLE 9.2 DISC STYLES IN A FACILITATED SESSION.

Style	At Their Best in a Session	At Their Worst in a Session	Prevention Strategies
D	Driving for efficiency Participating Directing Making direct comments Giving end point first	Alienating by being forceful Not letting people catch up Making snap decisions Killing creativity Being unaware of what's happening with the group	Keep session fast paced, well planned Lay out the process and the benefits Get them on your side to go with the flow
I	Participating Creative Talking Keeping energy up Cheerleading and supporting	Don't stop talking Don't listen Don't want to take time for important details Blue-skying, unrealistic	Give lots of chances to talk Enlist help for out-of-box thinking and getting others to speak Have ground rules: keep discussions relevant, give end point first, avoid bar discussion Take reality check
S	Friendly Supportive, nodding, agreeing Paying attention, listening well Tolerant Acting as peacemakers	Going along with what they don't believe Being the silent martyr Checking out Acting passive-aggressively in response to change	Check for agreement Use teams to avoid putting on the spot Use their name a lot Reinforce with praise
C	Looking at the details Constructive critiquing Identifying impacts of decision Keeping on task Providing reality check	Bogging down in details Giving all the reasons why something won't work Not allowing intuitive judgment Holding unrealistic expectations of quality, details	Set the expectation that more detailed analysis will be done outside the session to confirm directional decisions Remind of the level of detail needed for each decision

Techniques for Clean Resolution

How you deal with dysfunctional behavior will vary depending on, for example, the nature of the dysfunction, when it occurs, the number of people affected, and the probable root cause. However, the general formula for addressing dysfunction is our next secret.

The Secret to Resolving Dysfunction

Approach the participant privately or generally; empathize with the symptom; address the root cause; get agreement on a solution.

Steps to Resolving Dysfunction

Let's take a look at each step in the general formula. As a backdrop for the discussion, let's use the example of Barry, who is busy signing purchase orders and not giving his full attention to the session.

Step 1: Approach the Participant Privately or Generally

For many dysfunctions, you will want to speak privately with the person during a break, as publicly calling attention to the person's behavior might get in the way of resolution. This would likely be the case with Barry signing purchase orders.

For other dysfunctions, you will be able to address the issue generally to the entire group, without pointing out the person specifically. For example, if the issue was that someone or several people arrived late for the meeting, you might say, "I would like to take a second to remind the group of the ground rules to which we agreed. We said we would have one conversation, start and end on time, and avoid bar discussions."

The person for whom the comment was intended may appreciate that you avoided putting him or her on the spot by including the reminder with a few of the other ground rules. In addition, you will probably want to speak with the person at the break to ensure that there was not an additional problem.

Step 2: Empathize with the Symptom

When people behave in a dysfunctional way, such as when Barry is signing purchase orders during the session, our natural tendency may be to say, "Stop that! Put that away. Behave like a functional person." Unfortunately, most adults would not react well to such an approach.

I strongly recommend that you start by empathizing with their situation. You can express concern about the situation in which they find themselves or praise an appropriate aspect of their behavior. In the case of Barry, you might say, "It looks like you have some important work to get done, and this session has gotten you behind." Notice that this comment neither blames Barry nor says that the behavior is unacceptable.

Step 3: Address the Root Cause

Now that you have empathized with the symptom, the next step is to address the root cause. You will want to make an effort to get at the real issue. Attempt to do this by asking a question that will yield a response that confirms the issue.

In the case of Barry, who is doing outside work during the session, his actions seem to indicate that his work is more important to him than the work of the group. It could be that he values the work of the group but is facing a tight deadline (outside factor). Alternatively, it could be that he does not value the work of the group and is trying to do something productive to fill the time (session content or process). There may be other reasons for the behavior as well. Consider trying to get at the root cause by asking a question along these lines: "We do need your full participation if we can get it. Are we addressing issues that are important to you?"

Step 4: Get Agreement on a Solution

The final step is to get agreement on how the situation will be handled going forward. The agreement, of course, will depend on what the real issue is.

Let's go back to the example of Barry. We'll take the easy one first. If the real issue is that Barry has a critical deadline, the conversation might flow like this:

Sample Dialogue: Gaining Agreement I

Facilitator: We do need your full participation if we can get it. Are we addressing issues that are important to you?

Barry: The session is great, Michael. I just need to get these purchase orders out by noon so they can make this week's check run.

Facilitator: I see. I suspect some people have been a bit distracted by the work you are doing, and others may be encouraged to come back with their own work! Let me ask you, how long do you think it will take you to finish with the purchase orders?

Barry: I need at least another twenty minutes, thirty minutes max.

Facilitator: Well, we have another ten minutes left on the break. Why don't you step out now, get it done, and make it back as soon as you can. I'll let the group know that you had to meet a noon deadline, and I'll catch you up at the next break.

Barry: That will work. I'm sure I'll make it back here pretty quickly.

Now let's take the tougher issue. Suppose Barry doesn't want to be in the session and is there only because he was told he had no choice.

Sample Dialogue: Gaining Agreement II

Facilitator: We do need your full participation if we can get it. Are we addressing issues that are important to you?

Barry: I don't know why they asked me to be here in the first place. This is a waste of time. Nothing is going to change.

Facilitator: You know, I don't think I'd be too excited about wasting my time either. Part of my job is to try to figure out how to make sure that doesn't happen. So help me a bit here. Why is this going to be a waste of time?

Barry: The leadership team around here never implements an idea that didn't originate with them. I have seen it over and over again. I even tried to get off of this team. But my manager said I had to be here.

Facilitator: I wish I could guarantee you that the recommendations from the team were going to be implemented. I can't do that. But it sounds like there may be other people on the team who share your same concern.

I need your help in getting this out on the table. That way it will be a team issue, and we can take the team issue to the organization's leadership team and ask them to respond to it. When we come back from the break, I'll open up the issue and ask how many people believe this could be a concern. When we begin talking about solutions, I need you to suggest whatever you feel makes sense. Feel free also to suggest that we take the issue to the leadership team. Does it make sense to address the issue in this way?

Barry: Well, I'm not convinced that it will make a difference. But I'm willing to try.

Of course, I do not have Barry's full buy-in yet. More than likely, at the next break, I will have to continue to interact with him to keep him engaged. But I now understand the issue and have laid the groundwork for addressing it.

Finer Points in Resolving Dysfunction

Here are some of the finer points in resolving dysfunctional behavior. Be sure to keep these in mind as well.

- *Timing.*
  - Deal with dysfunctional behavior as soon as you recognize it and when the timing is convenient.
  - During each break, address any remaining issues.
  - If the dysfunction is severe, call for a break early.
- *Activities to avoid.* These can serve to exacerbate the problem:
  - Correcting the person publicly
  - Getting angry or speaking emotionally yourself
  - Losing your objectivity or neutrality
- *Continued monitoring.* In the early stages of dysfunction, bringing up the issue can be enough to remove the dysfunction. However, following resolution, do a dysfunction check periodically with the participant to ensure that the root cause was addressed as well. If the root cause wasn't addressed, the dysfunction may take another form.

Recommended Responses to Various Dysfunctions

I have talked about the general formula for responding to dysfunction. Now let's look at some very specific dysfunctions and how to address them. The next sections give suggestions for addressing fifteen common dysfunctions. The titles are adapted from the MG Rush *FAST Session Leader Reference Manual* and from my book, *The Secrets to Masterful Meetings.* For each of the dysfunctions, I have provided a description, its likely causes, strategies to take to prevent the dysfunction, what to do "in the moment" when the dysfunction occurs, and what to do "after the moment" to further address the dysfunction. Although most are individual dysfunctions, the last two are dysfunctions related to the entire group.

- Cell phone junkie
- Door slammer
- Dropout
- Interrupter
- Late arriver or early leaver
- Loudmouth
- Naysayer
- Physical attacker
- Storyteller
- Topic jumper
- Verbal attacker
- Whisperer
- Workaholic
- Group: low energy
- Group: time pressures

Study the various dysfunctions. Understand their common causes, the prevention strategies, and the actions to take in the moment. Advance preparation can help you prevent dysfunction and respond appropriately should the need arise.

The Cell Phone Junkie

Description	The person's cell phone constantly rings, or the person is on and off the cell phone frequently.
Common Causes	• The person has a high-priority activity that requires attention during the meeting. • The person is unaware of how cell phone activity can reduce the effectiveness of the meeting for all participants. • The person sees little value in the meeting and is attempting to make the best of having to be present.
Prevention	• Establish a ground rule: no cell phone calls during the meeting.
In the Moment	If a private conversation is possible: • "It looks as though people don't know you're in an important meeting, so they keep interrupting you. Have you been able to get the problem addressed? Is it okay then to turn the cell phone off for the rest of the meeting?" If a private conversation is not possible: • "When I heard Tony's phone, it was a reminder to me that we need to keep cell phones off if we can. I want to check in with the group to make sure this won't be a problem."
After the Moment	Discuss the issue privately to ensure that no additional problems exist.

The Door Slammer

Description	The person leaves the room in apparent disgust.
Common Causes	• The person has an issue unrelated to the meeting that needs immediate attention. • The person does not believe the meeting is worth investing additional time. • The person is dissatisfied with the meeting content or meeting process.
Prevention	• Establish a ground rule: everyone speaks about issues in the room; we will discuss the undiscussable.
In the Moment	• Name the behavior and then spend a few minutes with the group debriefing the event. The debrief helps form a common group view of the incident: what happened, why it happened, what will be done about it, and how we will prevent the rest of us from feeling the need to suddenly walk out. "Wow, Bill just got up and left the room. Given what felt like abruptness, I don't think it was because he had to go to the rest room." "We could try to continue working, but I bet many people are thinking about Bill's departure. So I would like to take a few minutes to get clarity on what just happened. Who can take a shot at explaining what happened and why you think it happened?" "So we have talked about what happened, and we have a guess as to why it may have happened. Now I have two other questions. What should we do about Bill? And what needs to happen differently to keep the rest of us from doing what Bill just did?"
After the Moment	• Afterwards, take a break. Meet with the project sponsor or project manager to discuss the issue and select a replacement if necessary. • Follow up to ensure that the agreed-on actions are taken. Consider meeting privately with the person yourself.

The Dropout

Description	The person does not participate in the discussion.
Common Causes	• The person has an introverted communication style and rarely offers comments in group discussions. • The person is typically talkative but is less involved in the discussion because of work pressures or other factors outside the meeting. • The person is dissatisfied with what is being discussed or the way the meeting is being run.
Prevention	• Establish a ground rule: everyone speaks.
In the Moment	• Remind the group of the ground rules (everyone speaks). • *Alternatively,* employ a round-robin brainstorming activity to get everyone involved. Begin with someone two or three seats away so that the dropout will speak third or fourth, to avoid putting the person on the spot and to provide the person time to prepare an answer. "Let's hear from everyone on this next point. With this question, I would like to start with [give the name of a person two seats to the right of the dropout] and go around the room to her left. The question is . . ."
After the Moment	• Discuss the issue privately to ensure that no additional problems exist.

The Interrupter

Description	The person interrupts others or finishes their sentences.
Common Causes	• The person agrees with the comment being made, gets excited, and wants to show support. • The person has little patience with the speed with which others speak. • The person feels that what he or she has to say is more important, or the person disagrees with the comment.
Prevention	• Establish a ground rule: have one conversation; respect the speaker.
In the Moment	• Validate the interrupter's desire to speak, while transferring the conversation back to the person who was interrupted. "Can you hold that thought for a moment so that the person speaking has the opportunity to finish? It's hard sometimes when you really want to say something, but let's remember our ground rules."
After the Moment	• Discuss the issue privately to ensure that no additional problems exist.

The Late Arriver or Early Leaver

Description	The person habitually arrives late to the meeting or leaves early.
Common Causes	• The person has meetings or other commitments that make it difficult to arrive on time or stay for the entire meeting. • The person does not believe that the meeting is worth making full attendance a priority.
Prevention	• Distribute the meeting notice ahead of time; indicate a gathering time of five to ten minutes prior to the start time; indicate the importance of the purpose and products for the meeting. • Contact the person ahead of time to gain commitment to be present for the entire meeting. Get agreement that the meeting should start on time with whoever is present.
In the Moment	• Remind the group of the ground rules in a respectful way. "I want to thank everyone for being here when you could get here and for continuing to do all you can to arrange your schedules so that we can start on time. Our next topic . . ."
After the Moment	• Discuss the issue privately to ensure that no additional problems exist.

The Loudmouth

Description	The person dominates the discussion.
Common Causes	• The person has an extroverted communication style and is not aware that a tendency to frequently speak first can limit the time and opportunity for others to speak. • The person is aware of the tendency and needs help in balancing time spent talking with time spent listening. • The person intentionally wants to dominate in order to limit time spent discussing other views.

(Continued)

Prevention	• Establish a ground rule: have one conversation; share the air.
	• Meet in advance to let the person know that you will be trying to get others to speak.
	"I appreciate you being willing to speak, especially given that most have been pretty quiet. I need to get other people speaking more so that we can get their views on the table. So, during this next meeting, there will be times when you might hear me say, 'Nice point. Let's hear from some others on this.' This way, we'll get everyone's input."
In the Moment	• At the start of the next process, use a round-robin discussion to get everyone involved. Direct the round-robin away from the loudmouth so that everyone else will be able to provide input first.
	"Let's hear from everyone on this next point. With this question, I would like to start with [give the name of a person to the left of the loudmouth] and go around the room to his left. The question is . . ."
After the Moment	• At the break, solicit the person's assistance in getting other people to speak. Remember to empathize with the symptom. Let the person know that from time to time you will purposely not call on him or her to encourage others to speak.
	• Occasionally, make a point of acknowledging the person's desire to speak, but call on someone else.
	• Follow up to ensure that no additional problems exist.

Sample Dialogue: Gaining Assistance to Get Others to Speak

Facilitator: I appreciate your being willing to speak, especially given that most have been pretty quiet. I need your assistance, though. I need to get other people speaking more. Any thoughts on how we might do that?

Mark: You're right. I often find myself dominating the discussion because no one else is speaking up.

Facilitator: Why don't we do this: after the break, I'm going to be using a lot more round-robins to try to engage more people in the discussion. And from time to time, you might want to say something, but I will intentionally call on others to get them involved. Will that work for you?

Mark: That's fine. Thanks for letting me know.

The Naysayer

Description	The person makes audible sighs of displeasure or negative statements such as "That won't work," without offering solutions.
Common Causes	• The person has a communication style that focuses on identifying problems and risks.
	• The person opposes the idea suggested and is identifying reasons for the opposition.
	• The person opposes the idea suggested and is attempting to create stumbling blocks to prevent adoption.
Prevention	• Establish ground rules: benefits first (that is, give the strengths of an idea before identifying problems); take a stand (that is, rather than describe what won't work, describe what will).

In the Moment	• Naysayers often express negatively without offering alternatives. Avoid a debate about whether something is wrong by focusing their attention on creating something better.
	• Say with optimism, "You may be right. How do we make it better?"
After the Moment	• Seek to gain agreement to always state benefits before stating problems.

The Physical Attacker

Description	The person physically attacks someone.
Common Causes	• Disagreement during the meeting escalates into physical confrontation.
	• Tensions or issues with a source outside the meeting escalate during the meeting into physical confrontation.
Prevention	• Identify probable issues prior to the meeting.
	• Establish ground rules: discuss the undiscussable; be soft on people but hard on ideas.
	• Actively keep the conversation focused on seeking solutions rather than assigning blame.
In the Moment	When a physical attack occurs, it is important to take control.
	• Stop the meeting immediately.
	• Let the group know they will be notified when the next meeting is scheduled.
	• It is inappropriate to try to reschedule the meeting then, as a physical attack can restart while the attempt to reschedule is going on.
After the Moment	• Consider meeting with the parties separately to identify the issues and an appropriate course of action.

The Storyteller

Description	The person likes to tell long-winded stories.
Common Causes	• The person has an extroverted communication style and is not aware of the tendency to be verbose.
	• The person is aware of the tendency and needs help in getting to the point.
	• The person is aware of the tendency and believes each story is worth the group's time and should be completely communicated.
Prevention	• Establish a ground rule: share the air.
	• Meet in advance to let the person know that you will have limited discussion time in the meeting.
	"I can readily see how stories give people a stronger picture of the point you are making. One of the concerns I have is that I've noticed that sometimes people drop out when you begin a story. Is there a way that you can make your end point first and then shorten the story so that most will be able to follow? This may also mean that we can get to more things during our meeting. So, during this next meeting, if I perceive that you may be starting a story, you might hear me say, 'Let's give the end point first so that people will be able to follow you better.'"

(Continued)

In the Moment	Let the person know that he or she needs to shorten the comment. • Stand next to the person and privately, if possible, give the "circling finger" to indicate that the person should wrap up the comment quickly. • Remind the group of the ground rules (state the end point first). "Let's remember the ground rule to give the end point first and keep it brief so that people will be able to follow along better."
After the Moment	• Follow up to ensure that no additional problems exist.

The Topic Jumper

Description	The person frequently takes the group off topic.
Common Cause	• The person has a communication style that frequently shifts to a new topic before the prior one is complete.
Prevention	• Establish a ground rule: have one conversation; one topic at a time.
In the Moment	• Validate the person's point by offering to put it on the Issues list and then bring the conversation back on topic. "That's a good point. If it's okay, can we put that on the Issues list to be discussed later and get back to talking about . . . ?"
After the Moment	• Consider seeking an agreement with the person to make an effort to use the Issues list when new topics come up.

The Verbal Attacker

Description	The person makes a negative comment about or directed at someone.
Common Causes	• Disagreement during the meeting escalates into the verbal attack. • Tensions or issues with a source outside the meeting escalate into a verbal attack during the meeting.
Prevention	• Identify probable issues prior to the meeting. • Establish ground rules: discuss the undiscussable; be soft on people but hard on ideas. • Actively keep the conversation focused on seeking solutions rather than assigning blame.
In the Moment	• Move between the people to cut off the debate, then slow down the discussion and reestablish order. "Let's take a time-out here. We have important issues to discuss, and we have established ground rules to help us do this. One of our ground rules is to be soft on people and hard on ideas. We are unlikely to be successful if our focus is on blame or finger-pointing. I would like to continue the discussion, if we can, but only if we can do so respectfully and with an understanding of the problems and a focus on developing solutions. Can we do this?"
After the Moment	• Consider taking a break and reconvening the meeting later. • Consider meeting with the parties separately to identify the issues and an appropriate course of action. • Consider asking that the person be excluded from the session if you believe that the behavior is likely to persist.

The Whisperer

Description	The person holds side conversations during the meeting.
Common Causes	• The person did not hear or understand a prior comment and asks someone for clarification. • The person heard the prior comment and comments on it to someone. • The person is having an unrelated discussion.
Prevention	• Establish a ground rule: one conversation.
In the Moment	Take action in a respectful way to let the person know that the behavior is disruptive. • Move and stand next to the person. Often your proximity to the whisperer is enough to cause him or her to stop. • Privately, if possible, give the "shhh" sign with one finger to your lips if the whispering continues. • Remind the group of the ground rules (respect the speaker). "Let's remember the ground rule that we want to have one conversation in the room so that we are respectful of the speaker and other listeners."
After the Moment	• Discuss the issue privately to ensure that no additional problems exist.

The Workaholic

Description	The person does other work during the meeting.
Common Causes	• The person has a high-priority activity that requires attention during the meeting. • The person sees little value in the meeting and is attempting to make the best of having to be present.
Prevention	Establish a ground rule: meeting work only (that is, work on only the meeting during the meeting).
In the Moment	If a private conversation is possible: • "It looks as though you have some important work to get done, and this meeting has put you in a crunch. We do need your full attention if we can get it. Is this work something you can do later?" If a private conversation is not possible: "I know we established the ground rule of only doing meeting work during the meeting. I want to make sure that the ground rule will still work for everyone."
After the Moment	• Discuss the issue privately to ensure that no additional problems exist. (See the example under "Techniques for Clean Resolution" in this chapter.)

Group: Low Energy

Description	Energy in the room is low.
Common Causes	• The group members generally have an introverted communication style and rarely offer comments in group discussions. • The topic is of low interest to the group, or the speaker or facilitator is presenting in a low-energy style. • The discussion is occurring during a low-energy period (for example, right after lunch).

(Continued)

Prevention	• Ensure that topics and speakers are appropriate for the audience.
	• Plan the agenda to ensure that the group is highly engaged during low-energy periods.
	• Have the group establish a simple recharge activity (for example, "the wave") for use when the energy dips.
In the Moment	• Incorporate a highly engaging activity to raise the energy level, such as the whip or last person standing, as described in Chapter Seven.
	• Consider using a round-robin in order to get everyone involved (for example, "Let's go around the room and get everyone's answer to this next question . . .")
	• Use the group's recharge established in the ground rules.
	"I'm sensing that the energy in the room is dipping pretty low. Let's quickly do our recharge activity to get the energy up."
After the Moment	• During the evaluation of the meeting, look for other possible reasons for the low energy, such as lack of interest in the topic.

Group: Time Pressures

Description	You are running out of time.
Common Causes	• The agenda was packed with too many items to cover in the time period.
	• Too much time during the meeting was spent on items that were less important or were off topic.
Prevention	• While reviewing the agenda at the start of the meeting, establish target times for each agenda item.
	• Put the items that are less critical near the end of the agenda.
	• Use a timer to track time spent; alert the group when nearing the scheduled time for an item.
	• Be flexible, allowing additional time when warranted and acceptable to the group, but ending discussions when appropriate.
In the Moment	• Let the group know the issue and get participants' agreement on how to proceed.
	"We have hit our time limit with this item. Can we end the discussion here, or do we need additional time? . . . Okay, let's give it an additional five minutes, but let's see if we can wrap it up even sooner."
	"It looks like that at the rate we are going, we will not be able to spend the time we need to have a thoughtful discussion on the last agenda item. Does it make sense to move this one to our next meeting, or is another alternative more appropriate?"
After the Moment	• During the evaluation of the meeting, look for the causes of the time overrun. Identify knowledge to be gained about how much the group can tackle in a single meeting.

When the Unexpected Happens

Sometimes the unexpected occurs, and you as the meeting leader are at a loss as to how to proceed, especially when strong emotions are involved. These situations can arise when, for example, a participant

- Starts yelling or crying
- Has a medical emergency in the middle of the session
- Makes a revealing comment that greatly embarrasses one or more people

How do SMART facilitators respond? This is our next secret.

The Secret to Responding When the Unexpected Happens

Get the participants talking personally about the experience.

Facilitators often speak of unexpected events, such as an emotional outburst, as the "elephant in the living room" that no one wants to talk about. Of course, the wrong thing to do is to continue as if nothing has happened. Instead, SMART facilitators immediately take control and facilitate the group to a resolution.

When the unexpected happens in a session, SMART facilitators recover by taking the following steps:

1. Request the group's permission to detour from the agenda.
2. Facilitate a round-robin in which each participant is invited to answer the question, "Given what just happened, what are you experiencing right this minute?"
3. Facilitate a second round-robin in which each participant is invited to answer the question, "What needs to happen to allow us to proceed?"
4. Take a break and meet briefly with the meeting sponsor to ensure that the actions for proceeding are in line with the sponsor's goals.

Quick Tip!

With the first round-robin, you are requesting answers to the question, "How are you feeling?" Consider starting with someone who has demonstrated a propensity to be expressive, such as someone high in the Influence style (see Table 9.2 for descriptions of the four communication styles in the DISC model). With the second round-robin, the question is, "What needs to happen?" Consider starting with someone who has demonstrated a bias toward action, such as someone high in the Drive style. People with these styles will probably find their respective questions relatively easy to answer and may enable the discussion to flow more smoothly.

Sample Dialogue: Responding to the Unexpected

Facilitator: I don't know about everyone else, but I'm a little uncomfortable right now. Rather than continue as though nothing has happened, I think we should take a few minutes, if it is OK with the group. I would like to go around the room, starting with Chris, and have each person answer a simple question: Given what just happened, what are you experiencing right this minute? Some of us will be feeling a variety of things. But please, share whatever is topmost on your mind, and we will keep going around the room. Chris, get me started; be as honest as you can: What are you experiencing right this minute? . . .

OK, we've talked about what's happening with everyone; now let's answer, What needs to happen to allow us to proceed? . . .

All right, we're clear about what needs to happen for us to proceed. Why don't we take a break now, and when we come back, let's see if we can move forward.

Responding to Mistakes and Attacks

I have talked about responding to verbal attacks directed at a participant. What about attacks directed at the facilitator and the process? Or what about when you make a facilitation error, and a participant points it out? What do you do? Consider the following case study.

CASE STUDY: Making a Mistake as the Facilitator

The school board in a large urban area held a one-day team building session. The group had one facilitator working with them in the morning, and I was assigned to facilitate a session for them in the afternoon. Because it was the first time I was working with this group, I chose to sit in on the morning session. The facilitator for the morning session was clearly skilled in team building. However, her weakness in group dynamics became readily apparent. As she executed a very strong opening that covered informing, exciting, and empowering, I noticed that one of the board members read the newspaper during her entire opening. He seemed to be quite intent on ignoring the facilitator, and of course, other board members noticed. After the facilitator reviewed the ground rules, she started to go directly into the first agenda item. At this point, the board member who had been reading the newspaper piped up, "You didn't ask us for consensus on the ground rules."

I thought that this was a great opportunity to get the paper-reading board member engaged in the discussion by saying, "You are absolutely right. Thank you for pointing this out.

Let me correct this. I would like to entertain a motion to adopt the ground rules; would you mind making that motion?"

Instead of admitting the mistake, however, the facilitator responded, "These are such basic ground rules, I didn't think I needed to do it. Even third-grade children accept them." The board member responded, "Well, we are not children." At this point, the other board members came to the aid of the facilitator: "You need to put down the newspaper and become part of the team instead of throwing rocks at the facilitator." The session degenerated from there. At that point, I was not looking forward to the afternoon session. Fortunately, the tension in the room lasted only an hour, as the team exercises that the facilitator had planned proved quite helpful.

The role of a facilitator is to "make easy" the work of the group. This role is best played by facilitators who can place their ego in check whenever it is in the best interest of the group. How should facilitators respond when they are attacked or when someone points out a mistake?

The Secret to Responding to Mistakes and Attacks

Secret #44

Acknowledge that the person may be right, show support, and take it to the group for resolution if appropriate.

A Participant Points Out a Mistake

When one or more participants indicate that you have made a mistake, and they are right, there is a simple way to rectify it:

- Admit that they are right and thank them for the correction by saying, "You are absolutely right. Thank you for pointing this out. Let me correct this."

But what if you do not think they are correct? Keep in mind that the soul of the facilitator is egoless. If the so-called mistake is in the past and has no impact going forward whether you were right or not, sidestep the debate.

- Thank them for the correction and indicate that you will certainly give thought to it: "Thank you for pointing this out. Rather than take time now, let me give some thought to this for future sessions."
- If appropriate, contact them later for further discussion.

A Participant Thinks That the Process Should Be Changed

At times, participants will make recommendations to change the process. Although this in itself is not dysfunctional behavior, many facilitators may experience the request as an attack on the process.

If you are in favor of the change,

- Thank the participants for the suggestion.
- Indicate to the group that you favor the change and ask the group's permission to execute it accordingly.

If you are not in favor of the change, consider a different set of steps:

1. Thank the participants for the suggestion.
2. Name at least one advantage to making the change.
3. Explain why you believe it may be better to leave things as they are.
4. Indicate your willingness to following the group's direction.
5. Ask the group if they agree with the change. (To avoid the perception of bias, do *not* ask if they agree with leaving things as they are.)

Sample Dialogue: Responding to a Request for Process Change

Facilitator: Thank you for pointing this out. How would you suggest I correct this? . . . Taking that action could work because . . . Let me share with you why I did what I did, and if the group feels that a different action is needed, I'll be glad to do it.

A Participant Thinks That the Facilitator Should Be Changed

Now admittedly it is a little more difficult to remain egoless when one or more participants are questioning your appropriateness as the facilitator of the group. SMART facilitators try anyway. They know that their role is to "make easy," and if they are getting in the way, they humbly step aside.

When your role is threatened, it is important to show no defensiveness but instead to use language that focuses on your concern for the group. Consider the following steps:

1. Apologize that one or more members are uncomfortable with you in the role.
2. Indicate your willingness to step aside.
3. Indicate your desire to adjust based on what is needed for the group.

The sample dialogue that follows provides words for handling this very sensitive conversation.

Sample Dialogue: Responding to a Request for a Facilitator Change

Facilitator: First, let me apologize to the entire group. I have clearly not done my job adequately if even one person feels that the group is better off without me in the facilitator role. I am more than willing to step aside if that is the group's will. And even if there are only a few who feel that my performance has been inadequate, I believe the group should consider an alternative. If, however, there is an opportunity to identify what I need to do to perform differently, I am more than open to taking corrective action and would prefer to stay in this role. Since this is the group's decision about me, I will excuse myself from the room unless there are questions for me. Please consider assigning someone to guide this discussion and consider the strengths-weaknesses-merge process we've used so often [see Chapter Ten].

Rewarding Functional Behavior

When people stop engaging in dysfunctional behavior and begin to exhibit functional signs—for example, they begin participating, or they bring up issues rather than allow them to simmer—supply a wealth of positive reinforcement.

- Give them more of your attention.
- Give them head nods and smiles.
- Give them the floor when they request it.
- At a subsequent break, consider commenting on their participation.

Lesson Learned

Let's go back to the case study "The Chairman and the COO" that opened this chapter. Recall that the chairman yelled at the COO in front of the executive vice presidents, saying, "That's the stupidest thing I ever heard. It's limited thinking like this that has caused us to be in the situation we're in now!"

Let's ask the question, "What could I as the facilitator have done? What steps could I have taken in conscious prevention, early detection, and clean resolution?"

Conscious Prevention

I did my preparation work and understood that the CEO was new and that the former CEO had been demoted and was now the COO. I did not, however, execute any prevention strategies. To have prevented this dysfunction before the session even started, I could have spoken privately with the COO in advance. As always, I would have remembered to empathize first.

Sample Dialogue: Empathizing with the COO

> *Facilitator:* It speaks volumes that you care so much about the company that
> you have been willing to support the organization in a secondary
> role. During the session, I would appreciate it if you would make it
> a point not to be the first or second person to speak on any issue.
> This will clearly communicate to everyone that you are comfortable
> with not being in the lead role and will give the CEO a chance to
> let his desires be known. You should put your thoughts out there, of
> course, but it might be helpful if you spoke third or fourth rather
> than first. Are you comfortable with this?

These words are somewhat similar to what I would say to a CEO in an executive strategy session. But in this case, because of the issue of prior leadership, it
would have been helpful to share this version with the COO.

Early Detection

I had noticed the unease of the chairman, but I did not address it. After the
first or second display of discomfort, I could have asked the following: "Let's get
some input on what we are hearing. Joe, what do you think? . . . Jane, what about
you? . . . Bob [chairman], your thoughts?" This would have helped the uneasiness to come out in a functional way rather than a dysfunctional way.

Alternatively, during the break that occurred prior to the blowup, I could
have pulled the chairman aside for a brief conversation: "I noticed what I thought
was uneasiness about some of the things that were said. Is there an issue? What
do you think we should do about it? How about if . . ."

Clean Resolution

I had my first chance to address the issue through conscious prevention prior
to the session, but I missed it. I had a second chance through early detection
during the session, but I missed it. Because I missed prevention and missed the
early signs of dysfunction, when it came roaring back, the dysfunction was quite
ugly. I had a much bigger problem because I didn't address it early.

Once the blowup occurred, however, I still could have addressed it in at least
two ways. The first approach is direct and head-on. I could have responded,
"Wow. That was spoken pretty passionately. Help me understand: What do you
think we should be looking at? . . . Why are these things important? . . . Let's
go around the room and see if there are other things like this that we should
consider."

After the round-robin, I would then take a break to meet with the chairman, who in this person's case would have been more than willing to come back and publicly apologize for his behavior toward the COO.

Another way to address this issue is to respond as one would to any unexpected outburst, as described earlier in this chapter: "Wow. That was spoken pretty passionately. I don't know about everyone else, but I'm a little uncomfortable right now. Rather than continue as though nothing has happened, . . ."

Applying the Secrets to Managing Dysfunction

Dysfunctional behavior occurs in numerous personal and professional interactions. The example here focuses on the irate customer.

No matter how good your product and no matter how good your customer service, if you are in business for any reasonable period of time, you will face an irate customer. The customer will be upset because of something that you or your organization did or failed to do. The customer's concern may be valid or invalid; for that moment, to that customer, it doesn't matter.

Address this situation as one would a naysayer. Let's assume that this is a phone call, so the "approach privately" step is already addressed. Therefore, the remaining steps are as follows:

1. Empathize with the symptom.
2. Address the root cause.
3. Get agreement on the solution.

You might empathize with the symptom in a number of ways. The key is that the customer should feel that you understand the pain. This typically takes more than one sentence!

Sample Dialogue: Empathizing with the Customer

Service Rep: If I spent money on a class that didn't deliver what it said it was going to deliver, I would be upset too. Not only would I have wasted my training budget on a class that didn't meet expectations, I would have wasted travel money, and, more important, I would have wasted three days of time that I couldn't get back. I would not be a happy camper.

Once the customer feels that you understand the issue, and not before, you can move on to getting at the root cause and formulating a solution.

Sample Dialogue: Getting at the Root Cause

Service Rep: We certainly need to fix this. I need your help, though. I need to understand what happened that allowed us to get you in a class that wasn't right for you. Would you take a minute to explain to me what you wanted to get out of this class? . . .

OK, I understand that you were looking to learn how to build trust with clients and how to manage your client relationships. What did you see that told you the facilitation training class was the right class for you? . . .

OK, so you read the course description and signed up on the Web. Did one of our relationship managers contact you to confirm the registration? . . .

OK, so you were out of the country during the weeks leading up to the class and didn't have a chance to return the phone calls.

We have gotten to the root cause of the issue. The person signed up for the class over the Web, basing his choice on the course description. Yet judging from the description of what the client needed, we can see that the facilitation class wasn't going to satisfy this client. Our relationship manager would probably have figured this out in the follow-up call, but the follow-up contact was never made because the client was out of the country. Now we can move to getting agreement on a solution.

Sample Dialogue: Agreeing on a Solution

Service Rep: We will gladly refund your money. If we didn't meet your need at all, we don't deserve to be paid. I've gotten an idea, though, that I would love for you to consider. You saw the way our instructors teach: the thing we call PDI—*practical* techniques, *dynamic* instructors, *interactive* throughout? . . .

OK, so you were happy with the instruction and the dynamic class environment; it was just the wrong topic. As I have been listening to you, I realized that we probably had you in the wrong class. Whereas our facilitation class teaches group facilitation techniques, I think we should have had you in our consulting class, which focuses on client relationship management skills, building trust, defining the client's need, and so on. Let me give you a few examples of what is in that course . . .

If it is OK with you, rather than process a refund, we would love to transfer your registration fee to the next consulting class, because it sounds like it would teach the skills you really want. That way, you pay nothing extra, you get the class you want, and we get a satisfied customer. Does that work for you?

Facilitator's Checklist for Managing Dysfunction

☐ Understand what dysfunctional behavior is: *dysfunctional behavior* is any activity by a participant that is consciously or unconsciously a substitution for expressing displeasure with the session content or purpose, the facilitation process, or outside factors. Dysfunctional behavior is a symptom, not a root cause.

☐ Identify potential dysfunction during the preparation stage by learning of the following:

- The concerns of any participant who is not in favor of holding the session

- Participants who perceive that they stand to lose something if the session or project achieves its objectives

- Participants who are not on favorable terms with one another

- Participants who tend to point out problems rather than create solutions

☐ Execute strategies for preventing dysfunction from occurring:

- Assign seats.

- Add ground rules.

- Make sure you interact with particular people.

- Pay close attention to particular reactions.

- Hold informal meetings during breaks.

☐ Recognize the needs of the different communication styles:

- Drive—keep the session fast paced, well planned.

- Influence—give plenty of opportunities for discussion.

- Steadiness—check for agreement; don't put the person on the spot.

- Compliance—set the expectation that detailed analysis will be done outside the session.

☐ To detect dysfunction early, take dysfunction checks by actively and routinely looking for signs of dysfunction:

- Participants who are not speaking

- Participants who complain or object publicly to the group

- Participants who may be complaining or objecting privately to a neighbor through side conversations

- Participants whose outward expressions seem to indicate that they are not buying in

- Participants whose body language seems to indicate uneasiness with the session, such as folded arms, legs crossed, or bodies leaning away from the center of the room

☐ Quickly and routinely resolve dysfunctional behavior:

- Approach the participant privately or generally.

- Empathize with the symptom.

- Address the root cause.

- Get agreement on a solution.

☐ Use specific techniques to deal with the more common dysfunction types:

• Cell phone junkie	• Physical attacker
• Door slammer	• Storyteller
• Dropout	• Topic jumper
• Interrupter	• Verbal attacker
• Late arriver or early leaver	• Whisperer
	• Workaholic
• Loudmouth	• Group: low energy
• Naysayer	• Group: time pressures

☐ When the unexpected happens during a session, such as an emotional outburst, recover with the following steps:

- Request the group's permission to detour from the agenda.

- Facilitate a round-robin for answers to the question, "Given what just happened, what are you experiencing right this minute?"

- Facilitate a second round-robin for answers to the question, "What needs to happen to allow us to proceed?"

- Take a break and meet briefly with the meeting sponsor to ensure that the actions for proceeding are in line with the sponsor's goals.

☐ When one or more participants indicate that you have made a mistake or suggest a change to the process, take the following steps:

- Admit that they may be right.

- Thank them for the suggestion.

- If you agree with the change, make it once you have consulted with the group.

- If you disagree with the change,

  - Give at least one advantage to making the change.

  - Explain why you believe it may be better to leave things as they are.

  - Indicate your willingness to following the group's direction.

  - Ask the group if they agree with the change.

☐ When your role is threatened, it is important to show no defensiveness but instead to use language that focuses on your concern for the group. Consider the following steps:

- Apologize that one or more members are uncomfortable with you in the role.

- Indicate your willingness to step aside.

- Indicate your desire to adjust based on what is needed for the group.

☐ When people stop engaging in dysfunctional behavior and begin to exhibit functional signs, supply a wealth of positive reinforcement.

Exercise Your Skills

Conscious prevention, early detection, and clean resolution are the three keys to effectively managing dysfunction. To be effective at clean resolution, you will need to be able to recognize each of the dysfunctions and know how you would address them should they occur. To exercise your skills, consider taking the following two steps:

- First, read through each of the dysfunctions highlighted in this chapter, paying close attention to what is suggested to do "in the moment." Get to the point where you are confident that you know what action you would take should one of the dysfunctions occur in a meeting you were leading. This first step may require several readings and several weeks to accomplish.
- Then, in your next few meetings in which you are a participant, monitor the group dynamics in the same way you would if you were the facilitator. Identify dysfunctions occurring in the room, and the actions you would take if you were the facilitator.

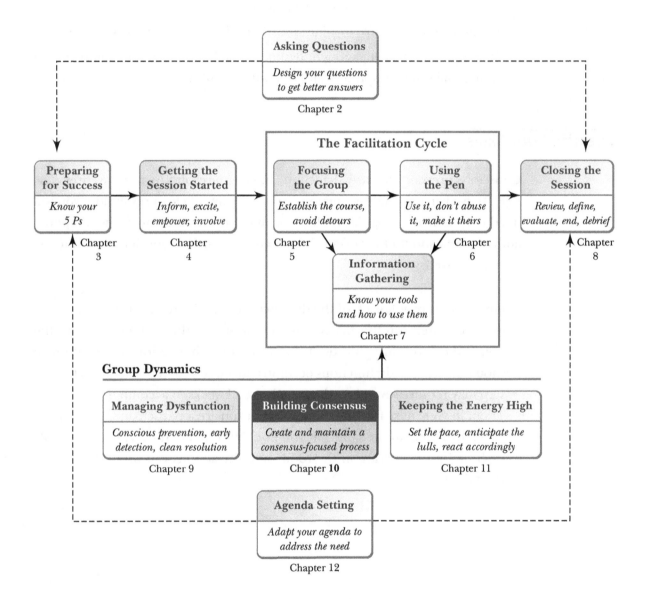

CHAPTER TEN

THE SECRETS TO CONSENSUS BUILDING

Create and Maintain a Consensus-Focused Process

Questions Answered in This Chapter

What is the definition of consensus?

Why might full consensus not be the recommended goal of group decision making?

What are the three reasons people disagree?

How do you address a disagreement in which the argument appears to be irrational?

How do you slow down a conversation to ensure that everyone is getting the facts?

How do you resolve a disagreement that is based on different values or experiences?

CASE STUDY: Consensus on Values

Two companies in the office and plant construction industry, one based principally in Europe and the United States, the other based principally in Australia and Asia, merged to become one of the largest construction companies in the world. Although the organizations had somewhat different cultures, part of the reason for the merger was that they had very similar values and beliefs.

Both organizations recognized the importance of having a set of well-articulated organizational values backed by the definition of desired behaviors that supported those values. A team of managers and executives from both organizations came together for a two-day meeting to merge the values of the two organizations into one set. The meeting was intended to produce two distinct deliverables: (1) consensus around a set of value statements and (2) a series of action plans at the organizational, regional, and individual levels for ensuring that the values were integrated into the organization.

As the meeting progressed, it was very easy to see that despite the differences in organizational cultures, there was considerable commonality among their aspirations and values. The session moved quickly and productively through the various stages of the agenda, until we came to the topic of integrity. Everyone in the room agreed that integrity was indeed "non-negotiable." When it came to discussing the behaviors that resulted from this value, however, there were distinct differences depending significantly on the region of the world in which the participants operated.

I took the team through our consensus building model (discussed in this chapter). We delineated alternative approaches to addressing integrity, identified the strengths and weaknesses of each alternative, and then merged the strengths to create new solutions that combined the key strengths of the original alternatives.

The discussion was very rich. Many of those who operated in some of the less developed countries of the world believed that you have to play the game based on the customs of that country. If providing indirect compensation and generous gifts to decision makers was the business custom of a country, these managers felt that the organization would be reducing its chances of success significantly if it did not play the game. Those who operated in some of the more developed countries, however, felt that the organization needed a definition of integrity that did not change depending on where one worked.

As a result of the discussion, there was a much clearer understanding of issues related to operating as a truly global player. The organization did reach consensus on one definition of integrity and one set of operating behaviors for the entire company. Through the consensus building process, they were able to define the operating behavior in such a way that it honored ethics and transparency while respecting the cultures of different countries.

Did you know that there are only three reasons people disagree? Every disagreement in the world can be classified as either a level 1, level 2, or level 3 disagreement. As facilitators, we need to understand these types of disagreements and the approaches for resolving them. For, unfortunately, if you try to resolve a level 3 disagreement using a level 1 approach, you are likely to fail. Likewise, if you try to resolve a level 1 disagreement using level 2 techniques, your chances of success are also very, very low.

In this chapter, you will learn the three reasons people disagree and four specific techniques for helping a group reach consensus. You will also see the consensus process in action as you follow a sample case through the process of achieving agreement.

Defining Consensus

My experiences have led me to conclude that consensus is a widely misunderstood concept. Many people think that for them to be in consensus regarding a decision, they have to believe that the decision is the best decision. Working with this definition, therefore, they believe that debate must continue until they convince the others or the others convince them.

The implications of this definition of consensus on organizational productivity can be staggering. Allow me to explain by way of an analogy. In the United States, a jury is made up of twelve people. After naming a foreperson, the jury members have only one decision to make. They have to decide whether the defendant is guilty or not guilty. Consider how long this one decision takes: sometimes a few hours, often several days. And, all too often, the process takes so long that they quit and declare a mistrial.

Let's come back to the work environment and consider the hiring process improvement team. They don't have just one decision to make; they have a number of decisions to make about each of the steps in the hiring process and how to make the overall process better. Let's suppose that if there were just two people on the team, and they had to debate until the two of them agreed that every aspect of the solution was the best that it could be, it would take them three days. If you were to add a third person to the team, would it now take five days? Probably not. It would probably take considerably longer, because the discussion couldn't stop until all three agreed on every aspect of the solution. Therefore, let's say that with three people, the process would now take seven days. Then let's add a fourth person and a sixth and an eighth, and so on. By the time you reach a team of ten or twelve members who all have to talk about every aspect of the solution until each one of the group agreed that every part was the absolute best it could be, how long would it take? Several weeks at least, and more likely several months. And quite possibly, like the hung jury, they might never get there!

To avoid the major investment of time and energy that 100 percent agreement on every aspect of a solution would require, SMART facilitators use a different definition of consensus.

Secret #45

The Secret to Understanding Consensus

Consensus means, "I can live with it, and I will support it."

How is this definition different from "I think this is the best solution that it can be?" With consensus, we want everyone in the room to be able to make a statement such as the following.

If I were making this decision on my own, I would not necessarily go in the direction that the group is going. However, I have had the opportunity to express my thoughts, and people have taken the time to understand my view. And though I have been unable to move the majority to my position, I believe I have been heard and my needs have been considered. Therefore, I am willing to support the group's decision now and in the future.

Let's go back to the group of twelve working on the hiring process, and let's assume they have completed their recommendations.

- There may be three or four team members who believe that the team came up with the best solution in every way.
- There may also be two or three who strongly favor the first three recommendations but would prefer to see the last two changed. After listening to their teammates, however, they understood why the last two recommendations are desired by some. They still don't particularly want the last two, but they can certainly live with their being among the recommendations.
- Another two people may think that those last two recommendations are the ones that are going to drive the greatest improvement. They think that the first three recommendations could be made stronger. But after discussion, it was clear that most members of the group wanted to leave them as they were, and these two members did not feel that the changes were essential.
- Despite these different views, all team members agreed that they would fully support all aspects of the plan through implementation. They even indicated that if someone were to ask them, "Do you think this is the best plan that it could be?" they could freely answer, "If it were up to just me to make the decision, I might change a few things. But for success in this organization, we need a plan that everyone can live with and support. I believe this plan will work, and it has my full support. Can we get yours?"

Deciding How to Decide

Early in its work, every facilitated group should choose the method it will use to make decisions. There are several alternatives.

Why Do This?

Why decide how to decide?

Whether you are looking to develop a recommendation, improve a process, resolve an issue, or generate any of a myriad of other group outcomes, at some point the group agrees that its work is done. What defines this agreement? Is it when *all* the heads are nodding at the same time? Or two-thirds of the heads? Or the majority of the heads? Or is it when the leader decides?

By establishing up front what constitutes a decision, the group will know how decisions will be made and typically is able to more effectively and quickly move through the decision-making process.

Leader Decides

The group will discuss the strengths and weaknesses of various alternatives, and the leader will make the final decision.

Leader Holds Veto Rights

The group will come to a decision based on one of the methods that follow, but the leader reserves the right to overrule.

Majority Rule

In some groups, decisions are made by majority rule. Whatever the majority of the participants want, that is the decision that is made. Majority decision making can be quick. It can also lead to less than optimal solutions, however, because not enough time was spent investigating potentially better alternatives. Majority decision making can also result in less effective implementation because there is not full agreement.

Supermajority

With the supermajority, the group debates until a large majority of the participants agree with one alternative. The supermajority target is typically 60, 67, or 75 percent. Although usually not as quick a method as majority rule, use of the supermajority can still lead to less than optimal and less effective solutions for the same reasons as majority rule.

Full Consensus

As described earlier, SMART facilitators define consensus as, "I can live with it, and I will support it." The strength of consensus is that it encourages discussion until we have created solutions that we are all willing to accept. Because we do reach full agreement, consensus typically increases the effectiveness of the implementation. Consensus also poses a major challenge, however. Often a potentially great solution that has the full support of nearly everyone can get watered down significantly because one or two disagree and are allowed to hold the process hostage until they get their way. And even though the watered-down solution gets full agreement, we can end up with a solution that is clearly not the will of the group.

Five-Finger Consensus

I have found five-finger consensus far more helpful to groups than the five decision-making methods I've just described.

The Secret of Five-Finger Consensus

Use five-finger consensus to reach agreement without jeopardizing the quality of a solution that has strong, but not unanimous, support.

Here is how five-finger consensus works:

1. Once an alternative has been proposed and discussed and the group is ready to check for agreement, the facilitator explains that on the count of three, each person should hold up between one and five fingers indicating the level of support for the recommendation on the table.

   5—strongly agree

   4—agree

   3—can see pluses and minuses, but willing to go along with the group

   2—disagree

   1—strongly disagree and can't support

2. In the first vote, if everyone shows a 5, 4, or 3, consensus has been reached, and we can move ahead. If there are any 1s or 2s, those who indicate such are given the opportunity to explain to the rest of the group why they gave the rating and make recommendations to change the alternative in order to make it acceptable to them. The originator of the alternative has the option to make the change or leave the option as it is, and explains the decision to the rest of the group. If changes are made, there is a new first vote. If changes are not made, move on to the second vote.

3. In the second vote, if everyone shows a 5, 4, 3, *or 2,* the decision is made, and we move ahead. Those who give a 2 vote are typically implying, "I don't think this is a good idea, and I want to register my vote that way, but if it is the will of the group, I won't block it." However, if there are any 1s, those who indicate such are given an additional opportunity to explain to the rest of the group why they gave the rating and make recommendations to change the alternative in order to make it acceptable to them. Once more, the originator of the alternative has the option to make the change or leave the option as it is, and explains the decision to the rest of the group. Once more, if changes are made, there is a new first vote. If changes are not made, move on to the final vote.

4. In the final vote, majority rules. The decision is made based on a majority of the participants.

Why Do This? | **Why use five-finger consensus?**

Five-finger consensus encourages the group to listen carefully when there is disagreement and encourages listening carefully twice if necessary. But the approach doesn't allow a solution to be watered down because a few disagree. Although admittedly there may be one or two who don't like the alternative, five-finger consensus helps ensure that everyone is heard, and heard well, and that the will of the group prevails.

Understanding Why People Disagree

Through our work with literally hundreds of groups over the past decade, we at Leadership Strategies have concluded that disagreements can be categorized into three basic types or levels. For simplicity, I will be using examples of disagreements that involve two people. The same principles and techniques are adaptable for disagreements that involve groups as well. Where there is a significant distinction in the techniques for resolving two-way and group disagreements, I will highlight the distinction. The following are the three levels of disagreement:

Level 1: the people involved lack shared information.

Level 2: the people involved have different values or experiences.

Level 3: outside factors are affecting the disagreement.

The Secret to Understanding Disagreement

Disagreements occur because the people involved lack shared information, have different values or experiences, or are affected by outside factors.

Level 1 Disagreement: Lack of Shared Information

In my experience, I have found more times than not that group disagreements are level 1: there is a lack of shared information. Fortunately, level 1 disagreements are also the easiest to resolve.

What Is the Cause?

In a level 1 disagreement, the people disagreeing have not clearly heard or understood each other's alternative and the reasons for supporting it. Level 1 disagreements are often a result of an assumed understanding of what the other person is saying or meaning. Take a look at the sample.

Sample Dialogue: Closing the Home Office

Joe: I've been thinking about this for some time. I think we should close down the home office in Denver and just operate the business out of our three satellite locations in Los Angeles, Chicago, and New York.

Larry: Are you out of your mind? That can't work.

Joe: Sure it can. You said yourself that there is a home office mentality that sometimes forgets that there's a customer. We get rid of the home office, and this problem goes away. We save a whole lot of money too, something we happen to need to do about now.

Larry: No, I don't think so. Joe, we've been partners for some time. But this has to be the craziest idea you've come up with in a while.

Joe: I don't understand why you don't like it.

Larry: Well, first of all, we have a home office because there are certain administrative activities that need to go on. So, genius, are we going to stop billing our customers? And what about legal counsel? Are we going to have each of the field offices have its own? That sounds pretty inefficient to me. And what about all the price breaks we get with central purchasing? Will we end up paying more because the field offices are buying their own stuff? And what about—

Joe: Hold on a second. I'm not sure you're hearing me. I said close down the home office, not decentralize. We still need to centralize certain functions. But let's centralize them in the field. For example, we could have New York take over billing activities and other administrative functions. We could have Los Angeles responsible for HR. Their HR coordinator out there is better than anyone we've ever hired here in Denver. And—

Larry: I get it. You would then have Chicago handle customer service and operations. You may be on to something. We could even offer jobs to those who are willing to make the transfer. By doing all this, we drop the overhead of the fourth office and increase our customer focus at the same time. I like it. But why didn't you say that in the first place?

Joe: I did say it. You just weren't listening. I said I wanted to operate our business out of the three satellite locations. What did you think I meant?

It is clear what Larry thought Joe meant. Larry assumed that the words "close down the home office in Denver and just operate the business out of our three satellite locations" meant that Joe wanted to close Denver and have each of the regions responsible for its own operation. He did not think that Joe meant to continue centralized functions and have each of the field offices responsible for one or more of the functions for the entire business. Once he understood what Joe meant, he quickly agreed.

Did you notice when the tone of the conversation changed? There was a statement made that shifted the entire conversation. People often think it occurred when Joe said, "Hold on a second. I'm not sure you are hearing me." But actually, the transition happened before then. Typically when two people argue, what is happening in the conversation is that each is making statements: talking *at* each other rather than *to* each other. If either party were to step back and begin asking questions, the talking at each other would stop, and listening could begin. Our role as facilitators is to bring this listening about by asking questions.

When did the change in the conversation occur? When Joe said, "I don't understand why you don't like it." Notice that even though it is a statement, it really is an implied question: "Why don't you like it?" Larry responds, and this leads to the recognition that they were not in disagreement at all. They simply didn't understand one another.

We use the term *violent agreement* to describe a level 1 disagreement. The parties really agree, but they don't know it, so they continue to argue. One of the common statements one hears following the resolution of a level 1 disagreement is, "Oh, is *that* what you meant? Why didn't you say that?"

How Is It Solved?

To solve a level 1 disagreement, SMART facilitators use questioning techniques that slow down the conversation to encourage careful listening and comprehension. When the disagreement is due solely to a lack of shared information, the parties quickly learn that they were not in disagreement at all. They were not hearing each other, hearing but not understanding one another, or not sharing relevant information.

In our example, Larry and Joe discovered their violent agreement when Larry began explaining why the suggestion he was hearing wouldn't work. Fortunately, Joe was alert enough to realize that Larry was not hearing the suggestion he was making. Otherwise, this violent agreement could have continued for some time.

Later in this chapter, I will focus on *structured* techniques for solving level 1 disagreements. But before discussing these techniques, let's take a look at the other two levels of disagreement.

Level 2 Disagreement: Different Values or Experiences

Level 2 disagreements are based on different values or experiences. These disagreements are significantly more difficult to address because the disagreement is based on beliefs or experiences that are not shared by all parties. Recall that a level 1 disagreement is resolved as soon as both parties identify the unshared information. In contrast, with a level 2 disagreement, once the parties identify the unshared experiences or values, they are just *starting* on the road to resolution!

What Is the Cause?

A level 1 disagreement is based on a lack of shared information, but a level 2 disagreement is quite different. In a level 2 disagreement, the parties have fully heard and understood one another's alternatives, but they have had different experiences or hold different values that result in their preferring one alternative over another.

Political parties often have level 2 disagreements. The parties typically understand each other's platforms and initiatives. They often just fundamentally disagree about how a country, state, city, township, or tribe should be run. In Australia, for example, the Labour Party values social democracy and ensuring social justice, especially for low-income earners. Therefore, members tend to believe that the government should intervene to provide more equitable outcomes. In contrast, the Liberal Party values social conservatism and encouraging a free market. In general, they tend to support business expansion and a limited welfare safety net.

Marriages are another arena for level 2 disagreements. My wife and I agree on a lot of things, but every so often, we have significant level 2 disagreements.

Sample Dialogue: Planning the Family Vacation

Sherry:	I've been thinking about our vacation for next year, and I've got it! There's a ten-day tour of Italy that takes us to eight cities, including Rome, Venice, Tuscany, and Florence. It's perfect. What do you think?
Michael:	That does sound like a wonderful tour. But I have really been looking forward to going to the beach this year.
Sherry:	Oh, come on, snookums. [This is what my wife calls me when she really wants something.] Let's go to Italy. We haven't been there before.
Michael:	Oh, sweetheart, darling, baby *(in my best impression of the deep baritone of singer Barry White)*. Let's go to the beach. It'll be quiet and restful.
Sherry:	Now, Michael, you've been out of town a lot this year, which has left me home to do both my job and take care of the kids solo, so we really should do what I want to do. Let's do Italy.
Michael:	You're right, Sherry. I *have* been out of town a lot this year, and it has worn me out. I really need a break. Let's go to the beach.
Sherry:	No, we are going to Italy.
Michael:	No, we are going to the beach.
Sherry:	Italy!
Michael:	Beach!
Sherry:	Italy!

Clearly, my wife loves to travel. She values vacations that allow her to see many things and have many new and different experiences. For her, the ten-day, eight-city tour is ideal. I, however, live out of a suitcase for major parts of the year. The last thing I want to do when I am on vacation is to pack every morning to go visit another city. *(That sounds like what I do when I'm working!)* I want the quiet, sandy beach. I want to be able to sleep late most mornings, get up when I want to get up, and do nothing if I want to do nothing.

Note that we understand each other's alternatives and reasons for supporting them. I understand that my wife values new and varied experiences, and she understands that I value rest and relaxation—a classic level 2 disagreement.

How Is It Solved?

The key to solving a level 2 disagreement is to isolate the most important underlying values and create alternatives that combine the values.

In the previous example, my wife and I have both taken positions. If the argument stays at the position level (Italy versus the beach), one of us is going to win (most likely my wife!), and one of us is going to lose. The real issue isn't the positions, however, but the reasons for supporting them. If, in consensus building, we can get beyond the positions and focus on the real issues, we may be able to create solutions that satisfy everyone's most important needs.

Think of the disagreement much like an iceberg. The tip of the iceberg—the part you see—is the position. But what is below the surface is what really matters, and these are the critical issues that we have to identify. How do SMART facilitators identify the key underlying values? They ask such questions as, "What benefit do you get from doing this?" and "Why is that important to you?" By working with the answers, SMART facilitators can help identify solutions that satisfy the key interests of, and provide key benefits to, all parties.

As an aside, whereas it appears that my wife and I are arguing about where to go on vacation this year, if you lift up the cover on this argument, you will see that the disagreement is really about the *purpose* of vacation. For my wife, the purpose of vacation is excitement—going to new places, experiencing new things. For me, the purpose of vacation is regeneration—having a chance to relax and recharge. Until we come to agreement on the purpose of vacation, we will have this disagreement every single year. (Trust me—I know from personal experience.)

Level 3 Disagreement: Outside Factors

Level 3 disagreements are by far the most difficult to resolve. Because the disagreement is based on factors that don't relate to the alternatives, resolution cannot be achieved by discussing them.

What Is the Cause?

Whereas a level 1 disagreement is based on a lack of shared information and a level 2 disagreement is based on different experiences or values, a level 3 disagreement is based on personality, past history, or other outside factors that have nothing to do with the alternatives. Sometimes a disagreement is not at all related to the discussion. Consider the example that follows.

Sample Dialogue: The Nominations Committee

Tom: One of the things I think we can do to improve our board governance is to add one or two board members with strong financial backgrounds. This way, we can better understand the financial ramifications of some of the proposals we're considering.

Frank: That won't work.

Tom: Sure it will; we just need to make sure we get the right people.

Frank: No, it won't work.

Facilitator: You may be right, Frank. Please explain why you believe it won't work.

Frank: It just won't work.

Facilitator: OK . . . Well, how might we improve it?

Frank: There's no way to improve it. It just won't work.

Facilitator: Help us understand, Frank. Why are you so convinced it won't work?

Frank: It just won't work. *He* thought of it. It won't work!

An extreme example to be sure. Frank clearly doesn't want to have anything to do with this idea, and the reason doesn't seem to be related to the idea. As it turns out, Frank had learned some time ago that when he was nominated to the board, Tom was one of the few people who spoke against the nomination. Since then, any suggestion made by Tom couldn't possibly work, at least as far as Frank was concerned.

A disagreement based on personality or past history (level 3) often calls for a deeper intervention and cannot be resolved in the typical facilitated session. It is therefore important that you determine the source of the disagreement as quickly as possible to avoid wasting time.

How Is It Recognized?

Level 3 disagreements tend to be irrational. The arguments in a level 3 disagreement don't seem to make logical sense; in many cases, the arguer doesn't offer *any* rationale for the position (as noted in our example). In addition, in a level 3 disagreement, one or more of the parties show no interest in resolving the disagreement, considering alternatives, or convincing the other side. Because the disagreement is not based on the issue, there is little desire to focus on the issue!

How Is It Solved?

A level 3 disagreement cannot be solved by an analysis of the issues. Therefore, SMART facilitators take the issue to a higher source.

The Secret to Resolving a Level 3 Disagreement

Take the issue to a higher source for resolution.

If you are in a facilitated session when an important level 3 disagreement is discovered, consider the following:

- Take a break. Meet with the parties together privately to indicate to them that you do not believe that the issue can be solved in the session.
- Seek agreement to go together to a higher source for resolution outside the session. In essence, let a higher-level person in the organization make the decision by having both parties go to that person together to explain the issue.

Issues based on personality or past history typically require more time than the group has agreed to give, or that you can give, depending on your contractual arrangement. Therefore, avoid attempting level 3 resolution unless the session was specifically designed for that purpose! Conflict resolution sessions are designed specifically to bring parties together to address level 3 issues. Although conflict resolution is beyond the scope of this book, level 3 conflict resolution sessions should, at a minimum, include the steps shown in Table 10.1.

TABLE 10.1   CONFLICT RESOLUTION STEPS.

1.	Give an opportunity for each party individually to identify and speak about the various issues, concerns, past actions, and present situations that have negatively impacted working together
2.	Gain agreement that a better working partnership is desired by all parties
3.	Identify the benefits of a better working partnership to each party individually and to all parties collectively
4.	Gain agreement by all parties that all important issues, concerns, past actions, and present situations have been identified
5.	Provide an interactive presentation and discussion of best practices for working together (this step brings outside insights on partnerships into the room)
6.	Develop a set of strategies and partnering principles that will govern how all parties will interact to address past issues, prevent future issues, and resolve issues should they occur
7.	Agree on a method for monitoring and intentionally making adjustments along the way

Which Level Is This?

Take a look at the scenario that follows. Pat and Chris work for the same organization. Pat is a manager in human resources, and Chris works in operations in one of the field offices. They are the first from their organization to attend a facilitation training course. As you read the scenario, decide if it is a level 1, 2, or 3 disagreement.

Sample Dialogue: The Training Course Disagreement

Pat: I think this training course is excellent. The methodology is sound, the way it is taught is interactive, and the techniques can bring results in a wide range of situations; in total, this stuff will make us more effective. I think everyone in our organization should take this course.

Chris: Everyone? That's a little extreme, don't you think? I could see having key managers take the course. At least they will actually have an opportunity to do something with it.

Pat: No; we can't limit this to managers. Everyone needs these skills. Everyone should take the course.

Chris: This is a business, Pat. You folks in HR sometimes forget this. We can't take everyone away from work for stuff they might not use. Only key managers.

Pat: I know this is a business, Chris. I'm not stupid. If you folks in the field were just more open to empowering your people, you might get better than mediocre results.

It looks like Pat and Chris are well on their way to a bitter argument. What started out as a friendly, enthusiastic comment to a colleague seems to have transformed somewhere along the way into a deep philosophical disagreement that has gotten quite personal.

Although this is a fictitious scenario, it is typical of disagreements that happen frequently in business, community, and personal interactions around the world. SMART facilitators can constructively address such disagreements because they understand the three levels of disagreement and techniques for addressing each level.

What type of disagreement did Pat and Chris have?

Level 3?

Given the tone at the end, one could easily decide that it is a level 3 disagreement. The tone has become harsh and tempers appear ready to surge. Recall, however, that the two signs of a level 3 disagreement are irrational logic regarding the issues at hand and a lack of commitment to reaching agreement. Both

Pat and Chris appear to have reasonable arguments ("Everyone needs these skills" versus "We can't take everyone away from work for stuff they might not use"). In addition, they each seem to be attempting to convince the other of the validity of his or her position. We conclude, therefore, that this is not a level 3 disagreement.

Level 2 or Level 1?

This scenario certainly *sounds* as though it could be a level 2 disagreement. Whereas Pat seems to value disseminating basic skills throughout the organization, Chris seems to value minimizing disruption to the organization's day-to-day operation by training only those who really need the skills.

Yet, as you will see, this very easily could be a level 1 disagreement. Pat and Chris think they understand each other's alternatives, but they may find they don't understand them at all.

Filling Your Toolbox of Consensus Building Techniques

As described earlier, if you conclude that a disagreement is level 3, take the issue to a higher source for decision making. Once you have ruled out level 3 as the disagreement type, however, you should assume that the disagreement is level 1 and apply appropriate consensus building strategies to ensure that the parties all understand one another. If level 1 techniques do not resolve the disagreement, then you can conclude that it is a level 2 disagreement and apply level 2 strategies.

There are several techniques for achieving consensus. In the remainder of this chapter, I will examine four of the most common techniques. Figure 10.1 shows the relationships among them.

1. Delineation
2. Strengths and weaknesses
3. Merge
4. Weighted scoring

Delineation

After eliminating outside factors as the source of the disagreement, you will want to take the steps to determine if it is a level 1 disagreement. In essence, you want to make sure each party clearly hears the other's alternatives. How do you do it? SMART facilitators use a process called *delineation*.

FIGURE 10.1   CONSENSUS BUILDING STRATEGIES.

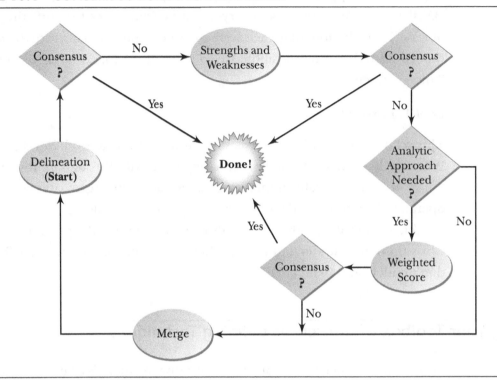

Secret #49

The Secret to Resolving a Level 1 Disagreement

Ask questions that delineate the alternatives.

Delineation has six steps:

1. Start with agreement.
2. Confirm the source of the disagreement.
3. Identify the alternatives under discussion.
4. Ask each party specific delineating questions: how much, how long, who is involved, what is involved.
5. Summarize the information.
6. Take a consensus check.

Step 1: Start with Agreement

Starting with agreement helps both parties see that they already have something in common. This initial agreement can serve as a bridge for constructing the final solution.

Sample Dialogue: Starting with Agreement

Facilitator: Let me make sure I'm understanding what I'm hearing. You both seem to agree that this is a valuable course; is that right?

Pat: Oh yeah.

Chris: Sure, I can agree with that.

Step 2: Confirm the Source of the Disagreement

Identifying the source of the disagreement shows the parties that they are not far apart, despite the fact that the discussion may have become somewhat strained.

Sample Dialogue: Confirming the Source of the Disagreement

Facilitator: Where you seem to disagree is on who should take the course; is that right?

Pat: Yes.

Chris: That's right.

Step 3: Identify the Alternatives Under Discussion

Once you have confirmed the source of the disagreement, you will then identify the alternatives that have been discussed. If, for example, there are two alternatives, create a two-column chart and label the columns with the name of each alternative. If there are more than two alternatives, create as many columns as you have alternatives.

Sample Dialogue: Identifying the Alternatives Under Discussion

Facilitator: So Pat, you are saying everyone should take the course.

Pat: That's right. *(Facilitator labels the first column "Everyone.")*

Facilitator: And Chris, you are saying something different?

Chris: Yes; I think key managers only should take the class. *(Facilitator labels the second column "Key Managers Only.")*

Step 4: Ask Each Party Specific Delineating Questions

For each alternative, you should direct specific questions to the supporter of the alternative and record the responses on the flip chart. The questions should result in the group's knowing the answers to the following questions:

- How much will it cost?
- How long will it take?
- Who is involved?
- What is involved?

Sample Dialogue: Asking Each Party Specific Delineating Questions

Facilitator:	Pat, you said everyone would take the course. How many people is that?
Pat:	All five hundred of our employees.
Facilitator:	Would each one take the full three-day course?
Pat:	Yes, that's right.
Facilitator:	How many people would be in each class?
Pat:	I understand that the vendor permits up to sixteen people per class. So let's assume that we will have fourteen to sixteen people per class.
Facilitator:	So to accommodate all five hundred people, does that mean there will be about thirty-five classes?
Pat:	That sounds right.
Facilitator:	How would people be assigned to particular classes? Would you go department by department, have people sign up when available, or use some other method?
Pat:	I would have people sign up when they were available.
Facilitator:	What are the out-of-pocket costs for the class?
Pat:	I think the vendor charges $10,000 per class. We would use our facilities, so there would be no out-of-pocket costs for this. There would not be travel costs or any other major expenses.
Facilitator:	And how often would you offer the class?
Pat:	Probably two classes per month.
Facilitator:	Well, that gives us a pretty good idea of how that would work. Now Chris, you said that you were for having only key managers take the class. How many people would that be?
Chris:	Eighty key managers.
Facilitator:	Who would choose the eighty?
Chris:	The executive team would select the eighty. But for the most part, I think it would be all the vice presidents, directors, and managers who have other managers reporting to them.
Facilitator:	Would they also take the three-day course?
Chris:	Yes, they would.
Facilitator:	Would you also have fourteen to sixteen people per class?
Chris:	Yes.
Facilitator:	So to get the eighty key managers trained, would that be five classes?
Chris:	No, I think we would need seven. We would schedule each manager for one of the first five classes, but I know that we would need at least two makeup classes for managers who missed the first round.
Facilitator:	Would the out-of-pocket costs be the same?
Chris:	Yes, $10,000 would be right.
Facilitator:	And how often would you offer the class?

Chris:	Probably one class per month.
Facilitator:	OK, I think I've gotten all that down.

Step 5: Summarize the Information

After getting the details for each alternative, summarize the key points at the bottom of the flip chart, as shown in Figure 10.2.

Sample Dialogue: Summarizing the Information

Facilitator:	So let's summarize the information we've learned. With the key managers alternative, we would have eighty people trained, it would take about seven months, and we would have about $70,000 in out-of-pocket costs. For the alternative in which we train everyone in the organization, we would have five hundred people trained, and it would take eighteen months at a cost of $350,000.

Step 6: Take a Consensus Check

Once you have delineated and summarized each alternative, check to determine if consensus has been reached. If consensus has been reached, you will be able to move on. If consensus has not been reached, you will want to move to the next consensus building technique.

Sample Dialogue: Taking a Consensus Check

Facilitator:	I know that we've talked only about the logistical and cost details without looking at some of the other issues. But it would be helpful to get a feel for what people are thinking at this point. Given the

FIGURE 10.2 RESULTS FROM DELINEATION.

Everyone	Key Managers Only
500 people	80 people
Sign-up when available	Executives select managers
3-day class	3-day class
14–16/class	14–16/class
35 classes	7 classes
2 classes/month	1 class/month
$10,000/class	$10,000/class
500 people	80 people
18 months	7 months
$350,000	$70,000

information we've talked about so far, how many people would be in favor of the first alternative, having everyone trained? . . . How many would be in favor of the second alternative, having only key managers trained? Well, it is clear we do not have consensus yet.

Why Do This?	**Why delineate the alternatives?**
	Delineation encourages people to listen to each other. When you delineate the alternatives, you slow down the conversation and ensure that everyone understands the alternatives under consideration. When done well, delineation dispels any assumptions that people may be making.

Key Points in Delineation

There are several points to remember when delineating alternatives:

- Prior to the facilitator's stepping in, Pat and Chris were talking *at* each other. The facilitator used a simple technique for getting Pat and Chris to listen. The facilitator took control of the conversation and then directed all the questions to one person, Pat. This encouraged Chris to be quiet and listen. Then the facilitator turned and directed all the questions to Chris, and it was Pat's turn to listen.
- When asking the delineation questions (step 4), rather than ask the direct question (for example, "How much does this alternative cost?"), instead ask the questions that provide the information needed to answer the direct question. For example, when the facilitator wanted to know the total cost of the alternative, the facilitator first asked the questions that would help the person figure out the number of classes needed and the cost of each class. This made it much easier to figure out the total cost.
- Note that the delineation questions focus on facts only. There are no evaluation questions (for example, "Why is that important?") during this stage.
- Consider waiting until you have gathered information for all alternatives before summarizing. If you summarize following each alternative, participants tend to focus on trying to ensure that their alternative "beats" the summary for the other alternatives.

Recall that delineation is designed to provide the information needed to resolve level 1 disagreements. Could this issue with Pat and Chris have been a level 1 disagreement? Certainly. For example, the discussion could have gone as follows:

Sample Dialogue: Discovering a Level 1 Disagreement

Facilitator: Pat, you said everyone would take the course. How many people is that?

Pat: All five hundred of our employees.

Facilitator: Would each one take the full three-day course?

Pat: No. I would want the vendor to create a special one-day class for our people so they wouldn't have to spend so much time away from work.

Chris: A one-day course? Why didn't you say that? I have no problem with that.

In this case, Pat and Chris would have been in violent agreement. They were in agreement but didn't know it. Chris had assumed that Pat wanted everyone to take a three-day course as they had. When Pat said it would be a one-day course, Chris was relieved. If the disagreement is truly level 1, delineation will likely resolve it by encouraging participants to take the time to fully understand one another's alternatives.

Strengths and Weaknesses

If consensus has not been reached through delineation, identify the *strengths and weaknesses* of each alternative.

Step 1: Identify the Strengths

In delineation, you focused on just the supporter of each alternative. When identifying strengths and weaknesses, however, the entire group is involved.

Sample Dialogue: Identifying the Strengths

Facilitator: Now that Pat and Chris have delineated the alternatives, let's all identify the strengths and weaknesses of each one. This will help us better understand the alternatives and the reasons for supporting them. Let's start with the first alternative, having everyone trained. Think about this alternative compared to the other. This alternative has unique strengths over the other one. There are particular benefits to this alternative that the other one doesn't have. Let's list them. What are the strengths of having everyone trained? . . .

What about the second alternative, having only key managers trained? What are the particular strengths of this alternative?

Step 2: Identify the Weaknesses

Once the group has identified the strengths of each alternative, have the group discuss the weaknesses of each alternative. The results of both comparisons are shown in Figure 10.3.

FIGURE 10.3 RESULTS FROM STRENGTHS AND WEAKNESSES.

Everyone	Key Managers Only
Strengths	Strengths
Common language	Less expensive
Everyone benefits	Completed quicker
Skills throughout the organization	Less time away from work
	Training focused on those who need it
Weaknesses	Weaknesses
More expensive	Focuses only on higher levels
Takes longer	in the organization
More time away from the company	Skills and language not shared

Step 3: Take a Consensus Check

Once the group has identified the strengths and weaknesses of each alternative, check to determine if consensus has been reached. If consensus has been reached, you will be able to move on. If consensus has not been reached, you will want to move to the next consensus building strategy.

Why Do This?	**Why use strengths and weaknesses in consensus building?**
	Recall that a level 2 disagreement is based on different experiences or values. *When you ask people for the strengths of an alternative, their responses typically represent the values they hold that result in their preferring one alternative over the other.* By asking for the strengths, you are actually requesting that people tell you about what they value.
	For example, those who prefer the "everyone" alternative place greater value on common language and everyone's benefiting. Those who prefer the "key managers only" alternative place greater value on saving dollars and limiting time away from the operation.
	Even if participants do not reach consensus at this stage, identifying these underlying values will give the group a clear basis for moving forward.

Key Points in Strengths and Weaknesses

The following are points to remember when using the strengths and weaknesses technique.

- It's very important to identify the strengths of all alternatives first before discussing the weaknesses. This method gives "value" to each alternative before the participants "devalue" either through the discussion of weaknesses.
- For many disagreements, especially when there are only two alternatives, the weaknesses of one alternative are equivalent to the strengths of the competing alternative. Notice in our example how the weaknesses of the "everyone" alternative reflect the strengths of the "key managers only" alternative. Once the group identifies this relationship, you can save time discussing the weaknesses.

Quick Tip!

If there are only two people involved in a disagreement, have them give the strengths of the alternative they oppose. This approach encourages active listening and helps the parties see the other side. The supporter of each alternative then adds any additional strengths that the detractor may have missed.

Merge

If the group does not reach consensus through strengths and weaknesses, the next technique SMART facilitators use is *merge*. Through merging, the group creates a third alternative that combines the key strengths of the original alternatives.

Secret #50

The Secret to Resolving a Level 2 Disagreement

Create a new option that combines the key strengths of the original alternatives.

To resolve a disagreement based on values or experiences (level 2), take the following steps:

1. Identify the key strengths of each alternative.
2. Create one or more new alternatives that combine the key strengths.
3. Delineate the top alternative.
4. Take a consensus check.

Step 1: Identify Key Strengths

Start the merge process by identifying the most important strengths of each alternative.

Sample Dialogue: Identifying Key Strengths

Facilitator: Now that we have identified the strengths and weaknesses of each alternative, let's see if we can use this information to help us come to consensus. For those who prefer the first alternative, would you raise your hand? I'm going to read through each of these strengths. When I'm done, I would like for you to tell me which are the one or two most important strengths. *(Read through the strengths; place an asterisk next to the one or two most important identified by the group.)*

For those who prefer the second alternative, let's do the same.

Step 2: Create One or More New Alternatives

Have the group focus on the key strengths to create one or more alternatives that combine the strengths.

Sample Dialogue: Creating New Alternatives

Facilitator: Is there a way to create a new alternative that combines these strengths? Is there an alternative that is . . . *(Reads the strengths and draws a single circle around all the key strengths, as shown in Figure 10.4)?*

Pat: Chris, I can see how having only the key managers take the class limits the time away from work. But I would still want everyone to be exposed to the skills. What do you think of having managers hold a two- to three-hour briefing for the members of their staff to focus on the skills they learned in the workshop?

Chris: That can work, especially if we can get the vendor to develop a briefing packet for the managers to use.

Facilitator: I've written that alternative. Are there other alternatives we should consider?

FIGURE 10.4   RESULTS FROM MERGING.

Everyone	Key Managers Only
Strengths	Strengths
Common language*	Less expensive*
Everyone benefits	Completed quicker
Skills throughout the organization*	Less time away from work*
	Training focused on those who need it

Step 3: Delineate the Top Alternative

Have the group select the new alternative with the most promise and delineate it.

Sample Dialogue: Selecting the Top Alternative for Delineation

Facilitator: Of these additional alternatives, is there one in particular that we might focus on first?

Chris: I think having the managers brief the rest of the staff is the way to go. It focuses the training on the most important group and provides a means for getting the training communicated throughout our organization.

Facilitator: Other thoughts? We seem to have strong consensus around the briefing approach. So let's delineate this alternative to make sure we all understand how it would work.

Step 4: Take a Consensus Check

Once the group has delineated the merged alternative, check to determine if consensus has been reached. If consensus has been reached, you will be able to move on. If consensus has not been reached, you will want to move to the next consensus building strategy.

Why Do This?	**Why use the merge strategy to reach consensus?**
	I have found that the merge strategy is a superb technique for getting people to think about creative solutions to solving problems. Whereas the strengths and weaknesses process helps you identify values, the merge strategy gets people focused on coming up with solutions that combine the most important values. Rather than promoting compromise, the merge strategy typically results in creative solutions on which all parties can agree.

Key Points in Merge

The following are points to remember when using the merge technique.

- Through merge, the group creates an alternative that combines the key values of the participants. We typically use the delineate–strengths and weaknesses–merge process in sequence. You may find, however, that the group is ready to take a shortcut by jumping from delineation to creating new alternatives right away.
- Be sure to delineate the new alternative before assuming consensus. The delineation will ensure that all participants understand how the new alternative will work.

CASE STUDY: Improving Customer Delivery Times

Charlie Tombazian is currently president of Innovative Strategies LLC, a management consulting firm based in Scottsdale, Arizona. He shares the following story, which took place during the time that he was vice president of a Fortune 200 technology distributor.

I facilitated a group made up of two teams that had been in conflict with one another over the past nine months. The sales and marketing team from our largest field office had lodged several complaints during this period that our integration center team (operations) at our corporate headquarters was not getting their orders for customers built and delivered on a timely basis. Until this meeting, the sales and marketing team had taken no responsibility for how they might be contributing to the problems, only expressing confusion and concern over how poor the timeliness of delivery had been.

After interviewing key members of both teams and realizing we might be headed for a session filled with contention and finger-pointing, I used the building consensus process I learned from Michael Wilkinson at the annual conference of the International Association of Facilitators in Fort Worth, Texas.

The session went something like this. After introductions, I defined consensus as being 100 percent commitment to support the group's decision, and explained we wouldn't have consensus if, after open and honest discussion, anyone in the group was unable to make that commitment. Once the group nodded their understanding and acceptance of this definition, I began by going over the agenda and asked the group if the agenda would achieve what they wanted to accomplish. Once a few items were clarified or added, everyone agreed we had consensus, so I moved to the next step in the consensus process, explaining that people disagree for essentially three reasons.

While I adapted the reasons using my own terminology, they are essentially the same: task orientation differences (what we are doing, the information included, and what we are trying to accomplish), process orientation differences (how we are going to work on it), and personality differences (cultural, gender, experience, values, attitudes). I stated that it was fair game to address differences in the first two categories, but under no uncertain terms were we going to spend time on personality differences. If personality issues did surface, I would take them offline between the people involved. I completed this point by stating that we would focus on the problem and opportunity, not the individual. Once there was consensus acceptance of this parameter for the session, I moved to the next step.

I used the delineation approach, which begins by building a foundation of agreement by asking the teams to list the facts of our lack of timely delivery with which they could all agree. After making an extensive list, we validated together the fact there was much the teams agreed on. This was a very positive and energizing step for the two teams, since most of their dealings to this point had been negative and contentious. This step, combined with the previous one, thrust the teams headlong into a discussion of the problem and opportunity with a very collaborative spirit. It was clear to me at this point that once the emotion was taken out of the interaction, the individuals could really work toward solving the problem and capitalizing on the opportunity. Had we started the process with the teams' differences and problems,

I would bet a paycheck things wouldn't have been nearly as productive. This was a great lesson for me as a facilitator; agreement can be very energizing!

Delineation then continued with clearly identifying where the two teams disagreed. A list was made and then the sources of their disagreement were identified by me soliciting the teams' observations about the list of disagreements. Individuals from both teams concluded that their differences resulted from differences in the team's perspective of the order and inventory control process. As is so often the case, people in a particular function have good visibility into the part of the process they deal with, but not so clear visibility into the parts of the process they do not directly interact with. When the order and inventory management process was mapped on a wall from beginning to end, the teams quickly saw where the breakdowns were and where mutual opportunities to improve the process existed.

We finished the delineation step by listing the alternative solutions for some process improvements, making certain there were plenty of alternatives to select from by breaking the two teams into smaller teams made up of members representing both sales and marketing and integration center (operations). They were charged with reporting out their solutions. As each team reported out, only new solutions not covered by a previous breakout group were listed. I checked for consensus by asking if there were enough good solutions to choose from, to which the group signaled not only their agreement but their delight at having come to this point so quickly and positively.

Next we promptly identified the strengths and weaknesses of each alternative, and even though there was some debate, I didn't dwell on the differences too much. This led right into being able to create a "merge" list of those solutions that incorporated the strengths and potential positive outcomes from the alternative solutions. Again, the group could see that one or two solutions were emerging that made the most sense. But it was only after going through this logical and unemotional process that they could more clearly envision and embrace the solutions to their problems.

We moved on to the selection of two best solutions and then to the development of an action plan to develop and implement the solutions selected. Owners for the various actions were determined and agreed to, and the final step put a timetable to the actions listed. This entire process took about five hours and included a thirty-minute break for lunch.

This situation showed me the true power of the consensus building process—in particular, starting with the general reasons why people disagree, taking personality differences off the table, and building from what people can agree on, rather than starting with and focusing on their differences. I sincerely appreciate the tool Michael provided me, and continue to use it in my facilitation our customers and suppliers.

Weighted Scoring

The merge technique is often adequate for resolving level 2 disagreements. In some cases, however, a more analytical approach is needed for assessing alternatives.

The Secret to Using Weighted Scoring

Secret #51

Score by criterion, starting with the alternative with the most favorable score.

You can use the five steps of the *weighted scoring* technique when structured comparisons and numerical values can help the team reach consensus:

1. Define the criteria.
2. Establish weights for the criteria.
3. Score the alternatives.
4. Apply weights to the scores.
5. Take a consensus check.

Step 1: Define the Criteria

Start weighted scoring by having the team define the criteria that will be used for evaluating the alternatives.

Sample Dialogue: Defining the Criteria

Facilitator: We will be using the weighted scoring technique to help us evaluate these alternatives. There are three major steps in this process. First, we decide what criteria we will use. Then we score the alternatives across the criteria. Finally, we apply weights to the scores to arrive at a final weighted score for each alternative. Let's go through these steps one at a time starting with selecting our criteria.

If we were purchasing a car, there are certain criteria we would use to decide whether to buy one car over another. For example, location of the dealer might be a criterion. What else might be criteria for a car purchase? . . . For our issue related to how best to implement the facilitation training course, we need criteria as well. Given our two alternatives, how will we determine which of them is best? What criteria might we use to determine whether one alternative is better than the other?

Step 2: Establish Weights for the Criteria

The next step is to define the weights for each of the criteria, as shown in Figure 10.5.

Sample Dialogue: Establishing Weights for the Criteria

Facilitator: We've just identified the criteria, so our next step is to determine the importance of each one. This will help us better assess the

FIGURE 10.5   CRITERIA AND WEIGHTS.

Criteria	Weight
Cost	H
Time	L
Improved Skills	H
Lost Work Hours	M
Employee Morale	M

alternatives so that we can reach the best alternative for this situation. All criteria are not the same; some are more important than others. Take a look at the criteria list. Of the items listed, which is of highest importance? I'm going to label this one with an *H*. Are there any others as high as this one? Which is of lowest importance? I'm going to label this one with an *L*. Are there any others as low as this one? Is it OK to label the others as *M* for medium?

Step 3: Score the Alternatives

With the weights and criteria defined, the team is now ready to score the alternatives across the criteria. Figure 10.6 illustrates the results of this step.

Sample Dialogue: Scoring the Alternatives

Facilitator: We have just finished identifying and ranking the criteria. Now we will use the criteria to rate each alternative. This will allow us to look at our alternatives against the needs of the organization. Let's do this one criterion at a time. We will score on a 0 to 10 scale, with 10 being the most favorable. We will give a score of 10 to the alternative that is most favorable in that criterion. The other alternative will be assigned a score based on its relationship to the alternative that received the score of 10. If it is half as good, the other alternative will receive a 5. If the other alternative is 80 percent as good, it will receive a score of 8.

Let's look at this first criterion. Which alternative should receive the 10? What score should the other alternative get relative to this one?

FIGURE 10.6   SCORING ALTERNATIVES.

(Score 0–10, 10 = Most favorable)			
Criteria	Weight	Everyone	Managers
Cost	H	2	10
Time	L	4	10
Improved Skills	H	10	3
Lost Work Hours	M	3	10
Employee Morale	M	10	3

Step 4: Apply Weights to the Scores

The next step is to calculate the weighted scores by assigning a value to each weight and multiplying the value by the score. The result of this step appears in Figure 10.7.

FIGURE 10.7   WEIGHTED SCORING.

(Score 0–10, 10 = Most favorable; weighted score in bold)			
Criteria	Weight	Everyone	Managers
Cost	H = 4	2 / 8	10 / 40
Time	L = 1	4 / 4	10 / 10
Improved Skills	H = 4	10 / 40	3 / 12
Lost Work Hours	M = 2	3 / 10	10 / 20
Employee Morale	M = 2	10 / 10	3 / 2
		72	84

Sample Dialogue: Applying Weights to the Scores

Facilitator: We have just finished rating the alternatives against the criteria. Now we will calculate a weighted score for each alternative. This will allow us to identify which alternative best meets our criteria.

We typically translate the high-medium-low criteria ratings into the following values: lows are given a value of 1; mediums are twice as important as lows, so they are given a value of 2; and highs are twice as important as mediums, so they are given a value of 4. Are these weight values appropriate?

Now let's calculate the weighted score for each alternative by multiplying the score by the criterion weight and adding down.

Step 5: Take a Consensus Check

Once the group has calculated the weighted scores, check to determine if consensus has been reached. If consensus has been reached, you will be able to move on. If consensus has not been reached, it may be time to take a break. See the section "Knowing When to Move On."

Key Points in Weighted Scoring

There are several points to remember when using the weighted scoring technique.

- Criteria
  - Use your PeDeQs with an example (see Chapter Five) to get the team started on defining the criteria.
  - Make sure each of the criteria is unique and without overlap to avoid double counting a criterion. For example, in the training course case study, it may not be appropriate to have both "improved skills" and "long-term impact on company," as much of the long-term impact will come from the improved skills.
- Weights
  - Note that when asking for the criteria weights, ask first for which criteria should be weighted the highest, then ask for the lowest, then get the others. This approach is preferable because weights are relative to one another. You should review the entire list of criteria before assigning the weight to a single one.
  - Avoid starting at the first criterion and assigning weights one at a time. You will not know whether to give the first one a high, medium, or low until you compare it to the other criteria.
  - Delay translating the high, medium, and low into numbers until after the alternatives have been scored. The delay prevents any highly analytical team members from calculating scores ahead of time in an effort to ensure that their favorite alternative scores higher.
- Scoring
  - Consider scoring from 0 to 10, with 10 being the "most favorable" score. The term *most favorable* should be used instead of *high,* as "high" is not always good. For example, going back to the case study, if we were scoring the two

alternatives against the criterion of cost, if we gave the 10 to the one with the *high* cost, then the "everybody" alternative would get the 10. If we use the term *most favorable,* however, and give the 10 to the one with the most favorable cost, the "key managers" alternative would get the 10 instead. And, in fact, we want the 10 to go to the "key managers" alternative, because low cost is more favorable. For some criteria, such as improved skills and morale, high is good. For other criteria, such as time, money, and lost work hours, high is bad. For *all* criteria, however, most favorable is always good!

- In scoring the alternatives, go one criterion at a time, not one alternative at a time. Once more, scores are relative, so to determine the score for an alternative, it is important to set the score relative to the other alternatives. Therefore, starting with the first criterion, determine the score for all the alternatives for that criterion before moving on to the next criterion.

- Be sure always to determine first the alternative that scores most favorably and give that alternative the score of 10. All other alternatives should receive scores relative to how well they perform compared to the highest-scoring alternative. For example, an alternative that is not quite twice as expensive might be awarded a score of 6; an alternative that is five times as expensive might receive a score of 2.

- Note that for some criteria, all the alternatives may score very high because there might not be much difference between the alternatives.

- Relative scoring versus absolute scoring
  - The approach I've described uses a relative scoring model. In this approach, the scores for an alternative are based on how it performs relative to the other alternatives being compared. This means that an alternative may score, for example, a 10 in cost with one set of alternatives because it has the lowest cost. But when another alternative is added, it may score only a 5, because a less expensive alternative was added to the mix.
  - In highly analytical processes, teams have chosen to create *absolute scoring* as opposed to relative scoring. In absolute scoring, the team defines what constitutes specific scores for each criterion. For example, the team might define the following four absolute scores for cost, leaving room for in-between scores. Using absolute scoring means that an alternative's score stays the same regardless of the alternatives being compared.

Sample Absolute Cost Scale

10 = under $25,000
7 = under $100,000
4 = under $500,000
1 = over $1,000,000

Knowing When to Move On

When all else fails, move on! If after repeated attempts the group is still unable to reach consensus, allow some time to pass. Take a break or move on and return to the topic later. A fresh look at the issue often yields a better understanding and a greater willingness to "live with" an alternative.

Revisiting the Family Vacation

Earlier in this chapter, you recall that my wife and I were disagreeing about where to go on the family vacation. My wife wanted to go on a ten-day, eight-city tour of Italy. I wanted to relax on the beach. Using the consensus building model from this chapter, following delineation we would have identified strengths and weaknesses, as shown in Figure 10.8.

After strengths and weaknesses, we then would identify the one or two most important strengths for each alternative, shown as asterisks in Figure 10.9.

FIGURE 10.8   RESULTS FROM STRENGTHS AND WEAKNESSES—FAMILY VACATION.

Tour of Italy	Beach
Strengths	**Strengths**
Excitement	Relaxation
Different places	Sleeping in the same bed every night
Various local activities	Water sports
Meeting new people	Scenery
Weaknesses	**Weaknesses**
No time to relax	Nothing new
Changing hotels every night	Same place entire week
Time riding on a bus	Boring

FIGURE 10.9   IDENTIFYING KEY STRENGTHS—FAMILY VACATION.

Tour of Italy	Beach
Strengths	**Strengths**
*Excitement	*Relaxation
*Different places	*Sleeping in the same bed every night
Various local activities	Water sports
Meeting new people	Scenery
Weaknesses	**Weaknesses**
No time to relax	Nothing new
Changing hotels every night	Same place entire week
Time riding on a bus	Boring

The merge question then would become, "Is there a third alternative that has excitement and different places, but also allows for relaxing and sleeping in the same bed every night?" You may have already figured out an answer. Our best family vacations these days are cruises! My wife gets the different ports of call; I get to sleep in the same bed every night and relax most days. Consensus building works!

Applying the Secrets to Consensus

(Adapted with permission from The Executive Guide to Facilitating Strategy.*)*

Getting a group to reach consensus on how something is worded can be very challenging. Whether developing a mission statement, gaining approval on an important statement to the media, or expressing values and guiding principles, it is easy for large groups to spend many hours trying to get the wording just right. Unfortunately, deciding whether "a" or "the" is better in a sentence is probably not the best use of a group's time. Therefore, it is important to have processes that allow for quickly and efficiently moving to consensus on wording. This leads to our next secret.

Secret #52

The Secret to Gaining Consensus on Wording
Use the informed majority process to efficiently manage the wording process.

I have found that breakout groups and the informed majority process combine to provide an effective tool for helping a team reach consensus on wording. For example, if I am facilitating a strategic planning session with a team and we need to develop the goal statements for five goal areas that we have identified, I would start by breaking the team into five groups and assigning one of the five goals to each of the groups to draft goal statements.

I would then reconvene and give the entire group a limited time (for example, a maximum of twelve minutes per goal) to modify or clean up the language using informed majority.

The Informed Majority Process

1. Introduce the Ground Rule
During the session opening, I introduce the ground rule "100 percent coverage—85 percent complete." This ground rule means that the team will cover 100 percent of the agenda. However, on any one agenda item—for example, with goal statements—we'll declare victory once we are 85 percent complete. This is because with the 85 percent, we'll have agreement on the concepts. The last 15 percent is typically just wordsmithing—trying to get the words exactly right. That last 15 percent is best done by a smaller group outside the room, not by a large group that can spend ten or fifteen minutes debating whether the right word is "a" or "the."

2. Get All Changes
I have the breakout groups record their draft statements on flip charts in large writing so that all can see and with adequate space between each line to allow for editing. I read the first goal statement and ask the rest of the team for any recommended changes. The objective is to get all the changes for this first goal statement before processing any of the changes. I record each requested change in a pen color different from the original to highlight the change.

3. Speak for Change
Once all the changes are recorded, I go back to the first change and say, "Someone has recommended that this change be made . . . Would someone speak for the change? If no one speaks for it, the change is dropped because clearly no one supports it."

4. Speak for No Change
If someone does speak for the change, I then ask, "Would someone speak against the change and leaving the wording as is? If no one speaks for leaving the wording as is, then the change will be made by acclamation."

5. Ask for Additional Comments
If someone speaks for leaving the wording as is, I then ask, "Are there any additional comments?"

6. Call for a Vote
Once all comments have been made, I call for a vote and go with the majority. The point of voting on wording changes is to go with the will of the group and to avoid significant time spent on wordsmithing. Having people speak for and against a change allows people to be informed prior to voting.

7. Process Multiple Alternatives
If a portion of a statement has several alternatives (for example, "Maximize revenue" and "Optimize revenue," and the original wording was, "Achieve revenue targets"), I'll ask someone to speak for each alternative and someone to speak for leaving the wording as is. As before, if no one speaks for an alternative, the alternative is dropped.

8. Hold a Runoff (If Needed)
If there are multiple alternatives and no alternative receives a majority of votes, then all but the top two alternatives are dropped, and I conduct a revote.

9. Check for Consensus
Once all decisions are made about the wording, I rewrite the statement and seek majority confirmation that we have at least reached the 85 percent completion mark before moving on.

Facilitator's Checklist for Consensus Building

☐ The definition of consensus: "I can live with it, and I will support it."

☐ Consider five-finger consensus as an approach for decision making.

☐ Understand the three reasons people disagree:

- Level 1: lack of shared information
- Level 2: different values or experiences
- Level 3: outside factors

☐ When there are disagreements based on outside factors (level 3), take the issue to a higher source for resolution.

☐ Use delineation to address a level 1 disagreement:

- Start with agreement.
- Confirm the source of the disagreement.
- Identify the alternatives under discussion.
- Ask each party specific delineating questions: how much, how long, who is involved, what is involved.
- Summarize the information.
- Take a consensus check.

☐ Use strengths and weaknesses to identify the source of a level 2 disagreement:

- Identify the strengths of each alternative.
- Identify the weaknesses of each alternative.
- Take a consensus check.

☐ Use merge to solve a level 2 disagreement:

- Select the most important strengths of each alternative.
- Create one or more new alternatives that combine key strengths.
- Delineate the top alternative.
- Take a consensus check.

☐ Use the weighted scoring technique when structured comparisons and numerical values can help the team reach consensus:

- Define the criteria.
- Establish weights for the criteria by designating the highest and lowest and then the remaining weights.
- Score the alternatives by scoring the most favorable alternative first and assigning all other scores relative to it.

- Apply weights to the scores.
- Take a consensus check.

☐ When all else fails, move on! Allow some time to pass and return to the topic later.

☐ Use the informed majority process to gain consensus on the wording of statements.

Exercise Your Skills

Over the next one to two weeks, consider paying close attention to disagreements that occur, whether in your professional or personal life, and whether they involve you or are between others.

- As you listen to the disagreement, make an effort to determine if the disagreement is level 1, 2, or 3.
- As with the consensus building process suggested in this book, first determine if the disagreement is level 3. Are the arguments irrational? Does there seem to be no commitment on the part of one or more of the parties to finding a solution? If so, this may indeed be a level 3 disagreement and resolved best by taking it to a higher source.
- If you are able to rule out level 3, assume that it is a level 1 disagreement. Are the parties certain that they understand the other's alternative, or are they just assuming they do? Are they listening to one another or just making statements?
- If you can influence the discussion, consider asking permission to delineate—for example, by saying, "We may very well understand exactly what each person is saying, but just to be sure, can we take a few minutes to have each person explain exactly how this would work? Let's start with Joe. Joe, how would we . . . Who would be involved . . . How would it work . . . How much would it cost . . . How long would it take . . . ?"
- If delineation does not resolve the disagreement, you can be certain that the disagreement is level 2 and can ask questions about strengths to identify the values and use the merge strategy to identify potential solutions.
- If it is not appropriate for you to play an active role in resolving the disagreement, consider taking time on your own to guess what the answers would be to the delineation, strengths and weaknesses, and merge questions.

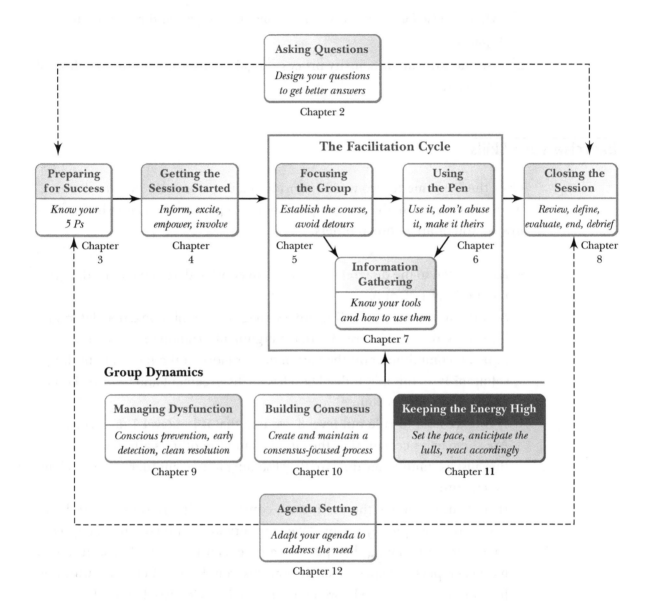

CHAPTER ELEVEN

THE SECRETS TO ENERGY

Set the Pace, Anticipate the Lulls, React Accordingly

Questions Answered in This Chapter

What is the impact of energy on the session topic, the session participants, and the participants' view of the facilitator?

How do you start a session with energy?

What are the lullaby times during the day, and what should you do about them?

How do you maintain energy throughout a session?

When are team building activities appropriate? How do you use them well?

CASE STUDY: Learning the Impact of Energy

I learned about the impact of energy the hard way, and it was deeply personal. I first began serving as a facilitator while a member of one of the national consulting firms. After about four years in the role, I was approached by one of the consulting partners, who said to me, "Do you know how much power you give up when you facilitate?" I was offended by the comment. I felt that I was a very good facilitator, thank you very much, and had the accolades of several clients to back up the claim.

But the partner was trying to teach me a valuable lesson that I wasn't ready to learn. It took another three years and two significant incidents before I fully understood and appreciated the gift he was offering me.

The first of the two incidents occurred a year later. I was attending my first facilitation class in an effort to round out my skills. Although I learned considerably from the class, the activity that affected me most took place on the last day. There were sixteen people in the class, and each of us had to facilitate the entire group for a portion of that final day. What I witnessed amazed me. Each time a new person got up to facilitate, the room would take on the personality of the facilitator. If the facilitator was energetic, the participants became more energetic. If the facilitator was low energy, the level of energy in the room would significantly decrease. If the facilitator was folksy, the group became more folksy, and so on. Here were the same sixteen people, yet the room would take on the characteristics of the person leading. I found it astounding. I didn't understand how important this was until the lessons came together two years later.

By this time I had become one of the founding members of the organization that I am a part of today. I was teaching our facilitation class several times a month, and the class included having people facilitate for an extended period on the last day. In one class during that first year, one of the participants chose to use our project planning methodology for his extended session. He started the session with high energy. But halfway through, he got tripped up in his efforts to take the group through the agenda item "critical success factor analysis." He became very unsure of himself, his energy level dropped significantly, and the session dragged terribly. During the feedback segment that followed, I asked him why he let his energy drop. He said, "I didn't know what I was doing. I just wanted to get it over with."

As it turned out, the next person to facilitate also used the project planning process. And when he got to critical success factor analysis, he also became confused. As I listened to the questions he was asking the participants, it was readily apparent that he didn't understand what he was doing. He was clearly lost. But he kept his energy up, and the people continued to follow him. It was like watching the blind leading the blind. He was leading them over a cliff, and they were going right along with him!

During the debriefing, he confessed that he didn't completely understand the process and got lost in the middle. But I turned to the group and asked them why they followed him. One person responded, "He seemed confident. He seemed to know what he was doing." At that moment, I finally understood what that partner three years before had been trying to teach me. And it is a lesson that we teach every facilitator we train.

Understanding the Impact of Energy

Through our work training hundreds of facilitators every year and providing facilitators for sessions in the United States and around the world, we have learned three key aspects of energy: it *energizes* the topic, *engages* the participants, and *elevates* the facilitator.

Secret #53

The Secret of Energy: The 3 Es
High energy energizes, engages, and elevates.

How Does High Energy Energize a Topic?

When a facilitator leads a session with energy, the energy transfers to the topic. Your energy around the topic encourages participants to think, "This topic seems to be important to the facilitator; perhaps it should be important to me." And just as high energy can make a topic more interesting, low energy can make a topic less interesting.

How Does High Energy Engage the Participants?

For most people, high energy is simply more appealing to listen to than low energy. In essence, high energy is just more fun. Of course, there is a point at which high energy goes "over the top," becoming less interesting and more irritating. But short of being overdone, high energy invites participants to listen and stay alert. Unfortunately, low energy can invite participants to check out or fall asleep. You have no doubt experienced this many times, as I have, with speakers in a variety of circumstances.

How Does High Energy Elevate the Facilitator?

Energy can have a significant impact on the participants' perception of the facilitator. This was the lesson the consulting partner was trying to get me to see. When I spoke with clients one-on-one as a consultant, I used a low-key consulting voice that was intended to project sincerity and concern. I wanted to let my clients know that I was concerned about their needs and wanted to be as helpful to them as possible.

Unfortunately, when I facilitated, I would speak with the same low-key voice. Whereas it was an effective consulting voice, it was a lousy facilitation voice. Why? Let's go back to the two facilitators who got confused when facilitating the project planning process. The first facilitator let his energy drop, and the session dragged. The second facilitator kept his energy up, and the participants followed him. Recall that when asked, one participant said he followed the second facilitator because *he seemed to know what he was doing.* SMART facilitators know that high energy projects confidence. In the case study, the facilitator's high energy gave the impression that he knew what he was doing. But the reverse is also true. *If high energy projects high confidence, then low energy can project low confidence.* And this was the point that the consulting partner was trying to get me to understand: my low energy during facilitation was projecting to the participants that I had low confidence. In his words, I was giving up power when I facilitated. Gift received.

Projecting Energy from the Start

How do you project energy from the start of the session? That's the secret to starting with energy.

Secret #54

The Secret to Starting with Energy

Think "level 3" with the first words out of your mouth.

What is level 3? Let's start by looking at levels 1 and 2. In the graph in Figure 11.1, the zero line represents the division between being awake and asleep. In ordinary conversation, most of us speak with just enough energy in our voices to keep people awake. I call this our level 1 voice. Over the course of a session, however, the energy in our voices tends to fall off dramatically. As a result, we often end up well below the zero line.

FIGURE 11.1 LEVEL 1 ENERGY.

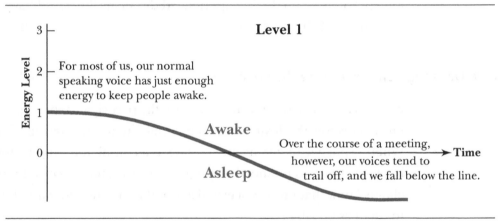

Let's say you raise your energy to level 2, as shown in Figure 11.2. At the beginning of the session, your energy level will be sufficient. But once more, over time it will fall off and quite possibly go below the line.

FIGURE 11.2 LEVEL 2 ENERGY.

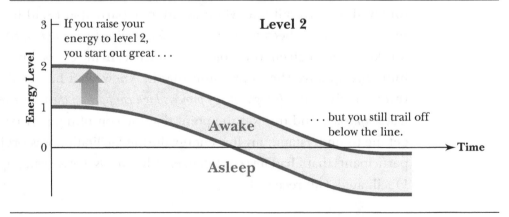

FIGURE 11.3 LEVEL 3 ENERGY.

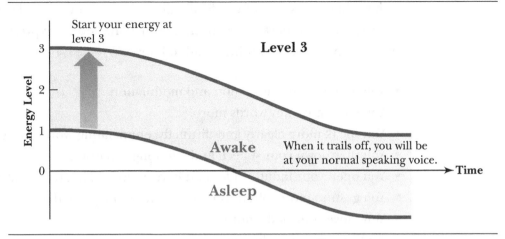

To maximize your impact, start a facilitated session at level 3 energy, two levels above your normal speaking voice. In this way, when your energy trails off you will likely fall back to your normal speaking voice, as shown in Figure 11.3.

Why Do This?	**Why start a session at level 3?**
	Your energy level is contagious. It spills over to the topic, to the participants, and to their perception of you. When you start with high energy, it indirectly says that the topic is important, that you are confident about what you are doing, and that the participants need to pay attention because something exciting is about to happen. If you start with low energy, it can indirectly say that the topic isn't important, that you are not confident in what you are doing, and that the session will not be very interesting.

Finding Your Level 3 Energy

Many people are not aware of what level 3 energy looks and feels like. Here is something to try to give you a starting point:

1. Imagine that you are sitting at a table with a close friend. Say the words, "Good morning. It is *great* to be here today."

2. Now imagine that you are standing in a moderately sized conference room with five people. Stand and say the words again as if you were speaking to all five.

3. Now imagine that you are in a much larger room, with five tables arranged in a semicircle and six people seated at each. Stand and say the words again as if you wanted the person furthest from you to hear your words and *feel* that you truly believe that it is great to be there.

People frequently think that energy is volume. But when we do this exercise with facilitators as part of our facilitation training, they quickly learn that there are several differences between their level 1 and level 3 expressions. When you speak at level 3, several things tend to happen:

- You have greater intonation and modulation.
- You emphasize key words more.
- You speak more clearly and distinctly, enunciating words more carefully.
- You slow down your speech and add longer pauses.
- You open your mouth wider and have a more animated facial expression.
- You gesture more, often using larger, more magnified gestures.
- You move your body more.
- And yes, you speak louder.

Is level 3 needed for every facilitated session? Certainly not. For example, in a session to determine the thirty people to fire in order to bring overhead costs in line with current reductions in sales, you probably would not open with level 3 energy. But for most facilitated meetings, SMART facilitators know that level 3 energy helps energize the topic, engage the participants, and elevate the participants' confidence in the facilitator.

Starting with Energy

The first words you speak to the group will establish the energy level for the session. If your first words come out at level 1, it is more than likely that you will remain at level 1 or lower for most of the session. Instead, consciously start at level 3. From the Secrets to Starting, you will have already decided in advance of the session what the first words of your opening will be. When you say these first words, consciously think, "Level 3!"

Energy and Authenticity

When we teach people about level 3 energy in our training classes, we often hear such comments as, "I'm not sure I could do level 3 energy in my sessions. It seems so inauthentic. It's not me."

Of course it is important for us as facilitators to be authentic and to be comfortable with the tools and strategies we use in our facilitation. So if level 3 energy is not for you, so be it.

Yet I would have you consider the following. The comment I receive most frequently after facilitating a group is something akin to "great energy." I think it is because I have learned the power of energy and adapted it to the point where it looks natural. As you recall from the case study that started this chapter, my natural style is that of an analytical consultant. I am a natural introvert who gets my energy from within, and I prefer a quieter, more analytical approach to solving problems.

However, I have learned that my natural quiet style is not nearly as effective when facilitating groups. So when I stand up to facilitate, it is showtime. It is the time for me to pull forth from within me what little extroversion I have, magnify it, and let it shine. It is work, and I'm exhausted when it's over. But I have seen the impact on groups. I find the group's response exhilarating and well worth it.

Is it authentic? My answer is yes—but not in the way one would traditionally mean. It is an authentic representation of my desire to be of maximum benefit to the group; and I believe the result is that the group feels my true desire to be of service.

CASE STUDY: The Low-Key Facilitator

In one of our early classes, there was a midlevel manager who was relatively soft spoken. Throughout the class, I could see that she was excited about the techniques she was learning and that she was looking forward to putting them into practice at work. In each practice facilitation, however, I noticed that her energy level was very low. I was looking forward to seeing how she would do with the energy exercise later in the class.

When we reached the energy module, I asked if there were people in the class who felt that their energy, when they facilitated, was not as high as they would like. Several raised their hand, including the manager. I then asked if one of them would be willing to work with me as a volunteer in front of the class to see if we could find a higher level that worked for them. I was pleased when she volunteered.

I had her read a three-sentence session opening at level 1, level 2, and level 3. I was surprised because she spoke with virtually the same energy for all three. I asked her to do just the first sentence at level 1 and then to give it all she had to demonstrate level 3. Her level 3 was about a level 1.5, if it reached that high. I had her do a few additional adjustments in tone, volume, and expression that got her to a solid level 2. She said something that I've heard many times since: "It sounds to me like I'm shouting." One of her classmates responded, "Shout some more!"

Adjusting to the Lullaby Times

SMART facilitators know that there are standard times during a day when the energy among participants is naturally low. Figure 11.4 shows the standard lullaby times.

FIGURE 11.4   STANDARD LULLABY TIMES.

Midmorning	10:30–11:00 (minor)
Just after lunch	01:30–02:00 (major)
Midafternoon	03:00–03:30 (moderate)

The Secret to Adjusting to the Lullaby Times

Plan high interaction during the low-energy times.

Arrange the agenda to accommodate the standard lull times:

- Schedule one of the following activities:
  - Team building exercise
  - Small-group breakout
  - Facilitated process requiring movement (for example, the rotating flip charts process)
- Avoid scheduling the following activities:
  - Presentations or long monologues
  - Reading
  - Individually assigned exercises

During the lullaby periods, you will find that people are generally willing to allow others to speak first. Of course, when everyone does this, you can have a fairly quiet room. Therefore, during these periods, avoid asking questions to the general group. Instead, direct questions more often to specific individuals (or teams). There are also specific activities to stay away from during the *major* lullaby time, which starts about thirty minutes after lunch: avoid starting a meeting or engaging in a visioning or creativity exercise.

Maintaining Energy During the Session

SMART facilitators consciously use a variety of techniques during the session to maintain the energy level:

- Resetting the energy level following breaks
- Establishing a recharge activity
- Employing praise
- Using applause
- Varying engagement methods and team size
- Taking additional breaks if necessary

Secret #56

The Secret to Maintaining Energy

Use energy-generating techniques throughout the session.

Why Do This? | **Why is it important to maintain a high energy level?**

Facilitators often seek to balance two goals: achieving the desired output from the session and maintaining high levels of engagement and buy-in. Energy is a key to keeping people engaged. And without engagement, you are more likely to achieve apathy than buy-in. Maintain a suitably high energy level to keep people engaged and actively participating.

Resetting the Energy Level

Following each break, you must start the next segment on at least the same energy level with which you began the day. By resetting the energy level following breaks, you can avoid long periods in which the energy is low. In addition, resetting the energy level can give people the *impression* of high energy throughout. Participants often ask me how I am able to keep my energy so high during a full-day session. The answer, of course, is that I don't keep it high. The energy level, in fact, modulates throughout the day, as shown in Figure 11.5. They are probably remembering the high points that occur at the beginning of the day and following every break.

FIGURE 11.5 RESETTING THE ENERGY LEVEL.

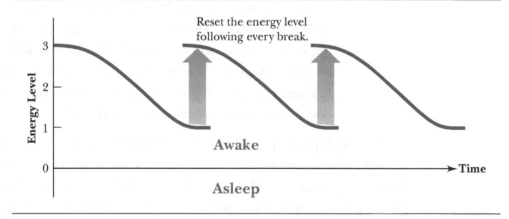

Establishing a Recharge Activity

Early in the session, and possibly as a ground rule, establish a simple recharge activity. The point of a recharge is to empower participants with a simple tool to raise the energy level whenever needed.

Sample Dialogue: Establishing a Recharge

Facilitator: This next ground rule is called "Recharge." I have to admit this is a little silly, but it works. A recharge is a quick activity intended to raise the energy in the room.

Let me ask you, what is going to happen to the energy in this room about 1:30 PM? . . . That's right, it will significantly drop off. Some people will have trouble staying alert, others will find themselves easily distracted, and some will even nod off. I call it the lullaby time. It is significant right after lunch; there is also a noticeable one around 3:30 and a small one around 10:45.

But we want to keep everyone alert. So I would like for us to create a recharge activity, and anytime anyone senses that the energy in the room is dropping, that person can call for a recharge. The recharge activity can be anything we want. It just has to combine some body motion with something you say.

I had a group of thirty superintendents decide that their recharge was going to be the wave. Another group chose the chicken dance. Another agreed that they would just stand up, stretch, sit down, and say "Thank you very much." And then there is the old facilitator standby, "choo choo." The way it works is, the facilitator says, "All aboard!" Then everyone, with locomotive arm motion and all, says, "Choo choo, chugga chugga chugga chugga." I told you that it was silly, but it works: it wakes you up.

Now, I'm setting the clock to one minute. We have one minute to get as many suggestions as we can for our recharge. After a minute for nominations, we will vote, and the one with the most votes will be our recharge for today. If we can't come up with anything, we have to do "choo choo," so please come up with something! Any questions? OK, I have set the clock to one minute. What suggestions do we have for the recharge?

Although participants with some communication styles may be initially turned off by the idea of a recharge, SMART facilitators know that when they have clearly explained the reason for the recharge, provided examples, and given the participants the opportunity to choose their own recharge, there tends to be buy-in or at least acceptance. There are a couple of additional nuances to having the group choose the recharge activity.

- Notice that nominations are limited to one minute. For those participants who may feel initially turned off by the idea of a recharge, it is typically helpful to them to know that this "silly diversion" will last only a few minutes.
- Note that the participants are given a subtle penalty if they are unable to come up with a recharge: they have to use "choo choo." This "penalty" increases the likelihood that people will create suggestions and that others will appreciate their efforts.

Quick Tip!

Make a point of using the recharge activity at least once in the morning and as many times as necessary in the afternoon.

Employing Praise

Praise can be an effective tool for maintaining the energy level. Although many facilitators avoid praise so as to promote the perception of neutrality and to avoid partiality, SMART facilitators use praise to maintain high, positive energy in the room. Praise can range from relatively neutral statements like "Thanks for the contribution; that's something we haven't heard before" to opinion-related statements: "That's helpful; great point." Another advantage to praise is that by modeling it, the facilitator demonstrates how participants might praise each other during the session and after.

Although praise has many advantages, it is still important to maintain a level of impartiality. Therefore, when you employ praise, do be sure to avoid frequently singling out the same team or individual.

Using Applause

Applause can also serve as an effective way to maintain the energy level in the room. With their applause, team members give a form of praise to one another. Initially, the facilitator typically has to take the lead in the applause. Once a consistent pattern is set, however, participants become accustomed to the timing and often applaud without prompting.

Consider using applause at the following times:

- Prior to a presentation
- At the end of a presentation
- After each team's report-back following a breakout session

I also use applause in introductions. I typically do introductions as part of a small-group exercise. Therefore, rather than asking the group to applaud after each person, I have them applaud after all members of a small group have introduced themselves.

Varying Engagement Methods and Team Size

As described in Chapter Seven, you can vary your engagement methods as a means of maintaining energy. Moving from listing to brainstorming to grouping to lobbying to prioritizing is one way to vary your engagement method. The whip and last person standing are two high-energy engagement strategies described in Chapter Seven that are superb at raising the energy level.

You also can change the group size and processing method by using round-robins, small-group breakout, and pairs to vary the engagement for participants. Round-robins get everyone involved, whereas small groups can allow more people to be engaged in discussion at the same time.

Taking Additional Breaks If Necessary

When the participants begin to wind down, you the facilitator may have to work doubly hard to keep the energy high. Should other techniques not appear to be effective at keeping the group engaged, call for a break, even if you have to do so earlier than planned. Because buy-in and consensus are our goals, it is typically better to invest time in strategic breaks to ensure full involvement than it is to continue to push ahead with only a few participants engaged.

CASE STUDY: A Team Building Mistake

Over a decade ago, before learning the Secrets of Facilitation, I was called in to facilitate an international team of twenty, who had come together to develop a strategic information systems plan. The international team included representatives from three companies in a joint venture proposing to become the second telecommunications carrier in a foreign country. The joint venture was competing against two other international teams who were vying for this country's business. In ninety days, the country expected to announce the winner. Once the contract was awarded, the winner would be obligated to have wireless service up and running within six months. This tight time frame for offering services to the public meant that all operational decisions for the organization would have to be made in advance so that the six months could be spent implementing those decisions and not deciding what the decisions would be. Therefore, the information systems team had a limited window during which to identify *all* the computer systems that the entire operation would need and to create a plan for implementation in case the consortium was awarded the contract. This was going to take a herculean effort, to say the least.

For any new team coming together, a team briefing is needed to get all members of the team clear on the 5 Ps: the purpose of the project, the product the team is to produce, the participants who will be involved, the probable issues the team will face, and the process the team will use. The actual briefing lasted two days. Late in the afternoon of the second day, I noticed the energy in the room falling sharply. As the facilitator, I selected a team building activity to raise the energy in the room. The activity I chose, Categories, had nothing to do with the work we were doing, and the results of the activity in no way contributed to the work product. Nor did I hold a debriefing following the exercise to try to explain how the activity related to our overall purpose. (I'm not sure it did.) After the activity, the project sponsor pulled me aside and said quite angrily, "We won't do anything like that *ever* again, will we?" I learned an important lesson that day about team building exercises.

Using Team Building Activities

Team building exercises are excellent tools for raising the energy of a session. As the preceding case study demonstrates, however, a team building activity that is not clearly tied to the session purpose can be met with disdain.

When you use team building activities, take the following precautions:

- Ensure that you select an exercise that is appropriate for the session purpose.
- Use your PeDeQs to define the purpose of the activity and clearly deliver directions.
- Monitor the activity while it is in progress to ensure that objectives are being met.
- Once the activity is complete, take several minutes for a debriefing session to help team members understand how the activity applies to the work of the team.

Secret #57

The Secret to Using Team Building Activities
Select for purpose; debrief for application.

Team building activities can serve several purposes. Some activities are designed to share a common experience, others to identify issues, others to resolve issues. The following are some common purposes:

- Learn more about team members
- Share a common work experience
- Share a common nonwork experience
- Reveal how the team behaves under stress
- Reveal team biases
- Improve communication
- Improve the dynamics working in the team

You will want to be sure to define your purpose clearly and select a team building activity that is designed to meet that purpose. For a source of team building activities, consider the works of John Newstrom and Edward Scannell, authors of a series on team building activities, starting with *Games Trainers Play;* and also Brian Cole Miller's team building series, starting with *Quick Team-Building Activities for Busy Managers.*

Crossing the River: My Favorite Team Building Exercise

Every facilitator and trainer has his or her favorite team building activity. Some facilitators like the more active interventions, such as ropes courses; others prefer the more "touchy-feely" ones like trust walks; still others like using blindfolded instruction, or simulations like Gold of the Desert Kings.

Of course, your selection of the most appropriate team building activity for a group depends on a number of factors, including your overall purpose, the nature of the group, the amount of time you have, the limitations of the space, and so on.

Yet of all the team building activities I have experienced, my favorite by far is an activity called Crossing the River. I first learned of the activity over twenty years ago from a Chicago consultant working with the leadership team of my church. We have refined the activity over the years, but the basic elements have remained the same. I'll describe the exercise first and then tell you why I think it is so great.

The Objective

The objective for the participants is to get all their team members safely from one side of a bank of a deadly river to the other.

Preparation

Create three islands by taping together four 8 ½″ × 11″ sheets of paper for each island. Create a pebble for each person by cutting sheets of paper in half lengthwise to form 4 ¼″ × 11″ sheets. Create one rock (an 8 ½″ × 11″ sheet) for every five participants. Tape off an open area at least ten medium strides (25–30 feet) long and six strides wide. Place the islands as shown in Figure 11.6.

FIGURE 11.6   SETUP FOR CROSSING THE RIVER.

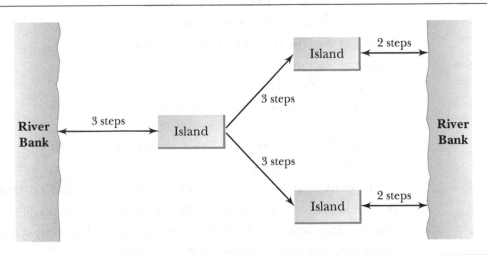

Instructions

Have all participants stand on the left side of the bank; hand out a copy of the instruction sheet to each person. Read through "The Situation" and "The Rules" together. Then give two minutes for questions. The clock starts after the last question is answered.

The Situation

You and your teammates are on one bank of a poisonous, deadly river. The river is so contaminated that if any part of a person's skin or clothing touches the river, he or she will die instantly! Each of the people on your team must cross from one bank of the deadly river to the other. You have twenty minutes.

The Rules

1. No part of a person's skin, clothing, or personal articles may touch the river. The only items that can survive in the river are islands, rocks, and pebbles.
2. Islands, rocks, and pebbles are safe spots (touchable).
3. Islands in the river may not be moved.
4. Rocks may not be moved once placed in the river.
5. Each team member owns a pebble.
6. Only the pebble owner may place a pebble in the river, take a pebble from the river, or move a pebble once it is in the river, and he or she may do so using his or her hand only.
7. All team members must step out of the river at the same time.

Execution

During execution, pay close attention to group dynamics. Some items to observe in particular follow.

Communication
1. How long did it take for there to be a single conversation going?
2. Did everyone who wanted to speak get an opportunity to be heard?
3. When suggestions were made, was a response given every time, or were some people's suggestions listened to while those of others were ignored?

Planning

1. Was a plan created? Who initiated the plan? How many people were involved in developing the plan?

2. How was agreement reached? Did the group check to ensure understanding and agreement from everyone before acting on the plan?

3. Did the plan provide a complete picture of how to start *and* how to end?

Execution

1. Was there a leader or multiple leaders? How was the leadership chosen? Was the leadership followed?

2. How willing were people to rely on one another, to help one another, and physically support one another?

3. Was the goal achieved within the twenty minutes? How much time was required? What was the key to achieving or not achieving the goal?

Debrief

At the completion of the exercise, debrief with the whole group. Have them identify their own observations. Be sure to offer your observations as well. Following observations, have them identify what they learned and how to apply their observations and learning to their workplace.

Why It Works

Crossing the River is ideal for eight to sixteen people. If you have up to twenty-four, you can choose several to be observers and assign them different sections of the items to observe described earlier. If you have more than twenty-four, you can split into multiple teams that do the exercise all at the same time, each with a separate river they have to cross. I have done this with sixteen teams simultaneously in a very large room. As each team completed the exercise, team members let out a team cheer, which spurred on the teams that had not finished.

What makes Crossing the River such a great team building activity?

-   The goal requires team planning and execution; the team has to come together for success.
-   No one can do it on his or her own; the team either succeeds or fails as a unit.
-   The exercise breaks down barriers; it requires people to share their thoughts, share their resources, and share their space.
-   Perhaps most interestingly, the time limit creates a sense of urgency that frequently results in participants' defaulting to the same behaviors that they

exhibit in the workplace. Those who typically take over do so in this exercise; people who drop out do the same; people who frequently serve as naysayers often take on this same role when faced with Crossing the River. As I watch teams engage in the activity, I find I am frequently watching a microcosm of how the teams operate in the workplace.

The Solution

I have executed this activity with more than fifty teams. Every team has come to essentially the same solution, and only one team ran out of time before completely executing it. There may be other solutions, but I'll describe the only one that I have seen teams use.

The key is to start with the end in mind. Because all people have to step out of the river at the same time, think about what the situation has to be the second before everyone takes that last step. In essence, everyone has to be lined up in the river, one step from the bank and ready to step out. This means that no one can be on islands; everyone has to be standing on a rock or a pebble (so the team should save the rocks for this lineup).

To get to the lineup, and I'll assume an all-female group to make the explanation easier, Person 1 lays her pebble between the bank and the first island. Person 2 then steps on Person 1's pebble and lays her pebble down toward the first island and then returns to the bank. Person 3 then steps on the pebbles belonging to Persons 1 and 2, then steps on the island, places a pebble toward the next island, then returns to the bank. This continues until there is a pathway to the second island, which typically requires Person 4's pebble as well. Person 5 then traverses all the other pebbles and places her pebble one step from the bank and lays a rock so that she can have one foot on her pebble and one foot on the rock. The additional team members follow suit until only Persons 1 through 4 are left on the bank. (Recall that there is one rock per five people, so five people will be huddled around a rock, each having one foot on her pebble and either having a toe on the rock or being supported by someone else.)

Persons 1 through 4 are the last to go, and they move to the islands in order, 4-3-2-1. Person 1 goes last and picks up her pebble as she moves to the island, but keeps going to the lineup. Then 2, 3, and 4, in that order, go back from the island and get their pebbles and move to the lineup. When Person 4 gets her pebble, she will move to the lineup, and everyone will be ready to take the last step. Typically, one person gives the "One, two, three," and everyone steps out of the river at the same time.

As I mentioned previously, every team I have worked with has been successful, except one. Interestingly, the team that failed was a nonprofit, and in the debrief the members concluded that they did not succeed because the group as a whole spent too much time focused on making sure everyone was comfortable instead of focusing on the goal. They concluded that this same issue was one of their major stumbling blocks in operating their organization!

Facilitator's Checklist for Energy

☐ High energy does three important things (the 3 Es of energy):

- Energizes the topic
- Engages the participants
- Elevates the facilitator

☐ In a facilitated session, the first words out of your mouth establish the energy level for the session. Consciously start at level 3.

☐ Following every break, reestablish the energy level by starting back at Level 3.

☐ During the lullaby times in a session, attempt to schedule small-group activities or activities requiring movement. Avoid extended "participant-passive" activities or activities requiring creativity.

- 10:30–11:00 AM (minor)
- 1:30–2:00 PM (major)
- 3:00–3:30 PM (moderate)

☐ Use a variety of techniques during the session to maintain the energy level, including the following:

- Reset the energy level following breaks
- Establish a recharge activity
- Employ praise
- Use applause
- Vary the engagement methods
- Take extra breaks if necessary

☐ When you use team building activities, take the following precautions:

- Select an exercise appropriate for the session purpose.
- Use your PeDeQs to define the purpose and deliver directions.
- Monitor the activity while it is in progress.
- Hold a debriefing session to help team members understand how the activity applies.

Exercise Your Skills

In this chapter, you learned about how I discovered the impact of level 3 energy. I have found that many facilitators are reluctant to try level 3 with groups for fear of going "over the top" or seeming inauthentic.

Although I addressed authenticity earlier, consider having the participants in your next facilitation serve as a sounding board to address your concerns about going "over the top." At the beginning of the facilitation, let the group know that you will be facilitating the session at a higher energy level than normal and that you would like to get their feedback at the end of the session. Then go for it! Start the session at level 3 and return to level 3 at the beginning of each agenda item and following breaks. At the end of the session, do a debrief. Ask them first, "What did you like about the energy level?" and have everyone respond. Then ask, "What adjustments would you suggest I make?" Finally, ask, "Do you think I should continue using level 3?" You may be surprised at the results.

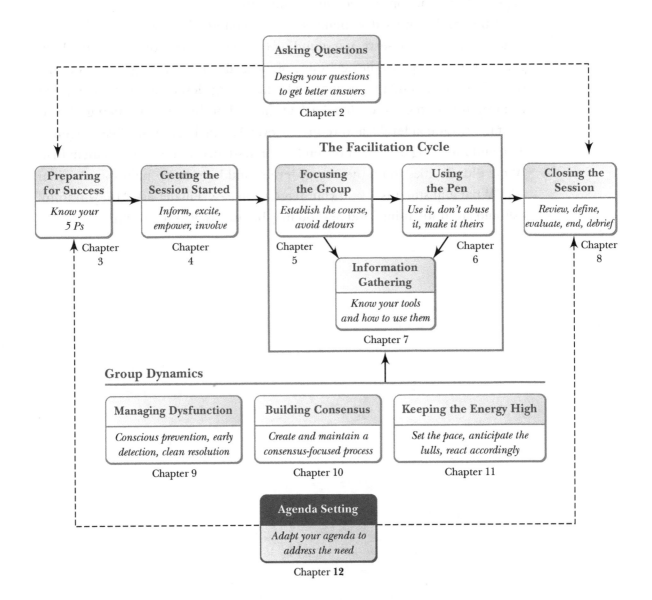

Asking Questions

*Design your questions
to get better answers*

Chapter 2

The Facilitation Cycle

Preparing for Success	**Getting the Session Started**
Know your 5 Ps	*Inform, excite, empower, involve*
Chapter 3	Chapter 4

Focusing the Group	**Using the Pen**
Establish the course, avoid detours	*Use it, don't abuse it, make it theirs*
Chapter 5	Chapter 6

Information Gathering

*Know your tools
and how to use them*

Chapter 7

Closing the Session

Review, define, evaluate, end, debrief

Chapter 8

Group Dynamics

Managing Dysfunction	**Building Consensus**	**Keeping the Energy High**
Conscious prevention, early detection, clean resolution	*Create and maintain a consensus-focused process*	*Set the pace, anticipate the lulls, react accordingly*
Chapter 9	Chapter 10	Chapter 11

Agenda Setting

*Adapt your agenda to
address the need*

Chapter **12**

CHAPTER TWELVE

THE SECRETS TO AGENDA SETTING

Adapt Your Agenda to Address the Need

Questions Answered in This Chapter

What is a standard agenda, and why do you need it?

How do you customize a standard agenda to meet a specific need?

How do you create an agenda from scratch?

How do you ensure that you know your process cold?

How does an agenda differ from a detailed facilitation guide?

What should be included in a facilitation guide?

How do you estimate time?

CASE STUDY: Pay for Performance

We were called in to assist a trade association that had about one hundred staff members. The board of directors had expressed concern that most people in the organization received pay-for-performance bonuses. The president was planning a meeting of his direct reports to determine how best to address the concern of the board.

On the surface, this session appeared to be straightforward issue resolution, and therefore we would be able to use our issue resolution approach (described in this chapter) as the working agenda for the team.

During our preparation work, however, we learned that there was a wide deviation among the departments, with 100 percent of some departments receiving pay-for-performance bonuses and less than 20 percent receiving them in other departments. The participant interviews also identified that different managers had different views of the purpose of the pay-for-performance program.

Accordingly, we combined the issue resolution approach with the current assessment and visioning components of the strategic planning approach (described in this chapter). The resulting customized agenda was as follows:

A. Getting started
B. Where are we today?
- The concerns of the board
- Our pay-for-performance results (three-year trend)

C. Defining our vision of pay for performance
- Our shared intention with pay for performance
- Indicators of success in achieving the vision

D. Assessing our recent performance against the vision
E. Identifying alternative approaches
F. Assessing and selecting an approach
- Strengths and weaknesses against vision
- Merging to refine alternatives
- Selecting alternative

G. Developing the implementation plan
H. Defining the response plan for the board
I. Review and close

The team, by necessity, spent considerable time on item C, "Defining our vision of pay for performance." Some of the managers felt that pay for performance was warranted anytime someone performed above and beyond his or her assigned duties. Others felt that pay for performance was warranted only when a person made an outstanding contribution to the success of the organization. These managers believed that clerical staff would seldom, if ever, qualify for a pay-for-performance bonus because they were not in a position to make a contribution that significantly impacted the success of the organization. There was one manager who strongly felt that the organization underpaid everyone and that therefore, pay for performance was a way to get everyone the extra compensation he or she deserved.

Once the team members reached consensus on a shared vision of the purpose of pay for performance, they were able to quickly identify alternatives, select an appropriate alternative, create an implementation plan for moving forward, and develop a plan for communicating back to the board.

Understanding Process

If purpose is the steering wheel of a car, process is the engine. Whereas purpose sets the direction, process gets you to your destination. A process is simply a series of steps to arrive at a result. To accomplish anything, people step through a process. Whether developing a strategic plan for a multibillion-dollar corporation or taking a hamburger order at the drive-through window ("Will you have fries with that?"), people move through a series of steps to arrive at the result.

Often we are not aware of the process in operation, as is the case with the process used to get a broadcast signal from the television station to our homes. Sometimes the process is relaxed, such as at a restaurant's buffet line: come and go as you please, take as much as you like. Other times the process is rigid and inflexible, such as the process used to disable a bomb. Often the process doesn't get our attention until it breaks down, such as the process used to get your luggage from the departure city to the baggage claim. The best processes work effectively and efficiently: they produce the desired result with minimal strain, wasting no resources.

Part of the job of a facilitator is to create the *process*—the agenda items and the methods that the team will use to accomplish its purpose. SMART facilitators use process as a vehicle for reaching a destination while also developing team relationships and building the team's ownership and commitment to the solution. If the facilitator is successful, the team will be able to execute the process effectively and efficiently. Participants will produce the desired result, wasting no resources and with minimal strain.

Using Standard Agendas

The team's work process may cover one meeting or multiple meetings, depending on the work to be accomplished. The agenda, or process, must be designed to achieve the purpose and must take into account the other three Ps—the product, participants, and probable issues.

For example, if the team's purpose is to streamline the hiring process, you might use a "process improvement" agenda. If the product you are trying to create is a plan for a program, you might use a "project planning" agenda. If the key to the session is to resolve a particular issue, you might use an "issue resolution" agenda. Each of these agendas is different because the purpose and products are different.

Secret #58

The Secret of Standard Agendas

Standard agendas create the starting point for addressing the specific needs of a meeting.

To maximize their effectiveness, SMART facilitators draw from a set of standard agendas that they can customize for a specific situation. Standard agendas have several advantages:

Advantages of Having Standard Agendas	• They reduce the amount of time needed to prepare for a session by giving you a starting point. • They help ensure that you do not miss a critical step. • They provide consistency from one assignment to another and from one facilitator to another.

What follows are standard agendas for six common organizational activities.

Standard Agendas

- Conference facilitation
- Issue resolution
- Process improvement
- Project planning
- Strategic planning
- Team building

Conference Facilitation Agenda

Purpose

- Have conference attendees understand a topic and identify actions to take collectively and individually to address it

Products

- Collective actions to be taken
- Short-term action plan

Process

A. Getting started

B. Current situation

C. Past successes and challenges

D. Potential solutions

E. Collective and individual action

F. Next steps

G. Review and close

Issue Resolution Agenda

Purpose
- Define an issue; identify alternative solutions; gain consensus on an alternative

Products
- Selection criteria
- Alternative definitions
- Selected alternative and justification

Process
A. Getting started

B. What is the issue?

C. What criteria should we use in selecting a solution?

D. What are the alternatives?

E. What are the strengths and weaknesses of the alternatives?

F. Are there other alternatives that combine key strengths?

G. Which alternative should we select?

H. Review and close

Process Improvement Agenda

Purpose
- Define the changes necessary to increase the efficiency and effectiveness of a business process

Products
- Existing process description
- New process description
- Implementation plan

Process
A. Getting started

B. How does the process work today?

C. What are the problems and root causes?

D. What are potential improvements?

E. How might we prioritize these improvements?

F. How will the new process work?

G. How will we implement this new process?

H. Review and close

Project Planning Agenda

Purpose
- Identify the objectives of a project and the resources and timelines needed to complete it

Product
- Project plan

Process
A. Getting started

B. Define project purpose and objectives

C. Determine project scope and deliverables

D. Identify critical success factors

E. Develop overall approach

F. Define resources, durations, dependencies, schedule

G. Identify risks and contingencies

H. Review and close

Strategic Planning Agenda

Purpose
- Develop a shared vision and document the steps to achieve that vision

Products
- Vision and mission statements
- Guiding principles
- Goals and objectives
- Strategies and priorities

Process
A. Getting started

B. Review situation analysis

C. Develop goals, mission, and vision

D. Develop objectives

E. Identify critical success factors and barriers

F. Develop strategies

    G. Define priorities

    H. Document action plans

    I.   Review and close

Team Building Agenda

Purpose

- Improve the ability of a team to work together

Products

- Our vision of an effective team—what we want to become
- Our action plan—the things we will do to move toward our vision
- Our team norms—how we will behave toward one another
- Our monitoring plan—how and how often we will check in to ensure that we are continuing to make progress
- Our accountability plan—how we will hold ourselves accountable

Process

    A. Getting started

    B. What makes teams work

    C. Our team vision

    D. Our issues and barriers

    E. Strategies to achieve our vision

    F. Our monitoring plan

    G. Our accountability plan

    H. Review and close

Customizing an Agenda

A standard agenda is designed with a focus on purpose and product. However, you should customize the agenda for a particular situation to address the other two Ps—participants and probable issues—more effectively. To tailor your agenda, you use your notes from the sponsor and participant interviews, and your understanding of the session purpose, to add, change, or delete activities in the standard agenda. For example, in the pay-for-performance case study, I used information gained in the participant interviews to modify the agenda to include both a discussion of the current situation and a visioning activity. The following are two other examples of customization.

Examples of
Customizing
a Standard
Process

- You are seeking to improve the hiring process, and you know that several participants are heavily invested in the old process. Therefore, you might include a process step after B, "How does the process work today?" such as C, "What are the strengths of the current process?"
- You are putting together a project plan for implementing new customer relationship management software, and you find out that the participants might be concerned about a lack of management support for the project (a probable issue). Accordingly, you could include a step H, "How do we ensure management buy-in?"

How do you customize an agenda? This brings us to our next secret.

Secret #59

The Secret to Customizing the Agenda

Design wide to narrow with early successes; establish common information and a base for decision making.

There are several principles to follow in customizing the agenda:

Principles of
Customizing
Agendas

- Ensure that the agenda includes standard opening and closing activities:
  - Include a "Getting started" segment to welcome participants, inform them about the process, get them excited about the objectives, set ground rules, understand their objectives, and establish the agenda.
  - Include a "Review and close" segment to review what has been done, ensure that objectives have been met, and get agreement on the next steps.
- The agenda should be designed to create a "wide-to-narrow" experience for the participants:
  - Early parts of the process should open the participants to a wide range of possibilities of what could be done. During this segment, the group should identify many potential approaches. You should use brainstorming, visioning, and other activities to help participants be creative and come up with many potential alternatives.

- Later steps of the process should narrow the possibilities of what *could* be done down to the strategies or recommendations that *will* be done. During the later steps of the process, you should encourage the participants to analyze and evaluate the possibilities and select those few strategies that have the potential to yield the greatest value.

- As discussed in Chapter Ten, people often disagree due to a lack of shared information. It is therefore important that you design the agenda to provide that base of information early in the process so that session attendees can work together to create solutions. For example, in the process improvement agenda, the item "How does the process work today?" is covered early, before the group begins to identify potential solutions.

- Arrange the agenda such that the session attendees achieve early successes and agreement before they tackle the more difficult issues. In our strategic planning model, for example, the group works on visioning and goal setting before taking on the very difficult task of establishing objectives.

- When the group is faced with making a decision, always have the session attendees build a common set of values they can use to guide their decision making. For example, in our issue resolution model, we use strengths and weaknesses and evaluation criteria to build a common set of values.

Developing an Agenda from Scratch

There will be times when none of your standard agendas, even with modifications, match the objectives of your session closely enough. When this is the case, you may need to construct an agenda "from scratch."

Secret #60

The Secret to Developing an Agenda from Scratch

Determine the critical question and the questions needed to answer it.

There are several steps in constructing an agenda from scratch.

Steps in Constructing an Agenda from Scratch	1. Determine the critical question. 2. Determine the preparation questions. 3. Determine the logical order of the preparation questions. 4. Transform the preparation questions into agenda items.

Determine the Critical Question

Your first step is to identify the key question that the participants must answer by the completion of the session. For example, the HR director states the following session purpose: "Develop a plan for fixing the hiring process. Make it less time consuming, less resource intensive, and more responsive to the needs of the department heads." Therefore, you might phrase the critical question as follows: "What are the actions necessary to improve the hiring process?"

Note that sometimes your critical question may have two parts. For example, if the purpose of the session is to set the organization in a new direction, the critical question might be: "What should our new direction be, and how do we get there?"

Determine the Preparation Questions

Once you have determined the critical question, you need to identify the questions that participants should answer first to prepare them to answer that critical question. Note that the last preparation question is the same as the critical question. The list of preparation questions might look like this:

- What's wrong with the hiring process?
- What's right with the hiring process?
- How does the hiring process work today?
- What things could we do to improve the hiring process?
- What are the actions necessary to achieve those improvements?

Determine the Logical Order of the Preparation Questions

Having identified the appropriate preparation questions, you now must determine their order. You should sequence the questions so that related questions are in close proximity to one another and questions that depend on answers from other questions are positioned later in the sequence. The following is the newly ordered list of questions:

- How does the hiring process work today?
- What's right with the hiring process?
- What's wrong with the hiring process?
- What things could we do to improve the hiring process?
- What are the actions necessary to achieve those improvements?

Transform the Preparation Questions into Agenda Items

The final step is to convert the list of questions into agenda items. You might choose to use the questions as they are as your agenda items. In other cases, you might change the wording so that all items appear as verb or noun phrases, as in the example that follows.

A. Introduction

B. Current processing steps

C. Strengths and weaknesses of the current process

D. Problems and root causes

E. Potential improvements

F. Implementation plan

G. Review and close

Knowing Your Process Cold: The Facilitation Guide

Although a standard agenda includes the activities to be covered, a detailed facilitation guide covers considerably more. The purpose of the facilitation guide is to ensure that you have thought through how you will facilitate each agenda item.

The Secret to Knowing Your Process Cold

Secret #61

Ensure that you know the process cold by having a detailed facilitation guide.

SMART facilitators use detailed facilitation guides to help ensure that they know their process cold. Along with purpose and product, a facilitation guide covers O-P-Q-R-S-T, as described in the following list, which outlines the contents of a facilitation guide.

Contents of
a Facilitation
Guide

- Purpose of the session
- Products to be created (and sample formats if possible)
- **Order** of the process steps to be taken (O; this is what most people think of as the agenda)
- Facilitation details for each process step (P-Q-R-S-T)
  - **Process** technique that will be used (for example, brainstorming, listing, prioritizing, grouping—see Chapter Seven)
  - **Question** to start the process step (that is, the type B starting question)
  - **Recording** method to document the responses received (for example, simple list, two-column matrix, having participants record on Post-it pads)
  - **Supplies** required to perform the process (for example, Post-its, dots)
  - **Timing** and estimated duration

Consider creating a facilitation guide for each of your standard agendas. Please note, however, that this level of detailed planning requires considerable time and involves using the techniques you will find throughout this book.

Why Do This?

Why take the time to create a facilitation guide?

The benefits of facilitation guides are similar to the benefits of standard agendas, but amplified. Facilitation guides

- Greatly reduce preparation time by giving you a starting point for starting questions, facilitated processes, and methods
- Help ensure that you do not miss a critical step or substep by giving you all the details
- Increase consistency from one assignment to another and from one facilitator to another, not only in what is done (the agenda) but in how it is done (the detailed steps)

See the Resource Guide for information on acquiring a set of facilitation guides for common sessions. Figure 12.1 is an example of a facilitation guide for the agenda item "How does the process work today?"

FIGURE 12.1   SAMPLE FACILITATION GUIDE.

Facilitation Guide for Process Improvement	
B. How does the process work today?	
What You Say	**What You Do**
• "We have just completed the introduction. Our next step is to list how the process works today. By doing this, we will all be starting from a common understanding before we move on to addressing the process. Let me give you an example. If we were discussing the accounts payable function, one major activity might include 'receive requests for payments from departments.' What else might be included in the accounts payable function?" —Processing and distributing checks —Reconciling bank statements —Interfacing with the general ledger —Producing reports • "Think about this process and the activities that occur on a regular basis. Let's build a list of these …"	• Label the page: "Steps in the *(Business Area Name)* Process." • Start with a checkpoint, PeDeQs, and listing. • Record responses on flip charts and post; the items on the list should be numbered for later use.
• "Now let's see if we can group these activities into a smaller group of categories, maybe three to five 'subprocesses'; the smaller group will allow us to analyze the information faster. What about the first activity … it sounds like it might be in a group called … What about the second activity … is it in this first grouping, or is another grouping needed?" • "So, we are saying that every activity in the business process is included in one of these subprocesses we listed; is that correct?"	• Label a separate page "Business Processes for *(Business Area Name)*"; list groupings as they are created, labeling the groupings A, B, C, and so on. • For each business activity on the business activities pages, indicate the letter of the group to which the activity was assigned. (Use a pen color different from the one used to list the business activities.) • Do a consensus check to confirm agreement. • *Note:* the department(s) may perform other activities outside the process under study (for example, personnel-related functions such as employee evaluations); because these activities are part of a different process, it is not appropriate to document these here.

Estimating and Tracking Time

I am often asked about methods for estimating the amount of time required to complete an agenda. Estimating time for a facilitated session is much like estimating time on a project: it is helpful to break down the whole into individual items.

The Secret to Estimating Time

Secret #62

Estimate based on the number of units and the amount of time per unit, being sure to add introduction and wrap-up time.

Estimating Individual Agenda Items

To estimate the duration of each agenda item, consider estimating four different elements. As an example, let's assume that we are using the process improvement agenda to address improvements to the hiring process, and we are estimating the time for the agenda item "How does the process work today?" Recall that this agenda item, as shown in the sample facilitation guide (Figure 12.1), includes both a listing activity (see the first section on the left side of the facilitation guide) and a grouping activity (see the second section). You will need to estimate the time for both activities. The four components involved in making an estimate are listed here:

The Four Components for Estimating Time	<ul><li>**Introduction.** How much time will it take to introduce the agenda item? Typically, this is two to five minutes, although some agenda introductions might take more time. Include in this estimate all the time needed before participants begin working. For example, the introduction would include your explanation and the time to divide into breakout groups. For our example, let's estimate three minutes for the listing introduction and another two minutes for the grouping introduction.</li><li>**Unit time.** How much time will it take to identify one item? For our example, let's assume that it takes us one minute to identify, record, and confirm each step, then another minute to decide which group it belongs to, for a total of two minutes.</li><li>**Number of units.** How many items are likely to be identified? Let's assume there are twelve to twenty steps in the hiring process. We will use the high number for the estimate, twenty units.</li><li>**Wrap-up.** How much time will it take to wrap up the discussion after all items have been identified? Let's assume that it will take another five minutes to wrap up the discussion.</li></ul>

The mathematical formula for calculating the amount of time is as follows:

Introduction + unit time × (number of units) + wrap-up = Agenda item time

For our example, the amount of time required would be calculated as follows (assuming twenty steps in the hiring process):

$$5 + 2 \times (20) + 5 = 50 \text{ minutes for this agenda item}$$

Adding Other Times

After estimating each agenda item, you should add other time required in the day, including break times and lunch. Consider including a ten- to fifteen-minute break every sixty to ninety minutes. Frequent breaks allow all members of the team to stay together during the discussion and work periods.

Tracking Time

As the session progresses, track performance against the time estimates.

- Record the actual start and end times as you proceed through each facilitated process.
- At each break, adjust the target start times and duration for future activities as necessary to respond to facilitated processes that are completed more quickly or slowly than originally anticipated.

I also recommend recording notes on the detailed agenda to improve your facilitated processes in the future. Notes may be related to variances in the estimation basis (for example, twelve items instead of the twenty estimated), areas that the participants found difficult, and ideas for improving the agenda or a facilitated process.

Applying the Secrets to the First Meeting of a Task Force

Over the past twenty years, my organization has facilitated hundreds of task forces through a series of meetings to create a specific product, such as a strategic plan, a new process flow, the requirements for a new information system, a community consensus around addressing a community-wide issue, or a team development plan complete with a team vision, team norms, and operating principles. Through this work, we have learned that the quality of the first meeting greatly impacts the success of the meetings that follow. The critical importance of the first meeting may not surprise you. However, what has been particularly surprising to us is that, over time, the way we facilitate that first task force meeting has become very consistent, despite the wide variety of session content.

Why has the first meeting become so consistent? Consider the goals of the first meeting. We believe it is important that the first meeting achieve a clear and common understanding of the following.

Questions to Be Answered in the First Task Force Meeting	<ul><li>Why have we been pulled together? What is the overall **purpose**?</li><li>What do we need to have when we are done? What are our **products**?</li><li>What are the most important topics we need to discuss or problems we need to address? What are the **probable issues**?</li><li>How are we going to go about doing our work? What is our **process** and what are our **ground rules**?</li><li>Who are the **participants,** and what do they bring to the table?</li><li>How will we go about making **decisions**?</li><li>Who needs to know about our progress? How will we **communicate** our activities?</li></ul>

Certainly there are numerous other questions that the group will need to address early on in the process. Yet we believe that answers to these core questions provide a solid foundation for the task force to move forward. How you go about answering these questions will differ from team to team. What follows here is a sample high-level agenda for the first task force meeting. With this clear focus on where you are going and a road map for how to work together to get there, your task force will be ready to begin its path to success!

Sample Agenda—The First Meeting of a Task Force

I. **Welcome**

II. **Charge to the Task Force**

What has the Task Force been asked to accomplish?

This is typically taken directly from the document that created the Task Force. During the facilitated session, a consensus check is taken to ensure agreement.

III. **Key Deliverables**

What are the critical documents or outputs that the Task Force must create to meet its charge?

A list of potential deliverables is created in advance, and they are presented as possible alternatives. Once deliverables are agreed on, sample tables of contents are also provided. This technique allows the Task Force to "start with the end in mind."

IV. **Key Issues**

What are the key issues that must be addressed in order to ensure that deliverables meet the charge?

We often use this as an interactive subgroup activity that allows the Task Force members to identify individual perspectives and hot buttons early in the meeting.

V. **Proposed Work Process**

What are the key activities that must be done to address the issues, create the deliverables, and meet the charge?

A proposed list of steps is presented to use as a starting point for the Task Force. Task Force members adjust the work process as necessary to ensure that the charge, deliverables, and key issues are addressed.

VI. **Ground Rules**

What are the guidelines we will use in our interactions with one another?

VII. **Gifts and Hooks**

What gifts does each participant bring to the group's work?

What has to happen for each participant to remain hooked and willing to attend and participate in all meetings?

VIII. **Communication Plan**

To whom should we provide updates on our status as we are going through the work process? How often should we communicate? What form should the communication take?

What should our policy be concerning communications about our status by Task Force members with others outside the Task Force, including the press?

IX. **Operating Logistics**

What will be our mode of decision making? Voting? Five-finger consensus?

How often should we meet? When? Where?

What information about each meeting will be documented? How?

How will information about each meeting be distributed, internally and externally?

If time permits, the work begins . . .

X. **Next Steps**

What are the things that need to happen between now and when we meet next? Who is responsible for ensuring that each happens?

XI. **Evaluation**

Facilitator's Checklist for Agenda Setting

☐ Maintain a set of standard agendas that you can use as a starting point for meeting the specific needs of a session.

☐ Use your notes from interviews and your understanding of the session purpose to customize a standard agenda.

☐ In customizing, ensure that you respect the following guidelines:

- Include standard opening and closing activities.
- Create a wide-then-narrow experience for the participants.
- Provide a base of shared information as early as possible.
- Design the agenda to achieve early successes and agreement.
- Build a common set of values or evaluation criteria for decision making.

☐ To develop an agenda from scratch, take the following steps:

- Determine the critical question.
- Determine the preparation questions.
- Determine the logical order of the preparation questions.
- Transform the preparation questions and the critical question into agenda items.

☐ Create your detailed facilitation guide, which should include the following:

- Purpose
- Product(s)
- Order of the process steps to be taken
- Facilitation details for each process step (P-Q-R-S-T)

  Process technique that will be used

  Question to start the process step

  Recording method to document the responses

  Supplies required to perform the process

  Timing and estimated duration

☐ To estimate the time required to execute a complete agenda, estimate the time for each agenda item individually, then add time for other items, such as breaks and meals.

☐ To estimate the time for each agenda item, use this formula: Introduction + unit time (number of units) + wrap-up

- How much time will it take to introduce the agenda item?
- How much time will it take to process one item?
- How many items are likely to be processed?
- How much time will it take to wrap up the discussion?

Exercise Your Skills

For your next meeting, use the steps in developing an agenda from scratch to build your agenda.

- Determine the critical question.
- Determine the preparation questions.
- Determine the logical order of the preparation questions.
- Transform the preparation questions into agenda items.

THE SECRETS TO FACILITATING VIRTUAL MEETINGS

Keep Everyone Focused and Engaged

Questions Answered in This Chapter

How do you help people who are not in the room "see" what is going on?

What are common technologies available to support virtual meetings?

How do you keep people fully engaged and participating in virtual meetings?

What special ground rules can be used to help with virtual meetings?

How do you apply the various Secrets of Facilitation in the virtual setting?

How do you facilitate a virtual meeting when you are the only person *not* in the room?

How do you address anonymity in a virtual meeting?

CASE STUDY: The Virtual Strategy Monitoring Session

The Drivers Model is the name we have given to our facilitative strategic planning methodology that covers all aspects of the strategy process, including briefing a management team on the benefits of strategy, performing a situation assessment, establishing the strategic direction, developing the implementation plan, and monitoring the execution. As part of the execution monitoring, the Drivers Model includes a monthly check-in that is done by phone, a half-day quarterly review typically done in person, and an annual two-day update to the plan.

For one particular government agency based in Cincinnati, its budget did not permit the travel expenses for the half-day quarterly review, so the agency asked if the sessions could be held via Web conferencing. In this case, the sixteen members of the planning team would be in a room in Cincinnati, and I would be "facilitating" the half-day session over the Web while in Atlanta. Although virtual meetings always present special problems for a facilitator, this particular case in which the facilitator was the only remote participant presented a new set of challenges. Not being in the room meant that I wasn't going to be able to observe the group dynamics, yet everyone else would.

The good news was that the quarterly review Drivers Model process comes with a highly structured agenda that helps maintain focus and control. The purpose and session agenda follows.

Session Objective

Review progress with the plan and reassess objectives and strategies for moving forward.

Session Agenda

A. Getting Started
   - Provide welcome and opening remarks.
   - Review session objective, deliverables.
   - Identify "Most prouds": What are you most proud of that has occurred in the organization since the last update?
   - Review agenda and ground rules.
   - Review the prior actions.

B. Assess Performance and Expectations
   By goal area
   - Assess each objective (measures): Are we getting the results we expected to get? What progress have we made? Where do we expect to be at year end?
   - Assess each strategy: Are we doing what we said we were going to do? What percentage complete are we? Where do we expect to be at year end?
   - What have been our significant issues or barriers in achieving the objectives and strategies in this goal area?
   - What adjustments do we make to objectives, if any?
   - What should we do with each existing strategy: keep, change, stop?
   - What strategies, if any, should we add to ensure accomplishment of the objectives?

C. Next Steps
   - Define the short-term action plan: What needs to be done immediately following the meeting to ensure implementation and follow-through?

Preparing

In advance of the session, I asked the plan coordinator to prepare a table listing all objectives. As shown on the next page, the table had five additional columns: the target, who is responsible, the year-to-date performance, expected performance by the end of fiscal year, and a grade column. The coordinator gathered the information and completed all sections except the grade column.

Objective	Target	Who	YTD Results	Expected Results	Grade

Likewise, in advance of the session, the plan coordinator prepared a table listing all priority strategies and their strategy leader, as shown in the table that follows. The plan coordinator had the strategy leaders indicate the percentage complete year-to-date and provide a recommendation whether the strategy should be kept, changed, or stopped.

Strategy	Leader	YTD % Complete	Expected % Complete	Keep, Change, or Stop?

I also prepared a Microsoft Word document that I would be using to record information from the session—much as I would prepare flip charts before a meeting began.

Starting

I asked that the meeting room in Cincinnati be set up in four teams with an LCD projector and screen. When people arrived, I had the meeting agenda and purpose shown on my computer's desktop, which was being projected in the meeting room via GotoMeeting Internet software.

At the beginning of the session, I asked the participants to say their names so that I would know who was on each of the four teams. I recorded the names in four groups on a sheet of paper in front of me as a visual to which I could always refer.

Following the sponsor's welcome remarks, I performed our classic IEEI: inform, excite, empower, involve. During the involve segment, I asked the participants to identify what they were most proud of that had occurred in the organization since the last update. I assigned team leaders and had them work in their teams for two minutes and record their responses on sticky notes, as I would do if I were in the room.

As teams reviewed their Post-its, I recorded the information in my MS-Word document for all to see. When another team indicated an item similar to one named by a prior team, I placed a 2 in front of the comment to indicate the number of teams making that comment. (No number, of course, meant that only one team made the comment.)

In reviewing the ground rules, I used our typical norms: everyone speaks, one conversation, take a stand, and so on. Because I had worked with the team before, I could easily associate voices with names, so it was not necessary for people to identify themselves before commenting—a norm we typically use in virtual sessions. I did, however, add a special ground rule given that everyone was in the same room except me. I called the ground rule "eyes in the room" and asked the plan coordinator to play this role. As my primary "eyes" in the room, he was to stop me—in midsentence if necessary—anytime he detected that I needed to speed up because people seemed to be disengaging or to slow down because people appeared to be lost, or to let me know that a hand was raised or that there was any other group behavior that I couldn't see. I also gave permission for others to do the same.

Running the Meeting

The bulk of the meeting was spent reviewing the status of each objective and establishing a grade, then reviewing the status of each strategy and deciding whether to continue, change, or stop the strategy. For each objective, I had the person responsible for tracking the objective take one to two minutes to review the status while I projected on the screen the information about that objective from the objectives table. Some people simply read the information on the screen. Most elaborated and gave a more complete explanation.

After the review of the first objective, I started with the first team and asked for someone from the team to suggest a grade (A through F) *based on the likelihood of achieving the target.* For example, if the target was 500 by the end of the year, and we were at the end of the first quarter and the performance was 100, but the owner expected to achieve the 500, the team might suggest an A grade, or an A– because the performance in the first quarter was lower than expected.

By asking the question to a particular team, I engaged that team in coming to a conclusion. Once someone on the first team suggested a grade, I recorded the grade in the table and then asked whether anyone wanted to suggest a different grade. My "eyes in the room" would indicate if others raised their hand to speak. If a different grade was suggested, I recorded that grade in the table as well. Once all grades for an objective were suggested (there were frequently only one or two), I used the informed majority process to have people understand the views and come to a conclusion, as follows:

- I asked each suggestor to indicate why he or she felt that the grade suggested was appropriate.
- I asked for any other comments, once more using my "eyes in the room" to indicate if other hands went up.
- After all comments were made, we used a simple raise-your-hand voting technique to allow the majority to decide the grade.
- My "eyes in the room" counted the votes and let me know the results. I removed all but the winning grade, and we moved on to the next objective.

When it was time to grade the second objective, I asked the second team to suggest a grade. With the next objective, I asked the next team, and so on, to involve all teams.

We used a similar process with the strategies, except that the strategy leader recommended whether to "keep, change, or stop" each strategy. I would then ask if anyone had a different recommendation. If there wasn't a different recommendation, we would move on to the next strategy. If there was a different recommendation, I would have the suggestor speak to the recommendation and then ask for other comments, and we would use the informed majority process as before.

For the next agenda item, issues and barriers, I had the teams pick team leaders, who then had their teams identify the key issues and barriers encountered in accomplishing our strategic plan during the quarter. After five minutes, I asked each team to share one barrier or issue (one that hadn't already been said). I recorded these in the MS-Word document for all to see until all unique barriers and issues had been identified.

After changing team leaders, I asked the new team leaders to discuss with their teams any recommended changes or new additions to the strategies or objectives, based on the issues and barriers identified, and to write these down. After five minutes, I asked each team to read their recommended changes, which I recorded in a two-column table, with the strategy or objective number going in the left column, as shown in the table that follows. If the team recommended a new strategy or objective, no number was given. I was then able to sort the table, and as a group we discussed all the recommended changes to each strategy and objective, using the informed majority process to decide which changes to implement. We then discussed the new strategies and objectives that were suggested.

Strat/Obj #	Recommended Change

Throughout the session, when issues arose that were not relevant to the discussion, I asked permission to place the issue on the Issues list, which was a separate document on my desktop so that I could easily access it and type in the issue. This document also contained the Actions list and the Decisions list.

Closing

At the completion of the session, I used the document to perform a standard close.

- I went back to the agenda to review what was done.

- I walked through the document to show the work that had been accomplished.

- I reviewed the Decisions list to remind people of any decisions made in the session.

- I reviewed the Issues list to address any outstanding items, asking the issue questions: Have we covered it? Do we need to cover it? Do we need to cover it now? All issues were covered.

- I reviewed the Actions list to ensure that a name and date were associated with all actions and to add any actions that were missed.

- We did a quick evaluation of the session.

  - We first did a round-robin person by person to identify what people liked about the session. I recorded these in the document.

  - When a comment was repeated, I placed a number at the beginning of the comment as described earlier.

- Following the round-robin, I went team by team asking for suggestions to improve the session. I recorded each improvement suggestion.
- To understand how much support there was for each improvement suggestion, I read each suggestion and asked people to raise their hands if they agreed with the suggestion. My "eyes in the room" counted the hands, and I recorded this with the suggestion.
- Finally, I turned the meeting back over to the sponsor, who thanked the participants, reminded them of the next steps, had them thank me for facilitating, and ended the meeting.

Following the monitoring session, it took me about two hours to clean up and merge items into a single document. I distributed the final document to the participants.

As this case study illustrates, in today's business world many meetings take place virtually using a variety of media, including the Internet, videoconferencing, the telephone, and other technology vehicles that allow participants to be in different geographical areas. Although these virtual media can reduce the cost of meetings, they can also present significant challenges to the facilitator. For despite the geographical dispersion, the facilitator must still find a way to get the participants excited from the very beginning, keep everyone engaged and focused on the objective, gather and document the critical information, build consensus, manage dysfunction, keep the energy high, and close with a clear understanding of what was accomplished, the value of the accomplishment, and the steps to be taken once the meeting ends.

Virtual meetings can be defined as meetings in which one or more of the people involved in the meeting are not in the same physical location as others. In some virtual meetings, you may have only one or two people who are remote and not in the same room with the rest of the group. In other virtual meetings, the number of people remote may be more than the number in the same room. In extreme cases, all of your participants and you may be in different locations.

For the majority of this chapter, I will be describing the extreme case in which all of the participants and you are in different rooms. Later in the chapter, I will describe how to handle cases when only a few people are remote or when you are the only one remote. However, in all these cases, two fundamental issues are common to virtual meetings:

- How do you help people who are not in the room "see" what is going on?
- How do you keep people who are not in the room fully engaged and participating as if they were in the room?

When it comes to virtual meetings, it is even more important to utilize the Secrets of Facilitation to maintain a consistency in your facilitation that will help those who are remote to be more engaged. This chapter covers strategies for adapting the Secrets to Virtual Meetings, starting with preparation.

The Secret to Preparing for a Virtual Meeting

In your preparation, select the appropriate technology and plan and prepare your facilitation methods so that everyone will be able to "see."

Choosing and Preparing Your Technology

Whenever possible with virtual meetings, consider using technology that will allow all participants to see the same information. In face-to-face meetings, flip charts serve as a major focusing tool; similarly, virtual meetings are far more productive when participants are seeing the meeting output created as the meeting is progressing. Having the meeting information visible can keep participants engaged, reduce off-topic conversations, minimize misunderstandings caused by people mishearing information, and provide a method for identifying and correcting when the facilitator has misunderstood a point that is made.

The number of tools available to assist facilitators with virtual meetings continues to grow. At the time of this publication, the more popular ones include WebEx, Live Meeting, Adobe Connect, GotoMeeting, Join.Me, Skype, Google Docs, Powernoodle, ThinkTank, TeamViewer, iLinc, and iMeet.

- For basic desktop sharing functions that allow others to see your screen while the meeting is progressing, tools that are free or relatively inexpensive, such as GotoMeeting, Join.Me, Skype, and Goggle Docs, may be more than adequate.
- When you need more robust capabilities, such as the ability to divide into breakout groups or have participants simultaneously record on a whiteboard, more powerful tools, such as WebEx, Live Meeting, or Adobe Connect, may be more appropriate.

Whatever tool you select, consider the following to help ensure that you are fully prepared with the tool. (These suggestions are adapted with permission from *Challenges of Virtual and Blended Meetings,* by Rachel Smith, director of digital facilitation services at the Grove Consultants International.)

- Spend time practicing with the technology before the meeting. Be sure to load any files you will be showing and to run through all the tools and options you think you might use. Consider practicing using two computers, one showing what you will see and one showing what participants will see, to ensure that you understand what you and the participants will experience.

- Offer to give a brief orientation session to participants in advance of the meeting to increase the comfort of those who are unfamiliar with the technology. The orientation session can also serve to identify potential technology problems early.

- If possible, arrange to have someone on hand during the session who can answer technical questions and help attendees who get stuck. Having a partner working with you to handle technical issues will allow you to keep the meeting running smoothly while your partner assists attendees in trouble.

- Ask attendees who are calling in from their computers to use a headset or earphones. When people don't use a headset or earphones, their computer microphone can sometimes pick up the output from the speakers and broadcast it back into the conference. Although the offender often can't hear this, others on the call will likely hear feedback or echoes.

- If some people simply can't use a headset or earphones, ask them to keep their microphone muted unless they are speaking.

Preparing for the Meeting

Along with preparing the technology, there are several other preparation steps, starting with identifying your 5 Ps.

- Define the 5 Ps for the session: the purpose, product, participants, probable issues, and process.
- When defining the process, think carefully through O-P-Q-R-S-T for the virtual setting.
  - What is the most appropriate **Order** of the processes?
  - What **Process** technique (for example, listing, brainstorming, or grouping) will you use with each agenda item?
  - What will be your type B starting **Question** for each agenda item?
  - How will you **Record** the responses for the agenda topic? Will you be using a Word document, PowerPoint, or whiteboard?
  - What **Supplies** do you need for the session? Although the session is virtual, consider what other tools you might need, such as pen and paper to diagram who is on the call.
  - What's your estimate of the **Timing** for each agenda item?
- Distribute a meeting notice in advance of the session, stating the purpose, the product, the agenda, and proposed ground rules, and that includes

any relevant handouts. The meeting notice should indicate what documents participants need to have for the meeting and any advance preparation required. If participants from multiple time zones are attending the meeting, be sure to specify the time zone when informing participants of the start and end times.

- As with face-to-face meetings, state a gathering time and a start time in the meeting notice. The gathering time should be ten to fifteen minutes before the start time to have everyone logged in and ready to go prior to the official start of the meeting.

- In planning the meeting, limit agenda items so that the entire call can be completed in two hours or less to help participants maintain focus. If necessary, break the meeting into several calls.

- Consider having participants do preliminary brainstorming and submit their ideas prior to the meeting. You can summarize these ideas into "brainstorm lists" and send them in advance to participants along with the agenda and other written materials. This advance preparation allows more time in the meeting to be spent grouping, prioritizing, or evaluating the brainstormed material.

- If there are multiple people at the same location, consider having them assemble for the meeting in a conference room or some other suitable environment. Having as many as possible in the same room promotes teamwork and helps people avoid the temptation to multitask (for example, answer emails) during the meeting. With each "call-in" location, consider appointing a scribe to document key points on flip charts during the meeting.

- Prior to the meeting, create a list that shows the name and location of each person expected in the meeting.

Starting the Meeting

As illustrated by the case study, the start of a virtual meeting includes the standard IEEI as you would execute in a face-to-face meeting. However, as you will see, there are a few additional steps due to the virtual nature of the meeting:

- Plan your setup time so that you are prepared and ready to go at least fifteen minutes prior to the start of the meeting. If this is the first time with a specific technology, you may want to plan to be set up thirty minutes prior to the meeting. This will give you extra time if you encounter unexpected difficulties.

- At the beginning of the meeting, conduct a roll call: ask participants to state their name and location.
- Try to address participants by name throughout the meeting to help others link names with voices.
- In getting the session started, perform a traditional IEEI: inform, excite, empower, involve.
  - Inform participants of the purpose and product of the meeting.
  - Get the participants excited about participating by explaining the benefits to them of a successful outcome.
  - Let them know the authority that has been given them.
  - Get them involved by asking a type B question that engages them in meaningful discussion that contributes to the work to be done. Use a round-robin and record responses so that all can see.
- If necessary, provide a quick orientation on how to use the virtual tool to help those not familiar with the technology or who did not attend a pre-meeting briefing.
- Consider adding specific ground rules to assist with "remote meeting etiquette," such as the following:
  - Announce yourself when joining the meeting and inform the group if you are leaving prior to the end of the meeting.
  - Always identify yourself before speaking.
  - Avoid using the "hold" button, especially when music or other sounds result.
  - Stay 100 percent focused during the meeting; avoid doing other work, answering emails, and so on.
- As discussed in the case study, if there are multiple people at one location, assign a person to be your "eyes in the room." Empower this person with the right to stop you—in midsentence if necessary—any time he or she detects that you need to speed up because people in the room seem to be disengaging or to slow down because people appear to be lost, or to let you know that a hand is raised or that there is any other group behavior that you can't see. Consider giving permission to all others to do the same.

Running the Meeting

As indicated earlier, one of the fundamental issues with virtual meetings is keeping people who are not in the room fully engaged and participating as if they were in the room. This brings us to our next secret.

The Secret to Engaging People Virtually

Every 10–20 minutes, lead a meaningful, interactive activity that engages everyone.

Just as with face-to-face meetings, there are several ways to increase interactivity in a virtual meeting. I have listed several common engagement strategies here.

Common Engagement Strategies for Virtual Meetings

- Use **round-robins** frequently to get input from everyone. For example, if the meeting is about improving the hiring process, a type B question might start as follows: "I would like to build a list of the strengths of the current hiring process. Let's go around the room starting with Joe. Think about . . ." With round-robins, you should vary the starting point so that the same person isn't always going first. However, follow the same order each time, calling people by name. This allows participants to be prepared to answer and for the meeting to flow quickly. Establish this order early in the meeting.

- The **whip** is an engagement strategy that can be just as effective in virtual meetings as it is in face-to-face meetings. With the whip, you ask a question and give people a brief moment (thirty seconds or less) to think about a one-word answer to the question. For example, "I would like to get the one word that best describes your opinion of the current hiring process. Think about . . ."

- Use **polls,** a feature of many virtual meeting tools, to have the group indicate their preferences or beliefs. For example: "In general, what has been the average time it has taken to hire someone? A. Under five weeks; B. Five to eight weeks; C. Over eight weeks."

- Employ the **whiteboard** feature of the technology to brainstorm. You can ask, for example, "What are the problems with the current hiring process?" The whiteboard allows many people to record answers at one time, making a round-robin unnecessary.

- Use **breakout groups** to have people work in teams. Again using the hiring process example, you might have each breakout group take a separate issue and identify potential solutions to the issue assigned. *Warning:* Be aware that at the time of this edition, the "breakout rooms" feature of a number of the virtual technology tools was not as reliable or user-friendly as other features. Often the splitting of audio and video between "rooms" and then pulling the information back required a higher level of skill for the facilitator. Be sure that you are both comfortable and competent in the use of this capability.

With the aforementioned engagement methods in mind, let's look now at strategies for running the virtual meeting.

- As with face-to-face meetings, do a **checkpoint** (review, preview, big view) at the start of every agenda item.
- Be extra clear with your directions, because people cannot see you. Use **PeDeQs** (purpose, example, directions, exceptions, questions, starting question).
- Consistently use type B **starting questions** that allow your participants to visualize their answers even before you are finished asking the questions.
- When asking questions, be very conscious of your wording, so as to avoid silence. Avoid asking a question to the group that no one person in the group can answer. For example, instead of asking, "Is *everyone* okay with the agenda?"—a question that no one person can answer—you might ask instead, "Would *anyone* like to recommend a change to the agenda?" If the group is small enough (twelve or fewer participants), use a roll call with direct questions, such as, "Would anyone like to recommend a change the agenda? Let's do a quick roll call with the question. Joe, any changes? Martha? Susan?"
- Establish a verbal method for doing consensus checks, such as a round-robin roll call, in which each person indicates agreement or disagreement.
- Do considerable summarizing and use frequent prompt and playback questions to make sure that everyone understands the focus of the discussion and what is being said.
- Review all issues, decisions, and action items prior to ending the meeting to help ensure full understanding and commitment to action.
- Publish a recap immediately after the meeting. As was true in the case study, you may very well find that most of the documentation has been prepared during the virtual meeting.

Special Cases

As indicated earlier, for the majority of this chapter I have described strategies for virtual meetings from the perspective of the extreme case in which all the participants and you are in different locations. Let's focus now on some special cases, including virtual meetings in which only a few people are remote.

If Only a Few People Are Remote

If only one or two people are remote and the rest of the participants are in the same room with you, it is very easy to overlook those participants. Consider the following strategies when this is the case:

- Consider adding the ground rule "Don't lose the remote." Explain that we don't want to lose those people who are remote, and we will always want to get their input. Also, give the remote participants the option to chime in at any time to get your attention because you can't see when they raise their hand.
- Consider always starting first with the remote participants when asking a question.
- Consider having a name card and chair at the table for the remote participants, as you do for the participants who are in the room. When you use round-robins, this setup will prompt you to ask for comments from the remote participants.
- Because there will be only a few remote participants, it is easy to forget that these people will not be in the room to receive any items handed out. Ensure that the agenda and all handouts are sent to remote participants in advance.

If You Are the Only Person Not in the Room

As was true of the case study at the beginning of this chapter, there may be times when all team members are in the same room for the meeting, and you—the facilitator—are the only one in a different location. This situation is especially difficult because, along with all the other challenges previously identified, everyone but you can see the group dynamics. For example, everyone else might see that the group is ready to move on, that you are going too fast, or that the group is not believing what you are saying, but you can't see these things.

When you find yourself leading a virtual meeting and you are not in the room, I recommend that you ask one person in the room to "be your eyes." Ask this person to call your attention to those things that you can't see. Let the person know that you are looking to him or her to point out what the group may be feeling or when the group appears to be in agreement or when there is a need to speed up or slow down.

If There Is a Need for Anonymity

As in face-to-face meetings, there may be times when the group would be best served by allowing anonymous comments to be made. This can frequently occur with organizations in which participants regularly defer to leadership or when fear of retribution or a lack of trust is present.

One way to create anonymity in a virtual meeting is to show participants how to send you a private chat message through the technology. Let participants know that you will copy these anonymous comments onto the screen for all to see.

Warning: I advise that you use this anonymity capability with caution. Generally, I find that although addressing the need for anonymity in a session can be helpful to that session, it can also mask deeper team issues that should be addressed to help bring about an atmosphere of open communication. By encouraging anonymous communication, you may instead be furthering the issue rather than helping resolve it.

This chapter includes more than forty strategies for running effective virtual meetings. Use these techniques to help make your virtual meetings as focused and engaging as your face-to-face sessions.

Facilitator's Checklist for Virtual Meetings

- ☐ Consider using virtual meeting technology that will allow all participants to "see" the same information; choose the technology that best meets your needs.

- ☐ Spend time practicing with the technology before the meeting; load any files you will be showing and run through all the tools and options you think you might use.

- ☐ Offer to give a brief orientation session to participants in advance of the meeting to increase the level of comfort for those who are unfamiliar with the technology.

- ☐ If possible, arrange to have someone on hand during the session who can answer technical questions and help attendees who get stuck.

- ☐ Ask attendees who are calling in from their computers to use a headset or earphones.

- ☐ Define the 5 Ps for the session: the purpose, product, participants, probable issues, and process.

- ☐ With the process, think carefully through O-P-Q-R-S-T for the virtual setting: order of the processes, process techniques, starting questions, recording technique, supplies, and timing.

- ☐ Distribute a meeting notice in advance of the session that states the purpose, the product, the agenda, and proposed ground rules, and includes any relevant handouts.

- ☐ As for face-to-face meetings, state a gathering time and a start time in the meeting notice; the gathering time should be ten to fifteen minutes before the start time to have everyone logged in and ready to go prior to the official start of the meeting.

☐ In planning the meeting, limit agenda items so that the entire call can be completed in two hours or less to help participants maintain focus.

☐ Consider having participants do preliminary brainstorming and submit their ideas prior to the meeting.

☐ Consider having multiple people at the same location assemble for the meeting in a conference room or some other suitable environment.

☐ Prior to the meeting, create a list that shows the name and location of each person expected in the meeting.

☐ Plan your setup time so that you are prepared and ready to go at least fifteen minutes prior to the start of the meeting.

☐ At the beginning of the meeting, conduct a roll call: ask participants to state their name and location.

☐ Try to address participants by name throughout the meeting to help others link names with voices.

☐ In getting the session started, perform a traditional IEEI: inform, excite, empower, involve.

☐ If necessary, provide a quick orientation on using the virtual tool to help those not familiar with the technology or who did not attend a pre-meeting briefing.

☐ Consider adding specific ground rules to assist with "remote meeting etiquette," such as the following:

- Announce yourself when joining the meeting and inform the group if you are leaving prior to the end of the meeting.

- Always identify yourself before speaking.

- Avoid using the "hold" button, especially when music or other sounds result.

- Stay 100 percent focused during the meeting; avoid doing other work, answering emails, and so on.

☐ If there are multiple people at one location, assign a person to be your "eyes in the room."

☐ Every ten to twenty minutes, lead a meaningful, interactive activity that engage everyone; some common engagement activities include round-robins, the whip, polls, the whiteboard, and breakout groups.

☐ In executing the meeting, use the same focusing and information gathering techniques you would use in a face-to-face meeting, such as checkpoints, PeDeQs for directions, type B starting questions, reacting questions, summarizing, and verbal checks.

☐ Close the meeting by reviewing all issues, decisions, and actions and reminding participants of the next steps.

☐ Publish a recap immediately after the meetings.

Exercise Your Skills

For the next virtual meeting you facilitate, use the approach described in this chapter to prepare, start, execute, and close the meeting. Expect that the preparation will take you about twice as long the first time, as you will be establishing new tools and approaches.

CHAPTER FOURTEEN

THE SECRETS TO FACILITATING LARGE GROUPS AND CONFERENCES

Use the Power of Process to Guide and Engage

Questions Answered in This Chapter

What are the key strategies for facilitating large groups?

How is planning the facilitation for a large group different from planning for a smaller group?

When is it best to have professional facilitators, rather than volunteers, lead the breakout groups?

How do you prepare the breakout group leaders?

What are best practices for facilitating conferences?

How do you maintain high levels of participant engagement when you have speakers and no control over how engaging they are?

How do you manage time during the conference, given that many speakers run over their allotted time?

CASE STUDY: Facilitating a Thousand People

Once a year, one of the largest national community-based organizations in the country convenes a meeting of its thirteen hundred affiliates and volunteers. At the conference this particular year, the organization was going to announce a new mission and vision that would likely change the nature of the work in local communities. Prior to the conference, the organizers had identified seven major issues that would affect the ability of the entire organization to realize this new vision. The organizers wanted the thousand or so people who would be convened at a general session to spend time discussing these issues and generating potential strategies for addressing them. They also wanted to have a meaningful report-back segment to hear some of the strategies that were identified. They wanted people to be able to address the topics that were of most interest to them. Finally, perhaps the toughest part, they wanted all this to happen in two hours and with one facilitator!

We knew that success in this endeavor depended on several critical factors:

- The purpose of the session and the deliverable to be produced had to be very clear to the participants.

- The directions for the process would have to be specific and understandable.

- The teams would have to be kept small because they would not be led by professional facilitators.

- We would need a rapid process for having people identify the topic of greatest interest to them and move to a team covering that topic.

- To avoid wasted time, each team would need to identify quickly the individuals who were to fill the roles of discussion leader, recorder, and reporter.

- We would need a process for hearing from a subset of the teams focused on each of the seven issues.

We undertook several strategies so as to execute this process effectively:

- The room was set up in 150 tables, with eight people per table. The tables were color coded with placards in seven different colors, each color representing one of the seven issues. Tables covering the same issue were clustered together in a section of the room.

- At each table, there were two sets of sheets. The first set, one copy per participant, included a one-page description of the steps in the process, the specific questions to be answered for the assigned topic, and a space for participants to record their individual responses. The second set of sheets, one page per question, provided space for recording unique comments from the group for each of the questions.

- At the beginning of the segment, I used our detailed process for giving directions (PeDeQs) to define the purpose of the session, provide an example of what we were seeking, give the general directions, identify likely exceptions and concerns, outline the report-back process, and recommend a process for assigning the roles.

- After quickly reviewing the topics, I asked the participants to select which topic they wanted to discuss and to decide which table they were going to join if they needed to move. They were then given two minutes to move to a different table. Somewhat surprisingly, very few people moved. Instead, most stayed with the topic assigned to the table at which they were sitting.

- After two minutes, I instructed the tables to select a discussion leader, recorder, and reporter. The discussion leader stepped through the five questions; the recorder wrote responses on the preformatted report-back pages.

- During this segment, I played the timekeeper role. The tables had a total of fifty minutes to respond to the five questions. We announced the completion of every ten-minute cycle and encouraged the discussion leaders to keep the discussion moving.

- At the completion of the fifty minutes, the report-back process began. To do the report-back effectively, we randomly selected five tables for each topic. The reporters from those tables became part of a panel onstage to engage in a structured, seven-minute discussion of responses to the questions related to that topic.

- At the completion of a topic report-back, those reporters departed the stage, and the randomly selected reporters for the next topic came on. To quicken the process of moving to a new topic, the reporters for the next topic were announced in advance and were seated near the stage in the "on deck" area.

- At the completion of the report-back process, the recorders submitted their information, which was later documented and made available for participants.

Facilitating Large Groups

Facilitating a large group can be quite intimidating. How does a single person influence the behavior of a group that includes hundreds of people? With large groups, well-defined processes become even more critical. Here are a few guidelines to use, starting with the Secret to Facilitating Large Groups.

Secret #65

The Secret to Facilitating Large Groups
Use the power of the process to help maintain focus, maximize productivity, and minimize dysfunctions.

In facilitating large groups, develop your facilitation process in three steps: first, define the process you would use if you were facilitating one team, then the process you would use if you were monitoring five others who were each facilitating a breakout group, and finally what the process would need to be if you had more teams than you could monitor. Let's take a closer look at each of these steps in developing the process to use with a large group. I'm going to assume that in your preparation you have already identified the first four Ps (purpose, product, participants, and probable issues) and are ready to focus on the fifth P, process.

- First, determine the process you would use if you were facilitating a single team of eight to twelve people. For this step, you need to cover only order and process techniques in the O-P-Q-R-S-T acronym for knowing your process cold.

- Next, consider how you would conduct the process differently if you had five breakout teams of eight to twelve people. This will probably mean having someone other than you serve as the facilitator for each of the breakout teams and another as a scribe. It is likely, however, that you would be able to monitor the process by spending some time with each team.

- Finally, consider how the process would have to change if you had more teams than you could possibly monitor. Then develop the rest of the O-P-Q-R-S-T: define your starting questions for each task, decide how to record information received, determine the supplies required, and estimate the timing for each task.
- Because you will not be facilitating the teams, the team processes should be very simple. Avoid complicated processes that require detailed explanation.
- If you are going to use a report-back process, consider employing one of these alternative methods to avoid having to hear from so many teams:
  - Have just a sample of the teams report back. The sample can be selected randomly or assigned based on topics, results, or group makeup.
  - Group each team with two others; have each team report to the other two and receive feedback.
  - Use a panel approach, as was done in the case study. If there are multiple topics and numerous breakout groups covering each topic, you could, for each topic, have five to seven groups that covered the same topic pick a representative to serve on a panel to whom you address questions about the topic. You would then have a different panel for each topic covered.

Often with large groups, as in the case study, it can be helpful if you supply the teams with written directions, a template for documenting their results, and guidelines for assessing the quality of their results. Depending on the complexity of the process and the skills of the team leaders, consider developing a team leader facilitation guide. Rather than just describing what to do, the facilitation guide would provide sample words to say when transitioning from one activity to another (checkpoints), when giving directions (PeDeQs), when asking starting questions (type B), and when executing the activity. Those team leaders who are more experienced or creative are likely to use the sample words only as a starting point for developing their own. Those less experienced team leaders are likely to find the sample words quite comforting!

Why Do This?	**Why is it important to do this level of detailed planning for large groups?**
	With large groups, your small errors are magnified greatly. Therefore, if you have not prepared a very detailed agenda for yourself and then practiced it, and if you do not have clear written instructions for breakout team leaders to use, you could be setting yourself up for significant failure.

If possible, you should select the team leaders in advance and hold an orientation for them as close to the event as possible. The orientation should explain the 5 Ps and take the leaders through the process they will use with their teams. If time permits, it is often helpful to give the team leaders an opportunity to practice using the process.

Finally, if the stakes are high or if teams will have more than about twelve people and will be spending more than twenty minutes in breakout, consider using professional facilitators as breakout team leaders. In these situations, expertise in managing group dynamics tends to become more necessary.

Facilitating Conferences

In both my professional and personal lives I have had the opportunity to attend a number of conferences. It seems that nearly all conferences are designed with the same format. A few well-known keynote speakers get up and give a talk— often amusing, sometimes thought-provoking, but hardly ever interactive. The keynote talks are then followed by concurrent breakout sessions in which other speakers, often less well known, get up and give a talk—often amusing, sometimes thought-provoking, but hardly ever interactive. Occasionally there is time left to ask questions. But for most conferences, the sessions include little interaction and engagement. Instead, participants become passive receivers of information. Frequently at conferences I have found myself sitting there thinking, "If only the conference planners understood how to use the power of facilitation, what a different experience their attendees could have."

Well, as the next case study reveals, I had the opportunity to put facilitation to use in facilitating a conference in my personal life.

CASE STUDY: Facilitating a Conference on Spirituality

Several of the top speakers and writers in the spiritual discipline that I follow were coming to Atlanta to headline a two-day conference. I was familiar with the conference organizers and met with them to gauge their interest in creating a conference experience that, for most attendees, would be unlike any other. I was pleased that they were excited about the sample approaches I shared with them, and appreciated their openness to my serving as their facilitator for the conference.

Although much preparation went into the conference design, a key success factor was the conversations with the various speakers to share with them ideas about how facilitation could be used to increase their impact as well as the audience's engagement and interaction.

During the two days of the conference, I used a number of different engagement strategies.

Introduction

Following the opening welcome by one of the organizers, who set the overall topic and reviewed the agenda at a high level, I was given the opportunity to set the expectations of the participants about the conference. I explained, "At most conferences, you are invited to come to hear great speakers. And you essentially become a passive recipient of information. This conference promises to be different. We don't want you sitting back receiving information. We want you to be an active participant in creating a conference experience that meets your specific needs. We want you reaching out so that you maximize this experience for you. For this to happen, however, it is important that you have in the forefront of your mind the specific question or insight you want addressed by this conference. Let's do this now. As you can see, you are broken into teams of about eight people each. Over the next five minutes, I would like you and your team to come up with up to three burning questions that your team members want answered by the end of the conference surrounding our topic. Here's how we are going to do it . . ." I then walked through the PeDeQs, had them select team leaders, and got them started. I let them know that during the morning session, I would group the burning questions and present them back.

Focusing the Audience

After introducing the first keynote, I explained, "Knowledge is good. Application is better. The key to change is to put into action what we are learning. As you listen to our first speaker, listen for tools that you can put in practice tomorrow, because after his talk, we will want to capture our learnings." By giving this information up front, I biased them to focus on actively listening to identify learnings.

Post-Questions

At the conclusion of the first keynote, rather than open the floor for questions, I had the prior team leaders choose the next team leaders and gave the teams two minutes to identify three questions they had for the speaker about his presentation. I then started with team 1 and had that team read one of the questions, then moved on to team 2, then team 3, and so on. I instructed team leaders to cross out any of their questions that were asked by another team. We exhausted all the questions from the teams within the fifteen minutes allotted, and I opened the floor for additional questions.

Reflection

I then gave one minute for people to reflect on the talk and to identify important tools or insights they heard that they could apply immediately to help them on their spiritual journey. I started with team 2 this time and asked one person from the team to share a tool or insight that he or she could apply. As a person from each team spoke, I captured the tool or insight by typing the information in a document that was being projected on the screen. Once we completed one from all the teams, I opened the floor up for anyone else who had something that had not been said. I used this reflection process after every plenary session to build our list of tools and insights.

Pre-Questions

With the second speaker, after giving her introduction and topic description, I introduced the pre-question technique: "Now that we have heard about the speaker and her topic, let's quickly identify the questions we would like to hear the speaker answer. Team leaders, you will have a minute with your teams to write down any questions your team would like to hear the speaker answer. You can record all the questions on one sheet. You will have just one minute. Think about . . . [starting question]. Now that you have recorded your questions, as you hear the speaker answer one of your questions, cross it out. At the end we will likely have an opportunity to take one question per team. So let's give a round of applause as the speaker comes up."

Panel Session

Halfway through the second day, we held a panel discussion that included five previous speakers. Prior to the panel discussion, I reviewed with the participants the burning questions that had been identified early on the first day and asked the teams to indicate whether a question had been addressed in some way. By the end we were left with only about a dozen questions that hadn't been addressed. During the panel session, each team had five minutes to have a Q&A session with the panel. The other teams listened in. The teams could choose one or more of the burning questions or any other questions team members wanted to ask the panel.

Brief Encounters

To provide one additional opportunity to help ensure that every person in the conference had an opportunity to have his or her most important issue addressed, we held a twenty-minute activity called brief encounters late in the afternoon of the second day. I described the activity this way: "You may still have a question that you haven't had answered yet. Wouldn't it be great to have about twenty people address your question? You will have that opportunity in just a moment. I am first going to give you a minute to write down the question you would love to have the answer to—preferably related to the last two days, but it's your question. When I start the clock, you will go to a random person and have what we call a brief encounter. You will first ask your question. That person will give you an answer. You will say thank you—no discussion—and then that person will ask you his or her question. And you will answer. The person will say thank you. This will end that encounter, and both of you will move on and encounter someone else. The key is to be present, hear the question, and give your best answer, and the person will do the same for you. *But no discussion;* once you are given an answer, say thank you, listen for the other's question, respond, and then move on. Try to have between fifteen and twenty-five brief encounters during our twenty minutes. Any questions? So think about . . . [starting question]." Brief encounters is a terrific way to raise energy in large groups and get people interacting.

Closing—Likes About the Conference

To close the conference, I had people work in their teams, with new team leaders assigned once again, to identify what they liked about the conference. I had the team leaders stand and read the items. To get through the reporting in a reasonable period of time, I had to give a thirty-second time limit to each team, as many teams had long lists! I would normally also ask for ways the conference could have been made even better, but due to time constraints, this question was covered later, on the evaluation form.

Closing—Actions

I then asked people to take a minute to identify the one action they would undertake as a result of the tools and insights gained over the two-day conference. The team members shared this with their fellow team members, who then selected one person from the team to speak his or her action to the entire conference.

The organizers considered the conference a tremendous success. As an aside, one person said that when he had heard that the conference was going to be facilitated, he was disappointed because he felt that it would negatively impact the conference; but he was pleasantly surprised at how much it had enhanced the overall experience.

This case study underscores the value of our next secret.

Secret #66

The Secret to Facilitating Conferences

Set the expectation of engagement early; use a variety of engagement strategies to ensure that each presentation is engaging and interactive.

In planning, designing, and facilitating conferences, I use the following steps with the design team to guide the program design effort.

1. Develop a clear purpose statement from the beginning.

   - Why are we holding this conference?
   - What is the issue or problem we want to see addressed?

2. Define the desired outcomes for the participants.

   - What do we want the participants to walk away with from this session? The "walk-aways" can be tangible (for example, an action plan, new tools they can use) or intangible (for example, beliefs we want them to hold).

3. Identify the key conditions critical to achieving the outcomes.

- If we are going to achieve the outcomes, what conditions must we create (for example, an understanding that the benefits far outweigh the "costs" of acting; time and a process for in-depth networking)?

4. Define the success strategies and program components for addressing the key conditions.

   - What steps should we take to create the key conditions?
   - What information or topics will the participants need to embrace, before and during the conference, to achieve the outcomes?
   - How should we group the topics?
   - What are our preliminary timings?

5. Identify the session speakers and facilitators who can relay the topics in a credible way that engages, provides interaction, and inspires the participants to action.

6. Explore creative opportunities for participants to engage with the content, interact with subject matter experts, share their experiences, network with one another, and create personal and collective action plans for applying their learning. Consider the following:

   - Using a banquet setup, with people seated around tables, in order to encourage teamwork and interaction.
   - Using the pre-questioning technique before speaker and panel presentations to engage the participants in a team activity, prepare them to listen, and give the presenters an understanding of what the participants are seeking.
   - Using a team round-robin Q&A activity following presentations to keep all participants engaged
   - Having three or four standing polls during a talk to get people out of their seats.
   - Having the speaker ask one or two questions that teams develop responses for, but take only three or four responses to save time.
   - Breaking out into small groups to identify collective and personal actions that can be taken based on the information gained in the conference. When using break-out groups, assign new team leaders each time to ensure that there is leadership responsibility and that the responsibility is shared.
   - Employing a variety of engagement strategies, such as brief encounters, to raise energy and to have participants gain valuable input from one another.

7. If participants need to reach agreement on conference outcomes, use the principles of consensus building: delineation, strengths and weaknesses, merging, and lobbying.

8. Hold discussions with speakers in advance to plan how you can best serve them in maximizing engagement and interaction.

9. During the session, pay close attention to your energy. Level 3 energy is typically essential for most conference facilitation.

10. Plan your time well. Plan for the potential impact of a delayed start by giving more time than needed for the start. Expect that it will take five extra minutes to restart following a break. Therefore, if you break for fifteen minutes, expect that you will need twenty before the group is productive once again.

11. Manage your time effectively. How do you manage your time when most of it is controlled by the speakers? This brings us to our next secret.

The Secret to Managing Time with Speakers

Inform speakers about the constraints; explain the process; take action as needed.

To manage your speakers, make sure that they know how much time they have been given and their expected start and stop times. Let them know that you will be giving them a five-minute warning and a one-minute warning, and that you will be standing once their time is up. If possible, sit in the front row and have three bright placards, one showing "5 minutes," the second showing "1 minute," and the third showing "Time Up." Plan to allow ten to fifteen minutes for Q&A, so that if a speaker goes over, you can adjust the Q&A accordingly.

In working with speakers, you will want to avoid offending them when asking how you can best serve them in increasing engagement and interaction with the audience. It is typically counterproductive to imply that they are not engaging! Instead, I have found it helpful to say words similar to the following.

You know how conferences can often be pretty boring with each speaker talking, followed by the same question-and-answer process, over and over again. Well, one of the things the organizers want is for each of the main sessions to engage participants in a different way. You may already be doing this, or may want to add something. In either case, if you are open to it, I would love to be your assistant. Some of the engagement strategies we have used in the past include engaging the group in identifying questions before you speak (we call this pre-questions); or you would ask a couple of questions, and I would have teams formulate their answers and take answers from three or four teams; or you would use two or three standing polls with true-false answers, and I would have people stand for true and then stand for false. These are just a few examples of the type of engagement strategies we can use. Are you open to including one or more engagement strategies in your talk? . . . Yes? Why don't we start with you letting me know what you have planned already . . ."

Are there organizations with conferences that tend to be highly interactive and engaging? Certainly. Conferences sponsored by the Creative Problem Solving Institute and the International Association of Facilitators are two that have come the closest in my experience. Although neither is perfect at ensuring that all their sessions and conferences are fully interactive, overall they both do very well at providing a highly engaging conference experience.

Why Do This?	**Why employ engagement strategies in conference design?**
	If you use these techniques once in a conference, the impact will probably speak for itself. You will probably find that your conference organizers, your speakers, and your participants will all comment on how much more value they gained and how much more beneficial the conference was.

One final note on facilitating conferences: recognize that the session planning time is typically two or three times more than would be the case if you were simply facilitating a session that lasted the same amount of time. As an example, with standard facilitated sessions, I find that the planning is about equal to the session time. That is, a two-day planning session would require a member of our core team about two days to prepare for the average session, perhaps one day if the session is relatively simple, and perhaps three days if the session is challenging. However, for a two-day conference, we would expect that it would require four to six days of preparation. Why so much more time? Primarily for two reasons:

- Conferences tend to have conference committees through which many elements of the program must be vetted. This means that you not only have to meet with the sponsor who guides you in the development of the agenda and the engagement strategies but also have to then gain the approval of the conference committee, a process that usually results in additional meetings and additional revisions.
- You will also have to spend extra time with speakers to plan with them the appropriate engagement strategies, given each speaker's topic, presentation goal, and presentation style.

Despite the extra time required, your use of facilitation techniques during a conference can significantly enhance the value and benefit gained by participants, speakers, and conference organizers. It's typically well worth the effort.

Facilitator's Checklist for Facilitating Large Groups and Conferences

Facilitating Large Groups

☐ Identify the first four Ps (purpose, product, participants, and probable issues).

☐ Develop the fifth P (process) through three steps: first, define the process you would use if you were facilitating one team, then the process you would use if you were monitoring five others facilitating breakout groups, then what the process would need to be if you had more teams than you could monitor.

☐ Use simple processes, as you will not be facilitating the breakout groups.

☐ If you are going to use a report-back process, consider one that avoids having to hear from every team.

☐ Consider supplying the teams with written directions, a template for documenting their results, and guidelines for assessing the quality of their results; depending on the complexity of the process and the skills of the team leaders, consider developing a team leader facilitation guide.

☐ If possible, select team leaders in advance and hold an orientation for them as close to the event as possible.

☐ Consider using professional facilitators as breakout team leaders if the stakes are high or if teams will have more than about twelve people and will be spending more than twenty minutes in breakout.

Facilitating Conferences

☐ Develop a clear purpose statement from the beginning.

☐ Define the desired outcomes for the participants.

☐ Identify the key conditions critical to achieving the outcomes.

☐ Define the success strategies and program components for addressing the key conditions.

☐ Identify the session speakers and facilitators who can relay the topics in a credible way that engages, provides interaction, and inspires the participants to action.

☐ Consider using a banquet setup, with people seated around tables, in order to encourage teamwork and interaction.

☐ Explore creative opportunities for participants to engage with the content, interact with subject matter experts, share their experiences, network with one another, and create personal and collective action plans for applying their learning.

☐ Plan specific engagement strategies for each component of the conference, especially for speakers and panels.

☐ If participants need to reach agreement on conference outcomes, use the principles of consensus building: delineation, strengths and weaknesses, merging, and lobbying.

☐ Recognize that the session planning time for conferences is typically two or three times more than would be the case if you were simply facilitating all components of a session that lasted the same amount of time.

Exercise Your Skills

When planning your next facilitation of a large group or conference, consider the strategies in this chapter. In particular, choose engagement strategies that will help keep the session interactive and your participants fully engaged.

CHAPTER FIFTEEN

THE SECRETS TO FACILITATING CROSS-CULTURAL GROUPS

Recognize Your Own Biases to Better Adapt to the Culture of Others

Questions Answered in This Chapter

What is meant by cross-cultural competency?

How does a national culture differ from an organizational culture or a team culture?

How do generational cultures impact facilitation?

How do you recognize your own cultural biases?

What are major dimensions that define different cultures?

How do you adapt the Secrets to the culture you are facilitating?

How do you facilitate groups whose culture encourages participants to defer to their leaders?

What is the dominance effect, and how does it play out in the groups you facilitate?

Introduction

How do you facilitate a group with a culture different from your own? To answer this question, I have asked three veteran facilitators with a wealth of experience in facilitating cross-cultural groups to make special contributions to this chapter.

- Dr. Eileen Dowse is the chair of the International Institute for Facilitation. She is an international consultant, writer, and speaker and president of Human Dynamics, a consulting company that specializes in organizational health and effectiveness. Eileen authored the first section in this chapter, "Understanding Cultural Competency."

- Eunice Shankland is a facilitator and trainer for the Food and Agriculture Organization of the United Nations. She is a principal of Shankland & Associates and a former chair and founding member of the International Association of Facilitators. Eunice currently works with organizations, associations, agencies, businesses, and United Nations agencies in the United States and internationally. In this chapter, Eunice teams with me to provide insights on applying the Secrets to cross-cultural groups.

- Nanci Luna Jiménez is recognized regionally, nationally, and internationally for her highly effective and insightful training, inclusive facilitation, and dynamic speaking with groups of diverse ages, industries, and cultural backgrounds. She has incorporated her unique approach to diversity, inclusion, and social justice in her work with such groups as members of the U.S. Congress, chiefs of Amazonian indigenous tribes, early childhood educators, students at every level, and leadership fellows from every sector. Nanci has provided the section "Interrupting the Effects of Institutional Power Through Facilitation."

Understanding Cultural Competency

In this section, Dr. Eileen Dowse shares her thoughts on cross-cultural groups.

As a Canadian with dual citizenship living in the United States and doing a great deal of facilitation work in Asia and Europe, I have found that the purpose and dynamics of a meeting depend on where participants come from. Britons and Americans commonly consider a meeting an opportunity to make decisions and get things done. The French typically use meetings as a forum for a briefing to cover and deliver important aspects of an issue. Germans are often more concerned with exactness and correctness, and hold meetings with the expectation of gaining compliance. Italians frequently use meetings to evaluate and gain support for their plans. Japanese and those in China regularly consider the first few meetings as an opportunity for establishing status and trust.

Each culture provides a code of behavior through its rules, values, and beliefs, to define what is right and wrong, proper and improper, respectable and disrespectable, and how things "should" be done. These rules, values, and beliefs are not necessarily made into law. Instead they become the thoughts and behaviors that must be adhered to and not broken in a person's culture. Essentially, unless they are eccentrics, people tend to conform to the values and beliefs of their culture. What does all this mean for a facilitator working with groups of people from across cultures? It means you must be sensitive to cultural expectations and be quick to define mutually shared goals.

There are no universal rules for facilitating meetings with cross-cultural groups. There are no hard-and-fast rules for structuring agendas, managing the process, or positioning participants in a meeting when people have gathered from different cultures and brought with them their different needs. Gaining allegiance with participants who do *not* share the same values, customs, habits, aspirations, preferences, and rules will clearly be more difficult for any facilitator. In fact, the level of difficulty could be compared to that of walking into a minefield—in this case, one of mammoth stereotypes, inaccurate assessments, and surprising exceptions.

Because the dynamics of cross-cultural facilitation can have such a profound effect on the process and the outcome of a meeting, we felt it was important to include it as a notable part of *The Secrets of Facilitation*. Our goal is to make you aware of some simple concepts for cross-cultural facilitation.

Definitions

It was the anthropologist Benjamin Wolfe who hypothesized that the language we speak largely determines our thinking, views, and perspectives. Sometimes our way of speaking and behaving might be seen as inconsiderate of, or even in direct contradiction to, what others hold sacred or consider appropriate. For example, after three long days of facilitating a strategic planning session together, a business partner and I decided to go to the hotel bar, where the program was held, for a glass of wine and a moment to review the events and outcomes of the last three days. After we had finished half a glass of wine, Barry (a born-and-bred male Australian now living in Hong Kong) turned to me (a born-and-bred female Canadian now living in the United States) and said,

"Hey Eileen, that was a ripper. What I need now is a nosh up, a top feed, and a blow. Whatdayareckon?"

Language determines our thinking, and at this point I was thinking that this colleague and friend was saying something that sounded offensive, but I couldn't believe that this was his intention. I looked at Barry, trying desperately not to let my eyes bulge out of their sockets, and asked, "What the heck are you talking about?" After he translated his message into "English," I learned that what Barry was really saying was,

"Hey Eileen, that was a ripper (good). What I need now is a nosh up (a celebration) a top feed (a meal), and a blow (a rest). Whatdayareckon? (What do you think)"

Barry's intention was to celebrate the hard work we had put into this project, followed by a well-earned rest. My intention was to clearly understand what he was saying before I slapped him across the face for being offensive! This kind of chaotic mix of dialects is often the source of miscommunication in all parts of the world. I can only hope that this story emphasizes the need for facilitators to be aware of the impact communication, language, and the use of slang has on others when their personality, gender, and culture interrupt the message being received. For this reason, I want to clarify the terms I will be using to communicate the concepts and insights in this chapter.

The terms related to cross-cultural concepts can be defined and understood in a variety of ways; the following are our interpretations:

Culture	The collective programming of the mind that distinguishes the members of one group from another. A culture comprises unconscious, taken-for-granted beliefs, perceptions, and thoughts related to the group and how it resolves issues. It can be the declared norms, operating philosophy, justifications, and values a group holds true. It can also include visible organizational structures and processes, long-held formal and informal systems, rules, traditions, rituals, routines, and customs.
National Culture	Incorporates such specific characteristics as language, religion, ethnic and racial identity, and cultural history and traditions. A person's national culture includes the value systems, beliefs, attitudes, and behaviors commonly held by people living in the country and is known to influence family life, education, economic and political structures, and business practices.
Organizational Culture	Incorporates the value systems, traditions, beliefs, attitudes, and behaviors commonly held by people working in an organization. Organizational culture is formed through experience, history, shared assumptions, and the meaning a group gives to symbols and objects, values, routines, informal norms and rules of conduct, habits, and traditions.
Team Culture	The sum of what people think, do, and produce. Team culture, when understood by all team members, allows a team to run smoothly in environments of stress and competing priorities.

Individual Culture	The integration of an individual's personality, traits, characteristics, idiosyncrasies, values, likes, dislikes, passions, talents, and knowledge. It is all these factors that make an individual unique.
Generational Culture	This term pertains to a group of individuals born and living in a specific time period. These individuals share or have shared similar experiences along with historic and social events. It describes what a generation generally thinks, how its members behave, and what they pass on to future generations.
Gender Culture	The set of social and behavioral norms considered to be socially appropriate for individuals of a specific sex in the context of a specific culture. These gender characteristics can differ widely between cultures and over time.
Racial Culture	Genetic and inherited features, such as skin, hair, and eye color, susceptibility to specific diseases, or other factors associated with race.
Dominant Culture	The culture of those who have the resources, assets, and economic or political power to impose their values, language, and ways of behaving on a subordinate culture or cultures. Dominant cultures have the institutional structures to shape and reinforce, through perceived benefits or real punishments, strong influence and effect on language, fashion, norms, values, behavior, and thinking.
Cultural Behaviors	Behaviors stemming from the common value systems, traditions, thoughts, beliefs, and emotions of the members of a defined group.
Cross-Cultural Competency	The ability to successfully communicate and interact with people from other cultures while being aware of and able to mitigate one's own prejudices. It entails being motivated to remain open to learning more about specific characteristics, different perceptions, and the ways members of other cultures think, feel, and behave, and to allow this learning to impact one's behavior and perceptions.

Cross-Cultural Groups Across Nations

Different cultures can require different facilitative approaches and different methods for engaging sponsors to increase the likelihood of achieving the desired outcome. As facilitators seize the immense opportunities that expertise in facilitating groups comprising mixed cultures can bring, they must be willing to increase their cross-cultural competency so that they can more effectively provide value to the sponsor and to the group being facilitated.

When it comes to identifying and understanding the traits of other cultures, often a person's mind tends to simplify the complex feelings and attitudes typically attributed to different groups. For example, it might not be uncommon for you to hear someone say,

> I facilitate for an international company, and there are some groups I just don't like to work with in meetings. I mean, those Italians are so smooth talking, while the Americans are arrogant and assertive. I'd rather hang out with the Brazilians, who are impulsive, body-centric, party animals, or even the Canadians, who are more agreeable, open minded, respectful, and law abiding. Let's just make sure we don't invite too many Greeks to the meeting, who in my opinion are disorganized and impossible planners. I know I'm supposed to be a neutral facilitator; it's just I always find these groups to act this way.

Stereotyping does exist, and the reality is that we cannot exist without it. We use stereotypes to fill in the gaps when we do not have enough information to make a decision. Stereotyping is not always a negative approach to thinking. It can be positive if it helps give facilitators a point of reference in determining how their own behavior might affect the cultures they are working with during a facilitation.

The important thing to remember as we consciously or unconsciously stereotype is that by having a working knowledge (or stereotype) of the basic traits of other cultures, a facilitator can minimize unpleasant surprises and gain advanced insight into a group. This insight can help a facilitator be more empathic and interact more successfully with different nationalities.

Empathy is the ability to coexperience and relate to the thoughts, emotions, or experiences of another person or group. When facilitators are empathic, they can appreciate the other person's situation and point of view and build on the differences in a positive way. You can tell when facilitators are using empathic skills because they will exhibit specific characteristics (see list on next page).

Ideally a facilitator will acquire insights into the culture and adapt a cultural mind-set when facilitating, especially when different national cultures are involved. If a facilitator is able to understand the typical preferences of a culture, then the opportunity for increasing objective thinking and removing cultural barriers can begin to occur within the group.

Empathic Characteristics	<ul><li>Sensitive to those around them</li><li>Flexible in their thinking</li><li>Willing to compromise</li><li>Polite</li><li>Tactful</li><li>Calm</li><li>Warm</li><li>Patient</li><li>Willing to clarify objectives</li><li>Observant of the other side's protocol</li><li>Careful to avoid irritants</li><li>Active listeners</li></ul>

With this thinking in mind, we present a self-awareness exercise to provide you an understanding of how your views as a facilitator align with other national cultural views and perspectives.

The Secret to Facilitating Cross-Cultural Groups

Understand how your cultural biases align with the culture of the group you are facilitating.

Cultural Awareness Assessment—an Exercise

This exercise is used and adapted with the express permission of Barry Brewster and Eileen Dowse from their book The Agile Business Leader.

Figure 15.1 is the Cultural Awareness Assessment. The objective of the assessment is to provide an understanding of how your views fit with other cultural perspectives and of ways to develop action steps toward building greater cultural competency.

Instructions

1. On each of the continuums in the figure, mark where you believe you are positioned in relation to the cultural dimension.

2. Being open to learning more about how others view the world and expanding your understanding of how to become more effective are what facilitators do to be successful. Consider asking the sponsor to go through the Cultural Awareness Assessment with you to identify where the group you will be facilitating falls on the various dimensions. In addition, ask yourself the following questions:

   - What will help me gain a better understanding or have a clearer picture of the diversity of the people with whom I will be working?
   - Given my own biases, how can I better open a dialogue between people of different languages, races, or cultures?

FIGURE 15.1   CULTURAL AWARENESS ASSESSMENT.

Respect Through Status vs. Accomplishments

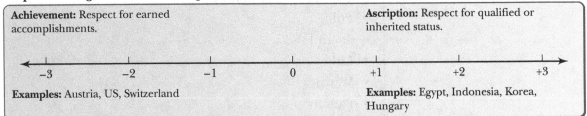

Achievement: Respect for earned accomplishments.

Ascription: Respect for qualified or inherited status.

−3   −2   −1   0   +1   +2   +3

Examples: Austria, US, Switzerland

Examples: Egypt, Indonesia, Korea, Hungary

Indirect Communication vs. Direct

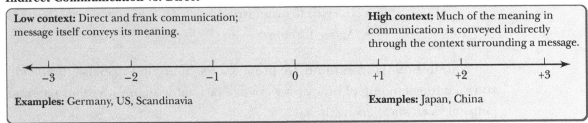

Low context: Direct and frank communication; message itself conveys its meaning.

High context: Much of the meaning in communication is conveyed indirectly through the context surrounding a message.

−3   −2   −1   0   +1   +2   +3

Examples: Germany, US, Scandinavia

Examples: Japan, China

Position Power vs. Shared

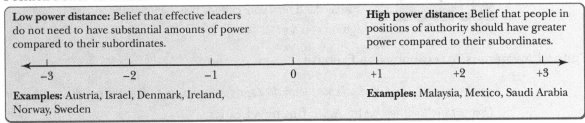

Low power distance: Belief that effective leaders do not need to have substantial amounts of power compared to their subordinates.

High power distance: Belief that people in positions of authority should have greater power compared to their subordinates.

−3   −2   −1   0   +1   +2   +3

Examples: Austria, Israel, Denmark, Ireland, Norway, Sweden

Examples: Malaysia, Mexico, Saudi Arabia

Communal Space vs. Territorial

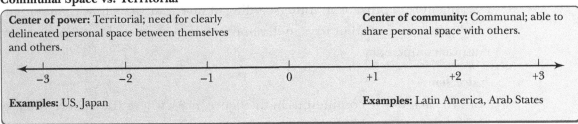

Center of power: Territorial; need for clearly delineated personal space between themselves and others.

Center of community: Communal; able to share personal space with others.

−3   −2   −1   0   +1   +2   +3

Examples: US, Japan

Examples: Latin America, Arab States

Long-Term Orientation vs. Short-Term

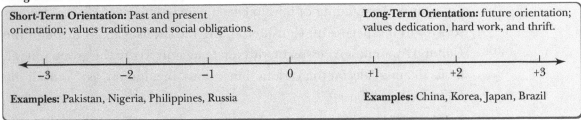

Short-Term Orientation: Past and present orientation; values traditions and social obligations.

Long-Term Orientation: future orientation; values dedication, hard work, and thrift.

−3   −2   −1   0   +1   +2   +3

Examples: Pakistan, Nigeria, Philippines, Russia

Examples: China, Korea, Japan, Brazil

(Continued)

FIGURE 15.1 (*CONTINUED*)

Intolerance for Ambiguity vs. Tolerance

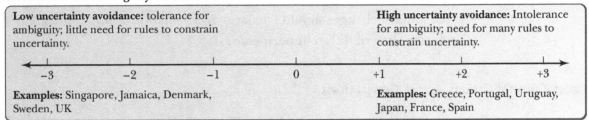

Low uncertainty avoidance: tolerance for ambiguity; little need for rules to constrain uncertainty.

High uncertainty avoidance: Intolerance for ambiguity; need for many rules to constrain uncertainty.

Examples: Singapore, Jamaica, Denmark, Sweden, UK

Examples: Greece, Portugal, Uruguay, Japan, France, Spain

Emotional Expressive vs. Refrained

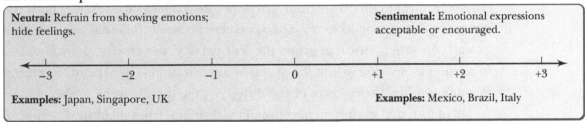

Neutral: Refrain from showing emotions; hide feelings.

Sentimental: Emotional expressions acceptable or encouraged.

Examples: Japan, Singapore, UK

Examples: Mexico, Brazil, Italy

Situational vs. Formal Rules

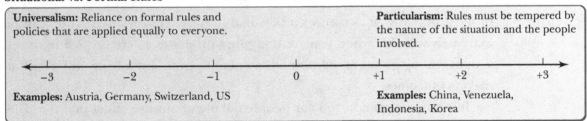

Universalism: Reliance on formal rules and policies that are applied equally to everyone.

Particularism: Rules must be tempered by the nature of the situation and the people involved.

Examples: Austria, Germany, Switzerland, US

Examples: China, Venezuela, Indonesia, Korea

Future Possibilities vs. Past Experiences

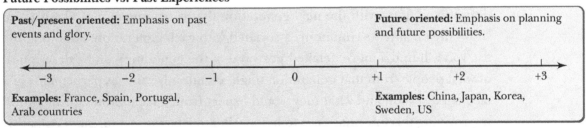

Past/present oriented: Emphasis on past events and glory.

Future oriented: Emphasis on planning and future possibilities.

Examples: France, Spain, Portugal, Arab countries

Examples: China, Japan, Korea, Sweden, US

Individual vs. Group Interests

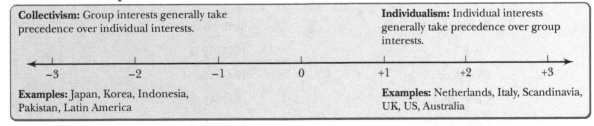

Collectivism: Group interests generally take precedence over individual interests.

Individualism: Individual interests generally take precedence over group interests.

Examples: Japan, Korea, Indonesia, Pakistan, Latin America

Examples: Netherlands, Italy, Scandinavia, UK, US, Australia

Note: The continuums in this exercise are an accumulation of the works of Kluckhohn and Strodtbeck, Hofstede, Hall, Trompenaars and Hampden-Turner, and Schwartz.

- How can I help the group work past cultural differences that may have contributed to the current situation? How can I assist in creating a better current state?
- What shifts or changes should I make in my facilitation to promote a greater understanding of different perspectives?

Cross-Cultural Groups Across Generations

We have talked about national cultural differences. Let's focus now on common generational differences. Facilitators can tell when they have ventured down the cross-cultural generation corridor when they hear a participant say, "This is the way we do things around here." This statement is usually followed by an attempt to teach the other person or group the "correct way" to perceive, think, and feel in relation to working within the group or organization. This type of "teaching" is common when the cultures of two different generations come together.

As mentioned earlier, generational culture describes a cultural period of a select group of people, one that spans all classes, races, nations, and people born in a certain period of time. Awareness of the cross-cultural perspectives of the group as well as your own personal preferences toward a group can be extremely valuable when you are designing processes to create positive interactions among group members and to enhance problem-solving and decision-making outcomes.

It is not uncommon to hear people talking about the effect that the Baby Boomers, Generation X, and Generation Y have on a group or organization. The list here names the five generations: four that are typically working in organizations today, along with the next generation that is coming along. The list also shows the birth years commonly associated with each generation. Following the list, you will find a more detailed portrayal of the generation and a description of what people from that generation might commonly value as participants in a facilitated session and what they would expect from a facilitator. Our intention in providing this information is to help facilitators be more aware and empathic to the needs of all group members.

Generation	Birth Years
Silent	1925–1942
Baby Boomer	1943–1960
Generation X	1961–1981
Generation Y	1982–2003
Generation Z	2004–2025

The descriptions that follow are adapted with the express permission of Barry Brewster and Eileen Dowse from The Agile Business Leader.

Silent Generation (Born 1925–1942)

This generation is also known as the Radio Babies, Builders, Veterans, Matures, Postwar Generation, Greatest Generation, Air Raid Generation, Seekers, Traditionalists, or Depression Babies.

People of the Silent Generation were influenced in their youth by the Great Depression and World War II. They grew up in serious times, when everyone had to do his or her duty (whether you liked it or not) and when children "should be seen and not heard." Many had fathers who served in World War I. They grew up as the suffocated children of war and depression. They came of age just too late to be war heroes and just too early to be youthful free spirits. They are conservative, hard working, and structured, preferring rules, order, and formal hierarchies. They have a "waste not, want not" mentality, and hate getting into debt. Their idea of progress is slow, incremental advancement, while minimizing risk. They also believe that it is "good" and "normal" to work hard. In fact, they believe they can achieve anything by sheer hard work. Their teenage years were marked by music, fashion, and entertainment that caused this postwar affluent group to adopt a consumerist bent. They are suspicious of those who make money by luck or by gambling.

Participants in This Generation Value the Following:
- Fairness
- Consistency
- Clarity
- Directness
- Respectfulness
- Honesty
- Loyalty

Participants from This Generation Expect Their Facilitator to Do the Following:
- Show dedication
- Place duty before pleasure
- Adhere to rules
- Work hard
- Provide and value law and order
- Respect the position and title of the person
- Be cautious in their actions
- Be self-sufficient
- Delay rewards

- Be modest
- Have patience
- Be reserved in expressing emotion
- Not be wasteful

Baby Boomers (Born 1943–1960)

Baby Boomers brought us the 1960s counterculture of a postwar generation renowned for drugs, sex, and rock 'n' roll. They had a hippie subculture that began in the United States during the early 1960s and spread around the world. They were disillusioned with traditional institutions and began to look for new, more authentic ways to live. These people created their own communities, listened to psychedelic rock, embraced the sexual revolution, and used drugs such as marijuana and LSD to explore alternative states of consciousness. They protested at anti-Vietnam rallies and were the initiators of the IT revolution. As they have aged, they have become greater consumers and have created more wealth (and accumulated more debt) than any other generation ever. They are a workaholic generation—driven, goal oriented, and focused on the bottom line. Boomers are passionately concerned about participation in the workplace; they are motivated by vision, mission, and strategy; and they care about creating a fair and level playing field for all who agree with them.

Participants in This Generation Value the Following:

- Excellence
- Idealism
- Optimism and positive attitude
- Autonomy
- Limited restrictions
- Self-expression
- Self-realization
- Image
- Personal gratification
- Personal growth
- Health and wellness
- Involvement
- Teamwork
- Work
- Nostalgia
- Political activism
- Free-market capitalism

Participants from This Generation Expect Their Facilitator to Do the Following:

- Show warmth and caring
- Be competent
- Be honest
- Demonstrate loyalty
- Treat people as equals
- Define purpose for every activity
- Use a democratic approach
- Create and maintain a positive, upbeat environment
- Ensure that the group gets the work done
- Provide plenty of opportunities to work in teams

Generation X (Born 1961–1981)

Also known as Baby Busters, Generation E, Nineties Generation, and the Boomerang Generation, Generation Xers grew up as "latchkey kids," many of them children of divorced parents who experienced an era of crises—from Watergate and Vietnam to the energy crisis and the collapse of communism. To them, it was clear that the adults didn't know what was going on. Adults had also become busier, and Xers experienced the first period in history when mothers could take a pill not to have any children. They are the MTV generation—influenced by fashion trends, music, and slang terms shown in music videos on the newly created cable channel MTV. After a brief period of living alone, frequently they boomeranged back to their place of origin by choosing to cohabitate with their parents. They grew up through an economic recession. As young adults, they dealt with the sexual consequences of AIDS. They dated and married more cautiously than previous generations. They are skeptical of corporations, realizing that long-term commitment is unlikely to pay the dividends it did to their parents and grandparents. They need options and flexibility, dislike close supervision, and prefer freedom and an outputs-driven workplace. They love change so much that they actually need it. Xers strive for balance in their lives: unlike many of their parents, who live to work, they work to have a life. They want rules, but from the right authorities only. Their "now" matters more than their future; they don't want to know "Is it true?" they want to know "Does it work?" They are spiritual seekers who believe in the supernatural. Music is significant in their lives: it is the "window to their soul" and the language they use to express themselves.

Participants in This Generation Value the Following:

- Willingness to challenge the system
- Willingness to create change

- Directness
- Competence
- Geniuses
- Informality
- Flexibility
- Results
- Learning opportunities
- Honesty
- Loyalty

Participants from This Generation Expect Their Facilitator to Do the Following:

- Be willing to change
- Be techno-literate
- Have a pragmatic approach to life
- Honor the individual
- Give them the ability to make choices
- Give immediate gratification
- Create a fun and informal setting
- Provide opportunities for learning
- Provide opportunities for global thinking
- Respect and honor the environment

Generation Y or N (Born 1982–2003)

Also known as the Net Generation, Nexers, Millennials, Bridgers, Echo Boomers, or New Boomers, Generation Y is the generation with the largest population in history. They are known as the "text generation," as they grew up with cell phones. They are defined as the generation growing up after the Cold War and in the new era of globalization, communication technology, and wireless connectivity. They are living in an age of unprecedented diversity and exposure to other cultures. They have an ability to filter out every command, every request, and every instruction that is not bundled with an acceptable rationale. They demand reasons and explanations. The traditional "because I said so" does not work with them. They are growing up in a world that is cracking under the strain of our lifestyles, and every day they are made aware of the fragile environment. In response, they are emerging as ethical consumers who want to change the world.

Participants in This Generation Value the Following:

- Motivation
- Collaboration

- Being positive
- Educated people
- Organization
- Receiving clear direction
- Achievement-oriented people
- Willingness to challenge the system
- Willingness to create change
- Congruency in words and actions
- Ability to be a coach
- Support and freedom
- Willingness to let them work at their own pace and in their own way
- Honesty
- Loyalty

Participants from This Generation Expect Their Facilitator to Do the Following:

- Exhibit optimism
- Offer opportunities for networking
- Provide opportunities for making changes
- Create an environment in which to achieve
- Include opportunities to be social
- Employ activities that produce collective action

Generation Z (Born 2004–2025)

Also known as Generation C for "click," "connected," and "computer," or the Digital Generation, this generation has grown up in a world with widespread equality of the sexes at work and at home, and where single-parent or same-sex-parent families are as commonplace as two-income families. Their lives are full of structured activities and parents using new technology tools as teaching aids and entertainment for their children. This new generation is being molded from the outset to be unique, as they are growing up with widespread broadband access, mass consumption of video games over the Web, and enormous online environments. They are both digital and virtual natives. They are exposed to an environment that is heavy on stimuli and weaker on interpersonal relationships. They are very active consumers, with a high degree of influence over their parents' purchasing decisions.

Participants in This Generation Value the Following:

- Willingness to create change
- Willingness to challenge the system

- Ability to coach
- Honesty
- Loyalty

Participants from This Generation Expect Their Facilitator to Do the Following:
- Create agendas and processes that are rational
- Provide opportunities to be proactive
- Minimize activities where social skills are critical
- Maximize processes where nonconformity is encouraged and respect for authority is discouraged
- Allow them to focus on self
- Provide opportunities to access and use the Web
- Allot time for careful planning

Conclusion

In our experience, having a cross-cultural perspective provides a way of understanding how a person thinks, behaves, and perceives the world. Facilitators who maintain this type of broadened perspective encourage awareness of how different groups of people are affected by cultural assumptions and foster cross-cultural cooperation. To ensure a smooth-running meeting when cross-cultural dynamics are in play, we suggest

- Setting clear, transparent aims and goals
- Insisting on an information sharing policy
- Providing practical, user-friendly tools
- Setting up time-efficient processes
- Recognizing contributions
- Preparing clear instructions
- Communicating instructions clearly
- Establishing ground rules related to multitasking

There is no doubt that cross-cultural dynamics will continue to influence the work of facilitators, and facilitators who choose to ignore the needs and perspectives of different cultures do so at their peril. Unfortunately, there is no universal formula or strategy for ensuring meeting success when such dynamics are involved. However, by understanding their own cultural biases and making appropriate adjustments in their facilitation style, facilitators will be able to guide the meeting process and provide a valuable experience for everyone involved. In the next section, we'll talk about strategies for adjusting the various secrets to the cultural needs of groups.

Applying the Secrets to Cross-Cultural Groups

In this section, Eunice Shankland joins with me in providing insights on applying the Secrets to cross-cultural groups.

The Secrets have been compiled from our combined experiences facilitating sessions for over three decades and from the experiences of hundreds of facilitators whom we have interviewed and trained. However, because we come from a Western culture, as do many of the facilitators with whom we have worked, the Secrets themselves are certainly designed with Western audiences in mind. So how do you apply the Secrets when facilitating across cultures? In this section, Eunice Shankland and I focus on strategies for facilitating cultures that are different from your own. We'll examine the use of key tools from each of the prior chapters in the book.

As indicated previously, it is important that you understand the environment in which you find yourself. However, avoid overgeneralizing cultural stereotypes. For example, if you are facilitating a session in Germany, there are certain national cultural norms of which you would want to be aware. However, although understanding a national cultural is helpful, understanding the specific company's culture is more important. For example, the culture of an engineering company is likely to be different from that of a marketing company. And cultures will vary even among engineering companies. Likewise, the culture of the specific team with whom you are working may have a greater effect on team members than the culture of the company. Therefore, use your understanding of broad cultural differences only as a starting point for understanding the culture of the specific group.

Let's look at how you might adapt key Secrets from each of the chapters of the book in a cross-cultural setting. For the sake of discussion let's assume we are going to be facilitating an English-speaking executive group of a Japanese manufacturer of handheld scanners in developing a three-year strategic plan.

Chapter Two—The Secrets to Questioning

The Starting Question
- Although the group is English speaking, we will record the starting question for each major agenda item on a flip chart to ensure that participants can

read and understand the question. We will want to be sure to avoid jargon and colloquialisms.

Reacting Questions

- Of the reacting questions, we are likely to find ourselves using the tag question, "That's important, isn't it?" more frequently. This question serves to constantly confirm that the group is moving together.
- We are likely to want to soften the use of the direct probe, "Why is that important?" to avoid its coming across as a challenge. This can be done by reducing our tone when asking the question or preceding the question with helping words, such as "Help me understand; why is that important?" Or, perhaps even better, we can changing the question slightly: "Help me understand; *how* is that important?" The point is that in a Japanese group, we want to be less confrontational in the approach.

Probing for Details

- If you find yourself in a high-context group where indirect communication is the norm, you may find it hard to get additional information directly when you ask the typical reacting questions. A different tack is to ask, "Tell me more about this," or "What story comes to mind about that? Describe it to me if you would . . ."

CASE STUDY: What Is the Objective?

How does culture impact the objective of the session? Eunice Shankland shares this story.

During a facilitation coaching session, a story about preparation was shared with the group. At the start of the session, the facilitator judiciously asked what the group was interested in achieving. He used the words, "Objective, result, and achievement" and gave illustrations to explain the terms.

The group kept telling him that their objective was to go through a process of working together. They were more interested in the path they were going to take and less interested in results. This was a departure from the usual understanding that a facilitated event has to deliver tangible results at the end of the session. It turned out that the group was made up of Buddhist monks.

The lesson we learned from this story was that you must strive to know your group; check assumptions and be clear about what you know and do not know about the group. Most important, before the event, be sure to get agreement on what the group wants—not what *you* think they should want!

Chapter Three—The Secrets to Preparing

Self-Preparation

- In preparing for this cross-cultural session, we will want to have done the Cultural Awareness Assessment. It will help us recognize our own biases and serve as a guide for identifying tendencies that we may need to adjust.
- For the session with the Japanese company, we recognize that it will be important to pay attention to people's titles when they comment. It probably will not be helpful for us to ask the top executive if it would be okay to put his unrelated issue on the Issues list. He or the group may perceive this as demeaning and insubordinate.
- Whereas we typically use "Titles left outside the door" as one of the standard ground rules to imply that titles are to be ignored in the room and that we should be treating all participants equally, this ground rule may not be appropriate for the Japanese session, as titles may be relevant to the participants. And for some groups, it is very important to address people by their titles. As always, check with the sponsor to ensure that you know what is and isn't appropriate.

Group Culture

- After making ourselves aware of our own cultural biases, we will want to understand the group's culture. One strategy to help accomplish this is to have the sponsor go through the Cultural Awareness Assessment to identify where the group falls on the various dimensions. Once we have a better understanding of the group, we will be better able to identify the adjustments we want to make to our facilitation style and approach.

Participant Interviews

- In interviewing participants prior to a session, you may find that members of some low-context cultures (those scoring low on the Indirect Communication Versus Direct dimension) are more likely to give you direct responses with details, whereas other cultures may be more indirect; in some cases, these group members expect you to probe further or to "read between the lines." This is especially true for high-context groups.
- Although group interviews are common in our practice, it may be important prior to this particular session to invite anonymous comments. Because transparency and openness are attributes that we highly value, we typically discourage anonymous comments, but it may be helpful to a high-power-distance group to allow them.
- Members of some cultures and with certain learning styles prefer to have the opportunity to read the interview questions in advance and write down their

answers in preparation. In that way, they do not look as though they do not know the answer and thus "lose face."

Room Setup

- Among other purposes, the room setup can serve to demonstrate your sensitivity to cultural norms. By creating a setting that is familiar to participants, you build an environment of safety and gain group members' trust.
- Some cultures tend to be more formal than others and would be more comfortable with a room setup that has such features as a head table with flowers, and microphones set up for each person. The opening session can be especially important in this regard.
- For cultures with a high need for territorial space, use roomy facilities that allow plenty of space between participants. Avoid room setups that seat people close to one another.
- As always, we want to consider how the session's purpose and desired products are served by the room setup. But, regardless of the purpose, we want to give considerable weight to cultural expectations and norms.

CASE STUDY: Facilitating the Strategic Plan for a Caribbean Government

I had the pleasure of facilitating the development of a national strategic plan for the government of one of the Caribbean islands. The planning summit included government ministers along with private sector and community leaders, 125 participants in total. I served as the lead facilitator for the session along with one other senior facilitator from our organization. We were assisted by seven breakout facilitators provided by the island-based private sector consulting firm coordinating the session. This session taught me two valuable lessons about facilitating in a different culture.

First, although the consulting firm briefed us on the culture of the country, I was not at all prepared for the challenges I faced in the opening. The session started with a greeting by the cosponsors of the summit. However, while the cosponsors were speaking, I noticed that a number of the participants at the various tables were engaged in side conversations, and that some of the conversations were quite boisterous. By the time I was introduced to review the summit agenda, the side conversations were completely out of control.

In a standard opening, I normally explain the agenda process before reviewing ground rules. However, I recognized right away that on this day the ground rules would have to come first. The ground rules included "Respect the speaker," and I underscored this particular ground rule by saying, as I described in Chapter Four, "If someone is speaking, it is considered rude to be speaking to your neighbor at the same time, because you are saying that your words are more important than the speaker's words. And my momma taught me that this is rude. So let's not make my momma a liar today. Let's agree that we will respect whoever is speaking by having one conversation. And if someone tries to speak to you while someone else is speaking, just say, 'Remember Michael's momma,' to remind that person of what my momma told me."

For most groups, I have found that this particular ground rule, when explained in that way, gains compliance almost immediately. Not with this group. We found ourselves constantly reminding everyone to keep my momma happy. We also had to modify our processes to minimize large-group time and ensure that we kept people highly engaged and interacting throughout. For this group, presentations longer than twelve or fifteen minutes were not a good idea.

Along with learning about the highly verbal nature of the group, I also learned the importance of understanding cultural norms with respect to behavior. In the United States, "fashionably late" refers to arriving after the official start time of an event to imply that you are a busy or popular person or to stage an entrance once most others have arrived. In this island nation, however, only the prime minister was allowed to be fashionably late. How was this enforced? For our social events in the evening, once the prime minister arrived, no one else was permitted to enter the room. And once in the room, no one was permitted to leave until the prime minister left. This gave new meaning to the term "captive audience."

Chapter Four—The Secrets to Starting

Starting on Time?

- In Western cultures, starting on time is preferred, although this rule varies according to corporate norms. As SMART facilitators, we do our part to ensure a timely start, and the Secrets suggest several strategies for bringing this about.

- For many cultures, however, the approach to time is very different from the Western view. For these groups, the start time stated on the agenda, and perhaps even agreed to in advance by all parties, is treated as a suggestion or guideline.

- To respect the time of those who arrive promptly, consider leading an engagement exercise early in the session that is valuable to the participants but doesn't require full attendance. You can also use this time to network or review the previous session or check the agenda for the day.

- For the session with the Japanese team, we will want to be diligent to talk about timeliness with the sponsor and others to ensure that we understand the group's view of timeliness.

What to Do First When Starting

- According to the Secrets to Starting, when people walk into a room, generally they want to know two things: why they are there and what will be accomplished. With this view in mind, the traditional start covers the following in this order:

- Inform: session purpose and product
- Excite: why it is important
- Empower: the role they are being asked to play
- Involve: their personal objectives
- Agenda: how their time will be used
- Ground rules and parking boards
- Introductions

- However, in the culture of your group, it may be more appropriate to focus first on who is in the room and on building relationships before focusing on why they are here, what they are going to accomplish, and how. Therefore, you may choose to have introductions occur first before anything else is done, and you may need to recognize that introductions may require more than just a few minutes. This can be particularly true for Asian and African cultures.

- For this particular strategy session with the Japanese manufacturer, the participants will know each other very well. However, coming from a culture that is high on the Respect Through Status Versus Accomplishments dimension, the group may want to know more about us and have us know more about them.

- In addition, when working in a high-context group, you might find it better to do a bit of "walking around the periphery and then moving toward the center" rather than starting directly with the core work.

Empowering

- The opening recommended by the Secrets includes specific activities that serve to empower the group. For example, during your opening statement, you empower the group by letting them know the role they are expected to play; in addition, you ask the participants for their personal objectives for the session and then offer to make adjustments to the agenda to ensure that all of their relevant objectives are addressed.

- These empowerment activities may not be as appropriate for cultures high on the Position Power Versus Shared dimension. These groups may expect that the work to be done has been set in concrete by those responsible and is therefore not open to discussion. Therefore, they may not understand the purpose of your typical empowerment efforts.

- Instead, empowerment in this context may look very different. As an example, you might listen for opportunities to open up group members by asking them to talk about their contribution to the topic at hand.

Ground Rules

- The selection and explanation of ground rules are critical activities for ensuring a successful session that reflects the needs of your group. The ground rules can communicate to the participants that you fully understand or completely misunderstand their cultural norms and how to maximize the session experience.

- Ground rules are frequently called operating principles, rules of engagement, group norms, and meeting criteria. The term you use should be one that is acceptable to the culture in which you are working.

- In facilitating a session for a culture different from your own, if you employ your standard ground rules, it is likely that you have not adequately adapted your facilitation approach to meet the needs of the group.

- As indicated earlier, for the session with the Japanese executives, we will probably drop "Titles left outside the door," one of the common ground rules. We might add a ground rule related to checking in periodically using small groups or a secret ballot to identify important issues that have not been discussed.

Chapter Five—The Secrets to Focusing

Checkpoints

- Using a checkpoint (review, preview, big view) for every agenda item helps keep everyone on the same page and provides a clear understanding of how each element of the agenda fits into the overall session.

- The checkpoint assumes that everyone is ready to move on and that people who are not ready will speak up.

- However, in some cultures, especially those high in the Indirect Communication Versus Direct dimension, people are highly unlikely to speak up if they are not ready to move on.

- Accordingly, with these groups, the Japanese manufacturing group included, it may be important to summarize and do a consensus check before the checkpoint. For example, we might say, "We have covered a number of points here, including . . . Is there more, or are we ready to move on?"

- Alternatively, you may find that the best approach is to do a round-robin when asking a question to the group. Some participants in certain cultures just won't answer unless they are specifically called upon.

Directions

- The PeDeQs method for giving directions (purpose, example, directions, exceptions, questions, and starting question) is explicit in giving participants the what, the why, and the how; it explains what they are being asked to do, why they are being asked to do it, and explicitly how to get it done.

- With groups that are low on the Intolerance for Ambiguity Versus Tolerance dimension, with little need for rules, the full PeDeQs may be viewed by some as being too simplistic or as treating them like children. For these groups, it may be adequate just to give the purpose, directions, and starting question.
- In contrast, for groups with high intolerance for uncertainty, such as the Japanese group in our example, you will want to use the full PeDeQs as a matter of course and to check that everyone is clear on the directions before starting.

Redirecting Comments

- As indicated earlier, the redirection question, which is used to move an irrelevant comment to the parking board, may be very appropriate for a group whose culture is low on the Position Power Versus Shared dimension.
- However, for a group with high power distance, which would likely be the case with the Japanese manufacturer, we will need to focus not only on what is said but on who says it, as it may be very inappropriate to redirect the comment of someone perceived to have high power.
- Our typical response to an off-topic comment is to redirect it by saying, "That's a good point; can we put it on the Issues list so we don't forget it and get back to our primary discussion on . . . ?" With a high power distance group, we might instead say, "Would you like to tell us more about that now, or would you prefer to save it until we talk about . . . ?" In this way, we are giving the power completely back to the speaker.
- Be aware that redirecting, even in this form, requires delicate intervention for some cultures, as you don't want to give the impression that you are discounting the person of power. It helps to consciously time your comment: have the person finish the comment and then respond, "We may need time to think out loud in smaller groups about this." This is like dancing: you don't want to step on your partner's toes. Giving some space is important as you flex to the situation the group is in, while keeping your purpose and outcome in mind.
- Finally, thinking again about the manufacturing strategy team, we will want to keep in mind that what we, coming from a Western culture, might deem as off topic might be very important to a high-context group.

Breakout Groups

- As described in Chapter Five, breakout groups serve as an excellent vehicle for increasing engagement when facilitating a large group and for getting more work done in a shorter amount of time if teams are working on different segments of the outcome to be achieved. For many cultures, however, breakout groups can serve two additional purposes.

- First, for cultures with a high focus on individualism (that is, high in the Individual Versus Group Interests dimension), breakout groups can serve to get people working together on a positive group outcome, rather than looking at the session through the lens of "impact on me."
- Second, a breakout group can provide a sense of empowerment that comes with anonymity. People who are reticent to speak in the large group for fear of offending someone in power often feel freer to speak up in a small group. This can be especially true of cultures high on the Position Power Versus Shared dimension.
- In the strategy session with the Japanese manufacturer, we will want to be on the lookout for times when respect for power may be blocking the flow of communication, and use breakout groups or other strategies to get ideas out on the table.
- We will also want to ask for insights in advance on how best to mix people. This may mean sometimes mixing different levels together, and other times having the same level together.

Chapter Six—The Secrets to Recording

Power of the Pen

- All the techniques surrounding using and not abusing the power of the pen apply to facilitating a culture different from your own. You will still want to write first, discuss second; write what they said, not what you heard; write so the group can read it; ask, don't tell; and so on.
- In some cases, you may ask the group to work in their language and make sure that they have good notes in English for the group report and for the final report. Consider having a bilingual member serve as the scribe. The small-group ideas can be written in English. Also consider using big cards and having participants write in two languages, theirs first and providing the English translation for the facilitator to track the conversation and what emerges from their ideas.

When Your Language Is Not the First Language of the Participants

- If you are facilitating in your native language and it is not the first language of the entire group, you may find times when you are unable to understand what someone has said. In these cases, it is of course okay to ask the person to repeat.
- However, it can become embarrassing and frustrating for the person if you are continually asking the same person to repeat, especially if, when the person repeats, you gain no greater clarity!

- If in the session for the Japanese company there will be people whose English is not strong, we would consider taking this issue off the table by adding a ground rule such as "Forgive my ears." We would explain this by saying the following:

  "I don't get the opportunity to facilitate in Japan very often and so haven't gotten completely used to clearly hearing the accents. Please forgive me if I have to ask you to repeat something. And if I still don't hear it, I may ask for you to write it down so I can get it."

- Another strategy for working with accents is to assign someone to be your "interpreter." Designate someone as the person to repeat the words if you don't understand them.

- You also might consider having someone else write for you. In this case, be sure to review with the scribe the Secrets behind how to use and not abuse the pen.

- Also constantly check in with the group to make sure your English is understandable to them: "Am I speaking slow enough to be understood? Is there something else I can do to make my message clearer?"

- Avoid catch phrases and slang, such as "That's cool," "Now there's an idea you can take to the bank," or "Let's do this and knock it out of the park." These work in your own country, but often don't make sense in other countries.

- Consider doing much more of the work in subteams so that participants are doing the writing rather than you.

Chapter Seven—The Secrets to Information Gathering

Setting the Context

- As the Secrets explain, when you want participants to provide you lots of answers, you do this by asking a type B starting question that allows them to "see" their answers. However, with high-context groups, it can be more beneficial to ask someone to build the context for the topic first.

- Therefore, with the Japanese executive team, we might ask a person of authority in the group, "Mr. Imaoka, would you talk with us about the importance of this topic?" or "We would like to invite . . . to . . ." (Of course we would have let the person know in advance that we were going to ask this question so that he would be prepared.)

The Influence of the Lead Person

- When we facilitate strategy teams, we often meet with the top executive in advance and gain agreement that this person will consciously *not* be the first, second, or third person to speak on an issue so that the others in the room will give their views without the direct bias of the top executive's view. This strategy typically works well.

- However, this approach can backfire for some groups. In cultures that are high social status and high power distance, people may be used to following the lead of the top executive. So if the lead person doesn't say anything, then they won't say anything either!

- In the strategy session with the Japanese group, we will want to have the conversation with the top executive on how to best encourage everyone's unbiased participation. Keep in mind, however, that the top executive may not want everyone's unbiased participation. In this case, facilitation may not be the best solution, as explained in the section "When Is Facilitation Not Appropriate?" in Chapter One.

Brainstorming

- In low-power-distance cultures, brainstorming is a frequently used practice to generate ideas. Following brainstorming, the facilitator typically leads the group through some type of grouping or prioritizing activity to identify the best ideas from the list.
- Typically, an important element of brainstorming is to separate an idea from the person who said it so that ideas are evaluated based on the quality of the idea, not on who said it.
- However, in some high-power-distance cultures, this type of brainstorming can be viewed as less desirable because of the implication that everyone is equal.
- Because there are numerous ways to brainstorm (for example, large group, breakout group, world café, silent brainstorming, rotating flip charts), you can reduce potential conflicts by holding discussions in advance to determine appropriate strategies for getting ideas on the table.
- When facilitating cultures high in the Respect Through Status Versus Accomplishment dimension, keep in mind that you may need to allot more time for small-group work. Participants will probably need to spend time making sure that all members agree with the items they will present back to the group.

Chapter Eight—The Secrets to Closing

The Closing Sequence

- Independent of the culture in which you are facilitating, the closing sequence is likely to remain the same: review the activities performed, review the participant's personal objectives, review the parking boards, evaluate the session, formally end, and then debrief with your project team. However, how you perform these activities may differ depending on the culture of the group.
- For some cultures, closing is just as important as the opening. Some cultures want and need more time to close a session and talk about what they have learned and how valuable it was to spend time with the group. Therefore, be sure you ask the sponsor about the group's preference in bringing the session to conclusion. Some will have formal talks, some will like to tell stories of what happened and what it meant to them, and so on. This is also a good time for

you to turn the up-front leadership back to the sponsor (having agreed with the sponsor beforehand).

Actions List

- At the close, there may be several actions to be completed following the meeting. Who performs these actions? In low-power-distance cultures, it is typical for people to volunteer to take on actions. In high-power-distance cultures, people are frequently assigned to actions by the leader, or "voluntold" (that is, "asked" to volunteer).
- Be sure you know how assignments will be made, so as to avoid assuming one way or the other. If you are not sure in the moment, defer to the leader by asking, "How should assignments be made for these actions? Are there particular people who you feel will fulfill the task best or who you would like to see handle each one? Or does it make more sense to ask for volunteers?"

The Closing Comments

- Regardless of the culture, it is typical to have a person of authority or influence formally close the session. Again, it is important that this person not be surprised by this role, but instead know in advance what is expected.
- For the strategy session with the Japanese manufacturing team, in the pre-meeting with the top executive, we will ask, "How shall we best close the session?" or "Who should do the closing comments at the end of the session?"
- It may be helpful in some cultures to have someone summarize in writing the key points from the meeting. The summary can then be handed to the leader, who can use it as a guide in giving the verbal summary.

Chapter Nine—The Secrets to Managing Dysfunction

Is It Truly Dysfunction?

- Recall the definition of dysfunction: *any activity by a participant that is consciously or unconsciously a substitution for expressing displeasure with the session content, the facilitation process, or outside factors.*
- What is considered dysfunctional is likely to differ depending on the culture of the group with which you are working. For example:
  - In some emotional expressive Latino cultures, interrupting and shouting may be considered functional communication styles.
  - By contract, in some Asian cultures, dropping-out behaviors might be more indicative of deference for authority than lack of interest.
  - Long-winded storytelling in some cultures may be a sign of an inability to focus, whereas for high-context cultures, stories are frequently used to convey meaning.

- It is important to consider the culture of the group you are facilitating when addressing what you believe may be dysfunctional behavior.

Preparing for Dysfunction

- To be better prepared to work with the group, review with the sponsor in advance the preferred style of the group and the list of common dysfunctions. Ask the sponsor to indicate the types of dysfunctions that you might encounter with the group. Also get the sponsor's counsel on how to best address the dysfunctions should they occur.

Addressing Dysfunction

- Although Chapter Nine provides strategies for preventing and addressing a variety of dysfunctions, be sure to view these strategies through the lens of the culture of the group.
- As indicated earlier, when working with cultures high in the Position Power and Respect Through Status dimensions, you will want to take extra care to ensure that you don't alienate yourself from the group by your manner of addressing dysfunctional behavior exhibited by a person of authority.
- For example, in the session with the Japanese manufacturing organization, we will want to avoid any situation that appears as though we are challenging a person of authority.
- When all else fails, it may be appropriate to solicit the sponsor's assistance in addressing a dysfunction, keeping in mind the second step in the general formula for addressing dysfunction: *empathize with the symptom.*

Chapter Ten—The Secrets to Consensus Building

What the Group Is Empowered to Do

- In some cultures, consensus is developed before the session occurs, through numerous conversations and negotiations. The purpose of the session is thus to decide on the terms of implementation. In other instances, the most important decisions are made during the break time. In your preparation, it is best to find out what level of consensus has already been reached and the role of the session. You must understand what the group is empowered to do, and choose the decision process that is appropriate for the group at any given time.
- For example, a group is often empowered in one of the following three ways: to create ideas, develop recommendations, or make a decision.
- If the group is charged with coming up with ideas, then a decision process isn't necessary. If one person suggests an idea, the idea would be on the list, regardless of the number of people who agreed with it. However, if the group has been charged with developing a recommendation or coming to a decision,

then a decision process is necessary, as some process is needed to decide when the decision is made or when a recommendation is agreed to.

The Decision Process the Group Will Use

- Once you determine that you need a decision process, the question then becomes, "At what point do we have agreement?" As Chapter Ten indicates, there are a number of ways of getting to agreement, ranging from pure consensus, in which 100 percent of the participants agree, to a simple majority.
- When working with cross-cultural groups, it is important to avoid making assumptions about how a decision will be made or even about the definition of consensus. For example, in some cultures, consensus simply means that after some discussion, a vote is taken and the majority rules. In other cultures, consensus means 100 percent agreement by all involved. Still other cultures define consensus as all participants having an opportunity to share their view, but the leader makes the final decision. This latter approach to consensus is frequently the case in high-context, high-position-power cultures, as would be likely with the Japanese manufacturer.
- To ensure that you are aligned with the way the group operates, review with the sponsor in advance the various ways decisions can be made (see Chapter Ten). Have the sponsor indicate the approach that best fits the culture of the group.
- It may also be helpful to coach the top executive to listen and affirm points of agreement to deepen ownership by the group. At the same time, if the boss strongly disagrees, it is better to find a way for the "No" to be stated during the meeting, rather than changing afterwards what appeared to be consensus among the group.

How Consensus Is Reached

- The Secrets to Building Consensus offer four strategies for reaching consensus: delineation, strengths and weaknesses, merge, and weighted scoring. These strategies for building consensus may be especially appropriate with groups who are low context and shared power, as is common in the West.
- However, for high-context, high-position-power groups, consensus building may best occur outside the room through side conversations and negotiations. Accordingly, you may find it more effective to have longer breaks during decision-making time to give space for people to come to agreement informally.
- Of course, this type of "consensus building" approach, which relies on conversations that exclude the entire group, may go counter to your "everyone is equal" sensibilities. However, it is helpful to recognize this sensibility as a potential cultural bias that can get in the way of serving the group.

Chapter Eleven—The Secrets to Energy

Level 3 Energy

- As described in Chapter Eleven, starting a session at level 3 energy serves three important purposes: it energizes the topic, engages the participants, and elevates the facilitator.

- However, whereas starting a session at level 3 may energize people from some cultures, it may do just the opposite for others. If your energy level is "over the top" for the group, it can de-energize the topic, disengage participants, and demote the facilitator in the eyes of the participants.

- Although the goal is to lift the energy of the group and in so doing raise the energy level of the session and increase the level of engagement of the participants, it is important to avoid going over the top and being perceived as "a typical rah-rah, touchy-feely facilitator," as we have heard it described before.

Adjusting to the Group

- How do you determine if you should start at level 3? We recommend that you pay close attention to the group conversation level. At what level do participants speak when talking in a group meeting? Level 1, level 2, or level 3?

- If you have concerns about level 3 being over the top, yet you still want to gain the advantages of the 3 Es, consider speaking one level above the group conversation level.

- For example, if you find during pre-meetings that participants predominately speak at level 1 or 1.5 when in groups, consider starting the session at level 2 or 2.5.

- A different strategy is to consider the metaphor of the symphony. Some symphonies start with a lot of fanfare. Others start quietly (*piano*), but then build into a crescendo (*fortissimo*). It is the facilitator's responsibility to track and guide the energy that is present in the room. You will therefore want to sharpen your sensitivity to the preferences of the group and compose the musical score accordingly.

CASE STUDY: Facilitating for Morehouse

You may wonder if there are groups who hold conversations at level 3. Only a few times have I facilitated such groups. One in particular was the board of directors of Morehouse, arguably the preeminent educational institution among the historically black colleges and universities. The board of this all-male college included Morehouse alumni, who were among the top in their chosen professions, including well-known actors, politicians, business people, researchers, and so on. Any time any one of them spoke, it was as though he were giving a speech: "My brothers of Morehouse . . . ," delivered at a resounding level 3.

Team Building

- As discussed in Chapter Eleven, you should choose team building activities that are tied to the purpose you are trying to achieve. In addition, it is important to hold a debrief following any activity to ensure that participants understand how the activity ties into the goal of the session.

- With high-context groups, it will be important to spend additional time at the beginning to provide the full context for why the activity is important. Although one or two sentences may be adequate for low-context groups, a full paragraph or two may be necessary to create the foundation needed for high-context groups.

- Give thought as well to how you assign leaders for team building activities. We often use random techniques for assigning breakout team leaders, but this approach may not be appropriate for all cultures. If the culture of the group you are working with is high in position power, consider having those in higher authority lead the first breakout groups. Then for each subsequent exercise, have the previous leader choose the next leader.

Chapter Twelve—The Secrets to Agenda Setting

Borrowing again from the Brewster and Dowse Cultural Awareness dimensions, let's examine how you might customize an agenda based on your group's position in each of the dimensions.

Respect Through Status vs. Accomplishments	
Ascription: Respect for qualified or inherited status. **Achievement:** Respect for earned accomplishments.	• If the respect is high for status or high for accomplishments, consider the impact this will have on general discussions, breakout groups, and prioritizing. • With general discussions, it may be appropriate to use round-robins to avoid allowing highly respected individuals to unduly influence the group. • With breakout groups, it may be important to ensure that the highly respected individuals are spread out. • When using prioritizing techniques, it may be wise to use techniques that increase anonymity.

Indirect Communication vs. Direct	
High context: Much of the meaning in communication is conveyed indirectly through the context surrounding a message.	• Provide more time in the agenda for participants to discuss and share their stories and reflect on meaning. • Recognize that sometimes you will have to "go slow at first in order to go fast."
Low context: Direct and frank communication; message itself conveys its meaning.	• Although less time is typically required for open discussion, consider checking occasionally to ensure that participants are not missing important contextual information.

Position Power vs. Shared	
High power distance: Belief that people in positions of author-ity should have greater power compared to subordinates.	• Consider using decision processes that acknowledge the role of authority. For example, you might employ a two-part process in which five-finger consensus is used for recommenda-tions that go to the leader, and then the leader reserves the right to accept or overrule the recommendations.
Low power distance: Belief that effective leaders do not need to have substantial amounts of power compared to their subordinates.	• Use standard consensus building processes, such as five-finger consensus.

Communal Space vs. Territorial	
Center of community: Communal; able to share personal space with others.	• No special adjustments may be necessary, as these groups are comfortable working closely with others as well as working separately.
Center of power: Territorial; need for clearly delineated personal space between themselves and others.	• Avoid team building exercises and other activities that require touching.

Long-Term Orientation vs. Short-Term	
Long-term orientation: Future orientation; values dedication, hard work, and thrift.	• With your opening and checkpoints, be sure to emphasize how the time the team is investing will be beneficial in the future.
Short-term orientation: Past and present orientation; values traditions and social obligations.	• Emphasize the short-term benefits of the work being done. • Be aware of both the traditions and the history of the group.

Intolerance for Ambiguity vs. Tolerance	
High uncertainty avoidance: Intolerance for ambiguity; need for many rules to constrain uncertainty.	• Be sure to design simple, easy-to-execute activities with instructions that can be easily understood.
Low uncertainty avoidance: Tolerance for ambiguity; little need for rules to constrain uncertainty.	• Avoid constraining the group with too many rules or providing too much process. Allow group members some degree of freedom in determining how they will tackle their work.

Emotional Expressive vs. Refrained	
Sentimental: Emotional expressions acceptable or encouraged.	• Avoid having the vocal minority make decisions for the entire group. Design consensus checks into the process to ensure that everyone is on board.
Neutral: Refrain from showing emotions; hide feelings.	• Avoid assuming that silence means consent. Use round-robins and other processes that encourage everyone to be heard.

Situational vs. Formal Rules	
Particularism: Rules must be tempered by the nature of the situation and the people involved.	• Be open to using ground rules only as needed and applying them as appropriate to situations and individuals.
Universalism: Reliance on formal rules and policies that are applied equally to everyone.	• Be specific with ground rules, with emphasis on how the group will be working together to create solutions.

Future Possibilities vs. Past Experiences	
Future oriented: Emphasis on planning and future possibilities.	• Spend less time focused on how things work today and more time on how they may work in the future.
Past/present oriented: Emphasis on past events and glory.	• Be sure that your processes take into account what has been done in the past. For example, more time may be needed to discuss how processes worked in the past before discussing how to improve them.

Individual vs. Group Interests	
Individualism: Individual interests generally take precedence over group interests.	• Although accomplishing the "will of the group" is typically the goal of facilitation, recognize that with cultures high in individualism, it will be important that everyone knows the WIIFM: "What's in it for me?" • Use processes that allow participants to recognize and verbalize their individual benefit.
Collectivism: Group interests generally take precedence over individual interests.	• Groups high in collectivism will naturally desire to develop solutions that benefit the entire group. Therefore, special adjustments to the process may not be needed.

What If You're Working with a Multicultural Group?

So far we've focused on facilitating a group from a culture different from your own. But what about multicultural groups? For example, what if the group is split between people from high-context and low-context cultures? What do you do? The following are strategies to consider:

| Facilitating a Multicultural Group | <ul><li>Be sure to plan additional time into the agenda.</li><li>Educate the group on cultural differences.</li><li>Encourage participants to laugh with one another as the differences appear.</li><li>Ask them to define what the meeting would look like if it were perfect for the other group or groups.</li><li>Have them determine how to incorporate the participants' diverse needs into the session.</li><li>Do activities that would draw on the energy of all cultures.</li><li>With breakout groups, be sure to pay attention to having a cultural mix in each group if appropriate.</li><li>You may find it helpful to have two types of agendas: one, detailed with a brief description of activities and a time log; the other, using images and more colorful language. Post both on the wall to engage both styles.</li></ul> |

Interrupting the Effects of Institutional Power Through Facilitation

Nanci Luna Jiménez provides insights on the dynamics of institutional power and how facilitation can be used to interrupt these dynamics.

Earlier in this chapter, you learned that cross-culturally competent facilitators own their cultural biases and make appropriate adjustments in their facilitation style. With both awareness and skills, facilitators can more effectively guide the meeting process and provide a valuable experience for everyone. By now you have begun to realize that facilitators have an incredible opportunity and even a responsibility to address power imbalances in a group. In doing so, facilitators model for others how to do so. We also have the ability to increase safety for people to participate no matter what role they play in the group. In this section, I am going to help you more deeply understand dominance and institutional power, how they impact groups, and some specific tools and processes you can use to responsibly interrupt them when facilitating.*

---

*Although many wonderful minds have influenced my thinking over the years, Lillian Roybal Rose has deeply influenced how I think about power, institutional oppression, and culture. I am grateful for her patient wisdom and gifted storytelling, and give her much credit for the ideas I express in this section. I also thank Barbara MacKay for generously reading and improving on earlier drafts and for introducing me to the world of facilitation.

Beyond Difference: Understanding the Dominance Effect

Conversations about cross-cultural facilitation will, at best, acknowledge differences, but they rarely do so with any awareness that not all differences are equal. Some differences carry more value; others are diminished. Those that carry more value are the ones that are reflected in the dominant group. The dominant group is simply the group that has power. It's important to remember that dominance has nothing to do with numbers—it's not the largest group, per se; rather, it's the group that holds institutional power. In an organizational setting, the dominant group would be the leadership or management team, or it might be the board of directors. In this discussion, though, I am referring to dominance at a societal level that shows up in any group regardless of the organizational structure.

If you are a facilitator working in the United States, it's important to remember that the dominant groups are men, white people, Christians (Protestants in particular), owning-class people (that is, those with enough investment income to support themselves without working), able-bodied people, heterosexuals, and adults (not too old, not too young). Before we go any further, check in with yourself: Are you experiencing a reaction as you read this list? Do you feel as though these are generalizations? Are you making a checklist of which groups you belong to? Which groups you don't? Have you had a variation of any of the following thoughts go through your head: "But I'm not dominant!" or "I don't have power just because I'm a (fill in the blank here with any one of the groups listed)." These are common responses, especially in a U.S. context. A dominant value is that being "progressive" or not prejudiced means that you don't see difference—evidenced by your ability to ignore or downplay it.

When I started my own business training and facilitating groups, I was twenty-six years old. Some of you may think that this is plenty old to be leading, but I struggled to think of myself as smart enough, skilled enough, or old enough. And a big part of that struggle was connected to my feeling too young to have anything of value to offer. I would hide my age and not reveal anything about myself that would enable someone to figure how old I was, for fear that my age would make me less credible in their view. When well-meaning participants older than I found out how old I was, they said, "I don't think of you as twenty-six years old" or "You are so smart for being twenty-six." As if this was an exception to my group. As if twenty-six-year-olds couldn't be that smart.

This comment reveals some important biases—and attitudes consistent with dominance. First, you might think it's a compliment that they didn't think of me as twenty-six. But I ask you: Why wouldn't I want them to think of me as twenty-six unless being twenty-six was negative? Yet that comment seeks to erase my difference (I was twenty-six years old, after all) and says, "I think of you like me, not like who you are."

Second, the person seeks to make me an exception to my twenty-six-year-old peers. If they must accept that I am a young adult, they are going to separate me from my group, "individualize" me and my experience, and therefore render me less threatening to them by divorcing me from a group that is different from theirs, experiences the world differently than they do, and has a different value system or way of knowing the world than they have. When they make me "just an individual," I become an oddity, not part of an experience of an entire generation that you would seek to understand. This is the dominance effect.

The Dominance Effect	The pressure or force for anyone not part of the dominant group to assimilate or conform to the group in power; the tendency to give more credibility, deference, access, or opportunity to those in the dominant group

An organization that I've worked with for many years is composed mostly of people of color and serves people of color communities. Although people of color make up the majority of the organization, there are usually one or two white staff members in any given meeting of twenty or so participants.

At a recent meeting I facilitated, the head of the organization was sharing her vision as part of a strategic planning process. The executive director is a woman of color who has more than fifteen years of experience running the organization and ample credentials and evidence of a successful track record. A white man, who was recently hired, challenged her vision as "out-of-date" and "misguided"—although he himself had no actual experience leading any organization, no credentials, and no track record. I watched the group members, all people of color, defer to him simply because he was a white man. The effect of his words—even though he couldn't provide any evidence or support to back up his comments or offer any real alternatives (he mostly criticized and questioned)—undermined the leadership and carried more weight with the group. This is an example of the dominance effect.

The dominance effect is an especially dangerous trap for those of us who are part of the dominant group. The trap is twofold: (1) if we don't talk about difference, then it isn't there, and if difference isn't there, then we can't be prejudiced or biased; and (2) we in the dominant group are systematically trained not to see difference—or the power granted to certain differences over others. To be in the dominant group is to be generally rendered clueless to the effects of dominance—both the unequal access, acceptance, validation, and material resources it provides for the dominant group and the exclusion, invalidation, and inaccessibility of material resources of the subordinate group.

The pattern of avoiding labels or denying difference doesn't make the power imbalance go away. Yet many of us, especially as facilitators, are trained to believe that to be effective we must be "neutral" and "objective." These very concepts—and an uncritical examination of the dominance intrinsic to this perspective (only certain groups are seen as "neutral")—can lead us facilitators to ignore the very differences in front of us—in the groups we guide and in ourselves—that will unconsciously or inadvertently give preference or deference to one person over another simply by virtue of their belonging to one or more of the dominant groups.

Beyond the Individual: Understanding Institutional Power

First, what do I mean by *institutional*? Every society is organized by its institutions. I am not merely referring to organizations but rather to the very building blocks that organize individuals into society as a whole. Some examples of institutions are families and marriage, the criminal justice system, education, health care, religion, politics, the military, and the media.

Given this understanding of institutions, what then do I mean by *institutional power*? This is different from individual power. Each individual is empowered to make decisions, act independently, and assess each new situation and context with fresh insights and learning. Institutional power reinforces norms and values that the dominant society views as "correct" or "right."

During the 1940s and 1950s in the United States, smoking was considered "cool" (perceived as highly positive and socially with the trend). You would see movie stars smoking on screen and off. Commercials on TV gave the impression that smoking a cigarette made you more attractive, more popular, and smarter. The media was the institution. The benefit that the media was attempting to sell us was "coolness," and smoking was the mechanism. Yet this benefit would be impossible to sell in the United States today. As more research demonstrated the overwhelming negative effects of smoking, the attitudes of the dominant groups shifted, and the media reflected this change in values. The dominant groups and their control over the institution didn't change—their values and feelings around smoking did. Now smoking, at least for most in the United States, is viewed as disgusting, unhealthy, and unattractive, and the people who smoke do so against the institutional norms and are penalized for it. For example, the so-called sin taxes make cigarettes more expensive. Even someone as individually powerful as the president of the United States, Barack Obama, hid his smoking habit, wouldn't let anyone take a photograph of him smoking, and was publicly emphatic about his desire to stop smoking.

Many of you may read this example and think that whether it is the 1940s and 1950s or today, smoking is an individual's choice. Technically, that is correct.

No one forced President Obama to buy cigarettes nor put a cigarette in his mouth and lit it nor made him inhale. However, I would offer institutional power as having an effect on his choice to do so. When we consider the effects of institutional power, we are not eliminating personal agency; however, our understanding of personal agency becomes more complex, more insightful, and more revealing when we look at the context and experiences shaped by the impact of institutional power on the individual. The challenge in talking about the concept of institutional power is that it debunks the myth of meritocracy[1] and the illusion of individual self-determination. And yet to ignore institutional power is to have only a partial understanding—biased as well as limited—of human beings.

How Institutional Power Reinforces Dominance

On the global and local scale, no two cultures are viewed or experienced as pure equals. In all societies, certain groups are granted additional credibility, access, and attitudes of entitlement or feeling "better than"—simply by virtue of membership in that group. These attributes are not earned or fought for; they are granted by the invisible hand of institutional power—and symbiotically, institutional power reinforces the dominance of the group in power.

The group in the position of "better than" is also the group that holds institutional power. That is to say, the group that benefits the most also controls the institutions of a society. As a USer,[2] I am most familiar with examples of dominance in a U.S. context. For example, the U.S. criminal justice system has the institutional power to judge whether a behavior is criminal or not, and it enforces this judgment with what it determines to be the appropriate response to this behavior—the level or kind of punishment, rehabilitation, or restorative justice. What is judged as criminal and how to respond to criminal behavior are determined by the values of the dominant group. And these values shared by the dominant groups in any society are reinforced with institutional power.

Because of the unique global position and influence of the United States, though, this dominance extends beyond U.S. borders. The list of dominant groups that I offered in the earlier paragraph is not limited to the U.S. context. Although there will be local variations, it is important to acknowledge that the United States exerts a larger, global dominance influence as well.

The Impacts of Dominance and Institutional Power on Facilitation

Now that we understand dominance and have a sense of its impact and how it is reinforced by institutional power, we must ask, What does all this mean for us as facilitators? Facilitation doesn't happen in a vacuum, absent of society's influences. Each individual has experiences that are shaped by the groups he or she belongs to: gender, sexual orientation, "race," ethnicity, class, religion, genera-tion, nation, and so on. Each individual is both aware and unaware of how he or she might be navigating the institutional power grid to decide when or whether to speak, what or what not to share, how vulnerable or transparent to be, and so on. Typically, we facilitators might consider these types of decisions on an indi-vidual, team, or organizational level.

Examples of Traditional Ways of Adjusting to the Individual or Team	• "That team is very analytical. They tend to process inter-nally, so we'll need to design a session that maximizes their optimal learning style even while we get them to share their thoughts with the other teams." • "She will be viewed as the expert in the room, so we'll need to make sure others get a chance to share their ideas early on; otherwise the rest of the group will defer to her suggestions."

In both these contexts, we are assessing a team's dynamics or an individu-al's influence on the process and therefore the outcome of a group's product. What if we considered facilitating with the added understanding of institutional power?

I was asked to facilitate a daylong session for the staff of a university department. The staff of about eighty people included an even mix of two groups: the first group was mostly white, African American, and Asian American professional staff (whom I'll call Group B); the second group was mostly Mexican, immigrant, or first-generation service or nonprofessional staff (whom I'll call Group A). When the staff gathered in the morning for the start of the session, almost without exception, Group A filled the seats in the back of the room while Group B took their places in the front. I was acutely aware of how Group A had physically deferred to Group B before the session had even begun.

What are the various dynamics of institutional power operating in this exam-ple? How would you facilitate so as to bring the group's attention to this dynamic in a productive way as well as to encourage equal participation from both groups, given the clear power imbalance?

Socioeconomic class imbalances are present in terms of both job responsi-bility and pay grade as well as the educational level of the participants. Another axis of dominance is language: in the United States, English fluency gives explicit priority in the meeting process. (Usually any flip charting or written documents are in English; the main presentation is expected to be in English; and if interpretation is made available, it is almost always the non-English speakers who will be expected to listen to the content in translation.) There is also the dynamic of "race" and ethnicity, especially as it relates to immigrants. Although the United States is a nation built by immigrants, Mexicans are viewed as "less than" by virtue of being darker, less educated, and "illegal." Even if they are first or second generation and born in the United States, they are still assumed to be foreigners.

Beyond Comfort: Embracing Discomfort and Ambiguity

In the session with the two groups described earlier, perhaps the very obvious segregation of the participants along these dimensions would have been blatant enough to get any facilitator's attention. However, the participants were following society's implicit expectations of how to divide based on status, preference, and dominance. Most people would think this was fine, even normal. Or at best, they would say that this is how the participants are most comfortable, so just let it be. However, "comfort" is not an indicator of correctness. An important aspect of skillful cross-cultural facilitation is learning to question comfort—in the group and in yourself as a facilitator.

A facilitator colleague shared a story of her experience of opting for "comfort" (instead of correctness) and how it played into institutional dominance. She was about halfway through a four-hour meeting when a few of the participants, in this case both nonwhite and not part of the organizational hierarchy, objected to the direction the meeting was going. They expressed that their concerns were not being addressed and were at times dismissed by the process. The facilitator patiently explained that they needed to get through the agenda and had only a couple of hours left to reach the outcome. She asked, "Could this be handled offline or in a later meeting?"

You can imagine how this meeting ended (not well), but let's use it as a learning opportunity for how dominance can lull us into staying with what is familiar or comfortable. When we are in an environment where staying on time is the value (which is also a U.S. dominant cultural pattern), most facilitators don't feel that they can easily address issues that come up unexpectedly, especially from groups that are structurally marginalized or when the person expressing the issue is angry or upset. Although in this case there may have been other motivations mixed in (for example, wanting to be seen as competent or to please the client), my colleague acknowledged that, primarily, staying on the agenda was simply more comfortable for her. Deviating from the agenda introduced too much ambiguity and emotion and wouldn't meet her task objective. These issues all relate to U.S. dominant values. It was within her comfort zone to continue to reinforce these norms—with little awareness that she, as the facilitator, was also reinforcing dominance.

This is just one small example of how comfort can confuse us as facilitators. Without understanding the intersection between comfort and dominance, we run the risk of colluding with or enforcing dominance. As you seek to develop cross-cultural fluency, explore your need to be comfortable or to make your group comfortable. Ask yourself some critical, probing questions, as follows.

Questions to Explore Your Need to Be Comfortable	• Who benefits from staying comfortable? • What is the worst that could happen if you (or your group) were uncomfortable? • What could you gain or grow from as a result of being uncomfortable?

Making Mistakes: Giving Up Perfection (aka Pretense)

Many of us are uncomfortable in an environment or situation where we might make a mistake. Think about how we were treated when we made a mistake, and this could explain why: How many times were we shamed for blowing it? How often were we made to feel stupid or incompetent when we missed the mark? It makes sense that we would work to avoid making mistakes—or at least letting anyone catch us making them. I think this is especially true where cross-cultural competency is at stake. The risks are high: we might be accused of being "sexist," "racist," or "prejudiced." To avoid this labeling, we tend to play it safe and not take too many risks—in other words, we'd rather appear perfect than be exposed for what we don't know.

Playing it safe, though, keeps us on the margins and in pretense. We act as though we "get it"—even if we don't—and as long as we stay on the margins, this image can't be tested. So we stay safe but also disconnected and ineffective. Making mistakes is human; it's how we learn. Without an opportunity to not get it right, how can we ever really know how to do anything?

Cross-cultural facilitation isn't any different. In fact, a willingness to make mistakes is a core competency—especially when the mistakes allow us to be vulnerable, learn from allies across differences, and become more aware of the blind spots created by dominance.

A facilitator colleague led a team charged with organizing and facilitating a dialogue in the community where he lives. The National Association for the Advancement of Colored People (NAACP), the oldest and largest civil rights organization in the United States, sponsored the event, and he was very conscious about getting a diverse group of volunteer community members to work with him. After several meetings, the group picked the date for the dialogue, and they sent out a press release. Within a matter of hours, he was getting phone calls and emails from members of the Jewish community because the date the group selected was on a high holy day—Rosh Hashanah. He quickly and respectfully responded to the emails and phone calls by setting up face-to-face meetings with the most vocal Jewish leaders. He listened, acknowledged his mistake, and apologized. In the process of holding these meetings, a couple of the leaders became interested enough in the project to become active members of the organizing committee. Working together, they set a new date and had a very successful community dialogue with all members of their community included.

Despite the team's diversity, no one from or connected with the Jewish community was part of the organizing committee. In part because of the dominance of Christianity, the organizing committee didn't notice the absence of Jews in an otherwise diverse group, nor were they aware of the Jewish calendar and high holy days when setting the meeting date. Unlike major Christian holidays, which are paid days off observed by government and commerce alike and well known to all whether you are Christian or not, Jewish holidays in the United States are mostly invisible to anyone who isn't Jewish.

This oversight wasn't my colleague's or the organizing committee's fault—it is important not to judge or assign blame or see the error as a sign of incompetence. Those attitudes toward mistakes will not create an environment where mistakes can happen and be learned from. Remember that in any of the places you are dominant, you are made clueless—this unawareness is institutionally constructed and reinforced. When you make mistakes, it's important to remember that there is no need to beat yourself up. Instead, simply acknowledge the mistake without defense, apologize for it without condition, and seek to gain new awareness from it. Each time you do this, your skills in cross-cultural facilitation develop and deepen.

Beyond Culture: Separating Culture from a Group's Patterned Response to Dominance

The last key concept to explore in our facilitator's journey toward cross-cultural competency involves a new perspective on and definition of culture. Let's go back to the definition of culture offered earlier in this chapter: "The collective programming of the mind that distinguishes the members of one group from another. A culture comprises unconscious, taken-for-granted beliefs, perceptions, and thoughts related to the group and how it resolves issues. It can be the declared norms, operating philosophy, justifications, and values a group holds true. It can also include visible organizational structures and processes, long-held formal and informal systems, rules, traditions, rituals, routines, and customs."

Although there are always exceptions to these definitions, there is also enough consistency that we assume that a definition of a group's culture, though dynamic and changing, is accurate to the extent that we either (1) observe these attitudes and behaviors enough to confirm the definition or (2) have limited or no contact with this cultural group, so we assume that the definition is accurate until proven otherwise.

A group's behavioral response to institutional power comes from a larger systemic effect than can be explained by the culture of a team, individual, or organization. These behaviors are often rooted in a group's sense of self or identity as shaped within and by the dominant culture. These behaviors eventually become so familiar that they are now mistaken for the group's "culture."

Unfortunately for all groups, whether "dominant" or "subordinate" in their relationship to institutional power, a definition of culture that centers on repeatable and recognizable attitudes and behaviors as the sum total of culture is at best limiting. Worse, without an understanding of institutional power, this definition of culture can reinforce these very power imbalances.

If we are successful in separating true "culture" from the responses to oppression, then we can allow people to fully claim their identities (for example, male, Canadian, working class, heterosexual, Jewish) and still reject any behaviors or attitudes that are negative toward themselves or others. This important separation gives everyone an opportunity to claim what is human, workable, whole, and benign about his or her group and fight against the oppressive attitudes and behaviors that impact his or her group—without confusing the two and losing a sense of pride and belonging along the way.

I grew up in a Catholic family. Both my parents were observant Catholics, as were my grandparents. I remember large family gatherings with scores of cousins at the church hall because no one's house was large enough to accommodate us all. Major family celebrations were centered around the church and usually involved mass, a priest, or both. My maternal grandparents died more than a quarter-century ago; yet every year to this day, a mass is celebrated in their honor, and the descendants, including great-great grandchildren who never even knew them, come together for this annual mass, followed by a family meal.

Yet despite growing up in a rich Catholic tradition, I rejected Catholicism years later due to what I viewed as homophobia and vicious antigay policies, sexism and discrimination toward women, anti-Jewish behavior, and collusion with policies of genocide, racism, and brutal colonization and attempted genocide of indigenous peoples. I decided I would no longer be Catholic, thereby rejecting all of these horrible oppressions. Yet I was still Catholic, because how do you leave who you are? I was unable to separate "culture" from "cultural patterns," but a brilliant nun made the distinction for me: "Come home to Catholicism. You can love all that is good and benign about what is Catholic and still say no to the oppression. But don't confuse that behavior with Catholicism, because it's not."

When I made the decision to "leave Catholicism," it was really my way of saying "I don't like this part of Catholicism, and I'm ashamed of it." I felt powerless to change it, so it felt as though the best option was to leave. Although leaving may have made me feel "better than" those Catholics who stayed Catholic, doing so, unfortunately, simply reinforced the shame.

As facilitators, we have the opportunity to clarify the difference between culture—something that distinguishes a group, a benign celebration or expression of difference—and cultural patterns, which are responses to institutional power and oppression, not an inherent part of the group's identity. If we accept and respect these cultural patterns as culture, we also reinforce self-destructive or oppressive behaviors within the group. We miss the chance to create a truly inclusive environment and opportunity for dialogue.

The Facilitator's Role in Creating a Just Environment

Recall the earlier example of the bilingual and bicultural university departmental staff meeting where Group A sat in the back and Group B sat in the front. Now that you've had a chance to reflect on the effects of institutional power and how it affects our role as facilitators, I'd like to return to this example. The question I asked was, *How would you facilitate so as to bring the group's attention to this dynamic in a productive way as well as to encourage equal participation from both groups, given the clear power imbalance?* What would you have tried?

Here are a few questions you might consider to guide your thinking. Please remember that which questions to consider will vary by situation, so use the ones here as a starting point for creating your own. You might also find it helpful to discuss questions like these with the sponsor or others who will be attending the session.

Questions to Ask to Identify and Address Power Dynamics

- What do I know about the power imbalances in this group? (Think in terms of "race," ethnicity, gender, socioeconomic class, education, language, literacy, religion, sexual orientation, age, ability, generation, region, seniority and years of experience, exempt or nonexempt payroll status, legal status, nationality.)
- With whom do I need to talk to better understand the unique ways the power imbalances play out in this group or might interrupt a truly inclusive process or meeting? (Make sure you are not just thinking about your client contact!)
- How unaware or clueless am I about the groups involved? (Be honest with yourself!) What additional research, reading, movie watching, or conversations do I need to do, see, and have to further my own learning about this experience?
- What activities do I need to add to my design to specifically address, interrupt, or mitigate against these power imbalances?
- What inoculations do I need to make (for example, anticipating and naming in advance the patterns of dominance or subordination that are predictable given the makeup of the group) to anticipate how the power imbalances will show up in this group during the meeting?
- How can I increase my own willingness as a facilitator to take risks and make mistakes with this group and allow others to call me out on my mistakes?
- How can I increase my skills in working in a highly emotional or conflicted meeting? How can I become more willing to listen to participants' feelings?
- How can I increase my capacity for facilitating in ambiguity?

Now that you've had a chance to use some of these questions to help you think about what you might have tried in the university example, let me share a few specific things I did to interrupt or mitigate the institutional power inequities in this situation.

Actions I
Took

1. I listened to the client about how these power imbalances were affecting his department. I invited him to think with me about the various aspects of the meeting that would need to change or would require additional resources in order to interrupt some of these dynamics.

2. I asked that there be enough translation equipment so that everyone experienced translation—not just the Spanish speakers—and I consulted with the interpreters about doing two-way interpretation.

3. I had all the written materials translated into Spanish in advance of the session.

4. Although I'm English language dominant, I also speak Spanish, so I started the session in Spanish. This would set a tone of welcome and inclusion for the Spanish-language speakers while also giving the English-language speakers the opportunity to learn experientially what it's like to participate in a bilingual meeting with the disadvantage of not speaking or understanding the predominant language in which the meeting was being conducted.

5. When we did our first pair sharing, I asked the Spanish speakers to stand as a group and pick an English-speaking partner. This allowed them to take leadership and initiative, and it impeded the English speakers in taking over or directing (although this still happened). I wasn't as explicit for later pairings, so most—but not all—group members tended to drift back to their own subgroups.

6. When I did the introductions, I started from the back of the room.

7. I introduced a "speaking order" that gave preference to Spanish speakers to ask questions first before I took questions from English speakers, and I asked the English speakers to count to five before raising their hands, to wait for the interpretation to finish.

8. I asked people to eat lunch with two people whose first language was different from their own.

9. When the content of the meeting created an opening for a discussion about these power imbalances, I asked participants to share their observations, personal experiences, and ideas for how to address them in the group going forward.

By now you have a keen awareness of the subtle and not-so-subtle ways that institutional power and dominance can impact you as a facilitator and your facilitation practice—despite your well-honed skills and passionate commitment. With this growing awareness, you can use the lens this section has provided to rethink and review how you might approach a facilitated session with increased cross-cultural fluency. At its best, cross-cultural facilitation can assess, mitigate, and even interrupt the impact of institutional power. At its most effective, a cross-cultural facilitation is one where all participants transparently and authentically contribute their wisdom, and the group's best thinking is truly representative of the whole group. At its most powerful, cross-cultural facilitation creates a space where everyone is seen, heard, and understood. And I ask you: Is there a more profound human experience?

At a break during that bilingual and bicultural university departmental staff meeting, I was conscious that I had been talking with someone on the first half of break and now had very little time before we were supposed to start again, and I really needed to use the facilities. Rushing into the restroom, I pushed open the door, and my eyes darted about as I desperately searched for an open stall. But when I entered the restroom, and the women in there, all Mexicanas and other Latinas, saw it was I, my break took another direction. The women turned toward me and began telling me what a difference it made to them that I was facilitating the meeting. In a mix of chorus and solo voices, they shared with me how proud they were that I was Latina too, that they could identify with me, that I understood them, and that I made it safer for them to share and be themselves. I stood there and listened. With tears in their eyes, without the least bit of self-consciousness as their tears began rolling down their cheeks, they thanked me. Over and over again, they squeezed my hands, gave me hugs. One by one the women thanked me, and I stood there until each woman had had her chance to say her words, touch me, and feel complete.

I don't know how much time went by, but at some point it was done, and I realized that I was now alone. And as I stood there in the middle of the bathroom, I noticed that my own cheeks were wet. I too had been crying. In some way I had done right by them. I had seen them, heard them, and known them. And I noticed that it made a difference. I felt both an extra weight of responsibility not to mess it up (which soon passed) and a sense of deep peace (which lingered for a long time). Without even looking at what time it was, I finally let myself go into the stall and get my much-needed break.

Facilitator's Checklist for Facilitating Cross-Cultural Groups

- ☐ Take the Cultural Awareness Assessment to recognize your own biases and identify tendencies that you may need to adjust.

☐ In preparing, learn as much as you can about the group and its cultural approach.

☐ Ask the sponsor to rate the group on the Cultural Awareness Assessment and review the results with the sponsor.

☐ Discuss with the sponsor the following:

- Room setup
- How decisions will be made
- What work has already been done
- How the session should open
- Whether a timely start is likely
- Ground rules to use
- Questions to avoid
- Likely dysfunctions and how to address them
- Methods for keeping the group focused
- How to avoid participants' deferring to leaders (if this is to be avoided)
- How the session will close
- How to handle assigning responsibilities at the end

☐ Adjust your start as needed.

- Use level 3 energy or adjust it as necessary.
- Adjust the agenda if a timely start is not likely and have appropriate initial activities for those who are prompt.
- For high-context groups, allow more time to focus on who is in the room and what has been done in the past.
- Define the decision process that the group will use.
- Select ground rules with the culture of the group in mind.

☐ Use appropriate techniques to keep the session flowing.

- Use the appropriate level of detail for checkpoints and direction giving, depending on the group's tolerance for ambiguity.
- Build context as needed before undertaking new agenda items.
- If you are facilitating in your natural language and it is not the first language of the entire group, and you are having difficulty understanding the participants, consider having someone "interpret" for you or assigning a scribe.
- Use consensus building strategies aligned with the culture of the group, avoiding full consensus if inappropriate.
- Address dysfunction as needed, paying close attention to adjusting your approach depending on how the group's culture rates on the Position

Power Versus Shared and Respect Through Status Versus
Accomplishments dimensions.

- Use breakout sessions to provide greater empowerment and anonymity
  as appropriate. Arrange the breakout groups so as to balance position
  power and respect for status as needed.

☐ Understand what dominance is and how it plays out in the group you are
facilitating.

- Identify what areas of dominance you share with the dominant culture
  that might create blind spots (areas of unawareness or collusion) for you
  as a facilitator.

- Question the idea that anyone is "neutral" or "objective" and especially
  understand where you are not "objective" or "neutral" in your own value
  system.

- Use tools (for example, constructivist listening,[3] speaking order,
  translated written materials, interpretation equipment for two-way
  interpretation) that structurally interrupt dominance patterns and build
  peer-to-peer relationships in the group.

- Learn to question where you are comfortable or keeping a group
  comfortable; gain skills that help you embrace ambiguity.

- Be willing to make mistakes, be called out on them, and learn from them.

- Separate culture (something that is a benign style or characteristic that
  distinguishes groups) from cultural patterns (a group's patterned
  response to oppression or systematic, structured institutional targeting)

☐ In closing the session, consider having an appropriate person (depending on
the culture) give the closing words. Be sure that the person is aware of this
role in advance.

Exercise Your Skills

Prepare yourself to work with cross-cultural groups by taking the Cultural
Awareness Assessment. The tool will raise your awareness of how your natural
tendencies and cultural biases may be very different from those of the groups
with which you may work.

In your next facilitation, consider adjustments you can make to your natural
facilitation style to better address the needs of the group. In addition, review the
questions to ask to identify and address power dynamics (listed in the section
"The Facilitator's Role in Creating a Just Environment"). What will you do differently so as to interrupt rather than support the dominance effect?

Notes

1. From Gladwell, M. *Outliers: The Story of Success.* New York: Back Bay Books, 2011.
2. Although "American" is a common term referring to people from the United States, dominance is reflected in this description because people from South, Central, and other parts of North America are also "American." The other term used is "North American"; however, North America includes Canada and Mexico, so using this term to describe people from the United States is both inaccurate and an example of dominance. I use "USer" in this chapter to refer to people from the United States.
3. For information on constructivist listening, see Weissglass, J."Constructivist Listening for Empowerment and Change." *Educational Forum,* Summer 1990, *54*(4), retrieved from www.nsrfharmony.org/fac_equity /constructivist_listening.pdf.

CHAPTER SIXTEEN

THE SECRETS TO BUILDING AN INTERNAL FACILITATOR CAPABILITY

Build the Case, Raise Awareness

Questions Answered in This Chapter

What is an internal facilitator capability, and how might it work?

What are the benefits to an organization of having a facilitator cadre?

How do you get a facilitator cadre started?

How many facilitators might you need? How do you recruit them and build their skills?

Who manages the cadre? How are the facilitators assigned to engagements?

How do internal customers learn about the cadre? What do they "pay" for the service?

What pitfalls must you avoid?

Introduction

Many organizations across the world have benefited from developing an internal cadre of facilitators. Organizations have established a facilitator network for a variety of purposes, including to increase productivity, improve employee engagement, enhance the effectiveness of meetings, implement change management, reduce the use of external consultants, address organization alignment, promote innovation, or roll out a company-wide initiative.

To identify best practices, I interviewed and gathered information from twenty-one organizations that have, or at one time had, a group of five or more facilitators whose primary role includes providing group facilitation assistance internally to their organization. In this chapter, you will find the stories of three of these organizations, which have taken different paths to get where they are. You will learn what is working and what is not working for them. Along with these three case studies, you will also find quotes from several of the other organizations interviewed. I end this chapter with a discussion of best practice strategies compiled from these three organizations and from the full group of twenty-one.

CASE STUDY: The Pull Strategy at Hydro One

Hydro One is accountable for the planning, construction, operation, and maintenance of the electrical transmission and distribution network for the province of Ontario, Canada. The company owns 97 percent of transmission in Ontario and delivers electricity over an area of 415,000 square miles, serving 1.3 million customers. Hydro One has approximately fifty-five hundred employees working in two hundred locations throughout the province.

Jim Rankin is the director of organizational alignment at Hydro One. He shares his story of how, starting as a department of one, he has developed a cadre of full-time facilitators who help drive positive, high-impact change throughout the organization.

The Beginning

The story of how this need came about goes back ten years to when Hydro One was making significant capital investments that, despite their size, were not producing the levels of return that had been presented to, and anticipated by, the board of directors. As a result, the board directed the organization to make changes in its management of capital investment projects.

In response, the organization initiated a number of changes. One of the changes was to hire change management consultants for some of the major projects to provide support in helping implement the needed change. This strategy proved to be effective especially in the implementation phase of projects, because resistance encountered in the past was significantly reduced due to initiatives introduced by the consultants.

With the success of these early projects, the organization decided to develop its own in-house change management capability, rather than continue to bring in outside consultants. The result was a department of one, me. Just prior I was an external change management consultant and winding down my involvement as the change management lead on a major project in Hydro One. As a department of one, I was given the mandate to establish a change management infrastructure. It would be resourced internally with a core body of consulting and facilitating expertise that would be available to facilitate the resolution of change-related issues.

Since I couldn't find identifiable models or experiences where other organizations had built a full-time facilitator infrastructure, I decided to start with a clean slate. One of the first things that I did was talk to people at various levels of the organization and learn what their experiences were with making change happen in Hydro One. I sought out any suggestions these people had on how to fulfill the mandate. There were numerous comments and suggestions, including the comment that there were too many consultants in the organization, resulting in too many models and too many definitions of what change and change management were, to the point that it was difficult for people in the different lines of business in Hydro One to talk with one another.

Common suggestions included disposing of the term "change management" since it had negative connotations from past change initiatives as well as a totally different technical meaning in this engineering-based organization. A second suggestion was to replace the multiple change management models with a single Hydro One approach to how to make change happen.

To address the first issue, I went back to the executive committee in the fall of 2007 with a definition of what I termed "organization alignment" rather than "change management" and with a model for how they should deal with change.

Organization Alignment and the Model

The definition of organization alignment I presented was the following:

Engaging people to achieve better results by aligning people, practices, policies, processes, systems, and strategies, through a structured approach to change that supports Hydro One's mission and vision, values, and strategic objectives.

The executive committee liked the definition and approved changing the term change management to what we now called organizational alignment in Hydro One. Over the last four years, organization alignment has become a very common term within the organization.

The next step was to eliminate the old models on how to make change happen, and to develop a new one. I presented the executive committee with a sequential eight-step model in the shape of a two-story house with a foundation, six rooms, and an attic. A description of each "room" follows:

The Foundation: Hydro One's mission, vision, values, and strategic objectives
How does the change support one or more the organization's mission, vision, values, and
    eight strategic objectives? Any change being introduced must be grounded by supporting
    one or a combination of these.
Room 1: The business case for change
What needs to be better? Where are the things that are not working? Why aren't they work-
    ing? Let's understand what the issue is and build the business case for change on the
    foundation of the mission, vision, values, and strategic objectives.
Room 2: The desired future state
Where do you want to be? What is the desired future state? What would "better" look like?
Room 3: Stakeholder readiness for change
What is the readiness for change among key stakeholders? (This was an area that had been
    ignored in the organization in the past: key stakeholders weren't identified and in most
    cases their needs weren't addressed, resulting in considerable resistance.)

Room 4: A strategy and plan to get to better

What is the strategy for improvement? How does it address the gap between where we are and where we want to be? How does it address key stakeholder readiness? What is the specific plan? What are the steps, when will they be done, and who is responsible for doing them?

Room 5: Implementation and results

Implementation and results include such activities as establishing accountability, ensuring engagement, taking a look at resistance as we go along, revising plans, and, most important, looking at results-based management. (When I interviewed the VPs and directors, one of the things that they noted was that on projects there was frequently a lot of activity and a lot of meetings, situations, and events. But all that activity did not often produce results; instead, *the amount* of activity had become a measure rather than the results of the activity being the measure.)

Room 6: Sustainment

What is the plan to ensure sustainment of the changes that were made? How will you ensure that the changes are still visible three months, a year, or three years later? How do you avoid having people go back to their old ways?

The Attic: Lessons learned

What are the lessons learned from this initiative, in terms of both the processes we followed and their impact and the results achieved and their impact? What went well? What could have gone better? Where did we encounter surprises? Where did things go awry? What should we keep in mind and apply in the future when situations arise that are similar in nature?

The model was approved by the executive committee in the fall of 2007 and has become the primary basis for how change happens in the organization. It is introduced and explained at the initial and subsequent sessions of all change initiatives. An important by-product of the "House" is that now people see the connection between the initiative that they are involved in and Hydro One's mission and vision, values, and eight strategic objectives. In the past, that connection was lost through the organization layers and rarely was translated down to the frontline levels where the change initiative was being worked or where the change initiative would have impact.

Staffing Up

To build the organization alignment (OA) team, I applied a principle of choice. I asked for expressions of interest for an eighteen-month rotation from knowledgeable and experienced managers who had dealt with the realities of good and bad change at the front lines.

I decided not to draw people from the traditional pool of human resources, for example. I wanted people who had worked in the business, had experienced and were required to contend with the highs and lows of dealing with change, and were respected by their colleagues and reports.

We conducted a session for those who expressed interest to outline what the opportunity was about. From the candidates who were still interested, I selected those who met our criteria. The respect piece was essential so that when they went back out to facilitate alignment issues, they had immediate credibility and respect.

We continued to have the OA resources report into their line of business instead of reporting directly to me. The reason for this was that I felt that the businesses needed to own their investment in their resources and would ensure that their people were working on issues that the business saw as important.

There was a need to build on the practical, work-based experiences of the new facilitators, so I researched various sources of development, augmented by in-depth coaching and tutoring. Their formal training includes three four-day courses on organization development from Queens University in Kingston, Ontario, a series that culminates in the awarding of a Certificate in Organization Development. In addition, OA staff members receive training through the following courses: Problem Solving and Decision Making, The Effective Facilitator, and Presenting to Groups.

By year end 2011, eight managers had worked through or were on the eighteen-month rotation in OA, with three of the eight staying on as permanent consultant-facilitators and two who returned to their previous positions as part of the plan to see facilitator resources seeded through the province. The executive committee has approved a plan that will see us adding four people on rotations each year for the next five years. Half will stay on as full-time facilitator-consultants and half will be seeded throughout the organization.

The Pull Strategy

We applied a pull strategy for moving alignment into the organization. This meant there was no requirement for any part of the organization to use this facilitation resource in dealing with change. I knew that if organization alignment was pushed on any level of the organization, it would be resisted and fail. A facilitated approach to change had to clearly add value as the basis for its growth so that alignment would be invited into the organization to provide support in resolving change issues.

This was a huge risk! If there was no interest, the Hydro One eight-step structured approach to change and the model for building a facilitator-consultant base would be stillborn! But I was determined to have the organization demanding our resources, as opposed to me demanding that they use us. Of course when we started there was no pull at all. I visited each of the organization's six VPs. Only one was interested in adopting this model of providing two respected, experienced people from his organization to join me for an eighteen-month rotation to learn and then work with me in facilitating change. But having gained his support, I still needed to get buy-in from at least one of his directors.

With the approval to proceed from one VP, I approached his directors with the same pull strategy in place. None were interested. I continued to supply them with different reasons for them to hop on board, but to no avail! Reasons for rejecting the opportunity included that the rotation would be seen as a career-ending move, that people resources were in short supply, and that no one would want to travel hundreds of miles from across the province to spend week after week in Toronto working on alignment.

Finally, I went to one of the directors and said, "I want you to give me one of the most difficult issues that you are facing right now—something important where people are not coming together to do what is required in the organization."

He selected an issue involving thirty-two people who were essentially in two polarized camps. They were finger-pointing in terms of who was the problem and were unable to even discuss how to resolve their impasse. We brought them together for three days. Through a series of facilitated processes, they initially addressed and overcame many of the relationship issues that had separated them. Working in teams of four, they worked through a facilitated process to analyze the main business issue that had divided them and develop plans to resolve it. All plans were presented to the director by the teams at the end of the three-day meeting.

When they presented their plans to their director, he was amazed by what he saw and heard. In place of finger-pointing, there was cooperation; in place of no accountability, there were detailed plans on what they were going to do to resolve his issue; in the place of complaining, there was commitment. His response was to ask me when I wanted him to send out an email to his managers, asking for expressions of interest in an eighteen-month alignment rotation! The pull strategy was under way. This director has since become the strongest advocate of alignment in the organization and has provided all of the eight resources to date, while other parts of the organization have been banging on our door.

Communication is one piece that contributes to making the pull strategy work. The organization is large and distributed across a wide range of territory. But word gets around very quickly on any issue. After this initial success, word spread, and demands for our services grew. The pull strategy was off and running.

But the most important contributor to the success of the pull strategy is quality work: respected, qualified facilitators; clear, effective designs; and results that support Hydro One's mission and vision, values, and strategic objectives. Good work means more work, and that's what the pull strategy is all about!

Sample of Projects

The following is a sample of projects that the OA group has supported:

- **Leadership team alignment.** Identify strengths and weaknesses in how the leadership team is working and design and facilitate processes that engage the team in resolving its weaknesses.

- **Office realignment.** Establish a structure and revise processes and integrate roles within the business centers to combine customer service and scheduling accountabilities in a single position.

- **Compliance with standards.** Identify gaps and issues in application and usage to ensure that work processes are in compliance with distribution standards and regulations; make recommendations; develop and monitor plans; measure results.

- **Barrier analysis.** Identify barriers to supervisors' spending more time in the field and make recommendations related to addressing them.

- **Process improvement.** Develop, implement, and measure the effectiveness of a centralized schedule for off-road equipment.

- **Common issues.** Assess the extent to which there are common issues among field business centers in four divisions within and across four of the eight provincial lines, and make recommendations on addressing those issues.

- **Time management.** Design a process (the work interruption tool, or WIT) to control the amount of nonproductive time of "wrench" and "wrist" employees that results from third-party requests identified within and outside the lines of business.

- **Customer service strategy.** Create a shared vision of a customer service delivery strategy.

Current Challenges

We have several challenges as we move forward:

- Controlled growth in the face of demands for alignment support. The challenge has been that we can develop resources only at a certain pace. We don't want to negatively impact the momentum we have gained by overutilizing our existing resources or using unprepared resources. The quality of our resources is a fundamental key to our pull strategy. At the same time, we want to be responsive to our customers and potential customers. So we find ourselves in a delicate balancing act.

- Maintaining a focus on learning and not turning the group into a "consulting house." (Our value states, "Thinking, learning, and results are our work.")

- Living by our values, especially "challenge and encourage each other to be the best that we can be."

- Ensuring that people who return to their previous jobs after eighteen months continue to apply their skills.

- Keeping the coaching and development of OA resources as the primary accountability for the director of organization alignment.

Results

We have been pleased with what our internal customers say about the OA group.

What Our Customers Have Said

- Connects multiple stakeholders to eliminate the siloed solutions frequently encountered in problem solving.

- Draws on employee expertise in their role and location to ensure that all the information gets on the table.

- Builds employee understanding of how they support Hydro One's mission and vision, values, and strategic objectives.

- Develops full-time, professional-level facilitators from the pool of field-experienced, respected managers and supervisors, who have "walked in my shoes."
- Eliminates "What's in it for me?" thinking and replaces it with "What's in it for the customer?" "How can we lower our costs?" and "What's in it for the organization?"

In the first four years of OA's existence, we have addressed 117 issues, trained sixty people in the Leadership Strategies workshop on facilitation skills, and driven the application of "consensus" decision making and "alignment" into the organization. Organization alignment terminology has become commonly used in the business. As a result of this initial success, we gained approval in 2012 to add four additional facilitator resources each year over the subsequent five-year period. Our reporting relationship has also seen us move from reporting to an executive vice president of services to the executive vice president of operations. This change was made to bring the alignment to the executive table for dialogue and decision making that would influence all lines of business.

In talking with Jim Rankin about his experiences, I discerned several keys to Hydro One's success:

- *The need was evident.* The board required change management for large projects, and the organization was creating confusion by bringing in outside expertise.
- *There was an internal driver.* Jim became the internal force with responsibility for creating the OA group.
- *Jim was proactive initially in finding opportunities.* Jim created internal "pull" through his early successes. However, gaining those initial opportunities for success required considerable hands-on activity.
- *Respected resources were tapped who were knowledgeable about the business.* Jim went after people who were already respected and had internal knowledge first and then skilled them up, rather than finding people with the skills and then trying to provide the internal knowledge and hoping they gained respect.
- *OA invested heavily in training.* Due to the focus on respect and internal knowledge, OA implemented significant training programs to bring people up to speed.
- *OA focused on pull rather than push.* Rather than attempt to mandate the use of OA's services, Jim took advantage of the positive results achieved and the informal communication network to create demand. I believe that an additional reason the pull strategy may have worked was the organization's internal mandate to increase employee engagement and productivity. OA offered a process to help people achieve these goals.

CASE STUDY: From Training to Something Bigger at Direct Supply

Based in Milwaukee, Wisconsin, Direct Supply is the leading provider of equipment, e-commerce, and service solutions to the long-term-care and senior living markets. Direct Supply has approximately one thousand employees.

John Rutkiewicz is the director of learning and development and the primary impetus in creating an internal facilitator network.

The Beginning

I started facilitating groups in the early 1990s. I believe in facilitation skills and what these skills can do. In 2006, I had the idea to create a facilitation network. It was my dream to create something that would help groups in the organization with their processes.

In 2009, the opportunity presented itself. We had an off-site, company-wide program teaching social dynamics. The program was eight days (reduced now to five days). I served as a facilitator along with a consultant and my boss. As a result of the impact of the program, the CEO decided that he wanted everybody in the company to go through social dynamics training.

I took this as the opportunity to train facilitators for the social dynamics programs and at the same time teach them skills that they could use in other areas. Our consultant had previously designed a facilitator training program. Although her program was primarily designed for trainers, it could also be used for meeting facilitation skills.

Selection and Development

We wanted facilitators from across the business. I solicited key leaders within the company and asked them to cascade down to their leaders and provide nominations. Then we opened it to the company and asked for nominations as well. People could nominate others or self-nominate. We had a vetting process that included self-analysis and analysis by the candidate's leader.

We looked at the facilitation personalities people tend to gravitate toward. Although I learned facilitation initially by facilitating support groups, there is also meeting facilitation, training facilitation, and team building–type facilitation. People tended to fit in one of the groups by nature of their personalities and preferences.

At the time of this writing, we have twenty-one facilitators. The skilling up is a four-day off-site training program and includes a ropes course, Meyers-Briggs Type Indicator analysis, and skills building.

People are facilitating for about 5 percent of their total time; their regular job is the other 95 percent. On average this amounts to about twelve days a year of facilitation per facilitator.

Serving Our Customers

I manage the facilitator network, though this will be turned over to one of my direct reports. I and two others look at requests and (1) check in with the client for more information or (2) put the request out to the network to take the job. Once assigned, we close the loop by telling the client who the facilitator is and that the facilitator will be contacting the customer.

Our facilitators are doing learning facilitation (training), team building activities, and meeting facilitation.

- Learning facilitation is primarily centered around the company's social dynamics program (eight weeks per year, three facilitators working in tandem).

- Team building may occur two to three times per month. Some of these sessions are formalized. As examples, we use a modified version of GE's New Leader Assimilation, which we call Fast Start and which has a team building component; DISC assessment has its own team building around the assessment; and we design for special needs.

- Meeting facilitation we do less of, perhaps once per month. Our meeting designs are typically done from scratch.

We get requests verbally, or they come through the request form, which covers six simple questions that give a baseline of information. Our services are free to the customer. Although we do a little advertising and marketing, the majority of our assignments come through word of mouth.

Examples of Benefit

One meeting facilitation involved designing an event for some of our people and one of our major vendors. Our sourcing group and the vendor generally were struggling with their working relationship—the feeling was that they weren't getting along in their interactions and negotiations.

In the meeting, one process the facilitator used was to have each side generate a list of the major obstacles that were in the way of their working relationship. They then shared their lists with each other, discussed them, and developed action items around them. The facilitator helped them move to a new relationship, and the relationship has held on.

This first session has become a template for work between our sourcing group and other vendors with whom they want to improve or enhance their working relationships.

Another example in which we created a benefit through facilitation involved a group of four managers from four different disciplines whose teams were a part of a process flow for information moving through the organization. These managers were having difficulty coming to agreement on how the process should work. They had worked together on and off for about six months and couldn't come to a conclusion. We brought in two facilitators (with different personalities) to cofacilitate. We held two sessions (two hours each), with homework between the sessions. By the end of the second session, we were able to help them solve what couldn't be solved over six months. I had the facilitator write up a description of what happened and the outcomes, so that we could use it as a case study for our other facilitators and to demonstrate to executives the value that facilitation can bring to the organization.

Keys for Success

Our experience has led me to believe that there are at least two keys to success if you are considering implementing an internal facilitator network.

- Develop the business case and get buy-in for the business case first from executive leadership. We parlayed the need for facilitators for the social dynamics training into something bigger. But occasionally we get pushback from managers who have facilitators in the network; they struggle sometimes to see the value of facilitation when it competes with the demands of a facilitator's full-time job. We are working now on this business case to see if we can get more traction for the network.
- Marketing is important. If you market something like this well, it can generate good activity. Then, when you have your successes, you need to build the case studies and promote those cases in your marketing. By showing the value of facilitation, our case studies have started to generate more interest and requests.

Along with the two key points that John makes, I would like to add two related ones:

- *How you start does not necessarily determine where you finish.* Although his facilitator cadre started out just focused on a specific program related to learning and development, John saw the opportunity to parlay this into a resource pool that could provide additional value to the organization in other areas.
- *Demonstrating value is not enough.* Communicating the value may be equally important. Capturing successes and then communicating them out to others allows you to leverage the good work you are doing through facilitation.

CASE STUDY: The Facilitator Development Program at Saudi Aramco

Saudi Aramco is the national oil company of Saudi Arabia. Through its fifty-five thousand employees, Saudi Aramco produces, manufactures, markets, and ships crude oil, natural gas, petroleum products, and chemicals to meet the global energy and chemical demand.

Steve Bushkul is chief of staff for the senior vice president of downstream and is the executive sponsor of a facilitation development pilot at Saudi Aramco. In this case study, he describes how the group got started and where it is today.

The Need

Over the years, Saudi Aramco has employed a number of very talented individuals who in addition to possessing technical and leadership skills have developed the ability to facilitate groups. These individuals have typically been moved to develop this skill set by business needs or projects with which they were personally involved. Most were self-developed. Some gained the skill set on the fly—just by the trial and error of leading meetings. And in our situation, a very small minority were formally trained and seasoned OE/OD practitioners. These men and women were deployed in various organizations all over the company.

In December of 2007, I was involved in preparing for an all-hands meeting for the leadership of the company's downstream business. The topic was safety. Over two hundred participants were to be involved. The new head of the organization aspired to go beyond the normal preaching about safety and wanted to achieve a high level of engagement with leadership and to drill deep into the DNA of the organization to identify things that needed to change. A feel-good, pep rally type of event wouldn't work. Neither would a typical lecture on the facts and figures. Engagement leading to buy-in and commitment was the order of the day. My first thought was, "We need very tight facilitation to herd these cats!"

Finding #1: Our facilitator bench strength was not as robust as we thought.

We called on the talented facilitator cadre I mentioned in the opening to help us. For a meeting this size we needed at least twenty-five facilitators—a lead facilitation group and a facilitator for each of the tables. Finding these individuals turned out to be harder than we thought. Locating enough facilitators who were available on relatively short notice was even harder. Through perseverance, arm twisting, and calling in favors, we managed to fill the facilitation roster.

Finding #2: We didn't have a common view of facilitation or a common language to help us be effective in planning and executing events requiring multiple facilitators.

In the weeks leading up to the meeting, as we prepared the group for this safety engagement, we found that not all facilitators are created equal. We didn't have a common language to describe the work needed and to effectively coordinate it. Our skill sets and backgrounds in facilitation were varied. We needed not only to "herd" the meeting participants but also to "herd" our facilitation team.

Finding #3: We were on the brink of a huge talent shortage in a key skill set, and no one was doing anything about it.

On the day of the event, the pieces did come together, and we did deliver to the customer's satisfaction. We changed the momentum of the organization's safety effort and today are reaping the benefits of the seeds that were sown during this event. That's the good news. As I surveyed the room, I was struck by a few observations that were not good news for the organizations or the company long term:

- Most of our facilitators (60 percent) were within five years of retirement.
- The overwhelming majority of our facilitators were expatriates, while most of our participants were Saudis.
- Many of the facilitators were from the HR, training, and development areas of our business, with few actually part of the downstream business unit.
- There were few up-and-coming facilitators.
- We had only one internationally recognized facilitator in the group.

The Response

In the weeks that followed the meeting, we pulled together a group of ten seasoned facilitators to review and validate the observations and findings. Their findings: the situation is direr than indicated by the informal observations of that one major interaction. Changes in focus by our training and development organizations and the accompanying structural changes were soon to take many of our dedicated facilitators out of play, as much less time would be available for them to facilitate. This trend highlighted the eroding of official support for dedicated experienced facilitators and a need to pursue a different course of action to develop the next generation of facilitators.

The team of ten evolved into a facilitator development "skunk works" of sorts. We engaged an outside facilitator, Dan Hogan, to help us keep on task and align with internationally recognized facilitation standards. We also licensed the Partners in Facilitator Development process from the International Institute for Facilitation.

Over the course of eighteen months, we outlined a set of key facilitator competencies, a development process for Saudi Aramco facilitators, an overall governance plan to keep things on track, a code of conduct, and a candidate selection process for the development program.

Some things to note at this point, which were used as the "guardrails" of our development process:

- Facilitation is to be a supplemental skill set—not a dedicated "job." Our corporate culture values facilitation, but doesn't see it as a full-time job.
- Responsibility for providing participants in the program is shared across the company.
- The program needs to address entry-level through highly skilled facilitators to create a pipeline of facilitation talent.
- Participants should be a balance of Saudi and expatriate talent, male and female, younger and seasoned.
- The overall program design should stress sustainability.
- Experienced facilitators would be expected to provide coaching and opportunities to facilitate for the less experienced facilitators.
- A system should provide a way for users throughout the company to quickly and easily connect with facilitation resources.
- The design must plan for significant attrition.

Another key component for success was the initial training for the candidate facilitators. As we surveyed the market, we found that a five-day version of The Effective Facilitator intensive facilitator development program from Leadership Strategies met our needs most closely in this regard. The program matched our philosophy of facilitation and provided a rigorous process that best assured success for new facilitators. The facilitation training company also offered more advanced training that could be deployed in later stages of our program development.

Buy-In

A skunk works can operate under the radar for only so long. Once the plan was in reasonable shape, the next step was to get buy-in to test-drive it. We engaged our senior executives with a description of the "burning platform" and our proposed solution. We had to sell both the value of facilitation (reasonably easy for this level of leadership) and the need for a structured development program (a little more challenging given all the other demands on the organization). In the end, we received wholehearted support for a pilot involving up to sixty candidates from across the company. This "support" amounted to a commitment of time and resources to train and develop new facilitators and allow them time to practice what they learned, and backing for the team to fully develop an overall facilitator development program concept.

Setting Up the Pilot

We had only one shot to do this right. Therefore, careful selection of initial candidates was the mantra for the pilot team. Since participation would require time away from "normal" work, it was imperative that a sufficiently high level of management endorsed each participant's nomination for the program. In the end, nominations came from vice presidents across the company. We had a healthy nominee pool of 135 for sixty positions.

Nomination, however, was only the first step. We needed to make sure that the candidates really understood what they were getting into. Process facilitation is a concept that is often misunderstood. We had many that assumed we would develop their public speaking capability so that they could become effective masters of ceremonies. Others thought that this would result in them being able to be totally freed from the current job. Some didn't have a clue at all but sought another set of letters to put after their name on their business cards. Education was definitely in order. To that end, we took all the nominees through a job explanation meeting (Job X) to give them the low-down. In a half-day session, we gave them the basics of process facilitation, the benefit to them, the code of conduct expected, and what the development plan would entail. The Job X was a brutally honest depiction of what their life would be like as a facilitator—something not to be taken lightly. At the end of the morning, each of the candidates was given a free pass to opt out without penalty. The remainder moved on to the next phase of the selection process. At this point we had a total of seventy-two candidates for sixty positions.

Interest and availability are vital but not sufficient for success as a facilitator. The next phase was set up to make sure that the candidate had what it took to become a facilitator. The interview process involved an examination of the candidates' ability to sell themselves, their passion and motivation as well as the ability to learn. A cross-functional set of existing facilitators interviewed each candidate and made the final assessment. Note, we didn't just rank the candidates and pick the top ones; we only took those we felt had the best chance to make it long term. In the end, we didn't fill all of the slots but ended up with thirty-six participants.

We used the interviews for some additional screening as well. The interview results allowed us to identify those who could be coaches immediately, those who were ready to deploy immediately, and those who would be our future coaches. We also divided the group into two balanced cohorts to go through the initial training. We were ready to go!

Launch

The excitement was palpable as the first cohort began their facilitation training. Pretty soon the flip charts were a whir of motion, and the rooms were resonating with the early practice of the Level 3 voices. The energy level was infectiously high. The candidates learned the basic practices of managing the clock, managing conflict, providing clear instructions, keeping the energy level up, and running a very tight engagement. They walked away well prepared and confident that they could take on the toughest meetings with the most obdurate client.

The coaches-to-be (mentors) received their own booster shot as well. In an accelerated version of The Effective Facilitator, the coaches (sixteen in total) were challenged to review their "go to" techniques and expand to include other means of facilitating. They had to unlearn some bad habits and were delighted to find solutions to challenges they had faced over the years. In doing this, they also learned a common facilitation language that would allow them to coach the fledgling facilitators more effectively. The 5 Ps of preparation, IEEI, and PeDeQs became part of their vernacular.

As the training of the second facilitator cohort was winding down, it was time to introduce the new facilitators to their coaches. Over dinner, the coaches and facilitators had their first "date" to learn about each other and to kick off their relationship. Pairings were purposeful, not random, to try to match temperaments and work interests. As a cornerstone of our program we intended to help nurture these relationships as much as possible.

Put Me In, Coach!

By the end of fall 2010, we had thirty-six facilitators and their sixteen coaches ready to go. With all this talent revving their engines and itching to practice what they had learned, the third leg of our program kicked in—connecting facilitators with business needs.

We devised a Web-based system to allow requests for facilitation assistance to be made directly. When users click on the "I Need a Facilitator" button, they are directed to provide basic information on the meeting and are connected to the facilitator network. The request is then distributed to the facilitators via email so that they can advise whether or not they are available for the meeting or interaction. This volunteer network is moderated by a dedicated senior facilitator who makes sure customer requests are handled in a timely and professional manner.

This new system allowed facilitators access to a wider variety and number of facilitation engagements than the previous personal network and organization-centric practice allowed. While this was still a volunteer effort, our facilitators were getting more opportunities to facilitate.

Success!?

This is definitely still a work in progress. As of this writing (in early 2012), we have many items in which we take justifiable pride. Other things have fallen below our expectations and need some further work. Here's our scorecard:

On the plus side we have the following:

- A new crop of facilitators who are adding value throughout the company with their facilitation skills

- A clear process for facilitator development

- A clear set of expectations for facilitators
- A process for linking facilitators to opportunities
- A heightened awareness in company management of what good facilitation looks like and its value
- A good start on a sustainable program

On the delta side, we don't yet have the following:

- A graduate from the program who is certified
- A governance process in place to carry this forward
- An organizational (customer) understanding of the lead time necessary to prepare for a facilitated engagement
- An effective coaching and mentoring program for ongoing development

In addition to the this scorecard, we haven't yet been able to institutionalize this. Our "skunk works" team has largely disbanded and moved on to other opportunities as a new corporate change initiative is now in full swing. The pilot hasn't yet been finalized as we are awaiting the certification of one of our new facilitators as a Certified Master Facilitator.

Out of the original group of thirty-six, only fourteen are regularly facilitating, in addition to eleven coaches. Those who aren't actively facilitating do use the skill set regularly in their jobs, but only to a limited extent. We haven't yet cracked the proverbial nut, but have made some good progress. We have a firm base to build on—something that didn't exist before.

Three Lessons Learned from Our Experiences:

1. *"Go slow to go fast."* Although admittedly eighteen months to begin implementing our facilitator development program is longer than optimal, once approved by senior management, the cadre was ready to be deployed within seven months—from nomination, interviews and selection, formalized training, facilitator and mentor matching, and execution with real clients.
2. *"Attrition and sustainability—plan for the minimum and hope for the optimum."* In our case of pilot participants, we planned for a 30-30-30 attrition rate, meaning that once we move into a sustained delivery mode, 30 percent of the cadre would leave the program within the first ninety days, 30 percent will become alternates and will participate sparingly in sessions, and 30 percent will become workhorses who continue to drive forward. The reader may be wondering about the other 10 percent; well, these are the folks who are seasoned facilitators who will carry the effort to the next level.
3. *"Contracting matters most."* A key predictor of success for an upcoming facilitated engagement occurs back at the entry and contracting stages—assuming of course that you have facilitators in the session with the right skills—especially for internally based facilitators. For all, but most important for internal practitioners, it is one of the most difficult and challenging aspects of the entire process. Contracting requires the facilitator to be a subject matter expert, diplomat, encourager, cheerleader, and coach, and to have credibility.

I want to highlight two key points from the Saudi Aramco experience:

- Saudi Aramco has in place a specific model for developing and mentoring facilitators, one that can serve long term for sustaining a high level of facilitator capability in the organization.
- Saudi Aramco's initiating goal was facilitator development and building a sustainable facilitator capability. There was not a specific business problem that the cadre was attempting to address. As a result, there was no ready-made focus for applying the skills once developed.

Best Practice Strategies

This section discusses several best practice strategies based on the insights gained from the interviews and other information submitted. I begin with the strategy I believe to be by far the most important.

Identify a Key Function and a Key Sponsor

The benefits to an organization of having an internal facilitation cadre are obvious to those who want to create the cadre. However, those benefits are important to point out when making the case for funding one. Benefits frequently cited in the interviews include the following:

Organizational Benefits of a Facilitator Cadre	<ul><li>Costs are reduced compared to using outside resources.</li><li>Facilitators typically have a stronger understanding of the business than do outside resources, and can bring insights from other areas of the business.</li><li>Knowledge gained is retained.</li><li>Those selected to be part of the cadre typically experience increased morale.</li><li>The organization develops its internal personnel.</li><li>There are ready resources for maximizing productivity and engagement in group sessions.</li></ul>

However, the stronger cadres appeared to have a key function they initially served that was tied to the success of the business. These cadres also had strong sponsors who supported them, as described in our next secret.

The Secret to Establishing an Internal Facilitator Cadre

Build a solid business case by identifying a key function for the cadre that will drive a specific business result, and a key sponsor who will steadfastly support the cadre.

The three companies highlighted in this chapter are listed in the table here, which also shows the initial function of the cadres and the level of sponsorship.

Organization	Initial Cadre Function	Sponsorship
Hydro One	Reduce the reliance on external consultants; improve delivery on capital projects	Steering committee of the board
Direct Supply	Serve as facilitators for the social dynamics program	Chief executive officer
Saudi Aramco	Develop facilitator skills	Senior VP downstream

Note that the initial cadre functions for Hydro One was closely tied to business results, and its cadre appears to be firmly established in the organization. The initial function of the facilitation network for Direct Supply was related to learning and development, but focused on improving soft skills in the business that the CEO saw as directly related to company performance. Saudi Aramco's first initial cadre function emphasized developing the skills of the facilitators and did not focus as much on the internal business. More recently the focus appears to be shifting more and more to opportunities to support the business, which in turn will provide greater opportunities for developing the skills of the facilitators.

In the case of Bowne and Company, the business case for building a facilitator cadre centered on transforming the HR organization to become partners to the business, as described here:

The head of HR wanted the HR people to be real business partners (not just generalists and transaction focused). I influenced the thinking around the idea that one way HR people could be closer to the business is to learn OD skills: how to diagnose issues, formulate solutions, facilitate business meetings and project team launches, and so forth. Why do this?

1. Savings: avoid paying $2K and up a day to bring in an outside facilitator.
2. HR transformation: let's teach the HR people these skills so they will be closer to the business, and so on.

3. Business climate: the increased level of complexity caused by changes in the industry created a need in a number of areas (for example, transforming from selling on relationship to selling on value of IT solutions)—which could be addressed with coaching, training, facilitation to support the business in the change.

Including myself there were eleven facilitators.

—Helen Materazzi, independent consultant working
with Bowne and Company

The importance of a function and executive sponsorship was underscored in another interview. Barrie Levinson used to be a member of an internal high-tech results center that included a team of facilitators. She describes the start of the center:

There was a recognition within the IT organization that the kinds of programs we were trying to drive (partnerships with business and technology) were complex and that there were challenges in decision making that were impacting the progress.

The CIO had staff do a best practices investigation to identify innovative ideas we might consider to address this set of problems. There was also an employee survey that said decision making could be more effective.

We found several centers, such as the Cap Gemini Accelerated Learning Environment and HP's Garage Works. We thought, "What if we had a place where people could get out of their daily routines and have focused events to help teams reach outcomes they needed—from early ideas to execution?"

The center got started as an experiment for one year. We leased a building with a one-year lease, which required an annual internal review to gain approval to continue. We were earning our way. The center ran for five years.
—Barrie Levinson

The center was a high-tech, open facility specifically designed to create an atmosphere conducive to collaboration and ideation. At its height, the center had six full-time facilitators and was bringing internal groups in regularly to innovate, create new products, and solve problems. The team also used the center to do its own innovation. Over the five-year span, team members documented over two hundred processes that they used to help their clients. The center was even featured in a *Wall Street Journal* article on effective meetings.

So why is the center no longer operating? Barrie explains.

The center was "decelerated" after a five-year run due primarily to environmental factors and sponsorship. We lasted more than a year after the CIO who started it had left. We were pleased we lasted so long. The sponsorship and measurable results were key.

—*Barrie Levinson*

This center was not the only organization that was impacted when the departure of a key executive coincided with the need to reduce staff.

The use of facilitators began when British Telecom (BT) started to use rapid application development techniques. They soon identified that they needed impartial people in the room to manage and record the process. From that they developed their own facilitation training, and this was used by many technical staff as they moved to a more people-management role and needed to have better interpersonal skills and run their own meetings.

The Facilitation Network was a list of everyone who had been on the training and was willing to be used as a facilitator. At its peak there were probably about one-hundred-plus people on it from all arms of BT. When someone wanted a facilitator they came to the trainers, who sent out a request to people on the list, who responded if they were interested or had the bandwidth to help. Everyone had their own day job.

This came to an abrupt halt with the introduction of a new CEO in 2004, who virtually made everyone apply for their own jobs. The main trainer and I took the opportunity to put together a business case for a small dedicated group of facilitators to continue with the training, manage the network, and respond to requests for facilitation. We got that and worked as a small team (three facilitators plus a manager) for about three years until the business focus changed to agile development with hothouses. They were looking for a 10 percent cut in staff, so we were an easy target to move into different roles.

—*Sally Murfitt, British Telecom*

Clearly Define Your Services

A few of those interviewed highlighted a key peculiarity about facilitation: people seldom buy it. What they buy are the things facilitation is used for: strategic planning, issue resolution, process improvement, team building, idea generation, and so on.

Find a way to have a valued-added offering around facilitation. You can't sell facilitation on its own. You should have a model to explain what you do; for us it was a circular model, with the core skill being facilitation (in the middle) with value-added services that leveraged facilitation into strategic planning, communications, program management, and mentoring.
—*Grant Barkman, formerly with Bell Canada Enterprises*

Some of the more successful cadres were able to clearly define the services they provided. Consider creating a list (brochure or PDF) that focuses on the three to five services you provide to your clients. Be sure to spend more words on the pain the client experiences and the benefit you provide than on the service you do. Although you might simply list other things you do, focus the majority of the piece on the three to five that you want your clients to know most about.

I worked in a group of internal facilitators in a large organization. A key point was that most of the team did not use facilitation as their main calling card. While the practice of facilitation was in many ways central to the work they did with client groups, the main advertised service related to topics like "team coaching," "organization development," "quality," and "knowledge management." This gave them other reasons for being of value to the organization, with facilitated meetings being a value-added service.
—*Michael Randel, Randel Consulting Associates*

Be Intentional About Marketing and Raising Awareness

We facilitators tend to be lousy marketers. So when a cadre of facilitators comes together, marketing tends to be the last thing on our minds. Our natural tendency is to focus on raising our skills, refining our craft, learning new methods, and developing our approaches in case someone calls, for most of us rely on our satisfied clients to tell others, who, we hope, will someday call us. And when they do, we will be ready!

Several interviewees highlighted the importance of having a strong marketing and communication channel.

Never underestimate account management. Never stop selling. Spend time with the customer. The more work we do, the more we see people who need to sit down in a workshop who have the same problem or interest; our understanding of the organization and issues allows us to see opportunities where work should be done.
—*Bjorn Blondell, Swedish Defense Material Administration*

Here are a few specific suggestions:

Marketing Suggestions

- Create client success stories from each relevant project that you can highlight, complete with quotes from the client talking about what you did. Consider having a "client of the quarter" whose story you circulate.
- Collect results for as many of your projects as possible at the highest level possible (see the Collect and Report Results section). Have these results available to report to others.
- Have an intranet page for the facilitator network that is customer focused. Include your client success stories, the specific services you provide, and the results you have achieved.
- Consider mounting posters in various departments that you replace quarterly to focus on different themes.
- Although satisfied customers will talk about you to others when the topic comes up, consider asking during the contracting phase whether they would be willing—if satisfied with your service—to help you share their success with at least three other organizations.
- When you are working with clients, always be listening for other needs they have that you may be able to support.
- If necessary, to get started consider doing what Jim Rankin at Hydro One did: ask to be given the toughest problem facing the organization, as a test. Okay, you may not want to start with the toughest, but you get the idea.

The Innovation Group started in 2010 with a new CEO. We have a value creation program going on in the corporation. One key thing is a winning culture, and one way to build it up is by identifying new ways of organizing things and people. This is where the facilitation comes in. The Innovation Group is quite visible in the corporate intranet site, magazine, posters all over the walls, and so on. We have put some effort into make it happen.
—*Mikko Vuolanto, Neste Jacobs, a division of Neste Oil*

As with most other things, if you are successful in your early marketing efforts and do a good job with each assignment, don't be surprised if your internal clients begin looking to you to do all sorts of activities, as noted here:

The team started out doing mainly strategic sessions. But when we became more known, we were asked for more activities—first to facilitate creative brainstorming within the organization, and now, with our organization in transition,

more and more sessions with a team development aspect in it, using theories like Tuckman's theory on group development. We're asked as well to facilitate sessions for external stakeholder consultations or workshops on conventions.
—*Rick Lindeman, Netherlands Agency of the Ministry for Economic Affairs, Agriculture and Innovation*

As described in the first case study, Hydro One used a pull strategy to create an environment in which their internal customers were proactively seeking assistance from the OA team. In his work with a client, Trevor Durnford used a similar strategy.

The client, SKF, wanted to bring some consistency in how they were implementing lean principles across the 130 factories globally. Most of their benchmark companies had used facilitators in some shape or form, and this was seen as a key to transferring ownership to the factories. Now there are seventy-five facilitators in Business Excellence, a program driven strongly by the CEO. Interestingly, facilitators are not forced on the business units. Local managers are encouraged to visit "Learning Platform" sites that have embraced the concepts (and have gotten great results from it too). This creates a hunger for help. There is no charge for the central facilitators, but there is a condition that the local businesses must provide full-time local facilitators who can sustain the journey.
—*Trevor Durnford, external consultant for SKF*

Collect and Report Results

What you collect and how you report is up to you. But collecting results and reporting them are essential. Adapting from the work of Donald Kirkpatrick, *Evaluating Training Programs,* you might consider measuring results at one of four levels, as shown in the table.

Level	Process	Sample Target
Level 1 *Reaction*	Evaluation form at the end of the session	At least 75 percent of participants indicate that the session was beneficial or highly beneficial to them
Level 2 *Session Outcome*	Evaluation form at the end of the session	At least 75 percent of participants indicate that the session achieved its stated outcome
Level 3 *Follow-Up Action*	Feedback 60 days after the session	At least 75 percent of participants indicate that actions to be taken in the first 60 days following the session had been taken
Level 4 *Results*	Research 120 days after the session	Documented evidence that the measurable business target set during the session was achieved

Without documented evidence of results, you may find it difficult to continue to justify the existence of the facilitation cadre. And the closer you can get to level 4 results, the stronger your case for continued investment will be.

At the end of every workshop, without exception, we gave every participant a survey. One key question: "Did your experience with the center drive to a better result faster?" There were subquestions about the environment, the facilitation, and so on. Measurable results are important. It comes back to justifying existence. If you know that 99 percent of the time people are getting to a better result faster, this is success that feeds on itself.
—*Barrie Levinson*

Make the Decision: Full-Time or Part-Time?

Some of the facilitator cadres had only part-time facilitators, as was the case with two of our featured organizations, Direct Supply and Saudi Aramco. Others had a full-time group; still others, like Hydro One, had both. There is no one right approach.

With organizations that used predominately part-time facilitators, the amount of time spent on facilitation was around one to four days per month. However, having at least one full-time facilitator does provide a level of consistency and momentum that can be more difficult to achieve without full-time support.

We recommend that our facilitators facilitate at least six workshops and cofacilitate four workshops a year. Unfortunately, for most of them this is not possible in combination with their regular jobs. There is one internal facilitator who works full-time for the cadre. It's her job to facilitate the facilitators. She is the one who receives the assignments and tries to match them with facilitators. Most of the time, the criterion is availability of facilitators.
—*Laura Zschuschen-van der Wel, Dutch insurance company*

If you do have full-time members of the team, however, heed the warning that follows about what facilitators do when they are not facilitating:

Having managed a facilitation group in a large telecommunications company for a number of years, and having to make the business case for their existence every year, I can personally tell you it is a very tough, but not impossible, sell. The key is *not* selling the value of facilitation but rather the value of what facilitators do when they are *not* facilitating. Most senior managers intrinsically "get" the value of facilitation—at least those who are concerned

about consensus. What they don't "buy" is keeping facilitators around when they're not facilitating—which is the greater percentage of their time.
—*Grant Barkman, formerly with Bell Canada Enterprises*

Have a Solid Recruiting and Vetting Process

Each of the organizations interviewed described a recruiting and vetting process that centered on one or more of the following components grouped into three dimensions.

Key Recruiting Criteria	**Knowledge and skills** • Knowledge of the business • Facilitation skills • Other nonfacilitation skills **Disposition** • Respect of peers • Values **Demographics** • Seniority in the organization • Department

For some selection processes, the disposition items were more important than knowledge and skills. For others, the reverse held true. In only a few cases were demographics the primary driver of selection.

In some cases, the organizations requested nominees from senior leaders. In other cases, self-nomination was the primary source of candidates. Having nominations from leadership serves the added benefit of encouraging management buy-in to the program. Self-nomination increases the likelihood that the pool will be filled with people who have a high interest in the work. One of the core issues is ensuring that people know what "the work" is. Some people think of facilitators primarily as instructors, others as meeting leaders, and others as discussion group leaders. As part of the vetting process, be sure that candidates are educated on what they are being recruited to do. Saudi Aramco used the Job X method to ensure full understanding on the part of its candidates.

Establish a Facilitator Development and Coaching Process

Take time to train the facilitators well; build solidarity among them so they support each other when the going gets tough; and educate the internal clients about what to expect, when to call on the facilitation team, and how to evaluate the results.
—*Beatrice Briggs, International Institute for Facilitation and Change*

Nearly all of the organizations interviewed had some type of skilling-up process for their facilitators, though in some cases the facilitators came "ready-made," as one organization described it.

The types and length of training varied widely. Some held a single training lasting two to four days. Others took a multistaged training approach that in one case totaled ten days. However, the most extensive initial training program, described in the Hydro One case study, included three four-day courses on organization development, followed by nine additional days of training covering problem solving and decision making, facilitation skills, and presentation skills, for a total of twenty-one days.

Saudi Aramco's coaching approach, coupled with its licensing of the INIFAC Partners in Facilitator Development program, provides an extensive model for implementing a structured development program for young facilitators.

Avoid the Pitfalls

Lander Stoddard, who was part of a cadre pilot in a U.S. government agency, started this list of pitfalls to avoid when setting up an internal facilitation network:

Twelve Pitfalls to Avoid in Establishing an Internal Facilitator Cadre

- Lack of an executive sponsor
- Not being housed in the right part of the organization
- Not picking the right people in the first place
- Not refreshing the cadre with new people as others move on
- Lack of commitment to training
- No formal mentoring
- Lack of criteria for staying a member of the cadre
- Unclear relationship of facilitation duty to regular job, especially when supervisor changes
- Not being clear about what skill level each person has and matching him or her appropriately to assignments
- Unclear process for internal clients to access the cadre
- Not contracting well at the front end of each assignment
- Not measuring and reporting results

Exercise Your Skills

If you are considering implementing an internal facilitator cadre, I would recommend that you carefully review the case studies of the three organizations included in this chapter. Their stories provide a wealth of insights into what can work and what might not work in your environment.

In addition, pay special attention to the best practices listed. Although it is not necessary to successfully address all eight, the experience of the twenty-one organizations suggests that missing one or two of the most critical is likely to significantly decrease your chances for success.

CHAPTER SEVENTEEN

SPECIAL TOPICS

Questions Answered in This Chapter

How do you apply the Secrets to running a simple meeting?

How do you apply the Secrets as a meeting participant?

How do you apply the Secrets to very small groups?

How do you apply the Secrets as a consultant or subject matter expert?

How do you become a certified facilitator?

Facilitator neutrality: fact or fiction?

Applying the Secrets to Running a Simple Meeting

The Secrets present a comprehensive approach to facilitating group sessions that often will take from half a day to multiple days to complete. But what about applying the Secrets to a one-hour meeting? Is there a simple checklist one can use?

In my book *The Secrets to Masterful Meetings,* I present the following vision of what a truly *masterful* meeting looks like. In today's business settings, the quality of the typical meeting is so low that bad meetings have become the standard. The vision elements that follow are intended to raise the bar on what should be expected from *every* meeting.

The Fifteen Elements of a Masterful Meeting

Preparation

1. **Advance notification**

   Participants know in advance the purpose, desired products, proposed agenda, and other important information about the meeting.

2. **Right people—prepared and present**

   The right people are at the meeting. They arrive prepared, they arrive on time, and they stay for the duration.

3. **Right information**

   All necessary information is available at the meeting.

Start

4. **Timely start and end**

   The meeting starts and ends on time.

5. **Clear purpose and products**

   At the start of the meeting, the meeting leader reviews the meeting purpose and desired products.

6. **Key issues identified**

   Either during the meeting or in advance, all participants have a chance to identify key issues or topics that need to be discussed to achieve the purpose and products.

7. **Agenda confirmed**

   The meeting leader confirms the agenda and establishes time limits for each item. (The leader may choose to adjust the agenda to ensure that all key issues are discussed.)

8. **Ground rules reviewed**

   The meeting leader reminds the participants of ground rules. Participants honor the ground rules throughout the meeting.

Execution

9. **Steady meeting flow**

   As the meeting flows from one agenda item to the next, the meeting leader reminds the participants of the purpose for each agenda item, how the agenda item fits into the overall meeting objective, and what the group is being asked to accomplish with the agenda item.

10. **Focused discussion**

    The discussion remains focused on the topic at hand. A topic is allowed to exceed its allotted time only with the expressed agreement of a majority and with full knowledge of the effect on the remaining agenda items.

11. **Positive, passionate participation**

All meeting participants are actively engaged throughout the meeting. They feel that it is safe to speak openly and honestly. People talk and listen with respect. There is energized discussion and debate. No one is allowed to dominate the discussion.

12. **Constructive conflict**

Disagreement is encouraged, and conflict is handled by participants asking questions, identifying strengths, defining concerns, and seeking new alternatives that maximize strengths and reduce concerns.

Close and Follow-Up

13. **Decisions and actions reviewed**

During the meeting, issues that arise that are inappropriate for discussion are deferred to an Issues list; decisions made and actions to be taken are documented. Prior to ending the meeting, all issues, decisions, and actions are reviewed, and appropriate actions are designated.

14. **Summary provided**

Following the meeting, a meeting summary is distributed to all participants identifying issues, decisions, actions, and relevant analysis.

15. **Follow-up on actions**

A follow-up process is put in place to ensure that all assigned actions are performed.

How many of the meetings that you attend in a typical week are truly masterful? Consider sharing these fifteen characteristics with other members of your organization. As you can see, the vision is well aligned with the Secrets from this book. (For strategies on transforming the meeting culture of your organization, consider providing a copy of *The Secrets to Masterful Meetings* to key meeting leaders.)

Checklist for Masterful Meeting Leaders

To create truly masterful meetings, masterful meeting leaders take the following actions:

Planning and Preparing

☐ Determine the meeting type, purpose, and products.

☐ Select participants.

- [ ] Identify probable issues that need to be addressed.
- [ ] Develop the proposed agenda.
- [ ] Select the processes that will be used in executing the agenda, and define the engagement strategies.
- [ ] Hold discussions as needed prior to the meeting.
- [ ] Select the meeting location, and handle other logistics.
- [ ] Prepare and distribute the meeting notice showing a gathering time and a start time.

Starting the Meeting

- [ ] Set up the meeting location, including any parking boards that will be used.
- [ ] Greet people when they arrive.
- [ ] Provide a two-minute warning prior to the start of the meeting.
- [ ] Start the meeting on time and state the purpose and products.
- [ ] Ask participants to identify key issues to be discussed.
- [ ] Review the proposed agenda; modify it as needed to address the key issues; establish time limits for each item.
- [ ] Remind the participants of the ground rules and parking boards.
- [ ] Make introductions if needed.

Running, Closing, and Following Up

- [ ] Review prior action items to ensure follow-up.
- [ ] For each agenda item, think FIRST CLASS:

  Focus the participants by providing an explanation of how the item furthers the meeting's purpose.

  Instruct by providing clear and concise directions on how the agenda item will be executed.

  Record the appropriate information gathered during the meeting, or ensure that the information is recorded.

  Step the participants through the agenda item, using the appropriate information gathering process.

  Track time to ensure that the participants are using time appropriately.

  Control and resolve any dysfunctional behavior quickly and effectively.

  Listen for off-topic discussions and redirect to a parking board to keep the meeting focused.

Address disagreements or conflicts that emerge.

Seek all opinions and invite people to speak.

Summarize the results.

☐ Close the meeting.

Review the items covered in the meeting.

Confirm the decisions made.

Address outstanding issues.

Ensure that all actions have names and dates assigned.

☐ Perform meeting follow-ups.

Document and distribute meeting notes.

Follow up to hold people accountable to assigned actions.

Form for Preparing and Starting a Session

Some items you create using this form are for planning purposes only; these items aren't lettered. Use the lettered items both in planning and in starting. The letters indicate the order in which you will say these items when you start the meeting.

1. Use the space below to record the purpose and the product for the meeting.

Purpose (inform). The purpose of this meeting is to . . .	
A	

Product (inform). When we are done, we will have . . .	
B	

2. Next, identify the people you will need in order to achieve the purpose and product.

Participants. The people who will be invited to the meeting are . . .	

3. Now, give some thought to why these people should attend this meeting. What's in it for them? What benefits will they gain if the meeting achieves its purpose? Give at least two sentences. Say the words "you" and "your" at least four times.

Excite. This is exciting because if we achieve our purpose, you . . .	
C	

4. Why were these participants selected, and what are they empowered to do? Are they being asked to represent a viewpoint? To be creative? To make a decision or recommendation?

Empower. You were selected to be a part of this meeting because . . .	
D	

5. Next, decide on the involvement question. Make sure to make it a type B question. You might ask participants to give thirty-second updates, key topics to cover, and so on.

Involve. Before going over the agenda, I would like to get you involved by asking . . .	
E	*Start with image building phrase:*
	Expand the image to the answers:
	Ask the type A question:

6. Next, think about the issues that will need to be addressed in order to achieve the purpose and product. What topics need to be covered? What will people want to talk about? What concerns are they likely to express?

Probable Issues. For the group to achieve the purpose and create the product, the following issues will need to be addressed or are likely to come up . . .

7. Decide on the agenda items you will have to cover during the meeting to achieve the purpose, create the product, and address the relevant probable issues.

Process. To help us achieve our purpose, I propose that we use the following agenda . . .	
F	

8. Decide on the ground rules you will use for the session to help ensure that the group works together effectively. See the sample ground rules in Chapter Four for examples.

Ground Rules. I would like to suggest several ground rules to help us work together effectively . . .	
G	

9. Decide on the parking boards that you will use. Consider the standard parking boards (Issues list, Decisions list, and Actions list) and add any others that may be helpful, depending on the session.

Parking Boards. During the session, some things may come up that we should document so that we can then move on. Accordingly, I would like to suggest that we use the following parking boards . . .	
H	

10. Now you are ready to start the session. Run through the eight elements (A–H) you have prepared, in order.

- In item F (Process), be sure to go back and have the participants indicate where in the agenda each of the issues identified in E will be addressed. Those issues not addressed can be added to the appropriate parking board.
- In item G (Ground Rules), be sure to ask the participants for any additional ground rules that should be covered.

Applying the Secrets as a Meeting Participant

There will be times when a meeting is not going well, but the meeting leader is not taking action. The reason for inaction on the leader's part might be a lack of skill or focus. In some cases, it might be that the meeting leader is the cause of the meeting's not going well!

The Secret to Guerrilla Facilitation
Ask questions that lead the group to action.

"Guerrilla Facilitation" is a set of techniques designed to help manage a meeting when you are not the meeting leader. The key to Guerrilla Facilitation is to *ask questions* that lead the group to take the action that is needed. Let's take a look at six situations that can be aided by guerrilla facilitation.

The Meeting Starts Without a Clear Purpose

You know from Chapter Three that everything starts with purpose. The agenda of a meeting, and the discussion that occurs, should be tied to the purpose of the meeting and the products to be created. Yet oftentimes leaders start a meeting either by going over the agenda or by diving straight into the first agenda item.

If the meeting leader starts the meeting without stating the meeting's purpose, you might say, "Excuse me. I may have missed it. Could you take a second to go over the overall purpose of this meeting and what we need to have when we are done? This will help me stay focused and make sure I don't go off on unimportant topics. What's our overall purpose for this meeting?" Note that a Guerrilla Facilitator never accuses—never says, for example, "You didn't state the purpose." Instead, a Guerrilla Facilitator asks a question to help gain clarity.

The Discussion Is Getting off Track

Chapter Five demonstrates how a facilitator uses redirection questions to keep a group on topic. Likewise, if the discussion seems to be getting off track but you are not the meeting leader, you can say, "These are excellent points we are discussing. I know we have to get back to our main topic, but I don't want to lose these points. Can we record them on an 'Issues list' or something so we can discuss them later, and then get back to our main topic?" Once again, asking the question can help take some of the sting out of the redirection.

One Person Is Dominating

Chapter Nine identifies techniques to use when a person is dominating the discussion. These same techniques can also be quite effective when you are a Guerrilla Facilitator. If the meeting leader permits a person to dominate the discussion, consider saying, "This is an important point we are discussing, and Joe has openly shared his views. It would be great to hear everyone else's opinion on this. Can we go around the room and have everyone give their view on this idea?"

One or More Participants Have Dropped Out

The round-robin technique you can use when one person is dominating the discussion will also work when you sense that one or more people are not participating. You might say, "This is an important issue we are discussing. It would be great to hear everyone else's opinion on this. Can we go around the room and have everyone give their view on this idea? I'll be glad to start."

Decisions or Actions Are Not Being Documented

Chapter Six discusses the importance of documenting all decisions made during the session and any actions that need to be taken. Sometimes, however, a decision can be made or an action indicated, and the meeting leader fails to record it. If this happens, you might say, "It sounds like we just made an important decision. Can we have someone repeat it so that the decision can be accurately recorded and we'll have documentation of the decision we made?"

The Meeting Is About to End Without a Review

Chapter Eight describes the proper ending of a meeting, which includes reviewing decisions made and actions to be taken. If a leader is about to end the meeting without a review, consider saying, "After such a productive meeting, I would hate to leave without being clear on what we decided or what is going to happen next. Could we take a minute to review the decisions we've made and the actions that need to occur once we leave?"

As you can see, Guerrilla Facilitation can be quite effective in guiding a meeting. These techniques serve as proactive strategies to help guide the discussion when the meeting leader is not providing strong facilitation. I have summarized these techniques in Table 17.1.

TABLE 17.1   ACTIONS OF A GUERRILLA FACILITATOR.

Problem	Action
The meeting starts without a clear purpose	Excuse me. I may have missed it. Could you take a second to go over the overall purpose of this meeting and what we need to have when we are done? This will help me stay focused and make sure I don't go off on unimportant topics. What's our overall purpose for this meeting?
The discussion is getting off track	These are excellent points we are discussing. I know we have to get back to our main topic, but I don't want to lose these points. Can we record them on an "Issues List" or something so we can discuss them later, and then get back to our main topic?
One person is dominating	This is an important point we are discussing, and Joe has openly shared his views. It would be great to hear everyone else's opinion on this. Can we go around the room and have everyone give their view on this idea?
One or more participants have dropped out	This is an important issue we are discussing. It would be great to hear everyone else's opinion on this. Can we go around the room and have everyone give their view on this idea? I'll be glad to start . . .
Decisions or actions are not being documented	It sounds like we just made an important decision. Can we have someone repeat it so the decision can be accurately recorded and we will have documentation of the decision made?
The meeting is about to end without a review	After such a productive meeting, I would hate to leave without being clear on what we decided or what is going to happen next. Could we take a minute to review the decisions we've made and the actions that need to occur once we leave?

Applying the Secrets to Very Small Groups

The Secrets of Facilitation are designed primarily for groups numbering from eight to thirty. As the case study that opened Chapter Five showed, applying the Secrets to a group of four or fewer may be a challenge. What makes these situations difficult?

- In such small meetings, there may not be a flip chart or other vehicle for recording what is said. This can lead to difficulty keeping the group focused and on track.
- The facilitator may view level 3 energy as too overpowering for a small group. Therefore, he or she may default to level 1 and have difficulty keeping the group energized.
- Formal information gathering techniques, such as rotating flip charts and dot prioritizing, may feel "canned" and artificial in a small group. The facilitator may tend to use only straightforward techniques that are less creative and that can become repetitive for participants.

The Secrets of Facilitation can be quite effective, even with smaller groups, but some adjustments are warranted:

- Consider letting the group know up front that you will be using facilitation techniques to keep the meeting focused. While sitting with them at the table, ask them to help you by providing feedback at the end concerning whether the facilitation was appropriate for a small group. Alerting the participants and asking for their help encourages them to go along with the process and reserve judgment until the end.
- To start the session, use a level 2 voice to inform, excite, empower, and involve, following the traditional steps of an opening. A level 2 voice is more appropriate with a limited-size group.
- Employ all other techniques as you normally would with a moderate-size group; avoid breakout groups, however, as the team is so small already.
- If you are working with a small group on a continuing basis, pay close attention to which Secrets work for that group and which don't. The lack of diversity in the group may warrant a tighter or looser approach to the facilitation, depending on the personalities of the participants.

Applying the Secrets as a Consultant or Subject Matter Expert

Oftentimes consultants are called in by an organization with the expectation that the consultants will apply their expertise to addressing some important problem or issue. Organizations often select consultants specifically because of their expertise in the topic area. In these cases, the consultants are not neutral. Instead, they bring a specific point of view and clear ideas for actions the organization might take. How does a consultant who is not neutral use the Secrets of Facilitation?

Most consultants have as their greatest desire that their clients implement the recommendations they make. For these consultants, the Fundamental Secret of Facilitation still applies:

> ### The Fundamental Secret of Facilitation
> You can achieve more effective results when solutions are created, understood, and accepted by the people impacted.

How do you gain maximum buy-in for your recommendations? In concept, the answer is simple: you involve the people in the process you use to create the recommendations you want them to accept. This way, the people own the recommendations, they understand them, and they accept them.

Although this is simple in concept, it is much more difficult in practice. How do you involve these people in the creation of the recommendations? How does this work, given that they have neither the knowledge you have from consulting with numerous organizations with similar issues nor the time you have to do the research and analyze the information about their problem?

CASE STUDY: The Strategy Firm and the Nonprofit

Several years ago, we had the opportunity to serve in partnership with one of the national strategy consulting firms. The customer was one of the nation's largest nonprofits, whose leader had recognized that after more than one hundred years, the nonprofit's business model was no longer sustainable. The organization had learned from its research that its share of the charitable dollar had been in decline across the country for over a decade. The long-term prospects for its hundreds of affiliates were not rosy. In essence, fewer and fewer Americans were seeing this organization as their top charitable priority.

To address this problem and build a new mission, vision, and business model for its entire system, the organization assembled a twenty-member panel that included CEOs and top community leaders and volunteers from around the country. Incredibly, this powerful group agreed to meet one to two days a month for seven months to build a new model for the organization.

The strategy consulting firm had a reputation for doing exceptional analysis and for crafting effective strategies in the for-profit world. It was used to engaging the senior team of an organization on the front end, doing its research, preparing recommendations, and presenting those recommendations for buy-in and acceptance by the senior team.

This task force, however, demanded that the work be done differently. They did not want merely to be engaged on the front end and the back end. *They* wanted to be the ones who created the recommendations, with the guidance of the consulting firm. My organization was called in to facilitate the task force meetings and provide the engagement opportunities for the task force members to understand the information and develop recommendations for implementation.

The consulting firm and our organization forged a strong working partnership with the help of the client project manager. As the facilitator, I was impressed to see some of the unique processes that the consulting firm used in developing alternatives and reaching conclusions. The consulting firm accepted new methods for engaging an executive team in defining the analysis, doing the analysis, and creating recommendations:

- In some meetings, task force members identified potential alternatives that the consulting team later researched and improved upon.

- In other meetings, task force members analyzed alternatives created by the consulting firm by defining strengths and weaknesses and eliminating alternatives they viewed as nonviable.

- Sometimes task force members modified recommendations, whereas other times they created new recommendations.

With the guidance of the consulting team, the task force created new vision and mission statements and a new operating model for the organization. They also developed strategies for engaging the entire organization for review and buy-in.

The task force members clearly created, understood, and accepted the recommendations. Following the completion of the task force work, the task force members went around the country gaining the buy-in and participation of hundreds of affiliates. Many of the recommendations coming out of the task force process have stood the test of time and continue to be implemented today.

This case study illustrates a number of strategies you can use to implement the Secrets of Facilitation as an expert consultant.

Using the Secrets as an Expert Consultant	• Assemble a steering committee or task force whose role it will be to develop the recommendations.
	• Develop a structured work process that educates the steering committee on the issues and engages them in the development—not just the approval—of recommendations.
	• In some cases, ask the steering committee to do the preliminary work. Have them come up with preliminary alternatives, preliminary decision criteria, preliminary recommendations, or preliminary implementation plans.
	• In other cases, the consulting team can outline preliminary thinking. In these cases, engage the steering committee in identifying strengths and weaknesses, defining implications, and isolating barriers, or in doing other work that forces them to focus on and improve the preliminary thinking. Steering committee members should be encouraged to modify the preliminary thoughts or create new thoughts based on their analysis. These activities influence understanding, creation, and acceptance.
	• Avoid presenting draft recommendations to the steering committee. If they are not involved in the creation, you are unlikely to achieve buy-in and commitment from the top level needed for the organization to gain full benefit.
	• Have steering committee members present the results to others. Steering committee members' presenting has the double advantage of increasing the commitment of the steering committee members and showing to others the top-level passion and commitment behind the recommendations.

Becoming a Certified Facilitator

In the mid- to late 1990s, there were many training organizations coming out with their own certification program for facilitators. By that time, my company, Leadership Strategies—The Facilitation Company, had trained a few thousand in facilitation skills. But I felt strongly that it didn't make sense for every training organization to have its own proprietary certification process. How could that help the profession? How could that help the customer?

In May of 1999, I was invited to serve on the North American Certification Panel for the International Association of Facilitators (IAF). The panel was tasked with reviewing a certification model from Europe and making a recommendation to the IAF board concerning adoption of the certification model for North America. To help our panel evaluate the model, four other panel members and I were taken through the process and became the first five Certified Professional Facilitators in North America.

The work our European colleagues had done in putting together the certification model was impressive. They had not only codified the skills and abilities facilitators required but also developed a process to ascertain whether a candidate facilitator showed evidence of these key elements. Assessors used a written application from the candidate, a facilitated role play, and two interview sessions to make pass/defer decisions.

Our panel recommended adopting the Certified Professional Facilitator (CPF) designation, which was later revised and continues to be improved to this day. The IAF has superbly overseen the development and execution of the CPF program, which has resulted in the certification of more than four hundred facilitators worldwide by 2012. (See www.iaf-world.org for more information.)

There was an additional recommendation from our panel. We recognized that the CPF was designed specifically to assess whether a candidate had basic, essential facilitation skills. As the IAF Web site explains, "The professional facilitator designation offers clients an assurance that those who are certified are qualified to design and provide basic group facilitation services." To support movement beyond the basic skills, the panel recommended the development of a higher-level certification to which all facilitators could aspire.

In 2005, this recommendation was picked up by the International Institute for Facilitation (INIFAC). An initiating committee, of which I was again a member, performed a study of existing certification programs and drafted thirty-two potential subcompetencies. Through a survey of 450 facilitators and users of facilitation services (that is, customers), the initiating committee gained input on the competency model. As a result, more than 40 percent of the drafted competencies were changed, resulting in the Certified Master Facilitator program.

The program includes six major competencies and thirty subcompetencies. (See www.INIFAC.org for more information.) As of 2012, fewer than two dozen people had achieved the Certified Master Facilitator (CMF) mark.

Both certifications serve their stated purpose. The CPF certifies that facilitators have the competencies required to design and provide basic group facilitation services. The CMF certifies that a facilitator has achieved the level of excellence required to facilitate both basic and advanced facilitated sessions. The requirements of the two certifications are summarized in Table 17.2.

I am both a CPF and a CMF, and I am an ardent supporter of the CMF program as a vehicle for raising the expertise level of the profession while providing clients with a true mark of excellence that carries a brand expectation of high facilitation performance. I recommend that those facilitators who qualify seek out the CMF program. *(Please note:* in full disclosure, I am a founding board member of INIFAC and continue to sit on the board.)

TABLE 17.2   CPF-CMF COMPARISON CHART.

	CPF **Certified Professional** **Facilitator**	**CMF** **Certified Master** **Facilitator**
Certifying Organization	International Association of Facilitators (www.iaf-world.org)	International Institute for Facilitation (www.inifac.org)
Intention	To offer clients an assurance that those who are certified are qualified to design and provide basic group facilitation services (IAF Web site)	To assess a candidate's ability to meet basic and higher-level skills for advanced facilitation
Target Audience	Competent facilitators with experience in the field	Advanced facilitators with significant or moderate experience (CPF not required)
Experience	Seven sessions in the prior three years	Thirty sessions in the prior three years
Organizations	No minimum	Five organizations; ten sponsors
Degree of Proficiency	Evidence of proficiency	Score a minimum 80 percent in all six competency areas
Written Assessment	Candidate provides examples of how he or she applied the core competencies in his or her work.	Candidate indicates his or her knowledge and specific experiences in responding to thirty questions related to the competencies.
Facilitation Assessment	Candidate facilitates at a scheduled on-site assessment event, with assessor interview and immediate feedback.	Candidate submits a video of a facilitated session based on an assigned topic and specific role-plays.

Why am I such a strong supporter of the CMF certification?

- **First and foremost, the competency model provides a vision for highly skilled facilitation.** A summary of the six major competencies appears at the end of this section. I believe that if every facilitator operated at the level described in those competencies, there would be little question about the value facilitators bring to the world.
- **Clients can rely on the certification to indicate high levels of facilitation expertise.** In my organization, we are so sold on the CMF mark of excellence that for clients who use a CMF through us, we guarantee the facilitator's work and will refund the fees if the client isn't satisfied.
- **The subcompetency model is based on observable behaviors and is rigorously assessed for consistency and reliability.** Each subcompetency can be assessed based on knowledge demonstrated through a written submission or a performance demonstrated in a video created by the candidate in a simulated session based on role plays provided by INIFAC. Assessors use a five-point scale with each competency, and the point system is clearly laid out with the assessor guide. This ensures a high level of scoring consistency among assessors.
- **The certification process is a development tool.** Every candidate receives a scored assessment in each of the thirty subcompetencies and is assigned one of four overall assessments:

  - Apprentice
  - Associate
  - Accomplished
  - Advanced

Those receiving the Advanced rating who also meet the experience requirement are designated Certified Master Facilitators. Those who meet all but the experience requirement are designated Provisional Certified Master Facilitators and given three years to complete the thirty-session requirement. Those who achieve an apprentice, associate, or accomplished rating receive feedback and recommendations on areas for improvement and can reapply at a later date.

Although the CMF certification isn't for everyone, it serves to distinguish those who have been assessed by their peers as possessing advanced facilitation skills. As noted earlier, the following six broad competencies are supported by thirty subcompetencies used for assessment.

CMF Competencies

Certified Master Facilitators bring PAC³E to every engagement.

Presence
- Master Facilitators bring compassion and authority to the room. Through their verbal and nonverbal expression, they exude confidence, energy, and self-awareness while also conveying a high level of warmth and caring. They make adjustments in their style to better serve the group.

Assessment
- Master Facilitators know and ask the questions necessary to accurately assess a client need. On the basis of their learning from past experiences, they create processes designed to address the client's specific requirements. They carefully plan and prepare sessions. They recognize when a planned process is not working effectively and are able to quickly define alternative processes to reach the desired outcome.

Communication
- Master Facilitators are skilled communicators. They actively listen, making sure to play back and confirm important points. They have highly tuned analytical skills that allow them to process information quickly, differentiate various content issues, and isolate critical points in a discussion. They ask questions that help groups engage effectively. They deliver instructions that are accurate, clear, and concise. They effectively identify and verbally summarize agreements.

Control
- Master Facilitators create and maintain a productive and safe environment in which participants with diverse styles and from different cultures can engage in interactions that stay focused on achieving the goal. They maintain control of the session and an appropriate pace. They understand causes of disagreement and can effectively guide a group through conflict. They consciously take action to prevent, detect, and resolve dysfunctional behavior.

Consistency
- Master Facilitators understand and consistently apply best practice techniques for such activities as starting the session, focusing the group, recording information, and closing the session.

Engagement
- Master Facilitators know and use multiple techniques for engaging a group, problem solving, decision making, promoting creativity, and raising energy.

Facilitator Neutrality: Fact or Fiction?

Many facilitators who have been guiding groups for a reasonable period of time have found themselves faced with the neutrality dilemma. Textbook facilitation dictates that the facilitator should be completely neutral, focus solely on the process and group dynamics, and at all costs avoid making *any* content suggestions.

But have you ever found that while facilitating a client session, ideas come to you that could potentially benefit the group? Have you wondered, "Should I say something? Would I be violating the primary role of a facilitator?" Herein lies the neutrality dilemma. Do you or don't you say something?

The traditional "facilitator school" would answer, "Absolutely not. It's not your role. You are not the expert. It is not honoring the wisdom of the group. If you want to participate, give the pen to someone else and sit down."

But there are other schools of thought. I had the pleasure of engaging with a group of facilitators in an online discussion about neutrality. In talking with them about this topic, I heard two distinct schools of thought. And of course there are likely to be other schools. For ease of discussion, let's give names to the two views: the traditional and the hybrid. Although in my practice I tend to facilitate using the hybrid approach, I think there are strengths and weaknesses to each.

The Traditional View

The traditional view, which I believe originated out of the organization development disciplines, is that facilitators must present themselves and conduct themselves as totally neutral parties.

- Facilitators are responsible for the process; participants are responsible for the content.
- Facilitators don't have to understand the content, and it is often best if they don't understand it so that they aren't tempted to engage in content discussions.
- Facilitators don't praise comments made.
- Above all else, facilitators never, ever, *ever* offer content suggestions.

The overall goal of facilitators who hold the traditional view is to take the group through a process that builds relationships, creates an atmosphere of trust, and produces results that have the support and the commitment of all team members.

The Hybrid View

The hybrid view, which I believe comes out of the management consulting arena, starts with the premise that facilitators, much like financial advisers, have a fiduciary responsibility to their clients to do all they can to help encourage positive outcomes for their clients.

Facilitators who hold a hybrid view believe it is better if the participants come up with the ideas because when participants create the ideas, they are more likely to own, accept, and implement them. At the same time, these facilitators believe that if they are aware of possible solutions that may be of help, they should, as a last resort, offer these possibilities. To this end, facilitators operating with a hybrid view might go to great lengths to educate themselves on their client's industry, operations, and business issues. They might consider in advance possible pathways clients might take to address their situation.

During the facilitation, if the group is overlooking a potentially suitable solution, facilitators operating under a hybrid view might ask a general leading question, such as "Are there solutions related to technology that we might not have yet considered?" Or if these facilitators are aware that a specific idea has not been brought forth, they might float the idea, being sure to record the idea only if participants take ownership of it. For example, a facilitator might say, "What do you think of doing X?" If there is a positive response, he or she might then say, "Why might you want to do X? What would be the benefits? How do you want me to write it . . . ?"

Facilitators who hold a hybrid view may use such techniques as leading questions and floating ideas, but do not care about the outcome. If the group takes the idea, great. If the group doesn't, great. However, these facilitators also recognize that these same techniques can easily be misused. Whether a facilitator uses them intentionally or unintentionally, these techniques can be employed to manipulate the group into agreeing to solutions that they don't own and, as a result, typically don't implement fully, if at all. Of course this type of manipulation, or facipulation as described earlier, can occur whether you follow the hybrid or the traditional approach; however, facilitators who adopt the hybrid view must take greater care not to abuse their role.

To summarize: in the traditional view, neutrality means *no* involvement in the content; in the hybrid view, neutrality means that the facilitator may offer content ideas, but has no investment in whether the ideas are used or not.

Strengths and Weaknesses

Table 17.3 lists the strengths and weaknesses of each approach. (Note that because there are only two views offered, the strengths of one are more or less equivalent to the weaknesses of the other.)

TABLE 17.3   COMPARISON OF THE TRADITIONAL AND HYBRID VIEWS.

Traditional View	Hybrid View
Strengths	**Strengths**
• Higher likelihood exists that the group will implement what they create because all ideas come from the group. • Higher likelihood exists that the group will look to themselves for solutions rather than to the facilitator. • Lower likelihood exists that the facilitator will become a "facipulator"—guiding the group to solutions that they don't create or own. • Less up-front effort is required by the facilitator to learn and understand the client's business and issues.	• The facilitator may be more likely to be active in facilitating and managing the discussion. • The facilitator is more likely to offer thoughts that stimulate the group's thinking. • Potential suitable solutions known by the facilitator are more likely to be brought out. • Clients may be more likely to perceive higher value from the facilitator's involvement.
Potential Weaknesses	**Potential Weaknesses**
• The facilitator is less likely to offer thoughts that stimulate the group's thinking. • Potential suitable solutions known by the facilitator may go unspoken. • The facilitator may be more likely to become less active in facilitating and managing the discussion. • Clients may be less likely to see the value of the facilitator beyond setting up the meeting agenda and ensuring that ground rules are followed.	• Higher likelihood exists that the group will look to the facilitator rather than to themselves for solutions. • Higher likelihood exists that the facilitator will become a "facipulator"—guiding the group to solutions that they don't create or own. • Lower likelihood exists that the group will implement what they create because some ideas may come from the facilitator. • More up-front effort is required by the facilitator to learn and understand the client's business and issues.

Boundaries

If you choose to use a hybrid approach, how do you avoid abusing the role? One facilitator explained it this way: "I have always felt that as facilitators we can never be totally neutral. We have our own values and beliefs that can seep out very subtly in our nonverbals. My answer to that with a group is to be very transparent up front about what my worldview and biases are, then ask them to call me on it if they see me inappropriately advocating. This way, I think I can use a hybrid approach without fear."

A second facilitator provided a different view: "A hybrid approach has the potential to offer greater value to clients if you establish and exercise a set of parameters." This facilitator recommends considering the following boundaries:

Some
Boundaries
to Consider
for
Maintaining
Neutrality

The facilitator may make content suggestions only if

- The facilitator has strong knowledge and experience in the area being discussed and can add value through the suggestion of ideas.
- The facilitator has a unique observation as an "outsider" that might be missed by those closer to the issue at hand.
- The facilitator offers these suggestions and ideas only after the group has stalled or is ready to move on, and the facilitator believes that they are potentially missing something that might have a significant impact on the group's output and success.
- The suggestion or idea is always posed as a question. ("What about . . . ?" "I'm wondering . . . ?")
- Suggestions and ideas are given sparingly and cautiously.

A third facilitator tells this story about how she handled the boundary.

> This issue came up last week during a facilitation. I felt there was an expanded suggestion from the one on the table that would benefit the group. As I was taking notes on the computer—projected during the discussion—I spoke and typed my suggestion/addition to the comments on the table. I announced that I was about to step out of facilitator mode for a moment and offer an suggestion, and that I would be happy to delete it from the notes if it didn't fit the group's perceptions of a suggestion they would like to keep. Given the option, the client chose to include the suggestion, and several folks mentioned that it was appreciated.

A Note of Caution

In thinking about a hybrid approach to neutrality, it is important to recognize the potential for widespread abuse. As one facilitator warned, "I think a lot of people who call themselves 'facilitators' just don't get the notion of neutrality as a defining characteristic of the role. Instead, they are looking for any excuse to parade their ego. So this line of reasoning opens the door wide for sloppy thinkers and undisciplined show-offs to call themselves facilitators."

What Do *Your* Clients Want?

It has been my experience that most of our clients want our facilitators to use more of a hybrid approach. However, one of the things that I now do more often is to gain agreement up front from the sponsor and the group with regard to their preference that I do or do not offer suggestions from my experience.

The bottom line: gain agreement with your sponsor on the appropriate approach and let the participants know early in the session.

EPILOGUE

I hope you have enjoyed *The Secrets of Facilitation*. I believe that the material provides substantial insight into the facilitation process. The numerous case studies were intended to help the material come alive, and the various "Why Do This?" lists provided the underlying reasoning behind many of the major concepts.

Veteran facilitators who take our courses often comment that they had no idea how much they didn't know. Others tell us that the material is overwhelming, and they have trouble determining where they should start. Here are some suggestions:

- *Become proficient one chapter at a time.* Choose a chapter from which you believe you can get the most benefit, such as the one on consensus building, getting started, or questioning. Read that chapter thoroughly from beginning to end once a week. Practice the techniques until you feel proficient. Then move on to another chapter.
- *Facilitate every opportunity you get!* When asked to facilitate, do it if at all possible. Real improvement can't come without opportunities to practice.
- *Seek quality feedback.* Following every facilitated session, hold a review session. Seek quality feedback from other facilitators. Identify specific areas for improvement. Focus on one area at a time.
- *Use the Secrets informally.* In conversations, use the question types and checkpoints. In meetings, make sure the purpose and process are clear. Use consensus building strategies any time you hear disagreements.

- *Consider joining a facilitation association and attending facilitator conferences.* There are regional facilitation groups throughout the United States and around the world. See the Resource Guide for additional information.
- *Sharpen your skills by taking a facilitation class.* The Resource Guide provides information on several exceptional courses.
- *Consider becoming certified.* Chapter Seventeen and the Resource Guide describe the Certified Master Facilitator and the Certified Professional Facilitator programs.

Please join us in "Sharing the Power of Facilitation with the World." I affirm for you much success as you continue to master the art and science of facilitation.

RESOURCE GUIDE FOR FACILITATORS

Leadership Strategies—The Facilitation Company

Following the publication of the first edition of *The Secrets of Facilitation*, Leadership Strategies—The Facilitation Company has emerged as the number-one meeting facilitation and facilitation training company in the United States. The author is the founder and serves as the company's managing director.

- *The Effective Facilitator* is the training course that teaches the Secrets of Facilitation and is taught monthly throughout the United States and in locations around the world.
- *The Facilitative Consultant* and *Facilitation for Trainers* are courses based on the same principles and were developed by the author.
- Leadership Strategies offers *The Facilitation Guides*—electronic versions of detailed facilitation guides that you can modify for use in your own facilitation.
- The company also offers free webinars monthly, including "An Introduction to Facilitation."
- Through the Web site (www.leadstrat.com) you can access a resource library of articles on facilitation, consulting, and leadership, and descriptions of all the organization's services. You can also sign up for the organization's free online newsletter.

The FindaFacilitator Database

The FindaFacilitator Database (www.FindaFacilitator.com), managed by Leadership Strategies, is the intelligent tool that simplifies the process of finding the right facilitator. Clients search the database to find the right facilitator, in the right location, with the right skills and experience, at the price they can afford. They can search for the top-rated facilitators in their industry or the least expensive facilitator in the location they desire. They can see which facilitators have received strong reviews from other clients and which have achieved the Certified Master Facilitator (CMF) or Certified Professional Facilitator (CPF) designations. There are over five hundred facilitators available through FindaFacilitator.com.

The International Association of Facilitators

The International Association of Facilitators (IAF) is the premier professional organization for facilitators and for organizations everywhere who want to benefit from facilitation methods and processes to increase participation and fulfill their mission. The IAF has more than twelve hundred members in over sixty countries. On the IAF Web site (www.iaf-world.org) you will find information about international conferences, facilitator certification (the CPF designation), joining the organization, and other topics.

The International Institute for Facilitation

The mission of the International Institute for Facilitation (INIFAC) is to maintain and promote a program of certification for facilitators at the master's level. INIFAC oversees the CMF certification and also licenses its assessment programs and competencies to organizations through its Partners in Facilitator Development program. INIFAC also accredits training classes that teach the thirty CMF competencies and provides video assessment services. The INIFAC Web site (www.INIFAC.org) contains information about the certification process and links to other resources on facilitation.

Training Courses in Facilitation

There are numerous organizations providing facilitation training. Listed here is information from five organizations that are arguably among the strongest, combining facilitation theory with quality facilitation practices.

Leadership Strategies

Leadership Strategies (www.leadstrat.com) offers eleven classes in facilitation-related topics.

- *The Effective Facilitator* is the flagship four-day course on which *The Secrets of Facilitation* is based. This course covers the ten fundamental principles of facilitation, over one hundred strategies and tools, ten detailed agendas, a three-hundred-page manual, six practice sessions including a videoed capstone session, the Refresher—a monthly online session for veterans of the class, and the Maximizer—a monthly reminder of a key class concept from the class. Public, open-enrollment classes are offered in cities in the United States, including Atlanta, Boston, Chicago, Dallas, Denver, Los Angeles, New York, San Francisco, and Washington DC and also in Toronto and Sydney. Private, on-site classes are available as well.
- *The Advanced Facilitator Workshop* is the natural two-day follow-on to *The Effective Facilitator.* The course provides training in facilitating advanced sessions, using a variety of engagement strategies and building top-level facilitator skills.
- *The Certification Preparation Class* is a two-day session that provides the foundation of skill and knowledge needed to prepare for certification by the International Institute for Facilitation (INIFAC) as a CMF. Participants in the class receive a certificate of completion from Leadership Strategies and can use the materials and the video from the course to apply for master-level certification by INIFAC.
- Other facilitation-related classes include
  - *Facilitation for Trainers*
  - *The Facilitative Consultant*
  - *Leadership Through Facilitation*
  - *Facilitating IT Sessions*
  - *Facilitating Virtual Meetings*
  - *The Secrets to Facilitating Strategy*
  - *The Secrets to Masterful Meetings*
  - *The Seven Separators of Facilitation Excellence*

Roger Schwarz and Associates

Roger Schwarz and Associates (www.schwarzassociates.com) provides facilitation training, consultation, and facilitation to help groups, organizations, and communities create fundamental change.

- *The Skilled Facilitator* workshop is designed for facilitators and consultants who want to learn a practical, powerful, values-based, systems approach to facilitation that they can apply to a wide range of groups and situations and that can create fundamental change in teams and organizations. Participants learn the principles and techniques of the Skilled Facilitator Approach and develop their skills in applying these principles and techniques.

- *The Facilitative Leader* workshop is designed for people who lead organizations, divisions, groups, or teams as well as for team members who want to fundamentally improve their group's effectiveness. Facilitative leadership involves using facilitative skills in cases where the leader has both a stake and a decision-making role in the issues being discussed. The course includes modeling a set of core values and ground rules, thinking and acting systemically, increasing responsibility and ownership while reducing unnecessary dependence, and creating conditions for learning.

Interaction Associates

Interaction Associates (www.interactionassociates.com) is a global provider of collaborative change consulting and workplace learning solutions.

- The *Essential Facilitation* course provides a solid framework and proven techniques for resolving conflicts, creating buy-in, and building lasting agreements—skills as valuable in everyday life as they are in business. These methods have been used by hundreds of organizations to generate faster decisions, increase creativity and productivity, and shorten cycle times.

- *Facilitating Change* is a course that shows how overcoming resistance to change is a function of building agreement around a projected outcome. Interaction Associates has helped hundreds of organizations overcome hurdles, build consensus, and take action to support change and transition efforts. The combined wisdom of more than thirty-five years of extensive research and consulting practice on collaboration has been distilled into this highly engaging three-day workshop.

MG Rush Systems

MG Rush Systems (www.mgrush.com), a division of Morgan Madison & Company, is a management consulting firm specializing in facilitated workshops (Joint Application Design–like) and facilitator training in the FAST technique.

- *The FAST Session Leader Workshop* is a five-day course designed so that the student will be able to perform as an effective session leader, demonstrate an understanding of FAST and its components and processes, demonstrate a basic level of proficiency in general facilitation skills, and use FAST in a variety of system development and non-system-related situations.
- *The Advanced Class* is a three-day session designed to review, refine, and enhance the facilitation and workshop-structuring skills of the experienced session leader.

The Institute for Cultural Affairs

The Institute for Cultural Affairs (www.ica-usa.org) provides services to promote revitalized communities, participatory organizations, transformative learning, and youth leadership.

- *Group Facilitation Methods* is a two-day course that teaches three proven processes for activating group participation: what the institute calls the focused conversation method, the consensus workshop method, and the action planning method. Gain hands-on experience practicing these methods and explore ways to apply them to your specific situation.
- *Mastering the Technology of Participation* is an intensive yearlong training program in the Technology of Participation (ToP) methods for those who wish to significantly increase their skills in facilitating group processes. The program provides a theoretical foundation for the ToP methods as well as opportunities for practice and feedback.

Facilitator Certification

- *Certified Master Facilitator.* The CMF certification is offered by INIFAC. The certification program is intended to certify facilitators at the master's level, indicating that they have the knowledge, skills, and experience to execute basic and advanced sessions. The certification covers the six competencies and thirty subcompetencies that make up the master certification program. Candidates are required to have facilitated thirty sessions in the three years prior to application. Applicants must provide a written submission in response to thirty questions that cover the competencies. In addition, applicants must document the required experience and provide a video of a structured facilitated session that meets the stringent guidelines of INIFAC. See the Web site (www.INIFAC.org) for additional information.

- *Certified Professional Facilitator.* The CPF designation is offered by the IAF. The certification process is meant to assess competency in a broad spectrum of skills and knowledge required to successfully facilitate a variety of basic sessions. The certification covers six competencies and eighteen subcompetencies. Candidates are required to have completed seven facilitated sessions and must submit an application. In addition, candidates must attend an IAF-sponsored certification event during which they are interviewed and are required to facilitate a practical workshop on a preselected issue.

Recommended Books

Doyle, M., and Straus, D. *How to Make Meetings Work! The New Interaction Method.* New York: Berkley Books, 1976.

Hall, E. T., and Hall, M. R. *Understanding Cultural Differences.* Yarmouth, Mass.: Intercultural Press, 1990.

Hofstede, G. *Culture's Consequences: International Differences in Work-Related Values.* Thousand Oaks, Calif.: Sage, 1980.

Hunter, D. *The Art of Facilitation: The Essentials for Leading Great Meetings and Creating Group Synergy.* San Francisco: Jossey-Bass, 2009.

Hunter, D., Bailey, A., and Taylor, B. *The Zen of Groups: The Handbook for People Meeting with a Purpose.* Tucson, Ariz.: Fisher Books, 1995.

Kaner, S., and others. *Facilitator's Guide to Participatory Decision-Making.* Philadelphia: New Society, 1996.

Kirkpatrick, D., and Kirkpatrick, J. *Evaluating Training Programs.* San Francisco: Berrett-Koehler, 2006.

Kluckhohn, F., and Strodtbeck, F. *Variations in Value Orientations.* Evanston, Ill.: Row, Peterson, 1961.

Miller, B. C. *Quick Team-Building Activities for Busy Managers.* New York: AMACOM, 2003.

Miller, B. C. *More Quick Team-Building Activities for Busy Managers.* New York: AMACOM, 2007.

Miller, B. C. *Quick Brainstorming Activities for Busy Managers.* New York: AMACOM, 2012.

Newstrom, J., and Scannell, E. *Games Trainers Play.* New York: McGraw-Hill, 1980.

Rees, F. *How to Lead Work Teams: Facilitation Skills.* (2nd ed.) San Francisco: Jossey-Bass, 2001.

Rush, M. G. *FAST Session Leader Reference Manual.* Self-published. Contact MG Rush, Chicago, Ill. Tel: 603-954-5880.

Schwartz, S. H. "Beyond Individualism/Collectivism: New Cultural Dimensions of Values." In U. Kim, H. C. Triandis, C. Kagitcibasi, S.-C. Choi, and G. Yoon (eds.), *Individualism and Collectivism: Theory, Method, and Applications* (pp. 85–119). Thousand Oaks, CA: Sage, 1994.

Schwarz, R. *The Skilled Facilitator: A Comprehensive Resource for Consultants, Facilitators, Managers, Trainers, and Coaches.* San Francisco: Jossey-Bass, 2002.

Trompenaars, F., and Hampden-Turner, C. *Riding the Waves of Culture: Understanding Cultural Diversity in Global Business.* New York: McGraw Hill, 1998.

Weaver, R., and Farrell, J. *Managers as Facilitators: A Practical Guide to Getting Work Done in a Changing Workplace.* San Francisco: Berrett-Koehler, 1997.

Weissglass, J. "Constructivist Listening for Empowerment and Change." *Educational Forum,* Summer 1990, *54*(4), 351–370.

Wilkinson, M. *The Secrets to Masterful Meetings.* Atlanta: Leadership Strategies Publishing, 2005.

Wilkinson, M. *The Executive Guide to Facilitating Strategy.* Atlanta: Leadership Strategies Publishing, 2011.

70 SECRETS OF FACILITATION

Secret #1   **The Fundamental Secret of Facilitation**
You can achieve more effective results when solutions are created, understood, and accepted by the people impacted.

Secret #2   **The Secret of When to Use Facilitation**
If more than a few people are involved, and understanding and buy-in are needed, so is facilitation.

Secret #3   **The Secret of the Starting Question**
Great starting questions draw a vivid image of the answers.

Secret #4   **The Secret to Guiding a Group**
Guide the group's flow by asking, not telling.

Secret #5   **The Secret to Influencing Idea Ownership**
When you float an idea, ask participants to identify its benefits and how to record it.

Secret #6   **The Secret to Preparation: The 5 Ps**
During preparation, define your 5 Ps: purpose, product, participants, probable issues, and process.

Secret #7   **The Secret Power of Purpose**
A clear purpose provides a solid basis for decision making.

Secret #8   **The Secret to Defining the Session Product: The 3 Hs**
To define the products desired from a facilitated meeting, ask the three H questions: What do you want people to have in their hands (deliverables), their heads (knowledge), and their hearts (beliefs) that they didn't have before the meeting started?

Secret #9   **The Secret to Managing a Sponsor's Presence**
Gain the sponsor's agreement not to be the first, second, or third person to speak on any issue.

Secret #10   **The Secret to a Strong Opening**
Inform, excite, empower, and involve in the first fifteen minutes.

Secret #11   **The Secret to Exciting in the Opening**
In the excite step of your opening, use the words "you" and "your" at least four times to ensure that you explain what is in it for the participants.

Secret #12   **The Secret to Gaining Agenda Buy-In**
Gain buy-in to the agenda by having the participants link their personal objectives to the plan for the meeting.

Secret #13   **The Secret to Using Ground Rules**
You start the list of ground rules; let them finish it.

Secret #14   **The Secret to Parking Boards**
Have a place to park decisions, actions, and off-topic comments that come up prior to the time when you want to discuss them.

Secret #15   **The Secret to Effective Introductions**
Have participants write first; set an introduction time limit.

Secret #16   **The Secret to Starting on Time**
Make the first time listed on the agenda the gathering time; make sure the first speaker is ready; give a two-minute warning.

Secret #17   **The Secret to Using Checkpoints**
Provide a review, preview, and big view at the beginning of each new agenda item or facilitated process.

Secret #18   **The Secret to Warming Up a Group**
Ask two questions that require a nonverbal response.

Secret #19   **The Secret to Giving Clear Directions**
When giving directions, use your PeDeQs.

Secret #20   **The Secret to Keeping a Group on Track**
Label, prompt, redirect.

Secret #21   **The Secret to Effective Breakout Groups**
Do, divide, direct: do one together; divide into teams; give final directions.

Secret #22   **The Secret to Rotating Flip Charts**
Have teams move from chart to chart to achieve a higher-quality review.

Secret #23   **The Secret to Using, Not Abusing, the Power of the Pen**
Write first, discuss second; write what they said; write so they can read it; ask, don't tell.

Secret #24   **The Secret to Knowing What to Record**
Record all decisions, actions, issues, and relevant analysis.

Secret #25   **The Secret to Keeping the Recording Concise**
Use templates, headlines, and abbreviations.

Secret #26   **The Secret to Avoiding Lulls While Writing**
Reduce the lull and get the participants to fill it.

Secret #27   **The Secret to Gathering Information**
Use the right tool in the most effective way to achieve your objective.

Secret #28   **The Secret to Getting the Details**
Ask, record, react.

Secret #29   **The Secret to Categorizing**
Ask, "Same or different?" one item at a time.

Secret #30   **The Secret to Q&A Sessions**
Use teams to identify the questions in advance.

Secret #31   **The Secret to Generating Ideas**
Ask, record, but don't react.

Secret #32 **The Secret to Prioritizing**
Define criteria; permit lobbying; check for consensus after scoring.

Secret #33 **The Secret to Reporting Back**
Increase feedback quality by assigning teams to review report-back.

Secret #34 **The Secret to Getting Quality Feedback**
Ask for strengths, areas for improvement, and level of consensus.

Secret #35 **The Secret to a Strong Close**
Review what was done; define what can be communicated; evaluate the value; end with next steps; debrief with the sponsor.

Secret #36 **The Secret to Confirming Commitment to Decisions**
Document the benefits, barriers, and success strategies for key decisions.

Secret #37 **The Secret to Clearing the Issues List**
Ask, "Have we covered it? Do we need to? Do we need to now?"

Secret #38 **The Secret to Assigning Actions**
Assign actions only to people who are present, with dates they have set themselves.

Secret #39 **The Secret to Understanding Dysfunction**
Dysfunction is a substitution and a symptom, not a root cause.

Secret #40 **The Secret to Preventing Dysfunction**
Identify potential dysfunction during preparation, then execute prevention strategies.

Secret #41 **The Secret to Detecting Dysfunction**
Take dysfunction checks at regular intervals.

Secret #42 **The Secret to Resolving Dysfunction**
Approach the participant privately or generally; empathize with the symptom; address the root cause; get agreement on a solution.

Secret #43 **The Secret to Responding When the Unexpected Happens**
Get the participants talking personally about the experience.

Secret #44 **The Secret to Responding to Mistakes and Attacks**
Acknowledge that the person may be right, show support, and take it to the group for resolution if appropriate.

Secret #45 **The Secret to Understanding Consensus**
Consensus means, "I can live with it, and I will support it."

Secret #46 **The Secret of Five-Finger Consensus**
Use five-finger consensus to reach agreement without jeopardizing the quality of a solution that has strong, but not unanimous, support.

Secret #47 **The Secret to Understanding Disagreement**
Disagreements occur because the people involved lack shared information, have different values or experiences, or are affected by outside factors.

Secret #48 **The Secret to Resolving a Level 3 Disagreement**
Take the issue to a higher source for resolution.

Secret #49 **The Secret to Resolving a Level 1 Disagreement**
Ask questions that delineate the alternatives.

Secret #50 **The Secret to Resolving a Level 2 Disagreement**
Create a new option that combines the key strengths of the original alternatives.

Secret #51 **The Secret to Using Weighted Scoring**
Score by criterion, starting with the alternative with the most favorable score.

Secret #52   **The Secret to Gaining Consensus on Wording**
Use the informed majority process to efficiently manage the wording process.

Secret #53   **The Secret of Energy: The 3 Es**
High energy energizes, engages, and elevates.

Secret #54   **The Secret to Starting with Energy**
Think "level 3" with the first words out of your mouth.

Secret #55   **The Secret to Adjusting to the Lullaby Times**
Plan high interaction during the low-energy times.

Secret #56   **The Secret to Maintaining Energy**
Use energy-generating techniques throughout the session.

Secret #57   **The Secret to Using Team Building Activities**
Select for purpose; debrief for application.

Secret #58   **The Secret of Standard Agendas**
Standard agendas create the starting point for addressing the specific needs of a meeting.

Secret #59   **The Secret to Customizing the Agenda**
Design wide to narrow with early successes; establish common information and a base for decision making.

Secret #60   **The Secret to Developing an Agenda from Scratch**
Determine the critical question and the questions needed to answer it.

Secret #61   **The Secret to Knowing Your Process Cold**
Ensure that you know the process cold by having a detailed facilitation guide.

Secret #62   **The Secret to Estimating Time**
Estimate based on the number of units and the amount of time per unit, being sure to add introduction and wrap-up time.

Secret #63   **The Secret to Preparing for a Virtual Meeting**
In your preparation, select the appropriate technology and plan and prepare your facilitation methods so that everyone will be able to "see."

Secret #64   **The Secret to Engaging People Virtually**
Every 10–20 minutes, lead a meaningful, interactive activity that engages everyone.

Secret #65   **The Secret to Facilitating Large Groups**
Use the power of the process to help maintain focus, maximize productivity, and minimize dysfunctions.

Secret #66   **The Secret to Facilitating Conferences**
Set the expectation of engagement early; use a variety of engagement strategies to ensure that each presentation is engaging and interactive.

Secret #67   **The Secret to Managing Time with Speakers**
Inform speakers about the constraints; explain the process; take action as needed.

Secret #68   **The Secret to Facilitating Cross-Cultural Groups**
Understand how your cultural biases align with the culture of the group you are facilitating.

Secret #69   **The Secret to Establishing an Internal Facilitator Cadre**
Build a solid business case by identifying a key function for the cadre that will drive a specific business result, and a key sponsor who will steadfastly support the cadre.

Secret #70   **The Secret to Guerrilla Facilitation**
Ask questions that lead the group to action.

ACKNOWLEDGMENTS

There have been many who have contributed significantly to this revised edition. First, to the reviewers of the first edition, Jim Rankin, Eileen Dowse, and several others, thank you for your critical insights and your recommendations. I hope you have seen your imprint throughout this revised edition.

To the many who agreed to talk with me about their experiences in creating or being a part of an internal facilitator cadre, your input has resulted in a thoughtful piece, perhaps the first of its kind, that documents the successes and challenges with building and maintaining an internal network of facilitators. I especially thank Steve Bushkul, John Rutkiewicz, and (again) Jim Rankin for agreeing to have their experiences highlighted in extended case studies.

To Eunice Shankland, Nanci Luna Jiménez, and (again) Eileen Dowse, my coauthors on the cross-cultural facilitation chapter, thanks for filling in the many holes in my understanding and allowing me to learn so much from the three of you.

To the hundreds of clients who allowed me to learn with them through my facilitation and to the thousands of individuals who provided feedback after attending our facilitation classes, I say thank you.

A special thanks to my editor, Kathe Sweeney, for her wisdom, guidance, and *patience,* and to the rest of my editing, production, and marketing team at Jossey-Bass, especially Rob Brandt, Mary Garrett, Michele Jones, and Dani Scoville.

I also thank the entire team of employees and contractors at Leadership Strategies, who have been supportive throughout this revision process, especially Richard Smith, the head of our training and development group, whose recommendations have touched many chapters of the book.

Although a solid professional support base is important, a solid home front is even more so. And so I say thank you to my two teenage daughters, Danielle and Gabrielle, who know how to make me smile even after a tough writing day. And to Sherry, my wife: words cannot express how much I appreciate all that you are and the life we continue to build together.

Finally, as a believer that good ideas come through us and not from us, I thank our Creator for using me as the channel for this gift.

THE AUTHOR

Michael Wilkinson is one of the nation's leaders in the facilitation industry. He is the founder and CEO of Leadership Strategies—The Facilitation Company (www .leadstrat.com) and author of the firm's highly acclaimed course The Effective Facilitator. He is the founder of the national facilitator database (www.FindaFacilitator.com) and serves on the board of the International Institute for Facilitation (www.INIFAC.org).

He has been awarded both the Certified Master Facilitator and Certified Professional Facilitator designations and is a frequent presenter at the conference of the International Association of Facilitators. In 2003, the Southeast Association of Facilitators (www.seaf.org) named him Facilitator of the Year for achievement and contributions to the field.

Wilkinson's personal facilitation experience covers over five hundred sessions with more than one hundred public and private sector organizations, including the Coca-Cola Company, KPMG Peat Marwick, the Centers for Disease Control, and the United Way of America. He is a much sought-after facilitator, trainer, and speaker, both nationally and internationally, having completed assignments in Bangkok, Brisbane, Glasgow, Hamburg, Helsinki, Hong Kong, Istanbul, London, Melbourne, Milan, the Netherlands, Oxford, Saudi Arabia, Singapore, Sydney, and Wellington.

Prior to entering the field of facilitation, Wilkinson spent eight years in Ernst & Young's Management Consulting Group. As an accomplished information technology consultant, he was selected by the governor of his state to serve for two terms on the governor's twelve-member Information Technology Policy Council.

His life is a storybook example of the positive results of affirmative action. Born in Washington DC, he spent his early years living in a government housing project. Along with his five brothers and sisters, Wilkinson worked odd jobs from an early age to help supplement the family's very modest income. While a newspaper carrier, he received a scholarship through the help of the *Washington Post* to attend St. Mark's School, an exclusive New England preparatory school. The academic environment was much more challenging for him, as indicated by his early grades. Within three years, however, he was rated in the top quartile of his class. He was named a National Merit Scholar and was awarded a grant by the UPS Foundation to attend Dartmouth College.

Wilkinson resides in Atlanta with his wife and two daughters.

INDEX

Page numbers in italics refer to figures and tables.